# Mind-Body Problem Solved

**Groundbreaking Psychology and Spirituality
Practical Nurturing and Healing**

The Explanation with Sam Kneller

The day science begins to study non-physical phenomena, it will make more progress in one decade than in all the previous centuries of its existence.

Nikola Tesla

A successful understanding of the mind–brain relationship will necessarily involve understanding the brain as a transduction device in one way or another. Such an understanding could prove enormously fruitful and can help us move beyond the current materialist framework in which neuroscience is practiced, which has held us so far back in our understanding of the mind and the brain. The brain is obviously material but it is just as obvious that the mind has immaterial abilities.

Dr. Robert Epstein

That which I see not teach you me…

Job 34:32

# MIND-BODY PROBLEM SOLVED

**First edition. June 23, 2023.**
Written by Sam Kneller.

Copyright © 2023 Sam Kneller.

All rights reserved. Excerpts of this work are free to share, copy, distribute, and propagate so long as the following credits are included: Produced by The Explanation with Sam Kneller.

For other distribution proposals, lectures, teaching, and speaking opportunities. Don't hesitate to get in touch with Sam Kneller at sam@theexplanation.com
Website: TheExplanation.com

While we have taken every precaution in preparing this book, the publisher assumes no responsibility for errors, omissions, or damages from using this information.

Kneller, Sam.
  Mind-body problem solved : groundbreaking psychology and spirituality practical nurturing and healing/ Sam Kneller.-- France: The Explanation, c 2023.

  vii, 540 pages: illustrations; 22 cm.
  Includes index.
  Contents: Universal conundrums.--The source for answers.-- Neshama: consciousness defines human.-- Ruach: the power of life and mind.-- Ruach: the creation of everything.-- Psychology of neshama and ruach.-- Spiritual conversion.
  ISBN: 978-2-9587628-4-1 (paperback)
       978-2-9587628-6-5 (hardcover)
       978-2-9587628-7-2 (audiobook)

1. Mind and body. 2. Consciousness. 3. Theology. 4. Psychology. 5. Spirituality. I. Title.

128 (ddc)

# Table of Contents

**Preface.** Mind-Blowing Claim ........................................... 1

**Introduction.** Higher Power or Not? ............................... 9

**I. Universal Conundrums** ................................................. 18

    1. Fine-Tuned Universe. Where From? ..................... 19

    2. From Rocks to Cells. How? ..................................... 27

    3. Brain to Mind. How? ................................................. 35

    4. Animal Cognition & Human Minds ..................... 45

    5. No Explanation for the Mind ................................ 54

**II. The Source for Answers** ............................................... 63

    6. Where is the Full Definition of Mind? ............... 64

    7. God-intended Meaning of Scripture ................. 71

    8. The Deep Meaning of 'adam' ............................... 80

    9. Does God Exist? ......................................................... 87

    10. Biggest Hidden Truth ............................................ 97

    11. God Works & Humans Work ............................. 105

    12. The Complex Human Body ................................ 115

**III. Neshama - Consciousness Defines Human** ......... 123

    13. Who Possesses Neshama? ................................... 124

    14. Neshama. Discover Deeper Meaning ............. 132

    15. What is the Purpose of Life? .............................. 142

    16. How Humans "Should" Function ..................... 151

    17. Social Relationships. Why? ................................. 160

    18. Human Rulership. Why? ...................................... 170

    19. 5 Types of Reasoning ............................................ 180

20. What it Means to be Human .................................. 190
**IV. Ruach - The Power of Life and Mind** ..................... 200
21. Spirit in the Bible ............................................. 201
22. Neshama and Ruach ......................................... 210
23. Bible Definition of Spirit ................................... 219
24. Role of the Ruach in Living Beings ..................... 229
25. Ruach Creates Human Superiority ...................... 238
26. Living Soul. Bible Meaning ............................... 247
27. The Active Mind ............................................... 257
28. Role of the Human Brain .................................. 266
**V. Ruach and the Creation of Everything** .................. 277
29. Quantum Physics & God's Spirit ........................ 278
30. The Meaning of Ruach ..................................... 286
31. Fluctuations of S/spirit .................................... 295
32. Origin of the Material World ............................ 304
33. Vibrations. A Troubled Mind ............................ 315
34. The Theory of Everything ................................ 328
**VI. Psychology of the Neshama and Ruach** ............... 339
35. Psychology. Best Bible Definition .................... 340
36. God Desires Good for All People ..................... 354
37. Universal Code Defines Morality ..................... 365
38. Bible Ethics for Humankind ............................. 375
39. Proverbs. Rules for Life .................................. 384
40. Warring Proverbs. .......................................... 394
41. Satan Influences Human Minds ....................... 405
42. Everyday Psychology for Everybody ............... 417
**VII. Spiritual Conversion** ....................................... 428

43. Human Filth to Godly Purity ............................. 429

44. Spiritual Calling ................................................ 439

45. Makeover of Neshama & Ruach ....................... 449

46. Genuine Spirituality .......................................... 462

47. From Rags to Righteousness ............................. 472

48. Believe and Repent ........................................... 482

49. The Way to the Image of God .......................... 493

**Epilogue**

The Fabulous Story of Humankind ........................ 504

Mind Transformation. First Steps ........................... 512

**Index** ........................................................................ 525

Scripture Index
   Old Testament
   New Testament

Strong's Index
   Hebrew
   Greek

List of Figures

# Preface. Mind-Body Problem Solved. That's a Bold, Mind-Blowing Claim

**Mind-Body Problem Solved. Is it just an alluring title, or is there actual substance behind that affirmation? Read on to find out; it's 100% accurate.**

You're in for a shocker. It can't be anything else.

An ongoing 450-year debate launched by Descartes' philosophy asserts that the mind-body problem represents two separate, distinct entities as opposed to one. Nobody has settled this issue until now. So it's 2023, and time to broach this exciting, earth-girdling, current issue. Why? Because it's directly related to the No. 1 world health woe in the 21$^{st}$ century. Not Covid-19 but mental health.

## The Extent of Miscomprehension

Here's what the Encyclopedia Britannica relates about mind-body dualism[1]:

> The modern problem of the relationship of mind to body stems from the thought of the 17th-century French philosopher and mathematician René Descartes, who gave dualism its classical formulation. Beginning from his famous dictum *cogito, ergo sum* (Latin: "I think, therefore I am"), Descartes developed a theory of mind as an immaterial, nonextended substance that engages in various activities or undergoes various states such as rational thought, imagining, feeling (sensation), and willing. Matter, or extended substance, conforms to the laws of physics in mechanistic fashion, with the important exception of the human body, which Descartes believed is causally affected by the human mind and which causally produces certain mental events.

The accumulated brains of science, religion, and philosophy over the last 450 years have come up empty-handed, not to say empty-headed. Why? There must be a reason. Not only that, but the cause must be hidden; otherwise, these investigative disciplines would have found it.

Here's the evaluation. **Science** has spent centuries examining and measuring the PHYSICAL universe. **Religion** has drawn its

---

1. https://www.britannica.com/topic/mind-body-dualism

inspiration from a spiritual well. However, that well is a mixture of traditions going back thousands of years, causing the assessment to be tainted. Its self-enlightenment has guided **philosophy**, limited by the capacity of our brainpower, coupled with unlimited human imagination; this chatter has taken us into every contradictory cranny on a jagged path of human wisdom.

The solution is outside of science, religion, and philosophy! If it were not so, the collective intellect would have revealed it. But, instead, it is cacophonic.

If you're going to read this book, you've got to know from the outset that the approach will be totally different. The solution has few references to science, philosophy, or religion. Instead, there are call-outs to science when discussing material aspects, like cells, the brain, light, and other physical phenomena. The key is NOT in opposition to science; in fact, it includes many scientifically proven facts.

It goes far beyond science because the solution to the mind-body problem finds neither its ORIGIN nor its CONCLUSION in that discipline - no more than in philosophy or religion. Yes, we will refer to aspects of philosophy and religion, but those disciplines cannot and are not our starting point for this quest. As great as they may be, they are far too limited to solve the issue.

To start with, we will use observation to establish a working basis. We know there's a mind and a brain, hence the mind-body problem, but we don't know what they are precisely, especially the relationship between them. You can read Wikipedia to see the diversity of ideas on this subject: [2]

---

2. https://en.wikipedia.org/wiki/Mind

Mind or mentality is usually contrasted with body, matter, or physicality. Traditional viewpoints included dualism and idealism, which consider the mind non-physical. Modern views often center around physicalism and functionalism, which hold that the mind is roughly identical to the brain or reducible to physical phenomena such as neuronal activity. However, dualism and idealism continue to have many supporters.

Another question concerns which types of beings are capable of having minds. For example, whether the mind is exclusive to humans, possessed by some or all animals, by all living things, whether it is a strictly definable characteristic at all, or whether the mind can also be a property of some types of human-made machines. Different cultural and religious traditions often use different concepts of mind, resulting in different answers to these questions.

## The Explanation Starting Point

*The Explanation* has no intention of joining this cacophony. I am not about to argue or refute these claims. Instead, we will start with a few general statements I hope we all agree with. At this point, we're not even going to define them. This simple fact already shows the complexity of the mind-body issue.

1. The non-living, inanimate, material world exists. (water, earth)
2. Life exists (flora, fauna)
3. There are animals
4. There are humans
5. There are brains

6. There are minds

By the end of this book, you will have a clear definition of each of these elements, and, more importantly, you will know the relationship between them.

## A Warning about Reading This Book

Reading this book will be challenging. At some point, you may become upset! Because it does NOT follow your way of reasoning. You may disagree with some intermediary steps and the logic *The Explanation* develops.

Here's the deal. You can't tell what a painting or a puzzle is until you see the FINISHED object with all the details. You only get a glimpse of the final artwork from the outline, sketch, and pieces. Your judgment on those initial fragments, or even halfway or three-quarters of the way to the final chef-d'oeuvre, may be important to you but are irrelevant to a dilemma nobody has solved yet. You must see the WHOLE picture, the coherent completeness, as I call it, BEFORE you can make a valid judgment.

By the way, there's no point in criticizing the author, either. He's just a human being like you. Any criticism of his person is unimportant. It has NOTHING to do with the solution. Social media likes to take potshots at people because they're different! You've got to look at their ideas, acts, and messages. That's what you've got to weigh, NOT their being. Those who criticize people show their ignorance of *live and let live*.

Another quote from Rene Descartes is also appropriate since his name is associated with the mind-body problem.

> If you would be a real seeker after truth, it is necessary that at least once in your life you doubt, as far as possible, all things.

## Full Disclosure

I condense much of this book's content from *The Explanation* series of seven books[3]. That series is more the *Story of Humankind*, a chronological progression. This book focuses on the key element, the mind, in the mind-body problem. *The Explanation* will not limit itself to defining WHAT the mind is, nor HOW it works, but searches for a more profound understanding of WHY the mind exists and WHY each human being has one. We'll also discuss HOW humans should use their minds and how misuse can be so problematic.

The mind is the crucial piece, the capstone in the *story of humankind*. Ultimately, it is the only piece that counts because it is the only piece that will survive. So I'll leave you hanging there, for the time being, as an encouragement to solve the mind-body problem along with me.

## The Extent of the Mental Health Shambles

The mind-body problem is so significant because of the number one current predicament regarding humankind's mental health.

The numbers are staggering. The World Health Organization says[4]:

> Mental health is one of the most neglected areas of public health. Close to 1 billion people live with a

---

[3]. https://theexplanation.com/books

[4]. https://www.who.int/news/item/27-08-2020-world-mental-health-day-an-opportunity-to-kick-start-a-massive-scale-up-in-investment-in-mental-health

mental disorder and in low-income countries, more than 75% of people with the disorder do not receive treatment. Every year, close to 3 million people die due to substance abuse[5]. Every 40 seconds, a person dies by suicide[6]. About 50% of mental health disorders start by the age of 14[7].

We estimate that over 160 million people need humanitarian help because of conflicts, natural disasters, and other emergencies. The rates of mental disorders can double during such crises. 1 in 5 people affected by conflict[8] is estimated to have a mental health condition.

The World Bank indicates mental health is one of the most neglected areas of health globally[9]. This was true before COVID-19 (coronavirus), but the pandemic has further worsened the status of mental health.[10]

There are several reasons why we've ignored mental health. First, is an associated stigma. Second, is a perception of mental health disorders as "luxury goods,"

---

5. https://www.who.int/news/item/21-09-2018-harmful-use-of-alcohol-kills-more-than-3-million-people-each-year--most-of-them-men
6. https://www.who.int/en/news-room/fact-sheets/detail/suicide
7. https://www.who.int/activities/Improving-the-mental-and-brain-health-of-children-and-adolescents
8. https://www.healio.com/news/psychiatry/20190612/one-in-five-people-have-mental-disorders-in-postconflict-settings
9. https://blogs.worldbank.org/health/mental-health-lessons-learned-2020-2021-and-forward
10. https://unitedgmh.org/sites/default/files/2020-09/The%2BImpact%2BOf%2BCovid-19%2BOn%2BGlobal%2BMental%2BHealth%2BReport.pdf

as opposed to actual illnesses. The additional top reasons include a fragmented and outdated service model. Some of these include the provision of mental health services mainly in psychiatric hospitals, severe lack of preventative mental health service, lagging policy changes, and a shortage of human resources.

This is one of the most pressing contemporary problems we are dealing with, yet we are totally in the dark in the supposedly enlightened 21st century. What a paradox. Our number one health problem is the mental state of our population. And at the same time, we don't even know what the mind is. So how can we hope to solve this dilemma without such fundamental knowledge?

It's way past the time to solve the mind-body problem. That will be our quest.

# Introduction. Your Starting Point: Higher Power or Not? Spiritual or Secular?

Does your belief start with a Higher Power or not? There's no right or wrong answer. It's a matter of how we approach the mind-body problem.

Either way, *The Explanation* already says science, philosophy, and religion do not have the answers[1]. So, whether you start from the spiritual or the secular, you must make serious adjustments to solve the mind-body problem.

This book must address both starting points and guide us to harmony. That is no small task. Whether you start from science, philosophy, or religion, I hope you realize that all three disciplines have enormous knowledge gaps.

---

1. https://theexplanation.com/mind-body-problem-solved-thats-a-bold-claim/

1. Science does not know WHY or WHAT the mind is
2. Philosophy is in an identical dilemma to science
3. Religion doesn't understand Genesis 2:7, the Creation of the first human. I will expand on this point below.

The three mainstays of human reasoning are unaware of the extent of damage to their vehicle. Therefore, they don't know the problem, so we must be educated about the issue.

This book has two parts. I will use the analogy of a puzzle with 557,707 pieces to show you the value and reasons for each art.

1. The belief is that the puzzle pieces assembled themselves randomly, by natural selection, mysteriously, or by whatever process over some 14 billion years for the universe, 4.5 billion for Earth, and 3.5 billion for life. The belief is that solely **PHYSICAL** interactions took place to bring about the beauty and intelligence we see on our planet.
2. The belief is that a **SPIRITUAL** Higher Power assembled the puzzle pieces. Right now, this Higher Power's name and nature are unimportant. It is simply the belief that a spiritual dimension exists beyond the physical phenomena our bodily apparatus can sense. In other words, some essence exists beyond touch, sight, hearing, taste, and smell.

## The Physical

You cannot start a conversation with the 1st group talking about SPIRITUAL things. It would be best if you began with the physical. That's the first Part of this book.

## MIND-BODY PROBLEM SOLVED

*Inventory of the Universe*, *Audit of the Universe*, and *Audit of Humankind*, the first three books of *The Explanation* series, address this issue. In the *physical area*, this is the reason the mind-body problem has not and cannot find a solution; because there's a non-physical element involved.

Science and philosophy limit themselves to the PHYSICAL arena and HUMAN imagination. Granted, those are vast territories, and incredible discoveries have been and are being revealed. However, they are devoted to WHAT things are and HOW they operate. The WHY is missing. WHY does the universe exist? WHY do human beings function the way they do? Their endless imagination hems in science and philosophy, which, because of their aura, can assert statements like "the universe can create itself from nothing[2]" (Stephen Hawking in his book, The Grand Design[3]). Many accept it based on the scientific reputation of the individual.

In his superb book The End of Science[4], John Horgan addresses what he calls *ironic science:*

> He defined "ironic science" as "speculative" and "post-empirical," and I said that it is more akin to philosophy, literary criticism and even literature itself than to genuine science. Ironic science "offers points of view, opinions, which are, at best, interesting... But it does not converge on the truth."

This first group must understand they don't have the answers to the WHY questions. Furthermore, there are *extra-physical* phenomena

---

2. https://physics.stackexchange.com/questions/13013/stephen-hawking-says-universe-can-create-itself-from-nothing-but-how-exactly

3. https://en.wikipedia.org/wiki/The_Grand_Design_(book)

4. https://www.goodreads.com/book/show/250814.The_End_of_Science

that are FACTS the PHYSICAL SENSES cannot explain. Until science and philosophy understand this, there's no point in addressing the second Part of the mind-body problem. I'm exaggerating somewhat because it is possible that reading sensible information about the spiritual world might help.

The first Part of this book paints a physical portrait of our universe. *The Explanation* has gone to great lengths in *Inventory of the Universe* to focus on what appears to be stupid questions like which came first, the chicken or the egg? After all, there has to be an answer. Here's what one reader said about this narrative of the material universe:

> This book is amazing! First of all, as an evangelist who delves deeply into the Word of God (the Bible?), I had already surmised what Sam is saying in this book. Second, as a scientist, it makes so much sense that our universe could only have been created out of intelligent design, no other way. The detail that he writes is phenomenal; I understand every bit of it.
>
> I only wish that I had this book back in the 70s when I was teaching general science to 9th graders; they would have latched on to it with far more enthusiasm than those boring textbooks that we had that many of them could not even read. But I would have used this book instead to teach them a well-rounded science course from it. And they would be so much better for it because they would have appreciated and embraced science. Fantastic!

I will state upfront that the goal is to help these physicalists understand that there's something beyond materialism and matter.

It is not a quest to *convert* anyone to anything. The mind-body problem goes beyond the material, and unless science and philosophy *open their minds* (sic) to this eventuality, they will forever remain in the domain of confusion.

## Higher Power

Those who believe in a Higher Power may want to jump to the second Part of this book and get straight into the explanation of the mind-body problem. There you will find references to the physical aspect of this question.

But that doesn't mean our group of believers in a higher power is scot-free. Not by any means. These people are in the *spiritual-religious* category. And that is possibly even more complicated than the material group. The opposition of beliefs among this group is staggering. In *Audit of Humankind, How Humans Reason*[5], I address the cacophony in the spiritual domain. Between the beliefs of different churches, meditation, Western Christianity, Eastern esotericism, and spirituality, whatever form it takes, there is a universe of differences in spiritual beliefs. This group, just because it believes in the existence of the spiritual, is by no means out of hot water.

They believe *their higher power* created and assembled the puzzle in their particular way. The myriad beliefs in this field are thunderous. WHO devised, created, and assembled the puzzle? WHY did this god accomplish this task? WHAT is their purpose?

WHERE can we find answers to those questions? How do we know we have the correct SOURCE? How do we UNDERSTAND that source? Unfortunately, the answers by *experts* to those questions are plethoric. Hence total anarchy in

---

5. https://theexplanation.com/read-all-the-content-of-audit-of-humankind-online/

the spiritual and religious areas and the absence of an authentic response to the mind-body problem.

These spiritual people can begin in the second Part of this book. Still, they will remain lost unless we agree on WHERE to find answers and HOW to interpret what we FIND.

Whether it's science, philosophy, or religion, turbulence and turmoil of ideas, theories, and concepts reign.

Where do we start?

## The Mind-Body Problem Solved is Not Sam's Solution

*The Explanation* will explain why we must go to one source, the Bible. I realize that many will immediately feel negative about reading further. I mentioned answering the mind-body problem will be challenging and cause upset[6]. Are you already going to quit? We're only discussing the puzzle pieces; we haven't even turned them the right way up yet. Stay with me.

Once we consider the Bible, we face another barrier. How do we study it? *The Explanation* will show you a method, keys to master Biblical Hebrew to unlock Scripture's original God-intended meaning. Yes, the method is Sam's, but the *God-intended meaning of Scripture* is NOT. And it is ONLY the God-intended meaning of Scripture that can lead us to the answer.

**Here's the dilemma of the mind-body problem.**

Nobody understands Genesis 2:7.

Wow, Sam, that's a strong allegation. What do you mean? Let's take a closer look at this verse.

---

6. https://theexplanation.com/mind-body-problem-solved-thats-a-bold-claim/

**Genesis 2:7**

And the LORD God formed man of the dust of the ground, and breathed into his nostrils the breath of life; and man became a living soul.

- Who is the Lord? What is the Lord's relationship to the Higher Power?
- Why are *Lord* (Yahveh) singular and *God* (Elohim) plural?
- What does *formed* mean? For instance, why doesn't it say *created*?
- Why from the dust? What's the difference between dust and ground?
- Why breathe into the nostrils? Why breathe at all? God could've used any *method*.
- Did you know that *breathed* and *breath* are two different words in Hebrew? What does each mean? What is their relationship?
- The Hebrew says the *breath of lives*. It's plural. What's that all about? By the way, the Tree of Life is also the *Tree of Lives*. Again plural.
- Does *man* in Hebrew only refer to the masculine gender?
- What is a *soul*? That's the $1.000.000 question! Everybody talks about it, but for a definition, there's as much confusion as for the *mind*.
- *Living* soul is singular. So why and how can a singular soul have a plural *breath of lives*?

Many of these singulars, plurals, and variations for the same word are invisible in English. If we want appropriate answers, we have no choice but to delve into Biblical Hebrew. But you're not a scholar, and neither am I! That's why we need a method. I'll show you how to unlock the God-intended meaning.

Now tell me you understand this verse and can answer all those questions. Talk to a scientist, philosopher, pastor, or other spiritual figure and ask them for answers. We are not interested in responses. The solution must be coherent and relate to every human being, past, present, and future. God is the God of humankind, or He isn't.

We might have a *spiritual* component, but we live in a *physical* world; they must relate. How? One of *The Explanation's* readers asked a very pertinent question recently. What happens to people born with or who develop impaired minds? Do they get preferential spiritual treatment or none?

When you can answer all those questions about Genesis 2:7 and many others, like the impaired mind, you will answer the mind-body problem with assurance and verity.

- Understand the Higher Power and the relationship with the mind.
- Grasp WHAT the mind is and WHY the Higher Power gave it.
- Fathom WHO possesses a mind and WHY they have one.
- Realize HOW TO USE your mind to its greatest potential. You'll understand the role of the mind now and, amazingly, in the future.

This book, the *Mind-Body Problem Solved*, will explain Genesis 2:7 and answer all the above questions and many more.

## Sections I-VII

### I. Universal Conundrums

There are many questions but no answers from science, philosophy, or religion.

### II. The Source for Answers

No answers, or confused ones, is not the solution. Where to find the explanation.

### III. Neshama-Consciousness Defines Human

The spiritual component of humans.

### IV. Ruach - The Power of Life and Mind

The activator and motor of consciousness.

### V. Ruach and the Creation of Everything

Another major scientific enigma related to ruach.

### VI. Psychology of the Neshama and Ruach

Biblical psychology for stable mental health for everyone worldwide.

### VII. Spiritual Conversion

When God becomes real, His Word becomes real, and the Holy Spirit witnesses with your spirit when you're called. Then you can believe, repent and become a son or daughter of God.

# I. Universal Conundrums

There are many questions but no answers from science, philosophy, or religion.

# 1. Did a Fine-Tuned Universe Give Rise to Our Dazzling Earth?

**Fine-Tuned Universe**

**What does it reveal?**

TheExplanation.com

**What insight do we gain from the immense, observable, fine-tuned universe? Science reveals eye-popping facts and figures. How do we interpret them?**

On Dec. 24th, 2021, NASA launched the James Webb Space Telescope. Its revolutionary technology will study every phase of cosmic history - from within our solar system to the most distant observable galaxies in the early universe. As a result, we'll get closer to understanding the origins of our fine-tuned universe. It will gaze at galaxies formed over 13.5 billion years ago with unprecedented resolution and sensitivity.

We, humans, are minute specks in this vast arena. Still, to our knowledge, we alone have minds capable of launching such a venture and digesting the incredible amounts of data gathered from such a mission. Our investigations have already revealed astounding facts.

At the two extremes of this equation are two unknowns. The origin of the Universe and the source of the mind. Where did they come from? Why do they function as they do? Is there a relationship between the two? Are they "just there," or is there some underlying purpose for their existence? These are questions this book will elaborate on.

The fine-tuned Universe and humans interconnect because each of us is stardust. Yes, the same fundamental elements composing the Universe are part of our bodies and brains. Of the 92 naturally occurring elements, the human body contains about 60. These elements, or fundamental building blocks of matter, everything physical, observable by our senses, formed over billions of years as the Universe developed and continues to expand.

You can delve into the exciting details in *Inventory of the Universe*[1]: Expanding Finity[2], Atmospheric Cocoon[3]; the various layers of the atmosphere protect Earth's inhabitants from harmful waves while letting through just what's necessary. Planet Water[4]; the mystery of the origin of all the fresh and saltwater. Our Earth[5] is about 6,000°C at the core, with the sun's surface the same and Earth's surface just right to walk barefoot on the beach. From Big Bang, the point of departure, some 14 billion years ago, to our present-day 93 billion light-years[6] diameter universe, when life

---

1. https://theexplanation.com/inventory/read-all-the-content-of-inventory-of-the-universe-online/

2. https://theexplanation.com/imagine-the-unimaginable-big-bang/

3. https://theexplanation.com/earths-atmosphere-ingredients-life/

4. https://theexplanation.com/water-but-very-little-to-drink/

5. https://theexplanation.com/land-surface-temperature-just-right-for-your-bare-feet/

arrived on our planet, all the elements were already there. They became the raw material for life, which we'll discuss in the next chapter.

We must look at the sky and realize the unique circumstances leading to our presence on Earth.

## The Precision of the Universe

The premise of the fine-tuned universe assertion is that a slight change in several of the physical constants would make it radically different. As Stephen Hawking[7] noted:

> The laws of science, as we know them at present, contain many fundamental numbers, like the size of the electric charge of the electron and the ratio of the masses of the proton and the electron. ... The remarkable fact is that the values of these numbers seem to have been very finely adjusted to make possible the development of life.

Hawking attributes these fine-tuned episodes in the universe's formation to fortunate coincidences[8]. So, tell me, how many of these "lucky happenings" must occur before you begin to say, "wow, something extraordinary is going on here?" I will remind you of this remark because there are many such coincidences as we survey the processes of establishing the Universe, Earth, and life. For instance, the layers of the atmosphere are at precisely the proper distance from Earth and density to protect us from damaging gamma rays and nurture humankind with vitamin D.

---

6. https://en.wikipedia.org/wiki/Observable_universe

7. https://en.wikipedia.org/wiki/Stephen_Hawking

8. https://theexplanation.com/science-and-theology-agreement-on-real-evidence-for-big-bang/

And Earth is endowed with enough salt water for the abundant supply of fish that nourishes 40% of our world's population. Or sufficient renewable resources to provide 24,000,000,000 (billion) meals (breakfast, lunch, and dinner) daily[9] for eight billion people on Earth. Our regular thought patterns don't focus on such events, do they?

## The 25 Fundamental Constants So We Exist

Here's what Ethan Siegel, an astrophysicist, author, and science communicator, writes[10]:

> The Universe appears to be enormously fine-tuned.
>
> On the one hand, we have the expansion rate that the Universe had initially, close to the Big Bang. On the other hand, we have the sum total of all the forms of matter and energy that existed at that early time as well, including:
>
> - radiation
> - neutrinos
> - normal matter
> - dark matter
> - antimatter
> - and dark energy
>
> Einstein's General theory of Relativity gives us an intricate relationship between the expansion rate and the sum total of all the different forms of energy in it.

---

9. https://theexplanation.com/creation-environmentally-friendly-for-billions-of-humans/

10. https://www.forbes.com/sites/startswithabang/2019/12/19/the-universe-really-is-fine-tuned-and-our-existence-is-the-proof/?sh=7e856dae4b87

If you know what your Universe is made of and how quickly it starts expanding initially, you can predict how it will evolve with time, including what its fate will be.

A Universe with too much matter-and-energy for its expansion rate will recollapse in short order; a Universe with too little will expand into oblivion before it's possible to even form atoms. Yet not only has our Universe neither recollapsed nor failed to yield atoms, but even today, some 13.8 billion years after the Big Bang, those two sides of the equation appear to be perfectly in balance.

If we extrapolate this back to a very early time - say, one nanosecond after the hot Big Bang - we find that not only do these two sides have to balance but they have to balance to an extraordinary precision. The Universe's initial expansion rate and the sum total of all the different forms of matter and energy in it not only need to balance, but they need to balance to more than 20 significant digits. It's like guessing the same 1-to-1,000,000 number as me three times in a row, and then predicting the outcome of 16 consecutive coin-flips immediately afterward.

The odds of this occurring naturally, if we consider all the random possibilities we could have imagined, are astronomically small.

Scientists wrote the above descriptions and arrived at the betting odds. But, of course, science would in no way invoke a Higher Power with the capacity to set such a scenario in motion.

I don't understand any of the figures, and you probably won't either. Wikipedia says the following[11]:

> The complete standard model requires 25 fundamental dimensionless constants. At present, their numerical values are not understood in terms of any widely accepted theory and are determined only from measurement.

There's a list of the 25 constants. Here are just two to demonstrate the complexity and precision:

1. Up quark mass: $1.4 \times 10^{-22} - 2.7 \times 10^{-22}$
2. Down quark mass: $3.4 \times 10^{-22} - 4.8 \times 10^{-22}$

Note these are confirmed measurements but are not understood in a widely accepted theory. Scientists don't know how to assemble the pieces of the puzzle.

On the other hand, religion uses this as a watchmaker argument[12] to *prove* there's a Creator. And there's even a well-known narrative, Genesis 1, although most theologians would not take this at face value. And there again, interpretations are boundless.

The next chapter will discuss life and the fine-tuned biological world. Now, I want to leave you with a thought as we progress in our solution to the mind-body problem. The first step is the need for the physical, material substance. A second obligatory step is moving from the inert, inorganic to the alive, organic. From dead rocks to living cells.

---

11. https://en.wikipedia.org/wiki/Dimensionless_physical_constant

12. https://en.wikipedia.org/wiki/Watchmaker_analogy

## Geochemical to Biochemical Processes

This is one of those fundamental queries few talk about regarding evolution and the origin of life. It means, how do we turn a rock into a living creature? It has nothing to do with living creatures developing into higher beings like apes to humans. This is the transformation of a mineral into a living cell; the inorganic matter like sand, water, and sun into even the smallest form of life, like a one-celled amoeba. There is absolutely no evidence for this. There is no known process for this. No skeletons or archaeological artifacts, nothing, nada.

There are only maybes, could bes, suppositions, and I think. This absence of evidence is NOT proof of God. But it should prick your mind. This is a visible fact manifested to us by science that should tick a box; be a clue to the possibility there's something invisible out there.

It's impossible to develop such a subject here. Read this article for a scientific search for transforming minerals into life[13]. Always note the number of *could have* (3), *may have* (2), *plausible* (2), *possible* (1) in such articles. Notice terms like myriad *possible* combinations of environmental conditions to find those that *could* initiate life.

True, the above proves nothing. That's where we have to be extremely careful because of info-gap. We know we don't have all the knowledge, but we could discover it in the future. The widespread mythological idea, also spread by religion, that Earth is the center of the Universe[14] is one example; until science proved otherwise. Science is beneficial, but it has its limits that it should recognize.

---

13. http://elementsmagazine.org/past-issues/origins-of-life-transition-from-geochemistry-to-biogeochemistry/

14. https://en.wikipedia.org/wiki/History_of_the_center_of_the_Universe

I don't know where your beliefs stand. I'm not presenting the fine-tuned argument as proof of the existence of God. I am offering it as evidence there MIGHT be something we need to consider. How much evidence do we need to make a solid case? There's much more to come.

# 2. Life Biology: From Rocks to Cells, Sublime Simple Complexity

**Life Biology is stunningly complex. Beautifully organized, interconnected processes run your body 24/7/365. How did this happen?**

## Rocks to Cells, the Stuff of Life Biology

In the last chapter, I left you with an enigma; How to transform rocks into cells, geochemistry to biochemistry. Well, science hasn't found a solution yet to reach life biology. Watch this very lucid video[1] presentation from Dr. Nita Sahai about the challenges scientists face to accomplish this feat.

Let me note what I consider to be a few critical points on the road to life biology.

- 4:20 Which came first, genes or metabolism?
- 5:40 We can't do reactions of the 1st life from minerals;

---
1. https://youtu.be/CeVk9yC0_vk

only come up with plausible ideas. Everything is taken with a grain of salt.
- 19:45 What came first? What came second? It's hard to pin it down.
- 21:05 Minimum life needs 1. Membrane 2. Heritable and mutable (for evolution) 3. Metabolic cycles.
- 26:25 The main problem. You have the genetic molecule DNA that produces enzymes, but the enzymes are needed to make the DNA. Which came first? Chicken or egg? Actually, it's more complicated than that because DNA first transcribes to RNA. There's this very complex process in modern life, DNA > RNA > proteins, all involving enzymes.

Below is a diagram from Dr. Sahai's excellent presentation illustrating the interactions between these various individual chemical pieces that assemble perfectly in life biology.

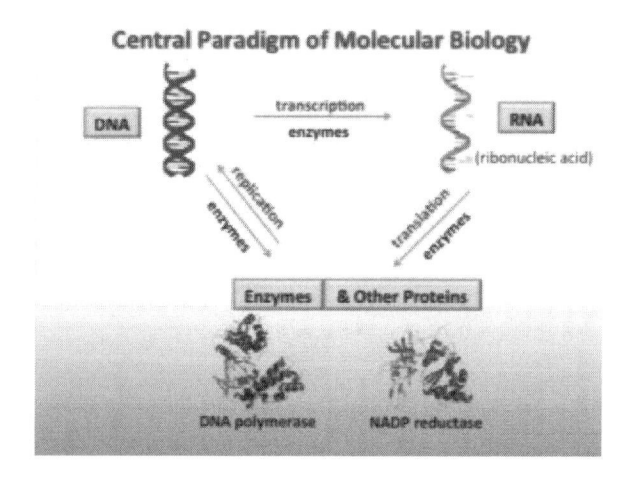

Figure 1. Central Paradigm of Molecular Biology

Once again, this transformation of geochemistry to biochemistry, life biology, like fine-tuning the Universe, doesn't prove anything. Instead, you can consider them as just two bricks of compelling evidence. Science hasn't yet figured out the how and will never know the why, but it recognizes some missing links.

## Processes in Processes

Let's move on to another brainteaser related to life biology. The first book in *The Explanation* series is *Inventory of the Universe*[2]. It is a journey from the vastness of outer space to the minuteness of the quark. From the physics of elementary particles to the psychology of the human mind. A portrayal of our known universal environment.

A 4* review of the book at Goodreads[3] said:

> This book is like an updated and longer "View from a Height"[4] by Isaac Asimov—an overview of the world and science from physics to biology.

I have to admit; it's nice to be compared to Isaac Asimov. His book covered 17 essays dealing with biology, chemistry, and physics. However, the reviewer missed the essential point, or maybe I wasn't clear enough.

Here's the crux of the matter I emphasized on numerous occasions. In Part 7, I wrote about Human Life[5]:

---

2. https://theexplanation.com/inventory/read-all-the-content-of-inventory-of-the-universe-online/

3. https://www.goodreads.com/book/show/31285784-inventory-of-the-universe

4. https://en.wikipedia.org/wiki/View_from_a_Height

5. https://theexplanation.com/imagine-human-life-human-element-on-earth/

To speak in terms of function and refer to sheer numbers is inadequate to describe the processes that perform like a battalion of flying trapeze artists in total sync, in our bodies, in human life, in flora, in fauna, and, indeed, in the Universe. The full gamut is breathtaking and awe-inspiring.

Regarding the human body, this is life biology[6]:

> Hundreds, thousands, and millions of timely processes are taking place night and day. This is the ultimate in chronobiology: very complex biological procedures and the clock being in the right place at just the right split second. It's so much more than simply mixing a few chemical elements together. Timing, the instantaneous coordination of umpteen intricate systems, is a decisive ingredient we cannot omit.
>
> I dare you to define life[7]. Scientists have synthesized certain DNA molecules mixed, matched, extracted, and implanted them to make a living entity. They've accomplished this process with bacteria that beat like in a heartbeat. Under such circumstances, we could say this organism is living, but it didn't last. Life is more than bringing elements together and having them beat the right beat; this has nothing to do with their tremendous biological breakthrough. But we need at least two additional functions.

# 1. Sustainability

---

6. https://theexplanation.com/imagine-human-life-human-element-on-earth/

7. https://theexplanation.com/i-dare-you-to-define-life/

An integral part of life is its capacity to sustain itself and have the ability to continue to live. Therefore, the organism must have access to and assimilate the correct fuel and the proper variety of food year-round. It then has to break down that food into chunks, transform it into energy, use its metabolism to digest and convert it to chemicals to run its machinery and produce extra energy to accomplish external activities. Not to mention, it must also be able to remove waste products.

## 2. Reproduction

Life biology must reproduce itself[8]. It must bring forth new life, of and by itself, with no external help manipulating the elements that are a part of the original living entity. We're talking about a reproduction system, be it asexual or sexual, but it must permit a second and third generation. Otherwise, it's not life. In that case, it lasts for a certain period and becomes extinct.

When the organism reproduces, depending on its complexity, it needs to copy itself, but not exactly. It needs some plasticity; otherwise, we'd have robotic dogs with robotic humans. Not only is there no variety, but it would end life with the problems arising from consanguinity and genetic disorders.

If it can't reproduce regularly and develop a self-sustaining population, we'd have to recreate life by assembling all the elements repeatedly.

## From Chemicals to Life Biology

DNA comprises five elements: oxygen, hydrogen, nitrogen, carbon, and phosphorus. The life biology cycle occurs in each of those 100 trillion cells of your body, especially amino acids and proteins,

---

8. https://theexplanation.com/two-must-characteristics-to-define-life/

which are vital building blocks. In a very simplistic way, this is the virtuous circle of chemical life: 5 elements > 20/100 amino acids > 500 / 1 000 000 proteins > DNA.

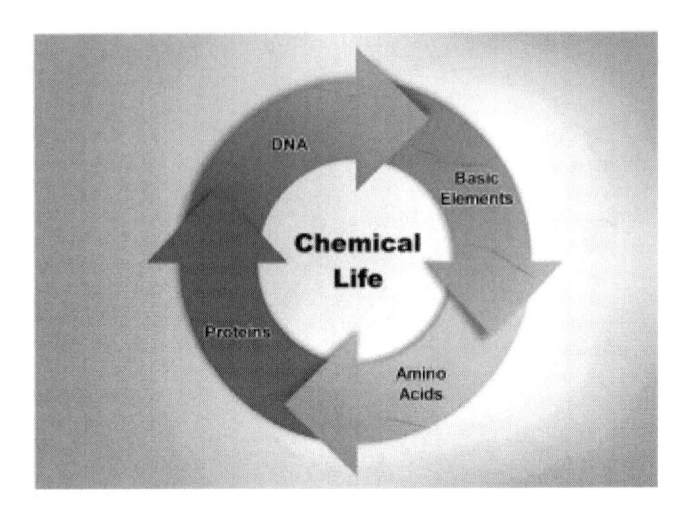

Figure 2. Chemical life

We don't know the precise number of amino acids or proteins in the makeup of our bodies, nor exactly how many are used for what purpose. The above are estimates. Notice that in this circle (in the image), IF you start with the FIVE basic elements and follow the circular path, it gets more complicated as you proceed. Still, after the most complex, DNA, it immediately leads back to the simplest, the FIVE elements.

This is precisely what happens in your body. In a nutshell, schematically, that's what digestion is: breaking down the food and water we intake. Of course, we might not think about digestion this way, but through multiple processes, your body is taking apart, breaking down food, metabolizing it into molecules and atoms,

## MIND-BODY PROBLEM SOLVED

then rebuilding, synthesizing those essential elements into DNA via the amino acids and proteins.

It's a very simplistic representation of life biology. The point is to explain chemical life is a virtuous, never-ending circle.

You cannot start just anywhere in the circle; go a certain distance, then end somewhere and say this is life. Life biology is the entire circle. It's not the chicken OR the egg; it's the chicken AND the egg with no interruption and no outside intervention, all or nothing. That's life.

That's the scientific, practical approach. But we really need to meditate on life's biodiversity to appreciate the complexity of its beauty. Look at the pictures or read a book like *Zoology* by the Smithsonian Institution. *Oceanology, the secrets of the Seas revealed*, or *Micro Life: Miracles of the Miniature World*. Discover the unique and beautiful kingdoms of life at a microscopic scale and how every organism meets the challenges of survival, no matter its size.

Life biology is a blaze of amazement. For example, in the Epilogue of *Inventory of the Universe*[9], I wrote:

> All the processes of each aspect of our environment fit together. For example, see the nitrogen and water cycles, butterflies, wasps, and bees pollinating flowers and plants.
>
> These processes impact, intermingle and create an interface so that other processes can express themselves. We live in a fully integrated, interdependent environment with no missing or redundant parts."

---

9. https://theexplanation.com/the-universe-an-infinite-number-of-puzzle-pieces-assembled-perfectly/

Are the chicken AND the egg evidence of something we're missing?

# 3. Brain to Mind. Can the Material Create the Immaterial?

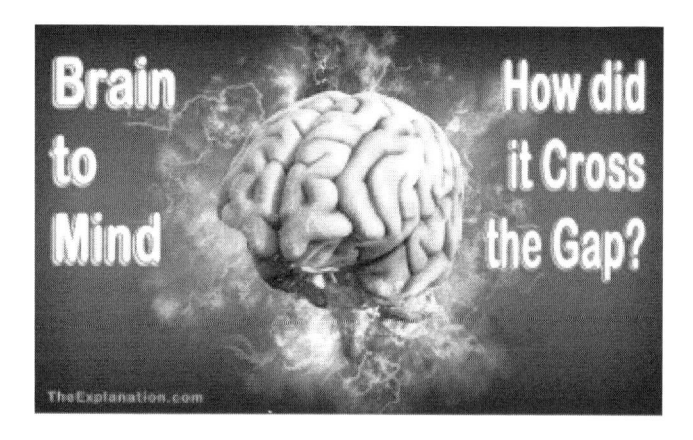

**Everyone agrees there is a brain and a mind. The disagreement arises in whether and how humans crossed the gap.**

Let's recap. We're discussing the mind-body problem. To find a solution, we can depart from the non-existence or the existence of a Higher Power[1]. Here we've started our trip with the former concept. So far, I've evoked two scenarios Science faces and still must resolve. First, a fine-tuned universe[2]. How? Why? Second, the transition from geochemical rocks to biochemical cells[3]. How? Why? This chapter marks another milestone in human development. From brain to mind. How? Why?

The last two chapters included many quotes. The reason is that I'm no expert in astrophysics or chemistry. And I want you to hear it

---

1. https://theexplanation.com/higher-power-starting-point-spiritual-secular/

2. https://theexplanation.com/did-a-fine-tuned-universe-give-rise-to-earth/

3. https://theexplanation.com/life-biology-rocks-to-cells-simple-complexity/

from the horse's mouth; it's eyewitness evidence from practicing experts in these disciplines. It is likewise in this exposé of brain to mind. Let's start with a short video[4] reminding us of the complexity of the brain. Pick up on some of the overriding statements.

- 4:00 On their own neurons aren't very bright but put 100 billion of them together in a small space and let them all start talking to each other (each communicates with up the 50.000 other neurons), and you get brainstorming. It's this complexity that allows us to think imaginatively. The trillions of neuronal networks, like an improvisational orchestra, create new ideas and connect different thoughts in a whimsical and sometimes inspired fashion. It's this impromptu ability to produce new things in our brain that allows us to progress.

The brain is truly unique, so much so that I hope you meditate on and analyze the idea that all this happened by natural selection over a relatively short period from an evolutionary point of view. The New Scientist writes[5]:

We can only speculate about why their brains began to grow bigger around 2.5 million years ago, but it is possible that serendipity played a part. In other primates, the "bite" muscle exerts a strong force across the whole of the skull, constraining its growth. In our forebears, this muscle was weakened by a single mutation[6], perhaps opening the way for the skull to expand. This mutation occurred around the same time

---

4. https://youtu.be/o9p2ou1IyC0

5. https://www.newscientist.com/article/mg21128311-800-a-brief-history-of-the-brain/#ixzz7JNRbjMMi

6. https://www.newscientist.com/article/dn4817-early-humans-swapped-bite-for-brain/

## MIND-BODY PROBLEM SOLVED

as the first hominids with weaker jaws and bigger skulls and brains appeared (*Nature*, vol 428, p 415[7]).

Remember always to note concepts like *speculate* or words like *perhaps*. The shots in the dark have no solid basis; it's ironic science[8]. Here's another quote from the book *Brain to Mind* by James Zull. Please take a few moments to reflect.

> My hope is to identify and explain how a brain becomes a mind through experience, and to create an educational agenda that will encourage and support that goal. Technology must serve development of the mind, not the reverse.
>
> The focus... on processes that are central to mental growth at any stage in life... we can claim success if learners... proceed to take actions, and ask questions when given a task. This is in contrast to getting it right.

There are two aspects here. Let me take the second paragraph first.

1. Should we (children and/or adults) focus on *getting it right or questioning the fundamentals?* Should we emphasize marks and grades or critical thinking[9]? I believe we'd agree it's the latter.
2. *Explain how a brain becomes a mind through experience.* Think about wording this phrase differently. How about experience(s) serves the development of the mind? Does the brain become a mind because of experiences an individual had or has? If the brain is a physical organ,

---

7. http://sapientfridge.org/chromosome_count/science_papers/myosin_gene_mutation.pdf

8. https://theexplanation.com/higher-power-starting-point-spiritual-secular/

9. https://theexplanation.com/critical-thinking-antidote-to-the-agony-of-humankind/

which it is, how can it experience anything without FIRST being connected to feelings, emotions, attitudes, and knowing perception? We run into our chicken and egg situation again.

Saying a brain becomes a mind through experience makes it sound like the brain is the originator of the mind. Is it? This is the heart of the brain to mind issue. Can a physical organ, even as sophisticated as the brain, engender the metaphysical output of reasoning, creating, and the many wonders the human mind is capable of?

## Are Brain and Mind the Same Thing?

In this video[10] Robert Kuhn, in his quest to get closer to truth, interviews brain scientist David Eagleman and Medical Professor Robert Stickgold[11], who states: "We don't know how matter gives rise to mind." It's a must-watch[12] to understand the brain-mind problem; an eye-opening 27 minutes well spent.

Here's the fundamental question. Can science explain the human mind?[13]

> People don't seem to regard the complexity of a natural phenomenon as a critical barrier to scientific progress. Instead, those phenomena that involve the unique characteristics of the reflective mind — such as introspection and conscious will — are the ones that are taken to present a real obstacle for science. And those

---

10. https://www.youtube.com/watch?v=2i9UPTDUFJo
11. https://youtu.be/2i9UPTDUFJo?t=1246
12. https://youtu.be/2i9UPTDUFJo?t=120
13. https://www.npr.org/sections/13.7/2017/11/20/565446970/can-science-explain-the-human-mind

that contribute to making us exceptional — more than a "mere" animal among many — seem to place us further beyond what science can explain.

Many articles ponder if science can resolve the problem of how the brain generated the human mind. The above and below quotes come from NPR, the National Public Radio, an American privately and publicly funded non-profit media organization.

The passage from the physics of the brain[14] to the corresponding facts of consciousness is unthinkable. Granted that a definite thought, and a definite molecular action in the brain occur simultaneously, we do not possess the intellectual organ nor, apparently, any rudiment of the organ, which would enable us to pass by a process of reasoning from the one phenomenon to the other.

They appear together and we don't know why. Were our minds and senses so expanded, strengthened and illuminated as to enable us to see and feel the very molecules of the brain, were we capable of following all their motions, all their groupings, all their electric discharges, if such there be, and were we intimately acquainted with the corresponding states of thought and feeling, we should be as far as ever from the solution of the problem. How are these physical processes connected with the facts of consciousness? The chasm between the two classes of phenomena would still remain intellectually impassable.

---

14. https://www.npr.org/sections/13.7/2017/11/29/567228138/science-and-the-mystery-of-the-mind

## The Hard Problem of Consciousness

Here's a comment from the Internet Encyclopedia of Psychology:

> The hard problem of consciousness[15] is the problem of explaining why any physical state is conscious rather than nonconscious. It is the problem of explaining why there is "something it is like" for a subject in conscious experience, why conscious mental states "light up" and directly appear to the subject.
>
> But even after we have explained the functional, dynamical, and structural properties of the conscious mind, we can still meaningfully ask, Why is it conscious? This suggests that an explanation of consciousness[16] will have to go beyond the usual methods of science. Consciousness therefore presents a hard problem for science, or perhaps it marks the limits of what science can explain.

I could continue forever giving you such quotes. I hope your critical thinking is running smoothly. So what do most people think explains the human mind if not science?

## Explaining How the Mind Works: A New Theory (Another One)

> The desire to understand the greatest enigma of all – our own minds[17] – has been the driving force behind many scientific endeavours, leading to the development

---

15. https://iep.utm.edu/hard-con/

16. https://iep.utm.edu/consciou/

17. https://researchoutreach.org/articles/explaining-how-the-mind-works-new-theory/

# MIND-BODY PROBLEM SOLVED

of theories and experiments aimed at explaining the mechanics of being human. Human thoughts, feelings, and behaviours are rooted in the brain, where a complex network of cells receives information from the internal and external environment, transforming this information into our experience of ourselves, the world around us, and our relationships with it. It goes without saying that how this happens is still being explored.

If you want to continue your study of science and its research about the brain to mind question, do a Google search for how does science explain the human mind.

I also suggest you read the chapters relating brain to mind in both *Inventory of the Universe*[18] and *Audit of the Universe*[19]. This material enhances your understanding of the body to mind issue. It is vital information related to the secular approach to the working of the brain and mind. But this book has no space to include all the relevant knowledge. The subject is simply too vast. Frankly, Part 1 of this book aims to demonstrate that science and philosophy cannot answer our questions.

Here are links to the chapters in the two books.

## Inventory of the Universe

- Brain and Mind[20]
- The Cerebral Cortex and the Geography of the Brain[21]

---

18. https://theexplanation.com/inventory/read-all-the-content-of-inventory-of-the-universe-online/

19. https://theexplanation.com/read-content-audit-universe-online/

20. https://theexplanation.com/the-brain-amazingly-small-amazingly-powerful-why/

21. https://theexplanation.com/the-brain-amazingly-small-amazingly-powerful-why/

- The Nervous System and the Multitasking Brain[22]
- Your Brain is Multitasking 100s and 1000s of functions all the time[23]
- The Acquiring Brain Has a Mind of Its Own[24]
- "Wired" Habits and Repetition[25]
- Think First[26]
- Critical Periods: When Babies and Children Learn[27]
- When a Child's Brain Accelerates its Development[28]
- Unique Brains[29]
- Mind and Cognition[30]
- Thoughts and Activity[31]
- Thinking Precedes and Activates Brain Activity[32]

---

22. https://theexplanation.com/neurons-communication-traffic-junctions-of-the-nervous-system/

23. https://theexplanation.com/your-brain-is-multitasking-100s-and-1000s-of-functions-every-moment/

24. https://theexplanation.com/your-plastic-brain-is-changing-constantly-it-has-a-mind-of-its-own/

25. https://theexplanation.com/your-wired-brain-praiseworthy-repetition-creates-good-habits/

26. https://theexplanation.com/think-first-think-repetitively-your-positive-or-negative-actions-follow/

27. https://theexplanation.com/critical-periods-when-babies-and-children-learn/

28. https://theexplanation.com/critical-periods-when-a-child-s-brain-accelerates-its-development/

29. https://theexplanation.com/unique-brains-and-minds-for-each-human-but-brain-and-mind-unity-in-human-diversity/

30. https://theexplanation.com/unique-brains-and-minds-for-each-human-but-brain-and-mind-unity-in-human-diversity/

31. https://theexplanation.com/thoughts-musing-and-cogitation-modify-our-physical-activity/

32. https://theexplanation.com/thinking-precedes-and-activates-activity-nobody-knows-the-

# Audit of the Universe

- Body and Mind—Are the Brain, Heart, and Gut–all Body Organs–the Mind?[33]
- The Human Mind–Is It a Body Part, Part of the Brain, or Somewhere Else?[34]
- Mental Health, You will be Surprised to Know what the State of the World is[35]
- In the Mind, each of us is Affected by the Violence and Sex We Encounter[36]
- The Mind-Body Dilemma, 400 Years Old and Still Unsolved. Why?[37]
- The Illusion of Artificial Intelligence and Transhumanism[38]
- Consciousness and Human Mind, You Can't Have One Without the Other[39]

---

mechanism/

33. https://theexplanation.com/body-and-mind-are-the-brain-heart-and-gut-all-body-organs-the-mind/
34. https://theexplanation.com/the-human-mind-is-it-a-body-part-part-of-the-brain-or-somewhere-else/
35. https://theexplanation.com/mental-health-you-will-be-surprised-to-know-what-the-state-of-the-world-is/
36. https://theexplanation.com/in-the-mind-each-of-us-is-affected-by-the-violence-and-sex-we-encounter/
37. https://theexplanation.com/the-mind-body-dilemma-400-years-old-and-still-unsolved-why/
38. https://theexplanation.com/the-illusion-of-artificial-intelligence-and-transhumanism/
39. https://theexplanation.com/consciousness-and-human-mind-you-cant-have-one-without-the-other/

This is the last chapter about science and philosophy directly related to the brain to mind issue. We must broach one pressing subject in the next chapter. Do animal intelligence and the human mind have anything in common? Could the former give rise to the latter?

# 4. Animal Cognition. Richly Similar & Different to Human Minds

**Animal cognition, animal mind. How intelligent are they? How does it compare with the human mind?**

Animal cognition has come to the forefront of scientific research. But is it a link between the brain and the human mind? What, if any, is the profound relationship between animals and humans?

In bygone years, many thinkers considered animals as automatons, each individual a robot replica of its progenitor. However, times have changed, and scientific research has established, without a doubt, that animals, including fish, birds, and insects, possess cognitive capacities. Here's what the Thinking Animals United[1] organization writes about animal cognition:

---

1. https://www.thinkinganimalsunited.org/about/

This involves the processing of information[2], problem solving: How the perceptual system (auditory, visual, olfactory, gustatory) receives data from the world it inhabits (including data from other individuals), and, with its species-specific neurobiology, uses its brain to process and act on that information.

This book will define what a mind is and why humans have it. At the same time, we cannot ignore animal cognition. We've all witnessed videos of animals expressing human emotions and feelings. Anyone who owns a pet knows how attached an animal can get to its owner-companion, how the animal can feel what you're feeling and react in consequence. Horses, dogs, donkeys, and dolphins are hugely successful therapeutic animals. It's far from having human company, but much better than being alone. So how does the human mind-body problem play out with animal cognition?

Once again, I will provide some quotes from capable experts to establish the reality of animal cognition. Of course, no explanation of the mind-body problem would be complete without clarifying what some call *animal mind*.

## Animal Cognition

Here are excerpts from a very informative and lucid article, A Journey Into The Animal Mind,[3] by Ross Anderson[4], deputy editor of The Atlantic:

> It was likely more than half a billion years ago that some sea-floor arms race between predator and prey roused

2. https://www.thinkinganimalsunited.org/what-is-animal-cognition/

3. https://www.theatlantic.com/magazine/archive/2019/03/what-the-crow-knows/580726/

4. https://www.theatlantic.com/author/ross-andersen/

# MIND-BODY PROBLEM SOLVED

Earth's first conscious animal. That moment, when the first mind winked into being, was a cosmic event, opening up possibilities not previously contained in nature.

There now appears to exist, alongside the human world, a whole universe of vivid animal experience. Scientists deserve credit for illuminating, if only partially, this new dimension of our reality. But they can't tell us how to do right by the trillions of minds with which we share the Earth's surface. That's a philosophical problem, and like most philosophical problems, it will be with us for a long time to come.

Yes, animal mind is a new dimension of reality. Anderson passes it off to philosophers. But they can't answer; hence it will be with us for a long time to come. Human reasoning cannot solve this problem, but *The Explanation* will. Anderson continues:

> But Eastern thinkers have long been haunted by its implications — especially the Jains, who have taken animal consciousness seriously as a moral matter for nearly 3,000 years.
>
> Mammals in general are widely thought to be conscious, because they share our relatively large brain size, and also have a cerebral cortex, the place where our most complex feats of cognition seem to take place.
>
> If these behaviors add up to consciousness, it means one of two things: Either consciousness evolved twice, at least, across the long course of evolutionary history, or it evolved sometime before birds and mammals went

on their separate evolutionary journeys. Both scenarios would give us reason to believe that nature can knit molecules into waking minds more easily than previously guessed. This would mean that all across the planet, animals large and small are constantly generating vivid experiences that bear some relationship to our own.

Scientists have sometimes seemed to judge fish for their refusal to join our exodus out of the water and into the atmosphere's more ethereal realm of gases. Their inability to see far in their murky environment is sometimes thought to be a cognitive impairment. But new evidence indicates that fish have minds rich with memories; some are able to recall associations from more than 10 days earlier.

Wasps, like bees and ants, are hymenopterans, an order of animals that displays strikingly sophisticated behaviors. Ants build body-to-body bridges that allow whole colonies to cross gaps in their terrain. Lab-bound honeybees can learn to recognize abstract concepts, including "similar to," "different from," and "zero." Honeybees also learn from one another. If one picks up a novel nectar-extraction technique, surrounding bees may mimic the behavior, causing it to cascade across the colony, or even through generations.

The first animals to direct themselves through three-dimensional space would have encountered a new set of problems whose solution may have been the evolution of consciousness. Take the black wasp. As it hovered above the bougainvillea's tissue-thin petals, a great deal of information — sunlight, sound vibrations, floral scents — rushed into its fibrous exoskull. But these information streams arrived in its brain at different times. To form an accurate and continuous account of the external world, the wasp needed to sync these signals. And it needed to correct any errors introduced by its own movements, a difficult trick given that some of its sensors are mounted on body parts that are themselves mobile, not least its swiveling head.

As Singh and I talked, the crow grew bored with us and turned back to the window, as though to inspect its faint reflection. In 2008, a magpie — a member of crows' extended family of corvids, or "feathered apes" — became the first non-mammal to pass the "mirror test." The magpie's neck was marked with a bright dot in a place that could be seen only in a mirror. When the magpie caught sight of its reflection, it immediately tried to check its neck.

These animal experiences are fact. However, please note that all the talk about how this state came to be is filled with *thought to be*, *may have been*, and a recognition of the immense coordination problems black wasps must overcome to sync hovering over a flower. As true as the hovering is, it's far from an explanation as to how a black wasp came to do this task in the first place.

## Animal Minds

In *Animal Minds*[5], Donald R. Griffin takes us on a guided tour of the recent explosion of scientific research on animal mentality:

---

5. *https://press.uchicago.edu/ucp/books/book/chicago/A/bo3640817.html*

Are animals consciously aware of anything, or are they merely living machines, incapable of conscious thoughts or emotional feelings? How can we tell? Such questions have long fascinated Griffin, who has been a pioneer at the forefront of research in animal cognition for decades, and is recognized as one of the leading behavioral ecologists of the twentieth century.

With this new edition of his classic book, which he has completely revised and updated, Griffin moves beyond considerations of animal cognition to argue that scientists can and should investigate questions of animal consciousness. Using examples from studies of species ranging from chimpanzees and dolphins to birds and honeybees, he demonstrates how communication among animals can serve as a "window" into what animals think and feel, just as human speech and nonverbal communication tell us most of what we know about the thoughts and feelings of other people.

Even when they don't communicate about it, animals respond with sometimes surprising versatility to new situations for which neither their genes nor their previous experiences have prepared them, and Griffin discusses what these behaviors can tell us about animal minds. He also reviews the latest research in cognitive neuroscience, which has revealed startling similarities in the neural mechanisms underlying brain functioning in both humans and other animals. Finally, in four chapters greatly expanded for this edition, Griffin considers the latest scientific research on animal consciousness, pro and con, and explores its profound philosophical and ethical implications.

Animals are the closest beings to humans in the way we live and act. Did our minds start within the animal kingdom? How similar are animal and human thinking? What explains the similarities and differences? Unfortunately, science, philosophy, and religion cannot answer these crucial questions satisfactorily.

## Animal Cognition Verse Human Mind

Once we've established, without a doubt, the existence and reality of animal intelligence, and their capacity to make decisions and adaptations, we need to compare this to our human capacities. And the fact is animal cognition comes up far short of the human mind.

I wrote this phrase to embody this chasm, fittingly, as the Summer Olympics were underway in Beijing in 2008:

> Animals will run off with all the Olympic medals, while humans will garner all the Nobel prizes. Animals have the physical advantage, but humans outdo them 100 to 0 regarding mental phenomena.

I will not spend time elaborating further on animal cognition or the vast impassible abyss separating animals from humans. The reason is that information is available in *Inventory of the Universe*, written to address this specific issue. Please read the following chapters in Parts 6 and 10.

## 6 Animal Ability

- Animal Ability[6]
- Communicators[7]
- Organizers[8]

---

6. https://theexplanation.com/animal-abilities-animal-communication/

7. https://theexplanation.com/animal-abilities-animal-communication/

# THE EXPLANATION

- Navigators[9]
- Climbers and Swimmers[10]
- Tool Makers[11]
- Home Builders[12]
- Weatherproofers[13]

## 10 The Human/Animal Dilemma

- The Human/Animal Dilemma[14]
- Amazing Animals and Less Amazing Humans[15]
- Animal Senses[16]
- Animal Bodies[17]
- Animal Movement[18]
- Animals' Survival in Extreme Conditions[19]
- Animal Stages of Life and Sociability[20]

---

8. https://theexplanation.com/animal-societies-community-organizers/
9. https://theexplanation.com/animal-navigation-defies-human-brain/
10. https://theexplanation.com/innate-capabilities-animals-leave-human-swimmers-their-wake/
11. https://theexplanation.com/animal-intelligence-tool-makers-home-builders/
12. https://theexplanation.com/animal-intelligence-tool-makers-home-builders/
13. https://theexplanation.com/animal-kingdom-will-never-cease-to-amaze-mankind/
14. https://theexplanation.com/mankind-sits-at-the-pinnacle-of-the-life-chain-why/
15. https://theexplanation.com/amazing-animals-less-amazing-humans-they-are-separated-by-a-gulf/
16. https://theexplanation.com/animal-senses-light-years-beyond-what-mankind-is-capable-of-why/
17. https://theexplanation.com/animal-bodies-all-shapes-sizes-forms-and-characteristics/
18. https://theexplanation.com/animal-survival-and-movement-capabilities-far-outshine-those-of-mankind/
19. https://theexplanation.com/animal-survival-and-movement-capabilities-far-outshine-those-of-mankind/

# MIND-BODY PROBLEM SOLVED

- Animal Accomplishments[21]
- Animal and Human Intelligence[22]
- What Is an Animal? What Is a Human?[23]
- Final Notions, Concepts, and Ideas for Thought[24]

The questions about animal cognition are real. *The Explanation* will address the existence of these facts. It will explain the mechanism behind the making of each species' survival, protection, hunting skills, and associated body development. How are animals so perfectly adapted to their environment and their capacity to survive there? What is behind their intelligence? It is an exciting and challenging subject.

---

20. https://theexplanation.com/animal-and-human-stages-of-life-and-sociability-what-do-they-tell-us/
21. https://theexplanation.com/animal-accomplishments-are-zero-compared-to-human-accomplishments/
22. https://theexplanation.com/animal-instinct-and-human-intelligence-the-insurmountable-gulf/
23. https://theexplanation.com/what-is-animal-intelligence-what-is-human-intelligence-do-they-compare/
24. https://theexplanation.com/mankinds-mind-the-key-to-final-notions-and-ideas-for-thought/

# 5. Human Reasoning has No Explanation for the Mind. Dreadful

**No Explanation from science, philosophy, or religion puts the mind-body problem to rest. So where do we turn for the solution?**

Human reasoning has been searching relentlessly, and no explanation for consciousness and mind is forthcoming. Not even close. We won't even wonder about an explanation of *why* the mind even exists.

Stardust is the composition of our body. Imagine that. Where did the original stardust come from? No explanation. What about the origin of the fine-tuning[1] for that stardust to become a life-supporting planet called Earth? No explanation. Then the inert minerals transformed into life[2]. Wow, no explanation. And then,

---

1. https://theexplanation.com/did-a-fine-tuned-universe-give-rise-to-earth/

2. https://theexplanation.com/life-biology-rocks-to-cells-simple-complexity/

the most significant leap in history, living matter developed ethereal consciousness[3] and mind. No explanation.

That's an awful lot of no explanation from enlightened scientific, philosophical, and religious reasoning of 21$^{st}$ century progressive humanity. Thankfully, we can count on science to explain material matters, just as we can look to behavioral science to describe human experiences. But, no explanation is prevalent, and I wrote in Part 5 of *Audit of Humankind: How Humans Reason* about this cacophonic collapse of communication and the presence of ironic science[4].

We must search for another source for profound, coherent explanations of the mind-body problem.

## Theology

The approach involves NONE of the methods above, no philosophy, science, or religion.

So, what's left?

The basis for further discussion is theology, one field we have not discussed yet.

Some might think this is akin to religion, but the two have a night-and-day difference. So, hopefully, let's explore this alternative option with an open mind. The first point to make is a clarification of the term.

Let's look at the word *theology* with its two distinct parts.

### *Theo* Means god or God.

---

3. https://theexplanation.com/brain-to-mind-can-material-create-immaterial/

4. https://theexplanation.com/science-facts-fiction-vital-human-reasoning/

Right away, we run into a thorny issue: the existence, or not, of some higher power. Then, if we agree, there is one: the nature of this higher power. If we took a poll, we'd get every idea under the sun - and then some. A factor of belief comes, assuredly, into play - an immensely personal feeling that characterizes each of us. As the author of this book, I want to respect your beliefs about G/god, science, religion, or any other concept, or lack thereof.

However, we took a step in the direction of some higher power when we decided that none of the principal ways humankind reasons (philosophy, science, religion) is fully working.

Theology means we continue in the direction of a higher power, fully aware that we don't know if this G/god even exists and that this power has yet to be defined.

## The Meaning of *logy* is

From a Google definition[5], we read: combining form: suffix: -logy; suffix: -ology

1. Denoting a subject of study or interest: psychology.
2. Indicating a characteristic of speech or language: eulogy.
3. Denoting a type of discourse: trilogy.

*Logy* involves the *study of*, or language and *discourse around a particular subject*. Here: god(s) or God.

We find a related word as part of logy: logo[6]

---

5. https://www.google.com/search?q=logy+definition&oq=logy+definition

6. https://www.google.com/search?q=logogram+definition

# MIND-BODY PROBLEM SOLVED

logogram ˈlɒɡə(ʊ)ɡram, a sign or character representing a word or phrase, such as those used in shorthand and some ancient writing systems.

As you can see, this word relates to a sign, character, word, phrase, shorthand, and writing systems. As seen above, this is part of the study of language and discourse. Company logos are everywhere - one identifying sign, frequently without a word - and we usually know precisely what or to whom it refers.

Theology is the sign or set of symbols, characters, words, or phrases relating to a higher power. In short, the writing system that identifies and expounds god(s) or God.

*The Explanation* is going a step further here because, within this concept of *logy* and *logo*, we find a familiar English word: logic.

> Late Middle English: via Old French logique and late Latin logica from Greek logikē (tekhnē) '(art) of reason,' from logos 'word, reason.' (Google definition)

> Middle English logik, from Anglo-French, from Latin logica, from Greek logikē, from feminine of logikos of reason, from logos reason (Merriam-Webster definition). Merriam goes on to add this:
> 
> 1. A proper or reasonable way of thinking about something: sound reasoning "There's no logic in what you said."
> 2. A science that deals with the rules and processes used in sound thinking and reasoning.

When we consider these concepts, we define theology as:

> The study of words related to God. not just any words, but rather sound, reasoned, logical ones.

*The Explanation* is NOT humankind's words about a deity. That's what Wikipedia[7] and the Science of Theology do.

> *The Explanation* IS about the sound, reasoned words of God. What does God have to say? What is His reasoning? Why does He want Peace and Prosperity? It's only the Source that can give real reliable answers.

For *The Explanation,* theology refers to the source's words. The source is a god with a small or capital *g*. Since it's generally associated with religion and its originator, it comes with a capital *G*. I don't expect non-believers to accept the capital *G* or even to believe that God has or could transmit the answers to the fundamental questions of life.

What *The Explanation* suggests: You've listened to all the 'no explanations' humankind has to offer about d/Deity as well as consciousness and mind; why not give an ear to what Deity has to declare to humanity? We're embarking on a fabulous story, some would say fabulation, about a Spiritual God and a Physical Universe, Earth, and humankind.

Is there Divine logic, sound reasonable words to explain not just the visible but also the invisible? A complete explanation of the brain, consciousness, mind, humankind, Earth, and the Universe? Not only the what, and how, but especially the why.

## Coherent Completeness

---

7. https://en.wikipedia.org/wiki/Theology#Definition

## MIND-BODY PROBLEM SOLVED

You've heard of the Grand Unifying Theory (GUT) and the Theory of Everything (TOE). They unify all the known physical forces governing our universe into one simple mathematical equation. Watch this informative video[8] by Dr. Don Lincoln from the Fermilab, the US national laboratory specializing in high-energy particle physics, to see the details and realize we aren't close to finding that answer.

The goal of *The Explanation* is obviously not on that scientific level but on a universal humankind mental and spiritual one. So, for now, I'll equate the spiritual level to the psychic or mental and leave open the possibility that other levels might not be readily visible to humankind.

This GUT, as scientists refer to it (*Inventory of the Universe*[9], Chapter 1) or Coherent Completeness, as I will call it, is a unique concept.

Coherent Completeness is the all-englobing-everything. Here are a few made-up words to try and describe this idea. It's monotheology, monoview, monomind, monotruth. Coherent completeness unifies, into one complete puzzle, a cohesive view of all the visible and invisible pieces. It renders a clear image of the why, how, and what of the Universe and humankind.

That is a tall order.

And I hear one of the critical counterarguments.

The religious-minded population, who believe in a Higher Power, often point out: The author - God - is mysterious, He's not a man. How can you expect to understand the mind of God? Or another

---

8. https://youtu.be/9LGBo7dLgYk

9. https://theexplanation.com/inventory/read-all-the-content-of-inventory-of-the-universe-online/

argument is that humans are just supposed to do our best and leave the rest to Him. He knows our hearts and will do what He has to do. There are 1001 other reasonings that drive us away from even thinking we can sound the mind of God.

Well, that is the task *The Explanation* has set before itself. To show how to reach and teach Coherent Completeness. Now, back to a more profound definition of theology:

> Theology understands the mind and concepts of the Originator. It is the all-encompassing WHY, the foundational motivation of the source, compared to the What and How of religion.

Theology goes deep into the mind and purpose of the author and answers the Why questions.

Whenever the Author thinks, says, or does something, there's a reason. He does nothing haphazardly. There is motivation, rationale, and an explanation behind each move.

Theology, the logical reasoning of God, the Source, will lead us to Coherent Completeness.

## Who is the author of The Explanation?

In conclusion, to this short Section on Theology, expanded in *Origin of the Universe*[10], I'd like to tell you about my dilemma when the idea of writing these books first germinated. First, what was I going to name it? Initially, it was to be one book, not a series. And the second question, as the author, how should I present my name? Maybe I should use a pseudonym. But, as you can see, I

---

10. https://theexplanation.com/deity-and-sound-reasoned-words-are-the-crux-of-theology/

# MIND-BODY PROBLEM SOLVED

decided against the latter simply because the teaching and videos accompanying the books would reveal my identity anyway.

I'm just as human as any person, be they a leader, philosopher, scientist, or religionist. My ideas are just as bad as anyone else's on this humongous subject of coherent completeness.

So, what's my relationship with this plan? I wanted the title of this book series to reflect that clearly: *The Explanation* **with** Sam Kneller. It looks like a minor detail - **with** - but it's not. Most titles would state "A Book Title BY ..." with the author's name. I'm explicitly avoiding the *by* to show that I'm NOT the author of *The Explanation* as such. All I'm doing is expressing *The Explanation* in different terms. I'm exposing it in a way to make it available to a broader audience; this is *The Explanation* WITH Sam Kneller. I'm just tagging along for its exposition.

In ABSOLUTELY NO WAY am I the author of the plan of coherent completeness. I'm a dummy when it comes to that. Your appreciation of, or argumentation with, the program of coherent completeness is not an issue to take up with Sam Kneller. That's why I will not debate, quarrel, or squabble about this plan. I will try to explain, but if you have a problem with it, you need to take it up with the real Author.

As I stated in Chapter 1, Higher Power or Not?[11] I wrote three books, *Inventory of the Universe*[12], *Audit of the Universe*[13], *Audit of Humankind*[14], and the first chapters of *Origin of the Universe*[15],

---

11. https://theexplanation.com/higher-power-starting-point-spiritual-secular/

12. https://theexplanation.com/inventory/read-all-the-content-of-inventory-of-the-universe-online/

13. https://theexplanation.com/read-content-audit-universe-online/

14. https://theexplanation.com/read-all-the-content-of-audit-of-humankind-online/

15. https://theexplanation.com/read-content-origin-universe-online/

summarized at the beginning of this book, *Mind-Body Problem Solved*, as an introduction to understanding *The Explanation,* and why we must delve into theology. We're almost there. But, to explore the divine, we must first determine where to find these sound, reasoned words related to god(s)/God.

## II. The Source for Answers

No answers, or confused ones, is not the solution. Where to find the explanation.

# 6. Where is the Full Definition of Mind-Body, Consciousness?

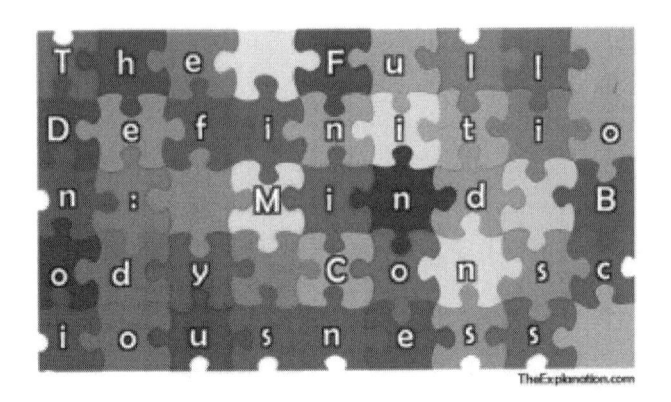

**Imagine finding a full definition of body, consciousness, and mind. What would that do for your trust in the document containing the complete description?**

Considering there are about 130,000,000 unique books, and we're not even sure the full definition is in any of these, we've got our work cut out. But we can systematically search for a full explanation of consciousness and mind.

Since we're looking to a Higher Power[1], sacred books are where we turn to pursue a study of Theology[2] (the words relating to g/God).

Sacred Books are historic writings generally penned by men or women to whom a higher power revealed the content. Followers

---

1. https://theexplanation.com/human-reasoning-no-explanation-for-the-mind/

2. https://theexplanation.com/human-reasoning-no-explanation-for-the-mind/

# MIND-BODY PROBLEM SOLVED 65

often worship the source of the works as g/God. These writings represent the foundation of knowledge, wisdom, and revelation from this divinity regarding the past, present, and future. They teach a way of thought and actions and are often the basis for a society applying principles to organize their daily lives individually and collectively.

The key to sacred books[3] is their inspiration derives from an *outside authority* - something beyond human capacity and reason. The idea is whatever the origin, their knowledge and wisdom are SUPERIOR to that of humans. Hence, these sacred writings contain more helpful information than humans can develop, investigate, or imagine. So let's reduce our choice of books.

## Here's a Non-exhaustive List of Sacred Books with Some of Their Followers:

- **Apocrypha**: Gospel of Thomas
- **Ayyavazhi**: The Akilathirattu Ammanai and Arul Nool
- **Buddhism**: The Tripiṭaka and the Dhammapada
- **Christianity**: The Christian Bible, especially the New Testament and the Gospels, Sacred Tradition
- **Confucianism**: The Analects of Confucius, also the I Ching
- **Epicureanism**, Principal Doctrines
- **Hinduism**: Shruti (Vedas, including the Rigveda; also Aranyakas, Brahmanas, Upanishads, Bhagavad Gita, Mahābhārata, Ramayana); Panchatantra
- **Islam**: The Qur'an, also Hadith and the Sunnah
- **Judaism**: The Hebrew Bible (Tanakh = Torah, Nevi'im, and Ketuvim), the Talmud, which includes Pirkei Avot
- **Mormonism**: Book of Mormon, Pearl of Great Price,

---
3. https://theexplanation.com/sacred-books/

Doctrine and Covenants
- **Satanism**: The Satanic Bible
- **Sikhism**: The Guru Granth Sahib and the Dasam Granth Sahib
- **Taoism**: The Dao De Jing, also Chuang Tzu, and the I Ching

## Identifying THE Sacred Book

Now to identify that ONE book. If you had a group of 100 people, how would you determine the one you're trying to find?

You'd look for evidence, proof, and identifying signs. For instance, if you know the person you're looking for is male, you're down to 50 people, has brown eyes, then you've eliminated another 20 people. If the person is between 1.60m and 1.70m, you're down to 10 people. And so forth: mustache, blond, teeth, DNA - until you've identified the *one and only*.

The identifying signs of the one sacred book we're looking for reveal answers to the why questions. The evidence is explanations of all the big questions in life. It must give us the WHAT and HOW of consciousness and mind, but especially the WHY. The full definition; we should expect nothing less from the Higher Power.

The fundamental reason I wrote *Inventory of the Universe* and *Audit of the Universe and Humankind* was to flush out the identifying signs. I summarized many of the why questions science, philosophy, and religion don't or can't answer. Click here for a partial list of dozens of questions[4] from *Inventory* and another with points to ponder from the *Audit* books[5].

---
4. https://theexplanation.com/the-why-of-human-life-the-biggest-unanswered-question-of-all-time/

# MIND-BODY PROBLEM SOLVED

Every single *why* question needs an answer, and the sacred text that answers ALL of those *why* queries with COHERENT WORDS in a SYSTEMATIC WAY is the ONE we want to use.

The why questions[6] are so much more vital than what or how. There isn't physical proof to offer because they are ideas, goals, desires, and plans established in the Higher Power's mind. We rarely, if ever, think about or consider the *why questions* regarding the motivation of individuals. This one sacred book must give a full definition of the answers.

## List of Basic Questions Humankind Cannot Answer

- Why are humans intelligent?
- Why are humans the only species that is worldwide?
- Why does humankind alone have the responsibility for the state of this planet?
- Why are humans sociable?
- Why do men, women, and children worldwide live in some form of relationship, generally marriage and family?
- Why are couples worldwide obliged to raise their children?
- Why do children take so many years to reach maturity?
- Why is this world in such an upset state? How is it possible to clear it up?
- And the key question of this book, unanswered by humankind's best brains: what is the full definition of consciousness and mind, and why do we possess them?

## One Sacred Book

---

5. https://theexplanation.com/the-nagging-question-how-do-humans-function-and-affect-the-universe/

6. https://theconversation.com/why-questions-good-and-bad-matter-147412

Our ONE sacred book must answer not just 25% or 50% or 72% but 100% of these questions and indeed even the issues that we don't think to interrogate!

The coherent, complete theology, the Source's sacred book, must answer these why questions. The holy book that gives us the correct answers points to the Source, who has recorded the answers to the why questions for humankind's benefit. We're going deep, deep, deep to search for a sacred book from a Source beyond humankind that can throw light on a full definition of subjects like why human life[7].

## The Bible

Let's cut through the Gordian Knot. In the Oriental world[8], their sacred books do not purport to answer why questions. In the entire Western world, the holy book is the Bible. Judaism limits itself to the Old Testament, but Christianity, in all its variegated forms, accepts and believes in both the Old and New Testaments. Some Christian religions also consider additional works as sacred. These works may illuminate some questions we are considering, but the Bible remains the cornerstone and common denominator of Western spirituality.

> The bottom line is the only book considered sacred, inspired by a Higher Power that answers all our questions, is the Bible.

I realize that's a huge statement you might not agree with. You could adamantly disagree. Many Christians and Christian theologians would take offense to such an affirmation. So here's the challenge: Show me writings that do answer ALL these questions.

---

7. https://en.wikipedia.org/wiki/Meaning_of_life

8. https://theexplanation.com/the-sacred-book-if-it-exists-could-it-possibly-be-the-bible/

# MIND-BODY PROBLEM SOLVED

I also understand that you might acknowledge the Bible as a unique work but not accept it as a sacred book and certainly not as one inspired by a s/Source beyond humanity with answers to all our mundane, earthly questions. This is where I need to ask you for patience. Such a subject takes time to develop; that's what the rest of this book, *Mind-Body Problem Solved*, is all about. So please, stay curious and keep reading.

Why would I focus on the Bible? On the Old and New Testaments? The Bible is an incredible paradox: the all-time best-seller and all-time champion of misunderstandings.

Maybe you're not a Bible advocate. You've had no interest in it or turned off involvement with this book. Many believe it's a myth, a collection of tales, many gleaned from other cultures. It's filled with errors and discrepancies. For now, I simply ask you to keep an open mind. We want and need writings that answer the big questions in life. *The Explanation* will show you the Bible does just that.

The identifying sign of the One Sacred Book we're looking for is that it will give accurate, coherent, complete answers to the BASIC questions for which humankind does not have answers.

Of all the sacred books I listed above, the Bible is the only one that has the answers to these fundamental questions of life - and, if you don't mind, I'll add death - because since we're all subject to that, it is a fundamental question which we cannot ignore: Why death? What is its purpose? Is there an afterlife? Why? How? Where? Under what conditions? Does everyone participate? And the list of questions goes on and on.

That I've focused attention on the Bible is nothing new. After all, many preachers are pounding out messages from the Bible. Hotel rooms carry a copy, and they'll even deliver one to your door free, accompanied by people who will explain certain teachings directly from its words.

So, why continue reading what *The Explanation* writes about the Bible?

Because whatever language translations you use, other than Biblical Hebrew, are incomplete and do not tell the entire story. Please don't get me wrong. I wrote INcomplete and the ENTIRE story. Oh yes, the English, French, German, Spanish, Japanese, Chinese, indeed all translations DO TELL A STORY - but NOT THE COMPLETE STORY.

Sorry for the capital letters; I need you to pay attention and stop, maybe even get a little irritated by what I just wrote and how I wrote it. I want to move you enough to become curious about what the Biblical Hebrew states and what you are missing in your comprehension of this one sacred book, and what it reveals about the full definition of consciousness and mind.

# 7. Fastest Bible Study Method to Grasp God-intended Meaning

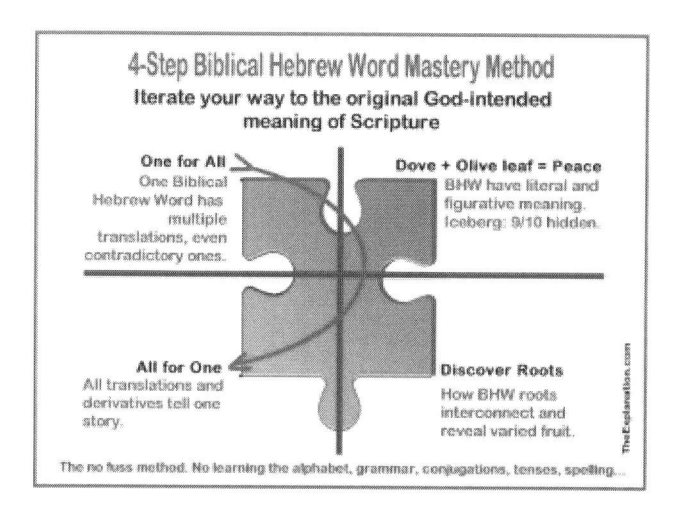

**4-Step Biblical Hebrew Word Mastery Method**
Iterate your way to the original God-intended meaning of Scripture

**One for All**
One Biblical Hebrew Word has multiple translations, even contradictory ones.

**Dove + Olive leaf = Peace**
BHW have literal and figurative meaning. Iceberg: 9/10 hidden.

**All for One**
All translations and derivatives tell one story.

**Discover Roots**
How BHW roots interconnect and reveal varied fruit.

The no fuss method. No learning the alphabet, grammar, conjugations, tenses, spelling...

TheExplanation.com

**The quickest Bible study method to unlock the original God-intended significance of Scripture is through mastering Biblical Hebrew words, with no fuss.**

This breakthrough Bible study method is easier than you think, takes less time, and all the Bible tools are freely available online. So if you want to understand what consciousness and mind are, give it a chance. Follow this Bible study through the next few chapters, and you'll definitely reach that goal.

Let's jump right in. Go to UnlockBibleMeaning.com[1], the only Bible Study method online 24/7/365 free toolkit we'll need to reach *The Explanation*. Find Genesis 2:7. We could switch

---
1. https://unlockbiblemeaning.com

(drop-down menu on the right) to either Strong's Concordance or the Interlinear Bible. Now choose the latter.

You probably don't know Hebrew, but maybe you want to learn it, which is commendable. But it isn't easy, starting with a brand new alphabet that reads from right to left. You'll be reading letter-by-letter, like a three-year-old, for months! It'll take you years of struggle, energy, and lots of $$£££€€¥¥ if you take a course. Furthermore, realize that Hebrew scholars disagree with the meaning of Hebrew Scriptures anyway, so, frankly, you're not much further ahead using such a Bible study method in your quest to unlock Bible meaning.

I suggest you give this unique Bible study method a try. Notice (reading from right to left) ...and breathed into his nostrils the breath of life. In English, we have the word *breath* twice, *breathed*... the *breath*... Now, compare the two Hebrew words וַיִּפַּח and נִשְׁמַת. It's not rocket science to see they are not the same. The Strong numbers H5301 and H5397 confirm this fact. See how easy that was?

The same English word, *breath,* is, in fact, two different Hebrew words. What you've discovered is essential for understanding the limits of translations and, therefore, your comprehension of the God-intended meaning. That's the reason you need this easy-to-apply Bible study method to unlock the original meaning of Scripture.

Let's continue with a search for the Bible expression *breath of life*. There are four instances. This time we'll use Strong's to compare the numbers.

Only Gen. 2:7 has H5397. The other three have H7307, although Gen. 7:22 has both H7307 and H5397 for breath. So what's going on here? Somewhere there's a translation anomaly. You cannot detect this in English.

Furthermore, from a humankind point of view, we're discussing the most fundamental aspect of what a human is, the *breath of life*. Have you ever heard of this dilemma, let alone a solution? No wonder nobody knows what a human is and what consciousness and mind are. But you will find clear definitions.

We've identified an enormous translation problem with one of the most fundamental Bible concepts, *the breath of life*: one English word, *breath*, translated from three different Hebrew words (H5397, H5301, H7307). We will clear up this dilemma.

For now, let's summarize the Bible study method we'll use throughout this book to arrive at the God-intended original meaning of the *breath of life* and many other biblical concepts.

## 4-Step Biblical Hebrew Word Mastery

We'll *use breath of life* in Gen. 2:7 to illustrate the efficiency and validity of the Bible study method. Click on H5397 (*breath* in Gen. 2:7), and the corresponding Strong's reference displays in the right column. *H* is for Hebrew (G = Greek), and it's the 5397th alphabetically listed word among the 8674 unique Hebrew words used to compose the Old Testament.

1. The first part of Strong's reference always presents the Hebrew, the literation, and pronunciation. Then Strong's annotation, his summary after his study, of the meaning of this word.
2. The second part starts with a bold (**King James Version**) followed by all the English language translations the KJV Bible scholars rendered that one Hebrew word. On

occasion, you'll also see [x], [+] signs, which are words in the Authorized and Revised Versions, including the American variations.

For our word *breath*, H5397, the English translations are *blast*, (that) *breath*(-eth), *inspiration, soul, spirit*; five different English translations. Some Hebrew words have 50+ renderings!

This brings us to the 4-Step Bible study method.

## 1. One for All

The first step is one Hebrew word can have multiple meanings. Our Hebrew word נְשָׁמָה - neshama - H5397 has five translations, that is, five meanings. Why not one-for-one? Many think it's simply a matter of finding the best translation, word-for-word, and substituting that English word every time we see the Hebrew one. This is decidedly not the way the KJV academics saw the translation process. We have multiple words. How do we explain this, and what's the implication for understanding the God-given meaning of the one Hebrew word?

Note that an aspect of this first step is among these multiple English word meanings; some can be contradictory or at least conflicting. We shall return to this in a moment.

## 2. Figurative Meanings

A flying dove is a physical bird. An olive branch is a physical twig with leaves. But put them together, and you have a figurative symbol for *peace*. Apart, they are simple physical objects; together, they have an unknown, hidden meaning. Most people know this, even if they don't know the symbol's origin. It is from the end of Noah's flood (whether you think it existed or not is not the point here), when a dove with an olive sprig returned to the ark, signifying dry land had appeared, the waters had receded, and the world was at peace.

A child knows a dove is a bird, and a piece of wood with leaves comes from a tree. But, it would not know, that together, they represent *peace*. The second step is figurative meanings are like the 9/10 hidden, underwater part of an iceberg. You simply do NOT know it's there unless someone explains it to you. Until you get *The Explanation*, you're flying blind.

That 9/10 of the iceberg is the most important. Here's why. Most Bible readers and students study their Bibles like they were steering the Titanic, with disastrous results. They do NOT see the 9/10 hidden figurative writing in front of their eyes.

Take *breath*, H5793, for example. Breath is physical; everybody knows what breathing is all about, we all do it. But the translations include *inspiration* and *spirit*. Those are invisible, hidden, non-tangible, and untouchable. I daresay few know *breath* is *neshama* in Gen. 2:7, and fewer know that it has the figurative meaning of *inspiration* and *spirit*. So 9/10 of understanding is hidden from you. In that situation, it is impossible to know what a human being is.

Mastering the figurative meanings of Biblical Hebrew words is one of the key reasons people do not understand their Bible. The 4-Step Bible study method focuses your attention on these hidden gems. Instead of sinking into Bible confusion, you will have eye-opening revelations of the original God-intended meaning of Scripture.

## 3. Root Meanings

Words in Biblical Hebrew build mainly on a three-letter base. For instance, in English, oculus, binoculars, and monocle come from the root word ocular (to see). Look at Strong's annotation for breath. Note *from H5395 (נָשַׁם)*; this always points to the linked root. Let's click and display it.

**H5395**

נָשַׁם nâsham naw-sham'; a primitive root; properly, to blow away, i.e. destroy:

KJV - destroy.

Note the primitive root with the three letters, נָשַׁם, which you'll find in all the derivatives like נְשָׁמָה (the מָ changes form to ם at the end of a word, but it's the same letter); this is Biblical Hebrew with no fuss. All you have to do is compare the letters.

Now for the clincher. In Genesis 2:7, God blew LIFE into the first human's nostrils. So what is the root meaning of neshama? DESTROY. Wow, you weren't expecting that, were you? That's Step 1, multiple, even contradictory meanings; this sure is paradoxical.

A personal note: I studied two years of advanced Hebrew with the Institute of Biblical Studies in Jerusalem to validate the Bible study method I'm teaching you. When I pointed out the contradictory nature of some words, my teacher and fellow students shunned the idea. I kept at it, and before long, they identified such conflicts and agreed with the principle. I guarantee you this Bible study method gives valuable results, as you can already see.

It's 100% sure the Biblical Hebrew word *neshama* means both *blow* and *blow away*. And we have a problem on our hands, which we will solve.

## 4. All for One

The fourth step of the Bible study method is the key destination for every Biblical Hebrew word. ALL the translations/meanings (multiple, contradictory, figurative, roots) for a given Biblical Hebrew word must tell ONE STORY. That's it. Bibles give us basically a word-for-word translation. However:

> Each Biblical Hebrew word tells ONE COHERENT STORY. ALL the multiple meanings weave together to narrate the original God-intended meaning.

We're praying, meditating on, and studying to reach that, and that alone. Each word is a puzzle piece with its one-and-only shape. The various meanings reveal the contours of each term. When we really tell the word story, we'll understand WHERE and HOW it assembles with ALL the other puzzle pieces. Religious and theological confusion comes from an incomplete understanding of the pieces and forcing them into the wrong place.

This Bible study method *The Explanation* uses for all its Bible commentaries narrates the word stories and assembles them with adjoining words until we build the complete puzzle, giving us the God-intended meaning of His purpose for the Universe and humankind.

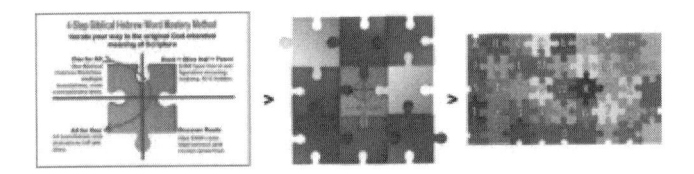

Figure 3. Puzzle of coherent completeness

In the Introduction, I asked ten questions about Genesis 2:7[2] and asserted religion and scholarly theology can't and don't answer them. Neshama, giving and destroying life, is the critical piece of our puzzle. We must get the narrative right, or we won't assemble the puzzle correctly. This image represents the answers to all those questions.

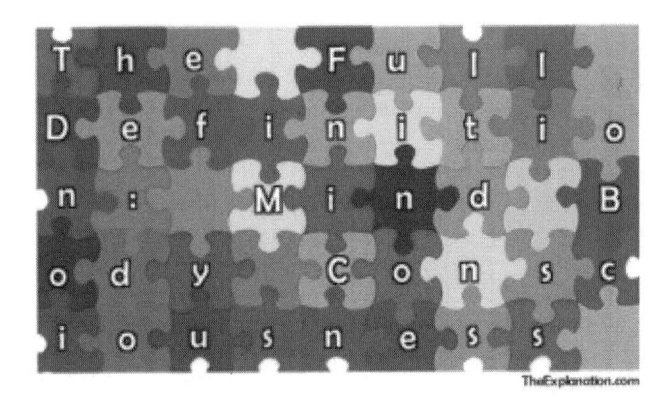

Figure 4. Coherent completeness

This book, *Mind-Body Problem Solved,* narrates the exciting stories of each Biblical Hebrew word and assembles them into the God-intended, original message of Scripture. Next, we will reveal the contours of neshama and explain why it's both a giver and

---

2. https://theexplanation.com/higher-power-starting-point-spiritual-secular/

snuffer of life. We'll then reach coherent completeness, illustrated by the image Full Definition: Mind, Body, Consciousness.

# 8. Men and Women Equality. Discover the Big Meaning of 'adam'

In Genesis 2:7, who received the breath of life, neshama? Does neshama play a role in men's and women's equality? What does *adam* mean?

Everybody knows the Bible indicates the creation of Adam as the first human being. How accurate is this affirmation, and what does this say about equality between men and women? We're in trouble if we just take the English version of the LORD God formed man of the dust of the ground, and breathed into his nostrils the breath of life (*neshama*); and man became a living soul. It looks like man, man, man.

Most Bible readers think this refers to Adam and naturally make the link that *man* refers to the male gender. Is that fact or an error? Maybe it's part of the problem of men's and women's equality.

# MIND-BODY PROBLEM SOLVED

Let's get the ball rolling with the 4-Step Bible study method[1] to understand the God-given meaning of *man*. At the same time, we'll see who the recipient of the *breath of life* is and focus on God's point of view regarding men's and women's equality.

At UnlockBibleMeaning.com[2], let's find our verse.

### Genesis 2:7

> And the LORD God formed *man* (H120) of the dust of the ground, and breathed into his nostrils the breath of life; and *man* (H120) became a living soul.

We saw the breath of life is the *neshama* (the inspiration). So the man - H120 (mentioned twice in this verse) receives this gift from God.

### H120

> אָדָם 'âdâm aw-dawm'; from H119 (אָדָם); ruddy i.e. a human being (an individual or the species, mankind, etc.):

> KJV - × another, + hypocrite, + common sort, × low, man (mean, of low degree), person.

- Use the *Hebrew Concordance for H120* link (move your mouse under *Prev. 5 - Next 5*) to locate all instances of *man - H120* in the Old Testament and see the word's usage in context.
- There are a lot of verses with *man* - H120. To help you out, focus on Numbers 31.

---

1. https://theexplanation.com/fastest-bible-study-method-god-intended-meaning/

2. https://unlockbiblemeaning.com

The 4-Steps for Biblical Hebrew Word Mastery are present. Identify them.

1. One Hebrew word has multiple meanings for *man*.
2. There are figurative or parallel meanings. What do you think of *hypocrite, low degree* in comparison to *dust*?
3. Root meaning; associated with *red*.

The goal is to tie ALL these meanings into ONE story; that's Step 4.

- I want you to discover a rather surprising *complementary*, some might say, *contradictory* meaning of *adam* translated *persons* in Numbers 31.

After your study, read what follows.

Here is a surprising meaning of man - H120

**Numbers 31:35**

And thirty and two thousand *persons* (H120) in all, of women that had not known *man* (H2145) by lying with him.

The *persons* - H120 - adam - אָדָם refers to... women! *Person*, in this context, refers solely to the 32,000 women who had not had intercourse with any man. As an aside, the Hebrew for *man* is H2145; look it up, it is *male*, again showing the limits of translations. This verse in Numbers is clearly referring to sexual relations, or rather their absence, between *women* and *males*.

What I want you to retain from this more complete comprehension of *adam* is we know the first human created was

# MIND-BODY PROBLEM SOLVED

Adam, a male, but the adam in Gen. 2:7 includes the meaning *human* and *person*. This means ALL humans, regardless of their gender, who they are, where they live, their culture, or anything else that characterizes them, receive *neshama*, the *breath of life*.

The Bible, at the moment of creation of the first human, establishes men's and women's equality without a doubt. Genesis 1:26, "In the image of God He created them male and female..." reinforces men's and women's equality.

I am spending a little time on this subject because some readers and Bible advocates or detractors of both the Old and New Testaments contest men's and women's equality in the Bible. And, I agree, there are ALL sorts of verses that SEEM to indicate their inequality. Emphasis on the word SEEM. I can only touch on this broad subject here. There are vast differences between the abilities, capacities, responsibilities, and obligations of males and females. Similarly, all men and no two women are alike. Each of us is a unique human finding and adjusting his or her place in society and life. This is an exciting subject. How and why does such diversity exist? We will go deep to answer these questions. But not today.

For now, bear in mind one biblical fact.

Each and every human, past, present, future, possessed, possesses, and will possess the *breath of life, neshama*. In this, men's and women's equality is the biblical reality.

Let's be even more precise. Infants possess neshama; even a baby that lives, unfortunately, for a few seconds possessed neshama. It had the breath of life for an instant, making it equal to all other humans. Sadly, some are born with mental deficiencies or, through life, fall into mental incapacities. They, too, carry neshama. Regrettably, some, through old age, develop Alzheimer's or some similar impairment; they, too, are endowed with neshama. No matter their state, every living human being is animated with the *breath of life, neshama.*

When we understand what neshama is and the role it plays for humankind, it is one of the most comforting comprehensions any of us can have regarding the sick, refugees, the troubled, tormented, harassed, mistreated people in the world, and there are many of them. They all benefit from men's and women's equality.

But know that *breath of life,* in Biblical Hebrew in Genesis 2:7, is not singular. It is *breath of LIVES -* (נִשְׁמַת חַיִּים). The key here is that the Bible establishes men's and women's equality right from the start, at the moment of Creation. All sorts of events happen to men and women later in the Bible story. Yes, God is responsible for some of them, like Numbers 31:35. This is another vital subject elaborated in *Origin of Woman*[3], *Agony of Humankind and the Antidote*[4], and *Evidence for Bible Wisdom*[5].

Through the possession of neshama by all humans, men's and women's equality is a fundamental biblical truth that, unfortunately, many are unaware of.

## Do Animals Possess Neshama? No

Let's answer this question unequivocally from the Bible, and then we will see the consequences for our understanding of the relationship between animals and humans. The following context in the book of Joshua enlightens us.

### Joshua 10:40, 11:11, 14

---

3. https://theexplanation.com/read-all-the-content-of-origin-of-woman-online/

4. https://theexplanation.com/sorrow-the-meaning-for-the-woman-in-genesis-316/

5. https://theexplanation.com/read-content-evidence-for-bible-wisdom-online/

# MIND-BODY PROBLEM SOLVED

**10:40** So Joshua smote all the country of the hills, and of the south, and of the vale, and of the springs, and all their kings: he left none remaining, but utterly destroyed all that *breathed* (H5397 neshama), as the LORD God of Israel commanded.

**11:11** And they smote all the *souls* (H5315 nefesh) that were therein with the edge of the sword, utterly destroying them: there was not any left to *breathe* (H5397 neshama): and he burnt Hazor with fire.

**11:14** And all the spoil of these cities, and the cattle, the children of Israel took for a prey to themselves; but every man they smote with the edge of the sword, until they had destroyed them, neither left they any to *breathe* (H5397 neshama).

As you reflect on these Bible passages, keep in mind Joshua 10:40. God commanded those crossing the Jordan to *destroy all that breathed (neshama)*. Reading this in English, we limit ourselves to physical *breathing*, which humans AND animals display. But, in the last episode[6], we saw neshama also carries the figurative or abstract meanings of *inspiration* and *spirit*.

In this episode, as the children of Israel entered the Promised Land, they utterly destroyed all the nefesh (souls) with neshama (*breathe*, as translated here, but it includes *inspiration*). HOWEVER, they took the cattle, which also breathe, for prey.

Since they destroyed ALL beings with neshama and kept the cattle alive, then cattle do NOT possess neshama.

---

6. https://theexplanation.com/fastest-bible-study-method-god-intended-meaning/

We will expand on this subject, but you've just learned a critical Bible concept. ALL HUMANS POSSESS NESHAMA; that's men's and women's equality. However, ANIMALS DO NOT POSSESS NESHAMA. Vital knowledge, which totally differentiates humans from animals and explains the impassible chasm separating them. Do you realize the impact of this Bible comprehension on sciences like social behavior, which studies animals to see why humans act the way we do? Do you see that saying chimps and humans share 98.8% of their physical DNA[7] completely omits the fact that chimps do not possess neshama, but humans do?

By understanding the full meaning of the Biblical Hebrew word *adam*, we see men's and women's equality because all humans are endowed with neshama. By the same token, we see that animals, with all their exceptional qualities, which we will discuss, do not possess neshama. This sets all humans completely apart as an exclusive race. The Bible is the story of unique humankind.

---

7. https://www.amnh.org/exhibitions/permanent/human-origins/understanding-our-past/dna-comparing-humans-and-chimps

# 9. Does God Exist? Yes, Who is the Higher Power YHVH Elohim?

**The question that changes everything. Can you even answer *does God exist*? How can you prove God exists? Even try?**

We're in the Second Part of the book *Mind-Body Problem Solved*. Here, there's a belief in a Higher Power, God exists, which remains to be defined. We have narrowed the search to a book answering all the big questions in life[1], the Bible.

From the Bible, we've answered one of our big 10 questions[2] regarding Genesis 2:7. Does *man* in Hebrew just refer to the masculine gender or something else? In the last chapter, we saw it relates to persons and humans, including women. In so doing,

---

1. https://theexplanation.com/where-full-definition-mind-body-consciousness/

2. https://theexplanation.com/higher-power-starting-point-spiritual-secular/

we've identified one of the critical characters of the Bible narration, all humans.

Now, using UnlockBibleMeaning.com[3], let's identify the other principal character.

**Genesis 2:7 - THE Key Character.**

And the *LORD* (H3068) *God* (H430) formed man of the dust of the ground, and breathed into his nostrils the breath of life; and man became a living soul.

This brings us to the most fundamental questions on our list about God's existence, which is essential to understanding the Creation of humans and the presence of consciousness and mind.

- Who is the Lord? What is the relation to the Higher Power?
- Why are *Lord* (Yahveh) singular and *God* (Elohim) plural?

I won't prove God exists, but I will explain some pertinent evidence—a few identifying signs from the book with the answers to see if God exists. The more pinpointing we do, the closer you'll come to believe, or not, in a Higher Power.

Genesis 1:1 to 2:3, the end of the seven days of Creation, refers to God, *Elohim*, plural, 35 times. Genesis 2:4 is the first time we read LORD God, *YAHVEH Elohim*, referred to in the singular. Many Bible scholars see this as proof of editorial dysfunction. They conclude there are two contradictory narrations of the Creation story, which, of course, the original author and editors would have seen and corrected IF there was an error. But there is NO anomaly.

---

3. https://unlockbiblemeaning.com

# MIND-BODY PROBLEM SOLVED

So, does God exist, and is His nature singular and/or plural? These are vital subjects. We're in the first five minutes of the Bible story establishing the characters and the plot that will play out over thousands of pages of the book and thousands of years of history. It behooves us to understand if God exists and His nature right from the start.

## Elohim

The first point to note is Elohim[4] is a plural noun in Genesis 1 and 2 and throughout the rest of the Bible. Please don't take my word for it; check it out. Here's Strong's.

### H430

אֱלֹהִים ’ĕlôhîym el-o-heem'; plural of H433 (אֱלוֹהַּ); gods in the ordinary sense; but specifically used (in the plural thus, especially with the article) of the supreme God; occasionally applied by way of deference to magistrates; and sometimes as a superlative:

KJV – angels, × exceeding, God (gods) (-dess, -ly), × (very) great, judges, × mighty.

### H433

אֱלוֹהַּ ’ĕlôwahh el-o'-ah; rarely (shortened) אֱלֹהַּ; probably prolonged (emphatic) from H410 (אֵל); a deity or the Deity:

KJV – God, god. See H430 (אֱלֹהִים).

### H410

---

4. https://theexplanation.com/yahweh-elohim-inseparable-relationship/

אֵל ʼêl ale; shortened from H352 (אַיִל); strength; as adjective, mighty; especially the Almighty (but used also of any deity):

KJV – God (god), × goodly, × great, idol, might(-y one), power, strong. Compare names in '-el.'

Elohim is plural in Hebrew, as we can see from H430. It means God, THE God, and gods.

The second grammatical point is the plural Elohim has a singular noun, *El*, as we see from H433 and especially H410, with which we are much more familiar. *El* is an integral part of many words, GaEL, IsraEL, and BethEL, including my full name, SamuEL. These are personal, national, and city names, all related to God.

The third grammatical point to consider is the plural ELOHIM takes a SINGULAR verb. In English, that would be the equivalent of *they does their homework*. To my knowledge, we don't have a word with these characteristics in English. Instead, we have a word like the animal *moose*. It is both singular and plural and can take a singular or a plural verb. But it doesn't have separate singular and plural nouns. A reader pointed out that the name United States is an excellent example of a plural word (50 States) using a singular verb. I like that idea.

But the real question is this. How can ONE God be plural? The concept of only ONE God is the basis of monotheism; this can be a somewhat controversial issue because of the ambiguity of Elohim (plural) using a singular verb. So what does the Bible say about this plurality?

**Genesis 1:26**

> And God said, Let *us* make man in *our* image, after *our* likeness ... male and female created He them.

The Bible, in its first chapter, the curtain-raiser, is unequivocal. The Author confirms the plurality twice by using the plural *us* and *our*. We cannot simply ignore or overlook this evidence. Throughout the 7-Day Creation week, until Gen. 2:3, it is Elohim plural with *us* and *our*. Then, from Genesis 2:4, we get a flashback to Creation week with much more detail, specifically of the Sixth Day Creation of the male and female.

## Who is YAHWEH?

Genesis 1 gives a global approach to Creation, whereas Gen. 2 and 3 concentrate on the personal, down-to-earth details. We learn the names of the male and female (Gen. 4:1), and we see their interaction with God, who now carries the name YAHWEH Elohim[5]. Chapter 1 gives a synthesis of Creation. Chapters 2 and 3 give exhaustive details about their Creation and the intimate interpersonal relationships between YAHWEH and Adam and Eve. I'll tell you right now that these two chapters' spiritual implications will blow you away. You can read about it in *Origin of Humankind*[6] and *Origin of Woman*[7].

Here's the Biblical Hebrew root and meaning of YHVH, YAHWEH, or YAHVEH.

**H3068**

---

[5]. https://theexplanation.com/yahweh-yahveh-meaning-identity-gods-name/

[6]. *https://theexplanation.com/read-content-origin-humankind-online/*

[7]. *https://theexplanation.com/read-all-the-content-of-origin-of-woman-online/*

יְהֹוָה Yᵉhôvâh yeh-ho-vaw'; from H1961 (הָיָה); (the) self-Existent or Eternal; Jehovah, Jewish national name of God:

KJV – Jehovah, the Lord. Compare H3050 (יָהּ), H3069 (יְהֹוִה).

**H1961**

הָיָה hâyâh haw-yaw; a primitive root (compare H1933 (הָוָא)); to exist, i.e., be or become, come to pass (always emphatic, and not a mere copula or auxiliary):

KJV – beacon, × altogether, be(-come), accomplished, committed, like), break, cause, come (to pass), do, faint, fall, + follow, happen, × have, last, pertain, quit (one-) self, require, × use.

YAHWEH, translated in English by the term LORD, derives from the verb *to be*. The translation LORD has no relation to the Hebrew meaning. God is the *Lord*, but that has nothing to do with this name, YAHWEH. In Biblical Hebrew, names have one or multiple meanings, just like any other word. A name describes and defines the person who carries that name.

The pronunciation is generally YAHVEH (the first letter, the 'יְ' (yod), is pronounced 'y', and the fourth letter, 'וָ' (vav), is pronounced 'v'). Over time and geographical location, the pronunciation can differ. For example, UK and USA English have the same vocabulary but different pronunciations. However, of utmost importance is the meaning.

Designated by this name YAHVEH / YAHWEH, the critical characteristic is His Eternity. The name is based on the verb *to be*. He WAS in the past; He IS in the present; He WILL BE in the future. He has always BEEN in the past. He is BEING in the present. He will BE in the future.

God Himself, in discussion with Moses, gives us the certitude that YAHVEH is one of the NAMES of GOD. Look at this confirmation in Exodus.

**Exodus 3:13-15**

> 13 And Moses said to God, Behold, when I come to the children of Israel, and shall say to them, The God of your fathers has sent me to you; and they shall say to me, What is his name? what shall I say to them?
>
> 14 And God said to Moses, *I AM* (H1961) THAT *I AM* (H1961): and he said, Thus shall you say to the children of Israel, *I AM* (H1961) has sent me to you.
>
> 15 And God said moreover to Moses, Thus shall you say to the children of Israel, The *LORD* (H3068) God of your fathers, the God of Abraham, the God of Isaac, and the God of Jacob, has sent me to you: this is my name for *ever* (H5769, everlasting), and this is my *memorial* (H2143, remembrance) to all *generations* (H1755, age, posterity).

The LORD God of Creation, the LORD who specifically created Adam and Eve and interrelated with them, carries the name *I AM* or, more simply, *AM*; the added descriptions confirm this in verse 15. I AM their father; I AM forever; I AM the memorial; I AM with all generations. I know that verse 15 does not say that. However, the ideas and word pictures tell us precisely that story.

I AM is הָיָה hâyâh (H1961) in verse 14, which is the root of LORD (H3068) in verse 15. It is clear that *I AM* and *LORD God* are the same; this is the ETERNAL God. *AM* refers to God ETERNAL, with no beginning, no end. The key is Step 4 to master Biblical Hebrew. All the meanings tell one story, that of Yahveh, God Eternal.

## Plural and Singular

How do we make sense of a plural *God exists* and a singular *Yahveh, I AM*? Let's see some Bible corroboration. Where else does the Bible refer to God's existence, Creation, Who was involved, and their relationship if it's plural? Furthermore, since Genesis 2:7 refers specifically to the Creation of humans, we'd also like a corroborative context.

### Hebrews 1:1-3

1 God, who at sundry times and in divers manners spake in time past to the fathers by the prophets,

2 Has in these last days spoken to us by his Son, whom he has appointed heir of all things, by whom also he made the worlds;

3 Who being the brightness of his glory, and the express image of his person, and upholding all things by the word of his power, when he had by himself purged our sins, sat down on the right hand of the Majesty on high;

In three verses, you have every single element of *the LORD God formed man...*

- **Plural**: God exists with His Son, Who sits on the right hand of His Majesty.

Clearly confirmed by verse 5, "You are my Son, this day have I begotten you? And again, I will be to him a Father, and he shall be to me a Son?" We have the relationship of two God Beings. Two singulars making one plural.

- **Singular**: ...spoken unto us by his Son, ... by whom also he made the worlds...

This context points explicitly to Jesus Christ, Who has the function of Creator through *making worlds* (plural). We're not talking about parallel worlds. Check the Greek; this refers to *worlds* and *ages*. There was an angelic age before our present human age, and there will be the millennial age after Christ's Return, followed by a Godly age when we will have a new Earth and heavens, Revelation 21-22. The singular Son is the Creator of all these ages, including the world during the seven days of Gen 1 and the Creation of humans on Day 6 mentioned in Genesis 2:7.

## Plural and Singular Together

The Father and Christ are one. The plural is singular.

### John 17:21-22

21 That they all may be one; as you, Father, are in me, and I in you, that they also may be one in us: that the world may believe that you have sent me.

22 And the glory which you gave me I have given them; that they may be one, even as we are one:

During His ultimate prayer before His Crucifixion, the Son refers to the Father, two singulars. He says the Father is in Him, and He is the Father. Christ expresses this entwining, meshing between the two with *we are one*.

Does this prove God exists? Absolutely not. Does this reveal the relationship between a Father and a Son, singular Entities of Elohim, a plural God? Yes. Does it show the relationship of a Creator Son (Who made the worlds) with His Creation, humankind? Yes. It gives you a theological perspective of WHO God is (Father and Son) regarding humans. *God formed man...* We'll see what *formed* means in relation to consciousness and mind.

# 10. The All-Time Biggest Hidden Truth. Elohim, God is a Family

*Elohim is plural* in grammar. *Elohim is a Family* of multiple individuals, a hidden truth in God's Word. Let's reveal it.

Unfortunately, the spiritual relationship between marriage, family, and God is a hidden truth. One reason is that these family ties reveal not only the future of humans but also the way to reach that goal.

*The Explanation* has expounded on this family relationship enormously because it is fundamental in comprehending why humans are on Earth (to develop relationships[1]) and why God instituted the marriage union, and family. In four words, *God is a family*. If you're hearing this for the first time because it is a hidden truth, I understand your amazement, especially your skepticism.

---

1. https://theexplanation.com/genesis-1-reveals-basics-social-relations-rulership/

There's one point to take away from this chapter; **God is a Family**. God gave humankind the family institution because He created us in His image. He's a family, and so are we.

### Ephesians 3:14-15

14 For this cause I bow my knees to the *Father* (G3965) of our Lord Jesus Christ,

15 Of whom the whole family in heaven and earth is named,

We know God is our Father, but look at the implication of the Greek. It goes much further and includes lineage, family, and kindred.

### G3965

πατριά patria pat-ree-ah'; As if feminine of a derivative of G3962; paternal descent that is (concretely) a group of families or a whole race (nation):

KJV - family, kindred, lineage.

### G3962

πατήρ patēr pat-ayr'; Apparently a primary word; a father (literally or figuratively near or more remote):

KJV – father, parent.

Biologically, if someone is a father, they are automatically a parent, whether they assume their parental responsibility or not. So, obviously, God, who is our Father, embraces that role toward each of us.

# MIND-BODY PROBLEM SOLVED

### Hebrews 11:23

> By faith Moses, when he was born, was hid three months of his *parents* (G3962), because they saw he was a proper child; and they were not afraid of the king's commandment.

In Greek, there is a direct vocabulary link between the words *father* and *family*. Not so in English; the spiritual reality is that the Father is the head of His family, of which we are the earthly children, for now. It would seem evident when reading Scripture, but instead, it's a hidden truth.

John 1 reveals the bond we humans can have with God. It, too, is a family relationship. Reading this chapter[2] will deepen your comprehension of this father-son (a generic statement, including father-daughter) family ties.

### John 1:12-14

> 12 But as many as received him, to them gave he power to **become the sons of God**, even to them that believe on his name:
>
> 13 Which were **born**, not of blood, nor of the will of the flesh, nor of the will of man, but of God.
>
> 14 And the Word was made flesh, and dwelt among us, (and we beheld his glory, the glory as of the only **begotten** of the Father,) full of grace and truth.

*Sons* of God, *born* - by the will of God, *begotten* - referring to Yahveh Elohim[3], **are all family terms**. Are there any other such

---

2. https://theexplanation.com/yahweh-elohim-inseparable-relationship/

expressions to corroborate this? Let's look at some fundamental descriptions of God and His environment that will help us better define What and Who this plural God (Elohim), Who has a singular verb, is. And how we humans relate to Yahweh Elohim and Elohim.

- God is called our *Father* (Mat. 6:8-9).
- Jesus, also God, is presently the only spirit-composed *Son* (Mat. 11:27).
- The term *Mother* describes the Church (Gal. 4:26).
- We are called His *children* (Rom. 8:16).
- In other words, His *sons* and *daughters* (2 Cor. 6:18).
- We are to be *brothers* of Christ, who is the *Firstborn* (Rom. 8:29).
- He called those who do the will of God *brothers*, *sisters*, and *mothers* (Mark 3:35).
- The Apostle Paul refers to Jesus Christ and the Church as *husband* and *wife* (Eph. 5:22-23), who will be *married* at the Messiah's return (Rev. 19:7).
- The terms *begotten* (1 Peter 1:3) and *born* (John 1:13-14) are employed, referring to Christians.

**Here we have the origin of the family institution**; this explains one of the critical pieces of the puzzle turned over and put in its rightful position. And you know what, in some ways, you're not surprised. Humankind knows very well that the *family* is the base of society. Doctrinally, nobody talks about this hidden truth. But you can't help knowing it. References to the family and its functioning fill the Bible. No other book contains more pertinent information about this basic building block of society and affirmations that God is a Family.

---

3. https://theexplanation.com/yahweh-elohim-inseparable-relationship/

## After His Kind

Here's another hidden truth in the first chapter of Genesis, the first five minutes of the story, where the author introduces the characters God, Elohim (plural[4]), and humans. Few stop to think about it, yet the family relationship between God and humans is right there.

To understand this context, we need to step back and make a point regarding the previous verses in Genesis 1, referring to fruit, herb, seed, fish, birds, creeping things, and beasts. There is an identical 3-word clause describing each of these reproductive creations. Between Genesis 1:11 and 1:25, it repeats no less than ten times, *after his kind* or *after their kind*. I highly suggest you read these verses to refresh your mind. Quickly click here[5], and go to UnlockBibleMeaning.com[6] to read this online. The frequent repetition of these words indicates a crucial reason the author wants you to recognize; this should not be hidden truth.

It doesn't take rocket science to understand the meaning of *after his kind* and *after their kind*. Orange trees grow oranges. Pepper vines yield peppers. Salmon breed salmon. Parrots produce parrots. Scorpions give birth to scorpions. Rhinoceros engender rhinoceros; this refers to the inviolability of one species giving birth to an entirely different species. We are not talking about the variety *within* a particular species that comes from cross-pollination, cross-breeding, or environmental adaptation. So, there's variety, but no, there's not, never has been, and never will be, a transformation of one species into another.

---

4. https://theexplanation.com/does-god-exist-yes-higher-power-yhvh-elohim/

5. http://unlockbiblemeaning.com/

6. http://unlockbiblemeaning.com/

### Sam's reflections

An axiom of Science is that experiments must work and must be reproducible in that they replicate the same results.

Although scientists have their controversy regarding the exact definition of the term *species*, one of the critical precepts is to what extent one species can crossbreed with another. The consensus in scientific circles is they cannot. The hidden truth is this runs amuck of the evolutionary process, which shows that man either descends from or has a common ancestor with apes. I don't want to get into such controversy.

The point is, whichever way you slice it, science has various species mutating into different species. There's no evidence, no reproducible experiment of this, and we hear no talk of when mutating species become a specific species (singular). They only reproduce among themselves, a fundamental precept for defining *species*. We have an example of horses and donkeys[7] (2 different species) producing mules, but they are sterile.

Ligers[8] (lions and tigers, also two separate species) are rare, and if you read the linked article, reproduction is nil. In this video[9], you can see other hybrid species. Notice the narrator's references to the necessity for human intervention for breeding or how the offspring are sick or infertile.

---

7. https://en.wikipedia.org/wiki/Mule
8. https://en.wikipedia.org/wiki/Liger
9. https://youtu.be/AMD6c9oN1Ys

According to what we just read in Gen. 1:25, "And God made the beast of the earth after his kind... " Apes can only give apes, in all their varieties granted, but all are always only apes. God's Word emphasizes this ten times for all floras and faunas. The Bible says apes cannot engender humans, only other apes.

Now reread a résumé of Gen. 1:26-27 with the concept of *species* in mind: And God said, "Let us make man in our image, after our likeness. So God created man in his own image, in the image of God created he him..."

Here's the question: What species are humans?

If you've never heard it put this way before, because it's a hidden truth, I can understand that you're conceivably having difficulty articulating an answer. In the above two verses, God repeats the two words *image* and *likeness* four times to help the answer take root and sink in. Why such emphasis?

> Humankind is of the God kind.

Why were humans created in the image of God? That is the question to ask. That is the question *The Explanation* will answer.

According to the Bible, we are not descendants of some ape, nor do we have a common ancestor, even if our genes and chromosomes are similar. We discussed this in *Inventory of the Universe* in the chapter about Human Life and a comparison of genes[10]. We know that just as we have chromosomes and genes similar to earthworms, scorpions, grass, and bacteria, the genome is typical of all life, but that does not mean we are their descendants.

---

10. https://theexplanation.com/mouse-has-more-genes-than-a-human-being-that-should-humble-us/

Also, in Genesis 1:26, where God tells us humans have the image and likeness of God, He tells us about our relationship to apes and earthworms. "Let *them* (humans created with the image of God) *have dominion* over the fish of the sea, and over the fowl of the air, and over the cattle, and over all the earth, and over every creeping thing that creeps upon the earth."

Even in King James English, this is clear. But, let's use Biblical Hebrew to sharpen the answer to the delicate but vital question: why were humans created in the image of God, with His likeness, after His kind?

So why haven't you heard this hidden biblical truth about the original model of humans? Excellent question. The Bible's knowledge that God is a Family, that He created humans in His image, is the critical reason humans possess consciousness and mind. We're seeing and will reveal more details about WHY humans have these two unique and precious elements.

# 11. God works & humans work. We Create Family & Rule Earth

**God works His relationship with humans and ruling Earth. Likewise, humans, created in God's image, accomplish the same social and rulership work.**

God works, what He does, and what humans do relate directly to the *mind* in the *Mind-Body Problem*. Science limits itself to WHAT the mind is, while psychology adds HOW the mind works. This book addresses both issues, but it also goes much deeper. WHERE consciousness and mind come from and especially WHY humans possess them. That's why we must delve into new territory like theology, God, how God works, humans in the image of God, and their work.

None of the classic approaches taken by science, philosophy, and religion have led to satisfactory and conclusive answers to all those queries. *The Explanation* involves an entirely different procedure.

Theology is based on a deeper understanding of Biblical Hebrew words, mainly in the first chapters of Genesis, the introduction, where God establishes His purpose for the creation of humankind. Many other contexts from both the Hebrew and Greek Scriptures, the Old and New Testaments, must corroborate God's purpose.

The chapters of this book are not isolated bits of information; they build on each other. The proper definition of theology[1] is what God says in His Word about Himself and His purpose. Two chapters ago, I pointed out that Elohim (plural) comprises the Father and the Son. Yahveh, meaning eternal, refers to Jesus the Creator. In the last chapter, we saw the relationship between these God Beings and those who will join Them. God is one Family, now two; in the future, Jesus will add multitudes more. Many Scriptures confirm these Bible facts. You know them, but unfortunately, most have overlooked the real meaning. For example, here's Christ's prayer just before His Crucifixion.

### John 17:1-11

1 These words spake Jesus, and lifted up his eyes to heaven, and said, Father, the hour is come; glorify your Son, that your Son also may glorify you:

2 As you have given him power over all flesh, that he should give eternal life to as many as you have given him.

3 And this is life eternal, that they might know you the only true God, and Jesus Christ, whom you have sent.

4 I have glorified you on the earth: I have finished the work which you gave me to do.

---

1. https://theexplanation.com/where-full-definition-mind-body-consciousness/

# MIND-BODY PROBLEM SOLVED

5 And now, O Father, glorify you me with your own self with the glory which I had with you before the world was. (Sam: The two God Beings BEFORE the Creation of this world. This is the one Family with two Beings.)

6 I have manifested your name to the men (Sam: a generic term including women) which you gave me out of the world: yours they were, and you gave them me; and they have kept your word. (Sam: Do you see how these two God Beings share everything? They have a common goal, and it involves humankind.)

7 Now they have known that all things whatsoever you have given me are of you.

8 For I have given to them the words which you gave me; and they have received them, and have known surely that I came out from you, and they have believed that you did send me.

9 I pray for them: I pray not for the world, but for them which you have given me; for they are yours.

10 And all mine are yours, and yours are mine; and I am glorified in them. (Sam: There's full sharing between the Two Beings.)

11 And now I am no more in the world, but these are in the world, and I come to you. Holy Father, keep through your own name those whom you have given me, that they may be one, as we are.

The plural individual Gods (Father and Son) are ONE Family. So likewise, the plural humans in Christ are ONE in the God

Family. Maybe you've never thought about it this way. This oneness is the spiritual, social bond that unites the God Family. It is the accomplishment of the two Great Commandments: Love God and love your neighbor—all Beings (love your neighbor) in the God Family (love God) for all eternity. We've got to learn those two lessons before we enter the God Family. God knows that because otherwise, He'd have chaos in the Family.

## Christ, God Works

Just as the chapters in this book are not isolated, passages in the Bible are not either. Everything connects. God works, illustrated by Christ worked (vs. 4), creating spiritual humans during His earthly Ministry. Similarly, Yahveh (the future Christ) worked in Genesis 1-2, creating physical humans and their environment, Earth.

This is *God works*. Most people don't meditate on this subject. Think. We know of Jesus Christ's total involvement in spiritual salvation with His Ministry 2000 years ago and since then in the individual lives of His people. Christ, God works over thousands of years. Who do you think worked with Adam? Abraham? Moses? David? Daniel? And all the other servants of God? Yahveh has always done Elohim's work. "I have finished the work which you gave me to do."

### 1 Corinthians 15:22-24

> 22 For as in Adam all die, even so in Christ shall all be made alive (Sam: *all* includes *all* the Old Testament servants with whom He worked).

> 23 But every man in his own order: Christ the firstfruits; afterward they that are Christ's at his coming.

24 Then comes the end, when he shall have delivered up the kingdom to God, even the Father; when he shall have put down all rule and all authority and power.

- God works on the Creation of the Environment: Gen. 1, Creation week.
- Yahveh God works at the Creation of humans: Gen. 1:26-27, 2:7 Creating them in His image and breathing the breath of life.
- Yahveh, God works, managing His Creation: Gen. 1:30 Animals were vegetarian[2] before becoming meat-eaters. Gen. 2:4-6 Watering Earth and bringing rain[3], setting up the water cycles; in modern terms, He's involved in the ecology of Earth. This is His rulership.
- Yahveh, God works at caring for humans: He placed them in the Garden of Eden[4] and gave them instructions; this is His socialization.

Please read details of God's role at the links or in *Origin of the Universe*[5] and *Origin of Humankind*[6].

**Sam's reflections**

Gen. 2:3 tells us, "And God blessed the seventh day, and sanctified it: because that in it he had rested from all his work which God *created and made*."

---

2. https://theexplanation.com/rain-falls-on-earth-entirely-because-yahveh-initiated-it/

3. https://theexplanation.com/rain-falls-on-earth-entirely-because-yahveh-initiated-it/

4. https://theexplanation.com/garden-of-eden-represents-much-more-than-a-garden/

5. *https://theexplanation.com/read-content-origin-universe-online/*

6. *https://theexplanation.com/read-content-origin-humankind-online/*

The translation of the end of this verse is somewhat ambiguous, *created, and made*. Please read this article for a clearer view of how God works and what the seventh day is all about[7]. Unfortunately, there is no space to cover this here. It concerns Christ upbraiding the Pharisees about their view of God's work on the Sabbath day.

**Matthew 12:5-8.**

5 Or have you not read in the law, how that on the sabbath days the priests in the temple profane the sabbath, and are blameless?

6 But I say to you, That in this place is one greater than the temple.

7 But if you had known what this means, I will have mercy, and not sacrifice, you would not have condemned the guiltless.

8 For the Son of man is Lord even of the sabbath day.

Priests then and pastors now work on the Sabbath day. They bring God's mercy to God's people, just as God cultivated His relationship with the first two humans right after their Creation and brought them mercy. God works; that's the essence of the story of the two Trees.

## The Lord God Formed Man

The third point about Gen. 2:7, in our list of 10[8], is about God works; *God formed*.

---

7. https://theexplanation.com/on-the-seventh-day-god-continues-finishing-his-work/

## Genesis 2:7

And the LORD God *formed* (H3335) man of the dust of the ground, and breathed into his nostrils the breath of life; and man became a living soul.

What does *formed* mean? Why doesn't it say created? Genesis 1:27 refers to God works, where we have *created* 3 times. "So God *created* (H1254) man in his own image, in the image of God *created* (H1254) he him; male and female *created* (H1254) he them.

*Bara Creation*[9] (H1254) refers to a *God-said* achievement in Gen. 1. It's instantaneous. Not so with formation; it involves time and other elements. Verify this at UnlockBibleMeaning.com[10].

### H3335

יָצַר yâtsar yaw-tsar'; probably identical with H3334 (יָצַר) (through the squeezing into shape); (compare H3331 (יָצַע)); to mould into a form; especially as a potter; figuratively, to determine (i.e. form a resolution):

KJV - × earthen, fashion, form, frame, make(-r), potter, purpose.

### H3334

יָצַר yâtsar yaw-tsar'; a primitive root; to press (intransitive), i.e. be narrow; figuratively, be in distress:

---

8. https://theexplanation.com/higher-power-starting-point-spiritual-secular/

9. *https://theexplanation.com/heaven-does-it-exist-yes-in-fact-there-are-three-heavens/*

10. https://unlockbiblemeaning.com

KJV - be distressed, be narrow, be straitened (in straits), be vexed.

The potter has a purpose for a lump of clay. They fashion and form it by narrowing it down with their hands. It's a time-consuming process equivalent to God as the Potter testing and challenging His servants to help them grow spiritually. "But now, O LORD, you are our father; we are the clay, and you our potter; and we all are the work of your hand" (Isaiah 64:8).

We will deepen our understanding of God's formation significantly; this is where consciousness and mind come directly into play, as we shall see.

But this chapter is to show God works. Yahveh works in two notable areas: ruling over His Creation and developing His relationship with His servants.

## Humans Form Relations and Rule

Keeping that in mind, remember God created humans in His image. Following that Creation in Gen. 1:27, in the very next verse, He establishes the roles of the male and female, and hence, of humankind.

### Genesis 1:28

> And God blessed them, and God said to them, Be fruitful, and multiply, and replenish the earth, and subdue it: and have dominion over the fish of the sea, and over the fowl of the air, and over every living thing that moves upon the earth.

Do you see that what God does (relationships and rulership) is precisely what humans are expected to do?

1. **Be fruitful and multiply.** God blesses them, referring to joining them in the marriage union as a new family, generally with children; this is developing relationships. God forms us, God's children, as the Potter, by developing our character. In the same way, parents form the character of their children. Have you ever wondered why it takes 16-20 years for a child to develop and become an adult, whereas animals often abandon their offspring at birth or after a very short time?

    God forms His children over time. In His image, humans do the same with their children. As a result, we're developing family relationships. Read about the extended family[11] and the role of children and grandparents. Human family relationships are to be a reflection of God's Family relationships.

2. **Subdue the Earth** and have dominion over everything. In modern terms, we refer to Environmental Sustainability or Ecology; this is rulership over our planet's resources - a worldwide concern in the 21st century. Climate control is directly related to rulership.

The world population significantly lacks training in social arts and government. Most national rulers have not been formed to govern. Is it any wonder families and nations are struggling? *Audit of Humankind*[12] addresses this issue. How are we doing? Is the glass half full or half empty? What's the tendency?

---

11. https://theexplanation.com/extended-family-many-generations-world-population/

12. https://theexplanation.com/read-all-the-content-of-audit-of-humankind-online/

God works and is specially equipped to do so. His Creation, humans, in His image, do the same work; therefore, God has endowed them physically and mentally so they can do just that. Thus, consciousness and mind directly affect how God works and how humans in His image work.

# 12. The Human Body. Incredible Complex Dust of the Ground

**The human body sends shock waves through science with its intricacy and coordination. The brain, the central controlling organ, is a marvelous headquarters.**

Words cannot describe the interconnectedness of the human brain. Does the brain, or any other organ or group of organs, generate consciousness and mind? Answer that query with certainty, and we're on our way to a solution.

In the last chapter, we saw "the LORD God formed man of the dust of the ground..." (Genesis 2:7). The Potter fashioned the exquisite human body from dust. This chapter explains what the fascinating human body is. If I can put it that way, the fabulous shell all human beings inhabit. All we need to do is add nutritious food, fresh water, and regular movement (less computer time), and it'll run for around seven decades.

*The Explanation* has written extensively about our human bodies. The human body, composed of stardust[1], defies imagination. Yet, we take it for granted. Eight billion of us function identically, yet each is unique. How can that be? For lack of space, please refer to these chapters in *Inventory of the Universe*[2] to learn more about our bodies' wonders.

- Human Life[3]
- Bodies Alive[4]
- Brain and Mind[5]

Many perpetual systems function in the human body, like proteins synthesized from the very amino acids they generate[6] (which came first, the chicken or the egg?).

Another marvel is protein folding[7] (watch the fantastic short videos), the split-second construction of a motor to run a specific process in your body, like a filter to allow only certain elements through the cell wall into the nucleus.

---

1. https://theexplanation.com/the-human-body-composed-of-stardust-so-intricate-so-perfect/
2. *https://theexplanation.com/inventory/read-all-the-content-of-inventory-of-the-universe-online/*
3. https://theexplanation.com/imagine-human-life-human-element-on-earth/
4. https://theexplanation.com/the-human-body-composed-of-stardust-so-intricate-so-perfect/
5. https://theexplanation.com/the-brain-amazingly-small-amazingly-powerful-why/
6. https://theexplanation.com/nucleotides-and-dna-millions-of-parts-assembled-perfectly/
7. https://theexplanation.com/protein-folding-machines-continual-movement-keep-body-running-smoothly/

# MIND-BODY PROBLEM SOLVED

When I wrote that book, the revelation that stunned me was apoptosis, the programmed death of cells[8] in the human body. When a fetus develops in the womb, we don't realize that cells are dying in specific locations, at just the right moment, to fashion fingers and toes.

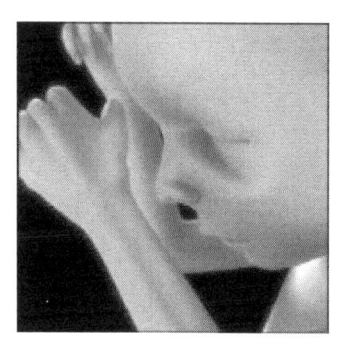

Figure 5. Apoptosis

Programmed cell death takes place in a baby's brain before birth. The University of Maine[9] tells us:

> A fetus' brain produces roughly twice as many neurons as it will eventually need — a safety margin that gives newborns the best possible chance of coming into the world with healthy brains. Most of the excess neurons are shed (apoptosis) in utero. At birth, an infant has roughly 100 billion brain cells.

## Your Brain, an Impressive Body Part

Your brain is multitasking[10] hundreds and thousands of functions right this moment (and every moment) without rest. In fact, your

---

8. https://theexplanation.com/apoptosis-programmed-cell-death-even-before-birth/

9. https://extension.umaine.edu/publications/4356e/

brain doesn't even relax when you are asleep! We function better after a good night's sleep because the brain continues to process the input received while we were awake, sifting, sorting, reinforcing what we learned, and allowing us to recall the information later.

No matter how trivial, each action or sense affects our neurons and activates synapses that we can see with neuroimaging. All these actions (feeling hungry, holding an apple, trying to guess what time it is) are given high, medium, or low priority and coordinated with all the other involuntary or voluntary actions occurring within our bodies.

You may think the coordination of New York City or Beijing traffic is complex, but your brain can integrate all the sensory information, mental processes, and motor skills you need to drive a car during rush hour and help you reach home safely.

A colony of weaver ants coordinating the building of a nest or a herd of wildebeest migrating long distances in Africa, or the vast internet network with about 5 billion people and the interconnected transmission of all the messages, email, and web pages certainly awes you. But consider that your brain's 100 billion neurons and the routing paths for your physical and mental activities act with split-second precision and coordination.

The number 10, followed by hundreds of zeroes, a number far greater than the total sum of atoms in the Universe, expresses the gargantuan quantity of neuronal circuits for communicating information. We've never imagined these sheer numbers of neurons or their speed, let alone the organization and coordination needed to make our body and brain run smoothly.

---

10. https://www.ninds.nih.gov/Disorders/Patient-Caregiver-Education/Know-Your-Brain

It's stupefying that your brain oversees all the wiring and connections. Your brain[11] is 1,4 kilograms of jelly tissue, of which 78 percent is water. It fills a space of 1,130 cubic centimeters in your skull, equivalent to a small balloon with a diameter of thirteen centimeters.

Imagine, right now, that 20 percent of your oxygen intake and 25 percent of your glucose consumption fuel your brain. Compare this with the size of the infrastructure and the energy input required to run the Internet or the world's most sophisticated supercomputer.

Pause for further thought and consider that this three pounds of jelly tissue is incredibly fluid and responsive, more so than the fastest Internet connection! The human body and brain are exquisite.

## What is the Composition of the Human Body?

The unique body with its 78 organs, systems, and networks, including your brain, runs perfectly in sync, but don't forget, God formed it, and it's nothing but dust.

"You are from dust and to dust shall you return." A pretty well-known Bible verse from Genesis 3:19. What does it really mean? If you asked someone what the Bible says about the composition of humans[12], I think the general answer you'd get is: of the ground. That's not far off, but it's not exactly right.

**Genesis 2:7**

---

11. https://theexplanation.com/your-brain-is-multitasking-100s-and-1000s-of-functions-every-moment/

12. https://theexplanation.com/from-dust-you-came-biblical-meaning/

And the LORD God formed man of the *dust* (H6083) of the ground, and breathed into his nostrils the breath of life; and man became a living soul.

Why did Yahveh choose dust and not the ground? Because coming from dust teaches us several characteristics. Not just for man but for all humans. Let's first see the Biblical Hebrew and how the King James translators rendered it.

**H6083**

עָפָר 'âphâr aw-fawr'; from H6080 (עָפַר); dust (as powdered or gray); hence, clay, earth, mud:

KJV – ashes, dust, earth, ground, morter, powder, rubbish.

There is a vivid contrast that God wants humans to understand. Our origin is in stark contrast to the:

- LIFE-GIVING mist and rain in the preceding verses 5-6
- The breath of LIFE He was going to infuse
- The LIVING souls He formed

We'll get to a much deeper explanation of the *breath of life* and *living souls*, but dust is dead. In dust, there's NO life. On Day 6[13], God said, "Let the earth (not the dust!) bring forth the living creatures." Of course, God created the animals, but even the fauna comes from *living matter*, whereas humans don't get that distinction. We come from the dead dust of the ground. So humankind begins rather austerely, even compared to animals.

---

13. https://theexplanation.com/creation-day-5-and-6-god-created-fish-fowl-and-fauna/

# MIND-BODY PROBLEM SOLVED

Did you notice the last word in the KJV list of translations for H6083, *rubbish*? Pretty graphic. Nehemiah 4:10 says, "The strength of the bearers of burdens is decayed, and there is much *rubbish*; (H6083) so that we are not able to build the wall." That's what we humans are, what we humans do. Here's another piece of the puzzle you can assemble in this context, Isaiah 64:6, "But we are all as an *unclean thing*, and all our righteousnesses are as *filthy rags*; and we all do fade as a leaf; and our iniquities, like the wind, have taken us away."

Please understand that the intention is not negative, but we must call a spade a spade. Humans start from an inferior position, in some ways lower than animals because they came from the ground. Dust is synonymous with *rubbish, unclean things,* and *filthy rags.*

The human story starts from the most humble origins but includes potential far beyond animals. We'll get to that in the rest of this verse. Yahveh, man's Creator, could've used ground, wood, or grass to form the human body, but He used *dust*. *The Explanation* has just given you a reason for this choice, but there are others.

In the list of verses containing the Hebrew word for *formed* (H3335), read Isaiah 44:9-10 and see what humans *form*: idols from molten metal and other materials, including clay like a potter. "They [humans] that *make* (H3335) a graven image are all of them vanity (Sam, *this corresponds to the dust, rubbish, filthy rags*); and their delectable things shall not profit; and they are their own witnesses; they see not, nor know; that they may be ashamed. Who has *formed* (H3335) a god, or molten a graven image that is profitable for nothing?"

God formed humankind from dust; humankind turns around and forms valueless graven images from dust. Instead of forming things to glorify our Creator, humans form anti-gods.

## THE EXPLANATION

The human body is sophisticated, complex, strong, and delicate. Yet, at the same time, it is just dust from the ground. Our brains are intricate and complicated dust. Consciousness and mind are elsewhere.

## III. Neshama - Consciousness Defines Human

The spiritual component of humans.

# 13. Breath of Life. The Unique Possessors of Neshama on Earth

*Breath of Life*
*Neshama*
*Genesis 2:7*
*Who Alone Possess It?*

**The breath of life in Genesis 2:7 is neshama. God gave it to humans. Does it animate anything else?**

Yahveh[1] formed humans[2] out of dust[3], the most sterile part of the ground. He then breathed in the breath of life, the neshama, a unique ingredient we will identify in the next chapter. The question is, who are the lone recipients of this gift of God?

Let's first identify the Biblical Hebrew for *breath* of life because, as you will see, translations are anything but complete in this domain.

**Genesis 2:7**

---

1. https://theexplanation.com/yahweh-yahveh-meaning-identity-gods-name/

2. https://theexplanation.com/god-created-man-bible-god-formed-man/

3. https://theexplanation.com/from-dust-you-came-biblical-meaning/

# MIND-BODY PROBLEM SOLVED

And the LORD God formed man of the dust of the ground, and *breathed* (H5301) into his nostrils the *breath* (H5397) of life, and man became a living soul.

We have to take the time and, step by step, look at the meaning of neshama. In this verse, the KJV translators used the same English word for two different concepts. God *breathed* (וַיִּפַּח - yifach, H5301) and the *breath* (נְשָׁמָה - neshama, H5397) of life. In Hebrew, these two words are distinct and grammatically unrelated. Here's Strong's entry for neshama.

## H5397

נְשָׁמָה nᵉshâmâh from H5395 (נָשַׁם); a puff, i.e. wind, angry or vital breath, divine inspiration, intellect. or (concretely) an animal:

KJV - blast, (that) breath(-eth), inspiration, soul, spirit.

We know what *breathe* and *breath* are; we do it many times each minute of our lives. So we give it no further thought. Great error. The 2nd Step to master Biblical Hebrew[4] is present, figurative meanings. Note neshama means *inspiration* and *spirit*. That is one reason I said neshama is a gift from God.

The question today is, who possesses the breath of life? I believe Strong made a serious error in his entry for H5397 by referring to the neshama as *(concretely) an animal*. We'll see why I think he made this error; I also made it until Genesis 7:21-22 became clear. Maybe you've made it too. Perhaps you're unaware of it, but we must clear it up. So here's that error-prone context. It's the very next time, after Gen. 2:7, where the author uses the word neshama.

---

4. https://theexplanation.com/fastest-bible-study-method-god-intended-meaning/

### Genesis 7:20-23

20 Fifteen cubits upward did the waters prevail; and the mountains were covered.

21 And all flesh died that moved upon the earth, both of fowl, and of cattle, and of beast, and of every creeping thing that creeps upon the earth, and every man:

22 All in whose nostrils was the *breath* (H5397) of life, of all that was in the dry land, died.

23 And every living substance was destroyed which was upon the face of the ground, both man, and cattle, and the creeping things, and the fowl of the heaven; and they were destroyed from the earth: and Noah only remained alive, and they that were with him in the ark.

I've reproduced verses 20 and 23 to show you we're discussing the beginning of Noah's flood. Verse 22 includes *neshama*. Does this verse include animals and every man? Or do animals possess neshama? In Genesis 2:7, God gave the *breath* of life (neshama) to the first man, but had He already given it to the animals He created?

Here's an image of verse 22 from the Interlinear Bible. I'm doing this so you can see the Biblical Hebrew because there's a massive problem that the KJV translators missed and didn't know what to do. You can NOT see this in English.

## Ge 7:21

| H776 | H5921 | H7430 | H1320 | H3605 | H1478 |
|---|---|---|---|---|---|
| hā-'ā-reṣ, | 'al- | hā-rō-mêś | bā-śār | kāl- | way-yiḡ-wa' |
| הָאָרֶץ | עַל־ | הָרֹמֵשׂ | בָּשָׂר ׀ | כָּל־ | וַיִּגְוַע |
| the earth | on | that moved | flesh | all | And died |

| | H3605 | H2416 | H929 | H5775 |
|---|---|---|---|---|
| | ū-ḇə-ḵāl | ū-ḇa-hay-yāh, | ū-ḇab-bə-hê-māh | bā-'ō-wp̄ |
| | וּבְכָל־ | וּבַחַיָּה | וּבַבְּהֵמָה | בָּעוֹף |
| | and of every | and of beast | and of livestock | both of birds |

| H3605 | H776 | H5921 | H8317 | H8318 |
|---|---|---|---|---|
| wə-ḵōl | hā-'ā-reṣ; | 'al- | haš-šō-rêṣ | haš-šer̄eṣ |
| וְכָל־ | הָאָרֶץ | עַל־ | הַשֹּׁרֵץ | הַשֶּׁרֶץ |
| and every | the earth | on | that creeps | creeping thing |

| | | | | H120 |
|---|---|---|---|---|
| | | | | hā-'ā-ḏām. |
| | | | | הָאָדָם׃ |
| | | | | man |

## Ge 7:22

| H2416 | H7307 | H5397 | H834 | H3605 |
|---|---|---|---|---|
| hay-yim | rū-aḥ | niš-maṯ- | 'ă-šer | kōl |
| חַיִּים | רוּחַ | נִשְׁמַת־ | אֲשֶׁר | כֹּל |
| of life | of the spirit | the breath | that [had] | all |

| H4191 | H2724 | H834 | H3605 | H639 |
|---|---|---|---|---|
| mê-ṯū. | be-hā-rā-ḇāh | 'ă-šer | mik-kōl | bə-'ap-pāw, |
| מֵתוּ׃ | בֶּחָרָבָה | אֲשֶׁר | מִכֹּל | בְּאַפָּיו |
| died | in the dry [land] | that [was] | of all | in the nostrils |

Figure 6. Genesis 7:22, the breath of the spirit

I checked the KJV, NIV, Modern English Version, Douay-Rheims, and the Living Bible[5]. They all say *breath* or *breathed*. Unfortunately, not one has translations for both neshama AND ruach. My French Louis Segond is better, *respiration, souffle* de vie. At least it attempts to translate both words.

Interestingly, the New KJV[6] has the *breath* (a) of the *spirit* of life, and there's a footnote (a): Genesis 7:22 LXX (the Septuagint, the

---
5. https://www.biblegateway.com/passage/?search=Genesis+7%3A22&version=TLB

6. https://www.biblegateway.com/passage/?search=Genesis+7%3A22&version=NKJV

first Greek translation of the Old Testament), Vg. (the Vulgate, the official Latin translation) omit *of the spirit*. The New KJV has two words here, *breath* and *spirit*, as in the interlinear image above. Whereas the footnote indicates the Septuagint and the Vulgate omit *of the spirit*. It would appear the KJV translators followed the LXX and Vg rather than the Biblical Hebrew in Genesis 2:7.

You must ask yourself why the KJV translators omitted one of these words. I will explain this later. We're reading this verse to see if ANIMALS have NESHAMA. If you skim it, as it is written, the answer appears to be yes; animals do have neshama. But let's take another look, especially at the end of verse 21. *and every man:* Notice the colon. The thought about man CONTINUES into verse 22.

A better reading of Genesis 7:22 in the KJV would be, *and every man, all in whose nostrils was the breath (H5397) of life*. If we follow the Biblical Hebrew, it would be "and every man, all in whose nostrils was the *breath* (H5397 - neshama) of the *spirit* (H7307 - ruach) of life." Quite a difference. Humans have neshama, not animals. Verse 22 continues and ends with: *of all* that was in the dry land, died. The *of all* is a summary that includes all animals and all humans.

Maybe you think I'm twisting scripture. Let's look at Joshua.

### Joshua 10:40, 11:11,14

> 10:40 So Joshua smote all the country of the hills, and of the south, and of the vale, and of the springs, and all their kings: he left none remaining, but utterly destroyed all that breathed (H5397 - neshama), as the LORD God of Israel commanded.

> 11:11 And they smote all the souls that were therein with the edge of the sword, utterly destroying them: there was not any left to *breathe* (H5397 neshama): and he burnt Hazor with fire.
>
> 14 And all the spoil of these cities, and the cattle, the children of Israel took for a prey to themselves; but every man they smote with the edge of the sword, until they had destroyed them, neither left they any to *breathe* (H5397).

In this episode, as the children of Israel entered the Promised Land, they utterly destroyed all the souls (11:11) with neshama (*breathe*, as it's translated here). BUT they took the cattle for prey. If they destroyed ALL those with neshama and kept the cattle alive, then, by deduction, cattle do NOT have neshama.

Furthermore, cattle BREATHE. Therefore, the meaning of neshama cannot be limited to *breathe*. There is something humans possess, given by Yahveh, breathed into them that animals do not have. It is neshama, and it behooves us to know what this is. Neshama differentiates humans from animals. Do you see what this does for human knowledge in science, philosophy, and religion?

## God and Humans Possess Neshama

From what we've seen, God alone gives neshama, and it inhabits every single human being. But humans alone.

### Job 33:4

> The Spirit of God has made me, and the *breath* (H5397) of the Almighty has given me life.

God has given humans something He possesses. Remember, we discussed humans are Godkind[7]. God created humans in His image. He did so by placing a portion of Himself in each one of us through the breath of life.

### Job 27:3

> All the while my *breath* (H5397) is in me, and the spirit of God is in my nostrils;

Job was a wise man with the spiritual understanding of neshama. He knew he possessed it, unlike most people today. He also knew the spirit of God animated him; this is fundamental knowledge of what a human being is.

### Isaiah 42:5

> Thus says God the LORD, he that created the heavens, and stretched them out; he that spread forth the earth, and that which comes out of it; he that gives *breath* (H5397) to the people upon it, and spirit to them that walk therein:

Another context revealing God gives neshama AND spirit to ALL people on Earth. He is an inclusive God. All people are His Creation, and He has a purpose for each one of us. We are living a given instant in that Creation plan, but there's much more to come.

### Job 32:8

> But there is a spirit in man: and the *inspiration* (H5397) of the Almighty gives them understanding.

---

7. https://theexplanation.com/all-time-hidden-truth-elohim-god-is-a-family/

Both God and humans possess neshama, and this verse states that neshama, an immaterial essence, confers certain attributes associated with *understanding* on humans. That's what we'll see in the next chapter.

Can you see how the English word *breath* is far short of expressing what neshama really is? The Job 32:8 translation *inspiration* is closer. As it says in that same verse, *of the Almighty*, I think a better translation of neshama would be *divine essence* (the Almighty's breath).

**Psalm 150:6**

> Let every thing that has *breath* (H5397) praise the LORD. Praise you the Lord.

The last verse in the final Psalm refers to the end of God's plan for all humans. It opens up a new era. It reveals a state of peace, prosperity, and unity between all beings concerning their Creator, Savior, and God. All beings in that position will possess well-oriented neshama, and as a result, will know God and be able to praise Him. Instead of *breath,* translate it *divine essence*. Isn't it clearer?

This chapter is an introduction to the *breath of life*. There remain many other exhilarating and revealing human aspects related to neshama. We have much more in common with God, being in His image, than you've realized.

# 14. Neshama is Translated Inspiration. Discover Deeper Meaning

**Inspiration isn't a bad translation for Neshama. But it hides the essential element of humans.**

Genesis 2:7 exposes the elementary components of a human being. And *inspiration* is not one of them. The only two mentioned are *afar* and *neshama, dust,* and *divine breath or essence.* So it's time to grasp what a human being is and why each of us is composed of two extremes, the lowliest dust and the highest divine.

The King James Version of the Bible does not use the term *consciousness*, undoubtedly because etymologically, the word goes back to about 1600, the same time as the KJV translation. It comes from the Latin *conscius*, knowing, aware. The goal of *The Explanation* is NOT to depart from English or Latin but from Biblical Hebrew. But, much more than that, to reveal the exactitude of the meaning of Biblical Hebrew words related to

# MIND-BODY PROBLEM SOLVED

21st-century proven facts. So, what is neshama? And is it related to consciousness?

## Genesis 2:7

And the LORD God formed man of the dust of the ground, and breathed into his nostrils the *breath* (H5397) of life; and man became a living soul.

We can immediately recognize that whatever this *breath* is, the body does not generate it. God infused it. There are two separate origins of these two components. Think about what this does for scientific *knowledge*. What is the Bible's definition of neshama? Check UnlockBibleMeaning.com[1]

## H5397

נְשָׁמָה neshâmâh nesh-aw-maw'; from H5395 (נָשַׁם); a puff, i.e. wind, angry or vital breath, divine inspiration, intellect. or (concretely) an animal:

KJV - blast, (that) breath(-eth), inspiration, soul, spirit.

With words like *inspiration* and *spirit*, we're in the ethereal realm. Invisible, untouchable, intangible. We delve into the inner workings of humankind. In the last chapter, I showed you why Strong's allusion to *(concretely) an animal* is incorrect[2]; humans alone possess neshama. God's servant Job gives us a clue to define *neshama* - inspiration.

## Job 32:8

---

[1]. https://unlockbiblemeaning.com

[2]. https://theexplanation.com/breath-of-life-unique-possessors-neshama-earth/

But there is a spirit in man: and the *inspiration* (H5397 - neshama) of the Almighty gives them *understanding* (H995 - bain).

Here, the KJV translation of *neshama* is *inspiration,* with another immaterial allusion to *spirit*. It also adds the nature of WHO gives neshama and WHAT neshama is. Now, let's look at Biblical Hebrew because English is correct and, at the same time, incomplete.

Figure 7. Job 32:8 El Shaddai

In Hebrew, only three words are the origin of, "and the inspiration of the Almighty gives them understanding." *Neshama* = inspiration. *Shaddai* = Almighty. *Bain* = understanding. The verb *gives* is NOT present. Why? It comes down to the 4 Steps to Master Biblical Hebrew[3]. In this case, the word/Name for God, *Almighty*. It is Strong's H7706. Simply compare the three letters (שדי - shin, daled, yod) with H7699 and H7701. The *yod* is a vowel, the *shin* and *daled* (שד) are identical in all three words, and they are related. Now notice the meanings: H7699-*breast* and H7701-*desolation*. Total opposites: one gives life, and the other destroys life. That's

---

3. https://theexplanation.com/fastest-bible-study-method-god-intended-meaning/

Step 1 to master Biblical Hebrew[4], multiple, even contradictory meanings to the same word.

Genesis 49:25 has both words, *Almighty* (H7706) and *breasts* (H7699), with God giving multiple blessings to Israel. Check the identical Biblical Hebrew roots in the image for Genesis 49:25.

```
Ge 49:25
              H853          H5826              H1              H410
              wa 'êṯ        wə·ya'·zə·re·kā,   'ā·ḇî·kā        mê·'êl
              וְאֵת         וְיַעְזְרֶךָ       אָבִיךָ         מֵאֵל
              also you      and who shall help of your father  From the God

H5921    H8064         H1293          H1288              H7706
mê·'al,  šā·ma·yim     bir·kōṯ        wî·ḇā·ra·ḵe·kā,    šad·day
מֵעָל    שָׁמַיִם      בִּרְכֹת       וִיבָרֲכֶךָ        שַׁדַּי
and      of heaven     with blessings who shall bless you by the Almighty

H7699         H1293       H8478     H7257      H8415       H1293
šā·ḏa·yim     bir·kōṯ     tā·ḥaṯ    rō·ḇe·ṣeṯ  tə·hō·wm    bir·kōṯ
שָׁדָיִם     בִּרְכֹת    תַּחַת     רֹבֶצֶת    תְּהוֹם      בִּרְכֹת
of the breasts blessings  under     that lies  of the deep  blessings

                                                    H7356
                                                    wā·rā·ḥam.
                                                    וָרָחַם׃
                                                    and of the womb
```

Figure 8. Genesis 49:25 Almighty of the breasts

The figurative meaning of God's name *Shaddai* is God *Breastfeeds*. There is no better way for a mother to GIVE their child a better physical start in life than to breastfeed them. Unfortunately, space does not allow elaboration on this issue. But, figuratively, God did that with the first human being.

Job 32:8 expands on Genesis 2:7 by telling us God breastfed humans with understanding. Shaddai, Breastfeeding includes *giving*; that's why there's no need for the verb *give*.

---

4. https://theexplanation.com/fastest-bible-study-method-god-intended-meaning/

## El Shaddai Gave Understanding to Humans

Here is what humans received when God breathed neshama - inspiration - understanding into them.

### H995

> בִּין bîyn bene; a primitive root; to separate mentally (or distinguish), i.e. (generally) understand:
>
> KJV - attend, consider, be cunning, diligently, direct, discern, eloquent, feel, inform, instruct, have intelligence, know, look well to, mark, perceive, be prudent, regard, (can) skill(-full), teach, think, (cause, make to, get, give, have) understand(-ing), view, (deal) wise(-ly, man).

Rather than answer what neshama is, I want to walk you through an exercise; this is a profound yet fundamental subject for grasping what God breathed into humans and what this breath, the neshama, God's inspiration, allows humans to accomplish. Note that it *separates humans mentally*. It *distinguishes* them (H995).

Take each of the above translations as a verb and put yourself in the driver's seat. I (you or me) attend to, consider, I am cunning, am diligent, I direct, discern, am eloquent, feel, inform, instruct, am intelligent, know, perceive, teach, think...

How can these actions take place? Why can these processes function in humans? Remember that, according to Gen. 2:7, a human is *dust* and *neshama*, a physical component and God's neshama, His *inspiration*, or, as I suggested, God's *divine essence*. This incredible fusion of apparent opposites, *rubbish,* and *divine essence*, allows humans to do all of the above intellectual activities.

# MIND-BODY PROBLEM SOLVED

You should already know precisely what neshama is. But let's look at a real-life example that will help us reach our goal, taking us deep into God's power and how He works with humans. He has a plan for each of us; His ways are not our ways. Look at what God did with probably the most powerful King in history, Nebuchadnezzar of Babylon.

**Daniel 4:24-25, 33-36**

24 This is the interpretation [of a dream], O king [Nebuchadnezzar], and this is the decree of the most High, which is come upon my lord the king:

25 That they shall drive you from men, and your dwelling shall be with the beasts of the field, and they shall make you to eat grass as oxen, and they shall wet you with the dew of heaven, and seven times shall pass over you, till you know that the most High rules in the kingdom of men, and gives it to whomsoever he will.

33 The same hour was the thing fulfilled on Nebuchadnezzar: and he was driven from men, and did eat grass as oxen, and his body was wet with the dew of heaven, till his hairs were grown like eagles' feathers, and his nails like birds' claws.

34 And at the end of the days I Nebuchadnezzar lifted up mine eyes to heaven, and mine *understanding* (H4486) returned to me, and I blessed the most High, and I praised and honoured him that lives for ever, whose dominion is an everlasting dominion, and his kingdom is from generation to generation:

35 And all the inhabitants of the earth are reputed as nothing: and he [God] does according to his will in the army of heaven, and among the inhabitants of the earth: and none can stay his hand, or say to him, What do you?

36 At the same time my *reason* (H4486) returned to me; and for the glory of my kingdom, mine honour and brightness returned to me; and my counsellors and my lords sought to me; and I was established in my kingdom, and excellent majesty was added to me.

This account is impressive by any means. It revolves around Nebuchadnezzar losing and regaining his understanding/reason (verses 34 and 36). It is not the same Hebrew word as Job 32:8 (understanding H995). In English, H4486 (Daniel 4:34) and H995 (Job 32:8) are both translated with the same English word *understanding*. The king forwent his understanding/reason for seven years. He lost his human reasoning capacity. God transformed this powerful human king into a beast of the field, into an animal. How did he do this? Did He just wave a magic wand? NO.

Please consider and revise the chapter Breath of Life—the Unique Possessors of Neshama on Earth[5]. Animals do NOT possess neshama. God temporarily, for seven years, removed Nebuchadnezzar's neshama, the inspiration that separates humans mentally from all other beings. However, Nebuchadnezzar still had specific capacities, those of a grass-eating beast that survives in the wild. We shall discuss what animates all animals. But Nebuchadnezzar totally lost his understanding/reason (H4486). Precisely what is this understanding/reason?

---

5. https://theexplanation.com/breath-of-life-unique-possessors-neshama-earth/

## H4486

מַנְדַּע manda‛ man-dah'; (Aramaic) corresponding to H4093 (מַדָּע); wisdom or intelligence:

KJV - knowledge, reason, understanding.

## H4093

מַדָּע maddâ‛ mad-daw'; or מַדַּע; from H3045 (יָדַע); intelligence or consciousness:

KJV - knowledge, science, thought.

## H3045

יָדַע yâda‛ yaw-dah'; a primitive root; to know (properly, to ascertain by seeing); used in a great variety of senses, figuratively, literally, euphemistically and inferentially (including observation, care, recognition; and causatively, instruction, designation, punishment, etc.):

KJV - acknowledge, acquaintance(-ted with), advise, answer, appoint, assuredly, be aware, (un-) awares, can(-not), certainly, comprehend, consider, × could they, cunning, declare, be diligent, (can, cause to) discern, discover, endued with, familiar friend, famous, feel, can have, be (ig-) norant, instruct, kinsfolk, kinsman, (cause to let, make) know, (come to give, have, take) knowledge, have (knowledge), (be, make, make to be, make self) known, + be learned, + lie by man, mark, perceive, privy to, × prognosticator, regard, have respect, skilful, shew, can (man of) skill, be sure, of a surety, teach, (can) tell, understand, have (understanding), × will be, wist, wit, wot.

Compare the KJV translations of H3045 (know) and H995 (understanding); you will immediately see the similarity.

That is the meaning of neshama. God removed or suppressed the neshama, and the king became a beast. Neshama is a definite element that clearly differentiates animals from humans. It is consciousness. Note that Strong's annotation (which is not God-inspired like Scripture) for H4093 refers to consciousness. And one of the KJV translations (again UNinspired) of H3045 is *aware* or *awareness* which we associate today with *consciousness* and *mindfulness*.

This event with Nebuchadnezzar went so far that he could not even care for his physical needs. As a result, his hair and his nails grew tremendously. Some animals naturally have long hair, but you never see animals that have to trim their hair and nails regularly. Only humans have to groom themselves this way. Without neshama, a human being CANNOT take care of their human needs; this is what happens when humans lose their minds for whatever reason.

Verse 35 explains why Nebuchadnezzar went through this episode (trial) in his life. God wanted him to realize that one of the most potent kings on Earth (if not the most powerful, because of what he symbolizes prophetically) is nothing in God's sight and that God does as He wills. He will accomplish His plan for the King and all of humanity. That's why we and the world have trials. God wants us to come to our spiritual senses, like Nebuchadnezzar.

But the point here is that God TOOK Nebuchadnezzar's neshama, held on to it for seven years, and then GAVE IT BACK to him. Not only did He give it back during his lifetime, but God enhanced his neshama and kingdom with additional blessings, as the end of verse 36 points out. All other humans will have their neshama returned to them at the resurrection. God collects the neshama and the ruach on death (Job 34:14). For humans, this duo always stays together. In the meantime, God stores it just as He did with Nebuchadnezzar. Nebuchadnezzar still had his dust brain, but God removed his cognition, awareness, and consciousness, his ability to act like a human being.

In the next chapter, we start a mini-five series expounding exactly what neshama - inspiration - consciousness allows humans to do. What defines a human being; the consciousness that separates all humans mentally from all other beings.

# 15. What is the Purpose of Life? Why Humans Crave an Answer

The purpose of life. 2.5 billion entries in Google and only floundering results. Why do people care about their life's purpose?

Neshama is the divine essence (breath of life) God infused into human beings (Genesis 2:7). It confers on us five human features. The first overriding element our consciousness revolves around is the purpose of life. Is there one? What is it? Why am I here? These are the existential questions about our existence and the meaning of life. Why do humans even wonder about such issues? Here's the answer.

- God made humans in His image and likeness (Gen. 1:27).
- He accomplished this by infusing His neshama (breath of life) into humans.
- The neshama, consciousness, confers on humans godly

qualities (image of God).
- God forms with purpose; therefore, humans can form with purpose.
- That's why humans crave to know what their purpose in life is.

When God formed Adam from the dust of the ground, He already had a concept for consummating His creation. In Genesis 2:7, the Hebrew word *formed* signifies a potter[1] molding his clay with resolution and *purpose* (at UnlockBibleMeaning.com[2], see Strong's H3335 yatsar). God, with His infinite mind, imagines a framework and is determined to bring to fruition His original concept, "...I have *purposed* (H3335) it, I will also do it..." (Isaiah 46:11). *Purposed* is the same Hebrew word as *formed* in Gen. 2:7.

God creates because He has a purpose. He has a long-term, organized, coherent policy, which He has committed to writing in the Bible and preserved for us (Isaiah 30:8). He has an overall goal, and no one shall annul it (Isaiah 14:26-27). It includes you and me, and He's equipped each of us, through consciousness, with the attributes to accomplish His goals.

I devoted Part 1[3] of *Audit of Humankind* to these immaterial singularities of each human. In giving the neshama, consciousness, to human beings, God automatically gave us all the singularities necessary to pursue our purpose in life.

## The Singularity of Humankind is Associated with Their Purpose in Life

---

1. https://theexplanation.com/human-family-elohim-god-works-both-create-rule/

2. https://unlockbiblemeaning.com

3. https://theexplanation.com/read-all-the-content-of-audit-of-humankind-online/

Humans can only accomplish their purpose in life because all the singularities necessary for this task are part of the complete package God breathed into us. All these capacities are mental attributes. You cannot find them in the brain; they are inherent in our psychological makeup. God designed humans this way by breathing the breath of life, the *nishmat chayim*, the neshama, into them when He created the first human who represents all human beings.

A purpose in life has always characterized humans worldwide and down through history. Think about that fact. How can that be? Where did it come from? Genesis 2:7 answers that question. Here is a concise summary of the critical mental attributes that confer on humans the capacity to plan goals and entertain aspirations and ambitions for their future. Click the links for a more profound view of these human characteristics.

- Nature of Humans, Consciousness & Mind Reveal Adroit Humans[4] (1.1 in the book *Audit of Humankind*). This chapter exposes the nature of consciousness and the mind.
- Space-Time is Not Only a Scientific Theory, but It's Also a Human Singularity[5] (1.2)
  Each of us has 24 hours (our time) to manage whatever we want (our space). It consists of time at home, office, factory, in a truck, airport, ship, etc., wherever you spend your leisure time, sleeping, working (that's your space) hours (that's your time). Your space includes every physical item you use, including the invisibles like the air

---

4. https://theexplanation.com/nature-of-humans-consciousness-mind-reveal-adroit-humans/

5. https://theexplanation.com/space-time-is-not-only-scientific-theory-its-also-a-human-singularity/

you breathe, the electricity to run the tools, the kitchen's odors, or the gymnasium's heat. Humans alone manage their space time.

- Creativity Sets Humankind Apart from and Above All Other Life on Earth[6] (1.3)
I'm amazed by the inventiveness of human ingenuity, aren't you? The myriad ways to cook food, decorate a room, build a house, catch fish, turn wood, etc. God is the Creator, and the neshama equips every human with the ability to invent objects, ideas, and ways of accomplishing tasks. It's never-ending.

- Imagination—Another Singularity of Humankind in Your Consciousness[7] (1.4)
Whenever a writer throws words on a page, a painter dips their brush in paint, or a designer sketches lines on a serviette in a restaurant, they imagine. We've filled our consumer society with merchandise that started in someone's conceptualizing mind. Each product was first a figment of a creator's imagination, a flash of insight, a daydream, or maybe even a nightdream. Imagination is where everything starts. Humans imagine because they possess consciousness, neshama.

- Bears Don't Learn to Ride Bicycles. Humans Learn That and Much More[8] (1.5)
To learn is a lifelong endeavor. It starts with how to suck your mother's nipple and ends with how to get out of bed

---

6. https://theexplanation.com/creativity-sets-humankind-apart-from-and-above-all-other-life-on-earth/

7. https://theexplanation.com/imagination-another-singularity-of-humankind-in-your-mind/

8. https://theexplanation.com/bears-dont-learn-to-ride-bicycles-humans-learn-that-and-much-more/

with an arthritis-wracked body. There always was, is, and will be something new to understand. When humans look up at the cloudy sky and wonder about the weather, pick up their daily newspaper, listen to the news, or watch it on their mobile phones, they learn about the world around them and themselves. When consciousness stops, learning stops.

- Your Choices Tell Us Who You Are. In Fact, They Identify You[9] (1.6)

   Every human being has a choice over various aspects of their life. Humankind is one race, but through choice, we're 8 billion individuals. Through our consciousness, we choose our personal hairdo, what we read, or watch, the causes we support, and the ideas we propagate.

- Growth Mindset—A Frame of Mind Unique to Humankind[10] (1.7)

   Consciousness confers on humans the thrill of making progress. Seeing oneself and others improve their lives. Not just earning more money or living in a luxury house. But progress is like piling blocks one on top of each other, learning the alphabet, riding a bicycle, learning the waltz, and driving a car. So daily, we make incremental improvements to our life experiences.

- I Challenge you ... A Human Trait that Keeps Us Moving Forward[11] (1.8)

   Whether it's a face-off over a game of Monopoly or a personal test to obtain one's driver's license, the challenge is a uniquely human characteristic. Over two billion

---

9. https://theexplanation.com/your-choices-tell-us-who-you-are-in-fact-they-identify-you/

10. https://theexplanation.com/growth-mindset-unique-humankind/

11. https://theexplanation.com/challenge-accompanied-courage-needed-face-new-struggles-another-human-singularity/

people step up to the challenge of playing video games. That's about one in four people worldwide. Huge. Why do they play? It's fun, but it's also a challenge. We're trying to beat something. Better our score, faster, more accurate, more skill. We all have personal records that we're proud of, but we always try to improve; this is an aspect of consciousness necessary for the purpose of life.

- Rule Life Responsibly—The Key Human Singularity[12] (1.9)
  Rule life responsibly comes down to how each person exerts their dual nature over the space time they influence; how we take care of the living and non-living environments which we impact. Life is a labyrinth of choices, moves, and decisions. Negotiating life is meeting these daily, weekly, and yearly challenges responsibly.

Let me be forthright with you. It is not *standing upright* that defines a human; God formed humans upright from the dust from the start. But, Neshama, consciousness, the ability to have a purpose in life, defines a human being. The fact that you know you have to manage your space and time, that you can use your imagination, and learn to create, grow and face challenges to lead a responsible life in the human family, is only because of the consciousness you possess, which determines you are human.

Each of the five features of consciousness will end with a brief excursion into their application in real life. The Bible is anything but myths and pretty stories. God's Word exposes a practical way of life applicable in the 21st century. Scripture clearly outlines directions for each aspect of consciousness, including the why, how, and what. They are for all human beings regardless of gender,

---

12. https://theexplanation.com/rule-life-responsibly-the-key-human-singularity/

culture, race, or religion. The first section on psychology will group the overall directives.

The second Section will elaborate on the biblical spiritual approach to properly use each aspect of consciousness. God gave us neshama and expects humans to use it according to His will. Those who choose to follow God and adhere to His way of life receive specific instructions when it comes to serving Him.

## Psychology and Purpose of Life

Psychology is the study of the mind. We shall discuss what the mind is, but consciousness is the foundation of humans. It is like a car's motor, body, brakes, steering, or wheels. Each can exist in thousands, even millions of types, but each of the five features is fundamental to any car. So likewise, the purpose of life is a primary feature, one of the five that characterizes humans.

For a human to flourish, they must know their life's purpose. Therefore, education, in all its forms, from parenting to teaching, to maturing, to growing up, to apprenticing, to educating, to mentoring, to forming, to training, to development, to whatever we input into an individual's psyche, must first and foremost be to enhance that person's purpose of life.

Truth, love, authority, courage, power, intelligence, travel, experiences, etc., are not the purpose of life. They are tools we use to enhance and reach our purpose in life. Education is not about facts, exams, and diplomas. Yes, those are necessary, but they are stepping stones to helping young and old to KNOW and ACCOMPLISH their purpose in life.

Your life purpose is that *overriding desire to do something* in line with your personal ambitions, education, and skills. It motivates you to get out of bed, think, and plan your future. It's what you really want to do with your life.

Our imagination, choices, creativity, learning, growth mindset, and challenges lead us there. We are fulfilled, happy, and at peace because of the combination of our daily activities. Our work time, leisure time, home time, and bedtime satisfy our needs for ourselves and those around us.

Psychology, therapy, and education should put all people on track to their individual purpose in life.

## The Spiritual Purpose of Life

How can I assert, and you be confident, that knowing one's purpose in life is a God-infused characteristic of neshama, consciousness? Because, in the first five minutes of the existence of humans, God tells Adam what humanity's purpose on Earth is; to *dress* and *keep* the Garden of Eden. The Biblical Hebrew of that phrase means to *worship* and *serve* God. That meaning encompasses the entire purpose of God for humankind. In other words, the purpose of life for human existence on Earth.

Read Dress and Keep Garden of Eden. Man Destined to be a Gardener?[13] In reality, the spiritual purpose in life is identical to our psychological purpose in life. With the essential additional point that God is our main focus, this is not some spiritual wishy-washy babble or foolishness. God wants us to accomplish something real based on His directives. His message is simple, "Worshiping and serving God means to put God and our neighbor first in our lives."

---

13. https://theexplanation.com/dress-keep-garden-of-eden-man-destined-to-be-a-gardener/

That means whatever personal and professional purpose in life we choose should be aligned with the worship of God and the service of our fellow humans, near and far.

We still have four features of consciousness to cover. They will detail precisely what alignment with God and neighbor mean. Spirituality is not just attending church and singing hymns. Authentic spirituality is how you exercise your purpose in life. Is it God-oriented or not?

The first aspect of consciousness is that every single human who has ever walked the face of this Earth has an ingrained purpose for their life. Success or failure, worldly or godly, is not the issue here; the key is all humans have the inborn desire for a purpose in life. It exists only because humans alone possess neshama consciousness.

In the next chapter, we shall elaborate on the second attribute of consciousness; how and why humans worldwide function identically.

# 16. Human Conduct. How Creative Humans Worldwide "Should" Function

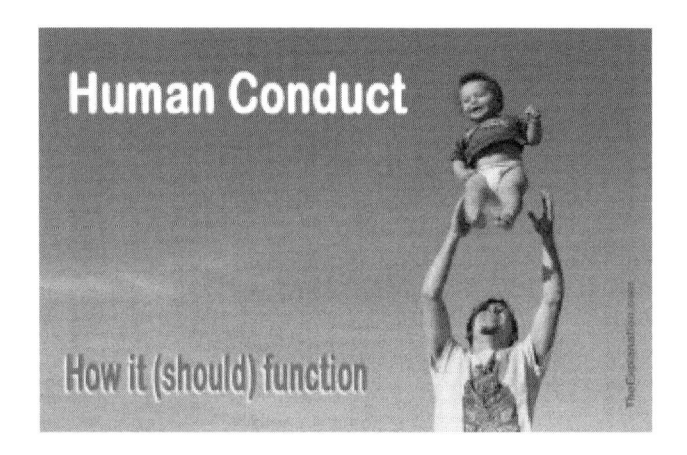

**Consciousness establishes the blueprint for human conduct. People's behavior has a definite pattern. Here's how it functions**

When God breathed neshama, the breath of life, into the first human, He conferred certain features or abilities on them. In the last chapter, we saw the ability to create a purpose for one's life[1]. Now we'll see **human conduct**, in other words, the primary or inherent features, characteristics, or qualities of a human being.

Have you ever asked yourself why humans, the planet over, function in the same way?

---

1. https://theexplanation.com/what-purpose-of-life-why-humans-crave-an-answer/

We all operate similarly because God made males and females in His image by infusing the neshama, the ability to accomplish specific functions God planned for humans. Remember, God is a Family[2], and we can become His sons and daughters here on Earth now, preparing ourselves for an eternal future as fellow members of His Family. That functioning mechanism characterizes each person on Earth. God is preparing humans now for their future with Him.

We are discussing WHAT consciousness is. We will discuss WHY we are imbued with it later. Consciousness is the model by which humans can live harmoniously with ourselves and with our neighbors. It is the way to having proper relationships with other humans, near and far. It is the inherent God-endowed features that identify humankind.

Human conduct is the second feature of consciousness, and like the five features of a car, the body, motor, brakes, steering, and wheels each has many components. Likewise, with human conduct, it's a 7-step method that I elaborated on at length in Part 2 of *Audit of Humankind*[3], and I ask you to refer to that book for details.

In this summary, each characteristic defines an aspect of human conduct and how they all work together harmoniously, like the parts of a car's braking system, to accomplish its specialized task. Humans possess the seven traits of human conduct because we have neshama, consciousness.

**1.** Two-faced Humanity—Depraved Priests and Kind Criminals[4]

Two-faced is not limited to a Batman movie. There exist good and bad individuals and those that exhibit both

---

2. https://theexplanation.com/all-time-hidden-truth-elohim-god-is-a-family/

3. https://theexplanation.com/read-all-the-content-of-audit-of-humankind-online/

4. https://theexplanation.com/two-faced-humanity-depraved-priests-and-kind-criminals/

grace and malice. The propensity to be virtuous and evil sets humankind apart from all other life forms on Earth. We reach out to fellow humans and the planet with proper or improper motives; this singularity of dual conduct has admirable or disastrous consequences.

**2. Free Will—We all Possess it, But We Can't Always Utilize it**[5]

Free will is the second characteristic human beings possess that affects how humankind functions. The ability to choose and freely make decisions endows each human being. We all possess this trait, but we cannot always exercise our free will because of our circumstances.

Each person can take infinite directions, including venturing into good and evil and everywhere in between. Some go one way, others in the opposite direction—we are all subject to decisions and course changes in our education, encounters, travel, profession, leisure, reading, and mates.

**3. Human Behavior is the Expression of Dual Conduct and Free Will**[6]

Human Behavior—how humankind conducts itself—results from a combination of the first two pieces of how humanity functions. Human behavior = dual conduct + free will. Human behavior is the cake each

---

5. https://theexplanation.com/free-will-we-all-possess-it-but-we-cant-always-utilize-it/

6. https://theexplanation.com/human-behavior-is-the-expression-of-human-nature-and-free-will/

human being bakes when they mix their particular dual conduct with their portion of free will.

The term human behavior is neither negative nor positive. It is totally neutral. Each person who walks the face of the earth has their specific behavior depending on dozens of factors—including heredity, environment, culture, and education—as well as decisions made in the individual's mind.

**4.** Ethics are the Blueprint for Behavior—How Humanity Should Function[7]

Ethics carries many other names: morals, values, rules, and virtues. They are the basis of the way each of us lives our life. Ethics exist whether you're playing a sport, driving, on a website, or washing dishes.

Ask yourself: What do referees in sports, stop lights in traffic, and terms and conditions on a website have in common? They all define the dos and don'ts of behavior. No society or organization, whether it be one person or billions, can run smoothly—with peace and prosperity—without rules and regulations.

**5.** Justice Goes Hand-in-Hand with Ethics to Obtain Peace[8]

Justice is the application of conformity to ethics. Since we need guidelines, a code of rules to regulate our behavior, we also need a way to adhere to that code. This adhesion is justice. Generally, this is equitable respect

---

7. https://theexplanation.com/ethics-are-the-blueprint-for-behavior-how-humanity-should-function/

8. https://theexplanation.com/justice-goes-hand-in-hand-with-ethics-to-obtain-peace/

for people's adherence to the accepted moral code. Justice comes with rewards and penalties to encourage right and dissuade wrong behavior.

**6.** Self-Reproach, the Essential Beginning Step toward Real Peace[9]

Self-reproach is a positive step to personal and collective peace. It's the realization that it's up to me to look honestly at my human conduct and choices for the ball to start rolling. It is the first element requiring introspection. Your mind looks deeply into your inner workings and discovers what your actual human conduct is accomplishing, both positive and negative, including mental decisions to follow your life warpath or peace path.

Humans take risks and face challenges. Everyone makes mistakes. I need to recognize my misbehavior. The reason we teach and why we need rehabilitation, including sanctions, is to reach our goal: change.

This awareness and change of heart must start with oneself.

**7.** Forgiveness; the Healing Bond for Humans to Function Peacefully[10]

You're walking around right now carrying a huge burden of guilt. If you have the least amount of sensitivity toward those in your entourage, your family, friends, colleagues, and acquaintances. You know you've done

---

9. https://theexplanation.com/self-reproach-the-essential-beginning-step-toward-real-peace/
10. https://theexplanation.com/forgiveness-the-healing-bond-for-humans-to-function-peacefully/

them wrong to one extent or another. That's when guilt hits. You're sorry for your wrongdoing; that guilt can be overwhelming, depending on the damage you've caused.

That's where forgiveness of oneself starts. Change and forgiveness go hand-in-hand. Exercising self-reproach and forgiveness takes concerted personal awakening, inner fortitude, and outward effort. The two ultimate steps of how humans function are a personal about-face decision of the first two steps.

Forgiveness caps off the entire process because it alone can begin to overcome and wipe away all the tears and hurt each of us has been subjected to during our lives. Of course, this can take time, but forgiveness alone permits a reduction and eventual eradication of negative thoughts in your mind.

The final chapter of How humans function in *Audit of Humankind* is Love is the Most Distorted English Word. Here's Why[11]. All the above seven characteristics together are the definition of love. The ability to love is inherent to our consciousness.

**Sam's reflections**

This chapter is one of the most important in the book. Why? Because it reveals not only how consciousness defines what a human being is but how the innermost aspect of our human conduct works.

It shows the autonomous conduct of each individual and the ability to make life-changing decisions at any point in their life journey; this is equivalent to plasticity, which is the other side of rehabilitation. The former

---

11. https://theexplanation.com/love-is-the-most-distorted-english-word-heres-why/

opens the door for the latter. God has built this ability to change direction into what a human being is.

## Psychology and Human Conduct

Human conduct goes hand in hand with the purpose of life. Psychology's role is to help people align their purpose and their conduct. When these two work together, a person begins to see positive results. Imagine transforming from a twisted personal and/or professional life (purpose), and a conflictual mode with outside people and inner self-doubt (human conduct). Putting your personal conflicts and professional misgivings in order is a pathway to reduced anxiety and depression.

When psychologists have to intervene, we're dealing with rehabilitation. Prevention is a much better solution, and that comes firstly from parenting and secondly from schooling. It's up to parents to help their children understand their dual conduct (1st step in how they function), make wise choices (2), and behave decently (3). As overseers, parents set rules (4) and apply rewards and discipline (justice 5). There's always room for change (6) and forgiveness (7) without fail. The entire 7-step procedure is called love.

The rules and behavior for how human life functions are found in the book of Proverbs[12]. This father-to-son fireside chat contains the most elementary ethics for a fruitful and happy life. There's not one single injunction that is not valid in the 21st century. Parents are primarily responsible for instilling these values, how human life functions in their children. Today, we've abdicated parenthood and teaching values. Our society is a reflection of the opposite of how human life functions.

---

12. https://theexplanation.com/rules-for-life-wisdom-for-living-abundantly-in-the-world/

## Spiritual Human Conduct

This 7-step blueprint characterizing each human being worldwide is not a wild guess. The Bible outlines this pathway immediately upon the Creation of Adam and Eve. Christ taught all these steps, and the Christian life is based on them. So, likewise, God uses these same criteria to judge His people. Here's a summary.

1. **Dual conduct**: Adam and Eve had a purpose for their lives and dual conduct to act like human beings and execute, or not, everything God revealed to them.
2. **Free will**: The two Trees in the Garden of Eden are the evidence. God counseled them on which to choose, but He left the decision up to them. Today, we can accept or refuse God's calling.
3. **Behavior**: The New Testament is replete with good and bad examples of Christian behavior. Acts of kindness and, unfortunately, discord are marks of God's Church.
4. **Ethics**: There are spiritual rules for Christians, the most vital being the Two Great Commandments. There are practical dos and don'ts (read Rev. 22:14-15 at UnlockBibleMeaning.com[13]) and the spiritual attitudes of the Beatitudes (Mat. 5) to develop.
5. **Justice**: God rewards and punishes before and after Christ's Coming. Luke 3:17 says, "Whose fan is in his hand, and he will throughly purge his floor, and will gather the wheat into his garner; but the chaff he will burn with fire unquenchable." Within God's Church, there's proper justice (1 Cor. 5).
6. **Self-reproach**: In the Christian era, we call this repentance. Acts 17:30-31, "And the times of this ignorance God winked at; but now commands all men

---
13. https://unlockbiblemeaning.com

every where to repent: Because he has appointed a day, in the which he will judge the world in righteousness by that man [Jesus] whom he has ordained." All humans are endowed with this trait of repentance as part of their consciousness. All humans will have the choice (2nd step) in God's time.
7. **Forgiveness**: It's part of the Lord's prayer, "And forgive us our debts, as we forgive our debtors." God's purpose revolves around the ultimate sacrifice of Jesus Christ, Who opened the way to forgiveness for all humankind. Romans 5:8 sums up God's love for each person who has walked the face of Earth, "God commends his love toward us, in that, while we were yet sinners, Christ died for us."

God-breathed consciousness is the sole reason we have all seven attributes of human conduct. God's neshama allows us to develop how we relate to our material world, other people, and our Creator to accomplish our purpose.

# 17. Social Relationships. Puzzling Humans Love & Hate. Why?

**Social Relationships are one of the most fundamental identifiers of humans. What is their origin? Why is it so essential and conflictual?**

God blew His own neshama (Job 32:8) into the first human (Gen. 2:7). Why? Because It is the primary agent that confers God's image on humankind (Gen. 1:26). What God does on His perfect spiritual level, humans can accomplish on their human level. Neshama confers *understanding* (Job 32:8), which means *discernment* and *perception*[1], the awareness of their surroundings; this is the equivalent of consciousness or cognizance of one's world in the broadest possible way with one's intellect, senses, and emotions.

---

1. https://theexplanation.com/neshama-inspiration-discover-the-deeper-meaning/

# MIND-BODY PROBLEM SOLVED

Consciousness empowers humans with specific attributes. So far, we've seen two of the five: purpose for one's life[2] and how each of us (should) function[3]. I will summarize this with three words: purpose to choose & change. Each human should be free to *choose* their *purpose* and *change* to accomplish it. I realize this is utopic. Why? Precisely because of the way humans function. We have dual conduct; therefore, we prevent others (the strong and rich prevent the weak and poor) from choosing and changing to accomplish their purpose.

## Social Relationships

Your purpose in life involves three major areas. Today we will discuss the first: **social relationships**. These are the interpersonal interactions with every other human being. Of course, you'll never meet and greet everyone! Your social relationships will be the circle of human beings with whom you'll be in contact throughout your life. It can expand and recede; in other words, you can *choose* and *change* your social relationships.

Through consciousness, each human comes pre-equipped with the capacity for flourishing and harmonious interconnections thanks to their emotions, feelings, and how we read others. Interpersonal relationships are in a state of flux, increasing and decreasing. They are dynamic.

The book *Audit of Humankind* elaborated on the many levels of interconnected kinships and affiliations, often based on affinities. As we go through this summary, ask yourself the question, how did humans acquire the capacity to have such a coherent variety of interpersonal bonds?

---

2. https://theexplanation.com/what-purpose-of-life-why-humans-crave-an-answer/

3. https://theexplanation.com/human-nature-how-humans-worldwide-should-work/

- Human Society, the Only Global Social Species[4] (*Audit of Humankind*, Part 3, Chapter 1)
  Human society exists because human beings are sociable. The presence or absence of proper social relations results in human turmoil or peace.
  We delve into how society, you and I, and the rest of the world population have organized ourselves to try to live in harmony with one another; this should lead to peaceful cohabitation. The word *society* comes from the term *social*. The origin of both these terms is the Latin *socius* meaning companion, friend, and ally.
- You are a Unique Individual among 8 Billion on Earth[5] (3.2)
  Each of us is a unique individual on planet Earth. Individuals are the first building block of human society. Social relationships start as soon as you have two unique individuals in the same room.
  Each one is a building block in the social network of human society that spans the globe. Your and my individuality mean each of us brings our qualities (and defects) to construct humanity. We pool our individualities—each individual is not diluted in the mass—our individualities are cumulative and represent the patchwork that is the diversity of society.
- Gender Equality, Gender Inequality, or Gender Compatibility?[6] (3.3)
  Gender equality makes headlines. Over the last few years, its come to the forefront as very controversial. How does it sit with human society?

---

4. https://theexplanation.com/human-society-the-only-global-social-species/

5. https://theexplanation.com/you-are-a-unique-individual-among-7-billion-on-earth/

6. https://theexplanation.com/gender-equality-gender-inequality-or-gender-compatibility/

How many genders are there, and what are they? The differentiation of gender and sex to denote human beings goes back to about the 50s but takes on fundamental differences around the 80s. Today gender identity and gender roles have become an issue for usage in language, responsibilities in religion, focus on poverty, and even a question in the discussion of climate change. Pandora's box has been opened.

- Bride and Groom is a Cross-Cultural, Worldwide Phenomenon[7] (3.4)

  Bride and groom spark engagement rings, engagement parties, and bridal showers. Celebrating this event is a milestone in a couple's life.

  Every girl and boy somehow aspire to be a bride and groom and eventually a husband and wife; this appears to be something built into the human psyche. Have you ever wondered why? And why is it so universal?

- Couple Relationship—Binding Husband and Wife in Marriage[8] (3.5)

  The couple's relationship is the strength of social relations. Marriage, the husband and wife together, is the twosome on which human society resides.

  The couple relationship between human beings is the foundation on which human society rises or falls. The ability of a male and a female to combine their capacities and complement each other in their family life endeavors is the mark of a stable society.

- Healthy Marriage, A Happy Twosome with Abundant Benefits[9] (3.6)

---

7. https://theexplanation.com/bride-and-groom-is-a-cross-cultural-worldwide-phenomenon/

8. https://theexplanation.com/couple-relationship-binding-husband-and-wife-in-marriage/

A marriage relationship has enormous benefits compared to living a single life. It's not a question of whether there are benefits but rather what those benefits are.

Joining the complementary contributions of the male and female partners has multiple benefits for a flourishing marriage. But the question still arises, why is it so?

- Family—The Cornerstone of Human Society[10] (3.7)
Family is the perfect structure on which to build human society. It alone assures stability to parents and children. The family unit is the cornerstone block in which the father, mother, and children can grow to be balanced and mature individuals. The social relationships spun therein are the foundation of the network of human society.
- Parenting, Father & Mother have Essential Complementary Roles[11] (3.8)
Parenting follows bride and groom, husband and wife. Father and mother have many challenges and responsibilities, but the benefits are incommensurable. Conceiving takes a few seconds; the consequences and parental responsibilities can last 20 years, but the rewards a lifetime.
- Extended family. Many Generations = World Population[12] (3.9)
The extended family, growing generation after generation, gave birth to our world population today. That's Human Society.
The extended family starts with the male and female,

---

9. https://theexplanation.com/healthy-marriage-a-happy-twosome-with-abundant-benefits/

10. https://theexplanation.com/family-the-cornerstone-of-human-society/

11. https://theexplanation.com/parenting-father-mother-have-essential-complementary-roles/

12. https://theexplanation.com/extended-family-many-generations-world-population/

# MIND-BODY PROBLEM SOLVED

marriage, babies, childrearing, youth, dating, and marriage, and the cycle continues from generation to generation. That's how the world population has passed eight billion people. We're all one family.

- Ethnicity, Clans, Tribes, Where Did They All Come From?[13] (3.10)

  Ethnicity is a significant subject today. Ethnic groups are in the limelight regarding minority rights, their treatment, and literal extinction.

  Ethnicity in a time of globalization should make us stop and think. Among the thousands of ethnic groups, many are on the brink. Society is dealing them a hard hand. Do we stop to think about where such diversity came from?

- Nations Are Identified by Their Own Patriotic Ethnic Culture[14] (3.11)

  Nations have their own heart. Their citizens are attached to their nationality, traditions, and culture.

  Nations and peoples are characterized by their values, foods, music, and sports teams; there's a patriotic fervor whenever there's any type of competition or conflict. Look at World Cup fever and flag-waving at the Olympic Games. But national identity even goes much further than that.

- Origin of Language, An Unsolvable Scientific Mystery[15] (3.12)

  Philologists are in total contradiction about the origin of language, while it is the basis of human relations. What a conundrum.

  The origin of language has stumped the most learned

---

13. https://theexplanation.com/ethnicity-clans-tribes-where-did-they-all-come-from/

14. https://theexplanation.com/nations-identified-by-their-own-patriotic-ethnic-culture/

15. https://theexplanation.com/origin-of-language-an-unsolvable-scientific-mystery/

intelligentsia for centuries. It was even forbidden to discuss this issue. Yet, language is the most common and apparent feature differentiating humans from animals. It allows the entirety of Earth's inhabitants to communicate with one another.

- Globalization: Integration Versus Segregation of People[16] (3.13)
  Globalization is a challenge. How do you integrate human beings when the natural tendency is to group them by ethnic language and culture?
  Globalization has its pros and cons. World travel and social integration are lovely ideas. What is the norm for such a utopia? We in the democratic, liberalized West might think that should be the norm. Unfortunately, many don't share our point of view. The fiber of human society and social relationships is in play with this world-encompassing issue.

There you have it, from individuals to world globalization, the basis of which is a couple of people birthing children in a family. All the parts assemble into visible and measurable social relations. But, innately, where does this impetus come from? Why is it hard-wired, the standard pattern across the planet, a permanent feature of humans down through history? The answer is God implanted it in us when He blew His neshama, consciousness, into the first human.

Is this conjecture? How can *The Explanation* affirm this? Check what the Bible says at UnlockBibleMeaning.com[17].

**Genesis 1:27-28**

---

16. https://theexplanation.com/globalization-integration-segregation/
17. https://unlockbiblemeaning.com

27 So God created man in his own image, in the image of God created he him; male and female created he them.

28 And God blessed them, and God said to them, Be fruitful, and multiply, and replenish the earth...

The model of proper social relationships is established and completed in the first five minutes of humankind's story, with God establishing marriage and family.

**Genesis 2:24**

Therefore shall a man leave his father and his mother, and shall cleave to his wife: and they shall be one flesh.

When I use the term *hard-wired,* it is in no way a reference to the brain. We saw God formed the first human from dust. The brain is dust[18]. Neshama is God's spiritual essence. You cannot locate neurons or anything else labeled social relationships. The brain, an electrical impulse or a chemical reaction through the synapses does not initiate them. These real reactions are the result of what is innate to consciousness. Social relationships have always been an integral part of the human psyche.

## Psychology and Social Relationships

Please listen to Jordan Peterson on loneliness and intimate connections[19]; his advice is sound. But beyond the counsel, statistics, the characteristics of singles, and their interactions, I want you to understand that social relationships are taken for granted as a defining element of all humans planetwide. There's

---

18. https://theexplanation.com/the-human-body-from-sterile-dust-of-the-ground/

19. https://youtu.be/-9l26VlF2to

no doubt humans are social creatures. And that inborn social inclination aligns with God's instruction to the first couple. Adam and Eve *understood* (Job 32:8, H995, the neshama gave them this feature of their psyche[20]) marriage and family because God's neshama implanted not only the concept but also the pattern of social relationships in their consciousness.

Our 21st century so-called progressive society has deviated (Matthew 24:37-39) from the basics of sane social relationships with the breakdown of societal well-being. Of course, there are many wonderful families with husband-wife, father-mother, and children assuming the benefits and responsibilities of family life. But, in general, with wayward dating and sex, divorce, parenting, delinquency, and dysfunctioning adults, we're paying a high societal price. The psychologist's role is to help people return to the basics of social relationships.

## Spiritual Social Relationships

Why did God instill the need for social relationships in humans via their consciousness? Because God is a family. [21] Family social relationships on Earth, in the image of God, are a training ground to prepare us for Godly Family relationships for all of eternity.

### Ephesians 5:25-6:1, 4

25 Husbands, love your wives, even as Christ also loved the church, and gave himself for it;

30 For we are members of his [Christ] body, of his flesh, and of his bones.

---

20. https://theexplanation.com/neshama-inspiration-discover-the-deeper-meaning/

21. https://theexplanation.com/all-time-hidden-truth-elohim-god-is-a-family/

31 For this cause shall a man leave his father and mother, and shall be joined to his wife, and they two shall be one flesh.

32 This is a great mystery: but I speak concerning Christ and the church.

6:1 Children, obey your parents in the Lord: for this is right.

4 And, you fathers, provoke not your children to wrath: but bring them up in the nurture and admonition of the Lord.

There are hundreds of Bible verses about social relations based on family values. However, the only reason all humans can apply interpersonal connections, whether spiritual believers or unbelievers, is because of the innate feature of social relationships conferred on each of us by God's neshama, consciousness.

# 18. Human Rulership has the Responsibility for People & Resources. Why?

**Human rulership has the management of themselves, other people, the environment, and Earth. So where did it come from, and why?**

Who decided on human rulership to govern other people, the world, and its natural reserves? It's no mystery that we're in a massive mess regarding the peace and prosperity of people and resources. Do you doubt it? Just ask a Ukrainian or any other oppressed minority. We are suffering at the hands of poor leadership.

We are the only species with a propensity for human rulership. Why is this ingrained in our being? What's the origin of this defining characteristic of humankind? In a word, consciousness. Human rulership is an embedded trait like human purpose for life, how humans function, and social relationships. It is a full-fledged attribute of the neshama God breathed into the first human[1].

God is The Ruler (1 Corinthians 15:27), and in His image, humans are also rulers; it is another identifying trait of males and females worldwide. This is the fourth of five features God endowed each human with by blowing His neshama into the first human. In the next chapter, we'll discuss the final characteristic, probably the most important.

## Human Responsibility

*The Explanation* has written *Audit of the Universe* and *Humankind* about how humans govern and the results. It's a mixed bag of progression and regression. Is the glass of peace and prosperity getting fuller or emptier? How is humankind managing space, the atmosphere, our planet's water, land, flora, and fauna? And what about managing humankind, the poor, elderly, handicapped, refugees, youth, and children?

You know the Bill of Rights, but have you heard of the Bill of Responsibility[2]? It's a universal declaration of human responsibilities proposed by the InterAction Council on 1 September 1997. Here are just two articles.

### *Article 1*

**Every person,** regardless of gender, ethnic origin, social status, political opinion, language, age, nationality, or religion, **has a responsibility to treat all people in a humane way.**

### *Article 7*

---

1. https://theexplanation.com/breath-of-life-unique-possessors-neshama-earth/

2. https://en.wikisource.org/wiki/Universal_Declaration_of_Human_Responsibilities

Every person is infinitely precious and must be protected unconditionally. The animals and the natural environment also demand protection. All people have a responsibility to protect the air, water, and soil of the earth for the sake of present inhabitants and future generations.

I encourage you to read through the entire document. Article 4 states "All people, **endowed with reason and conscience**, must accept a responsibility to each and all... " The responsibility is our individual duty and obligation to look after that for which each of us is answerable.

Read details of the practical application on a personal and national level of the fourth characteristic of consciousness, human rulership; this is the fourth Part of the book *Audit of Humankind*.

## How Humankind Rules

- Human Government for Personal and World Peace[3] (4.1)
  In all its shapes and forms, human government is responsible for bringing peace and prosperity to the people it rules. It is a key to understanding the state of Earth today. So do an audit of the universe. Are we further or closer to peace and prosperity?
- Governance Structure, Important Role in Rulership[4] (4.2)
  Governance structure occupies a prime position in human rulership. How functions and responsibilities are distributed in manageable parts. Each acts alone and also in conjunction with all the other parts. For example, pesticides are associated with agriculture but affect

---

3. https://theexplanation.com/human-government-personal-world-peace/

4. https://theexplanation.com/governance-structure-important-role-in-rulership/

# MIND-BODY PROBLEM SOLVED

industry and health. The governance structure must address this issue globally.

- Government for the People is Also Concern for the Poor[5] (4.3)
  Government for the people means those who rule consider the well-being of all citizens they oversee. It involves focusing attention on the welfare of all those you manage; family, school, company, neighborhood, city, or country. Whether you administer a prince or a pauper, all have conditions to lead peaceful and prosperous lives.
- Human Needs, the Basics Each Person Should Expect[6] (4.4)
  Human needs are what each human being worldwide should be entitled to as a citizen of the world. The essential requirements each person should expect as part of the human race. Those resources are present on the planet; governments should use them best to ensure all citizens' welfare.
- Inner Peace for Citizens is the Real Goal of Government[7] (4.5)
  Inner peace for every person you manage is an excellent motivation for looking at and working with those people around you. As a result, it is the most sought-after commodity today.
- Peace of Mind, the Tranquil Result of Good Leadership[8] (4.6)
  Imagine all citizens in your home, building, or neighborhood possessing peace of mind. Unfortunately,

---

5. https://theexplanation.com/government-for-people-concern-for-poor/

6. https://theexplanation.com/human-needs-basics-person-expect/

7. https://theexplanation.com/inner-peace-citizen-goal-government/

8. https://theexplanation.com/peace-mind-tranquil-result-leadership/

it's not happening today due to poor human rulership. Peace of mind is wishful thinking for many. We don't have the know-how or motivation to bring it to people around us.

- Prosperity for the Nation is Prosperity for Each Citizen[9] (4.7)
Prosperity is enough to live decently and handle emergencies. Imagine all families with this well-being, not for an elite or even the majority, but for everyone. Families in their own chosen home with satisfactory living conditions; that is a prosperous nation.

- History of Individuals and Nations[10] (*Evidence for Bible Wisdom* 2.4)
Does God work on a personal or national scale? History in the Bible tends to focus on individuals. It starts with Adam and Eve, Cain and Abel, and Noah, whose sons' descendants become nations. Likewise, spiritual conversion is an individual matter in the New Testament, but God also refers to nations.

- Individual Rights vs. Collective Rights[11] (*Evidence for Bible Wisdom* 2.5)
Human rights are a significant issue today. The question of whose rights come first, personal or community, colors the debate on many subjects. Can individuals do whatever they want and exercise their individual rights? Or, for the good of the community, are there collective rights to which individuals should adhere?

- Peace is a National & International Government Concern[12] (4.8)

---

9. https://theexplanation.com/prosperity-nation-prosperity-citizen/

10. https://theexplanation.com/history-of-individuals-and-nations-practical-bible-wisdom

11. https://theexplanation.com/individual-rights-vs-collective-rights-the-bible-balance/

Peace on a national and international level, for the last 70 years, has been a reasonably present phenomenon. What about the next 70? With the 30 glorious years following WWII and the rising standard of living, we have had an episode of relative peace in world history. Will it continue?

- Government, 2 Choices, Bottom Up or Top Down[13] (4.9)
  Government gives us two opposing choices. Autocracy or democracy. Top-down or bottom-up. Everything else is a combination of these extremes. Government in Western democratic nations is a system of checks and balances. Whenever the balance is out of kilter, there's turbulence. Today, we have worldwide turmoil.
- Best Form of Government, Aiming for the Common Good[14] (4.10)
  The best form of government brings peace and prosperity to all its constituents; humankind is still searching for this unique formula. Nations and international organizations have experimented with every type of governmental structure imaginable; what's left?

How can *The Explanation* affirm that a characteristic of consciousness is human rulership? To rule Earth is the reason you are here. After creating humans, God's very first directive was for them to dominate and reign over planet Earth.

**Genesis 1:26-28**

---

12. https://theexplanation.com/peace-national-international-government-concern/

13. https://theexplanation.com/government-2-choices-bottom-up-top-down/

14. https://theexplanation.com/best-form-government-aiming-common-good/

26 And God said, Let us make man in our image, after our likeness: and let them have *dominion* (H7287) over the fish of the sea, and over the fowl of the air, and over the cattle, and over all the earth, and over every creeping thing that creeps upon the earth.

27 So God created man in his own image, in the image of God created he him; male and female created he them.

28 And God blessed them, and God said to them, Be fruitful, and multiply, and replenish the earth, and *subdue* it (H3533): and have *dominion* (H7287) over the fish of the sea, and over the fowl of the air, and over every living thing that moves on the earth.

Go to UnlockBibleMeaning.com[15] and study Strong's H7287 (KJV: reign, rule over) and H3533 (KJV: bring into subjection). Human rulership is the calling of every person on Earth. God planted this fourth characteristic of neshama in humankind; along with social relations[16] (The third characteristic verse 28), they are our purpose in life[17] (1st characteristic). Note that these two verses (26 and 28) enclose verse 27, which clearly states God created both genders in His image. These characteristics of neshama reveal how He made all of us with the same attributes He possesses. Read these chapters for more details.

- Rule Earth – To Rule the World is God's Purpose for Humans[18] (*Origin of Humankind* 1.8)

---

15. https://unlockbiblemeaning.com

16. https://theexplanation.com/social-relationships-puzzling-humans-love-hate/

17. https://theexplanation.com/what-purpose-of-life-why-humans-crave-an-answer/

18. https://theexplanation.com/rule-earth-to-rule-the-world-is-gods-purpose-for-humans/

# MIND-BODY PROBLEM SOLVED

- God Blessed the Male and the Female – Here's the Meaning[19] (1.9)
- Rule the World. Humankind is on Earth for that Purpose[20] (2.1)
- Genesis 1 Reveals Basics: Social Relations & Rulership[21] (2.2)

## Psychology and Human Rulership

Most humans crave to know how to manage themselves and others better. There are many good books on this subject. Here are four best-sellers 21 Lessons for the 21st Century[22] by Yuval Harari, The Laws of Human Nature[23] by Robert Greene, Behave, the Biology of Humans at Our Best and Worst[24] by Robert Sapolsky, and 12 Rules for Life: An Antidote to Chaos[25] by Jordan B Peterson.

This brief Section on psychology is designed to show how all people worldwide can benefit from such teaching; this is a non-biblical perspective that is helpful for the general public. There are many other books in this field. In fact, we live in an era of *life coaches*, people who imagine rules of life for social relationships and management.

## Spiritual Human Rulership

---

19. https://theexplanation.com/god-blessed-the-male-and-the-female-heres-the-meaning/

20. https://theexplanation.com/rule-the-world-humankind-is-on-earth-for-that-purpose/

21. https://theexplanation.com/genesis-1-reveals-basics-social-relations-rulership/

22. https://www.ynharari.com

23. https://www.goodreads.com/en/book/show/39330937

24. https://infolearners.com/ebooks/behave-robert-sapolsky-pdf/

25. https://www.jordanbpeterson.com/12-rules-for-life/

The future role of God's people, for which they're being prepared now, is, "And have made us to our God kings and priests: and we shall reign on the earth" (Revelation 5:10). There's no space to expand on this here. Human rulership is in the image of godly rulership because as God rules, so should we now and when Christ returns. The above books are exciting and certainly have insights into human nature. But no book can touch the Bible and its laws and principles regarding human rulership.

It is replete with the history of Kings and Priests. The book of Proverbs[26] is the book par excellence for teaching both secular and spiritual principles of social relations and rulership to adolescents, young adults, men, and women. With up-to-date examples and principles, it should be the obligatory basis of a social studies class both at home and in school. It would go a long way to enabling a more stable society.

Human rulership is not some pie in the sky, going to heaven, gazing into some bright halo for all eternity. On the contrary, occupying the offices and functions of Kings and Priests are exhilarating occupations. They give you the ultimate opportunity to bring peace and prosperity to all people and resources you govern. But, unfortunately, I know you're not prepared or ready for that.

That's why God has given us physical life with consciousness to prepare us for such a role; this is the destiny of every single human being who has lived on this planet. How can we all be rulers? What are we going to rule? Let's leave that in God's hands; the Bible is the manual for humankind here and now. There will be a manual for Kings and Priests in due time.

---

26. https://theexplanation.com/fig-leaves-or-clothing-tinker-or-build-practical-bible-wisdom/

*Notes:*

# 19. 5 Types of Reasoning. Your Life Depends on Right Choice

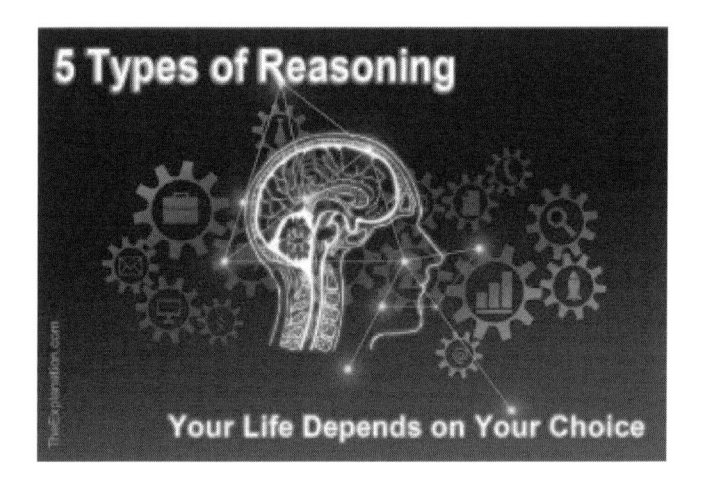

**You're a thinking creature, but strangely not always logical. So here are five types of reasoning. Which type are you? And where will it lead you?**

Your choice among the five types of reasoning is crucial. So let's examine them and see which one ultimately leads to life, real abundant life, with all its benefits.

We're discussing the divine essence, the *breath* (neshama) of life, which God blew into the nostrils of the first dust human He created in Genesis 2:7. Thanks to God's neshama, we possess His image. This image is ingrained and innate; we are all automatically born with these fundamental characteristics. They are our consciousness and define what it is to be human. Without neshama, consciousness, the image of God, we would act like animals.

The example of Nebuchadnezzar in Daniel 4[1] clearly displays the results of having and not having neshama. After regaining his mental senses, his neshama, his consciousness, the King declares, "At the same time my *reason* (H4486) returned to me; and for the glory of my kingdom, my honour and brightness returned to me; and my counsellors and my lords sought to me;" (Dan. 4:36). For seven years he lost the capacity to reason; he had no understanding (H995) which humans receive via the neshama (Job 32:8).

Thanks to the neshama, Adam, Eve, and Nebuchadnezzar, you and I all possess consciousness that confers the same five attributes on us. Like God, but on a human level, first, we have a purpose for life. Second, we have a human mode of functioning. Third and fourth, all humans can develop close (family) and far (friends) social relationships and rulership over their specific environment and Earth itself. The fifth attribute of neshama, the most important, is reasoning—our mental capacities.

Humans alone are born with this innate cognitive ability to think and figure out, extrapolate, deduce, perceive, solve, gather information, analyze, conclude, and decide. Only because we, in the image of God, can reason. From our earliest age, we are taught HOW to reason; it is a given we all come into this world with the ability to reason. Nobody explains its origin; mystery solved, from the neshama, the consciousness with which each of us is endowed.

Of the five types of reasoning, four are very well-known, recognized methods which *The Explanation* expounded on extensively in Part 5 of *Audit of Humankind*: Observation, Science, Philosophy, and Religion. To be open, I've always had difficulty naming the first of the five types of reasoning. We observe using our five senses: sight, sound, smell, taste, and touch, but then we

---

1. https://theexplanation.com/neshama-inspiration-discover-the-deeper-meaning/

analyze and decide. One way is intuition[2], "the power or faculty of attaining to direct knowledge or cognition without evident rational thought and inference. b: immediate apprehension or cognition" (Webster Dictionary[3]). Therefore, I will associate intuition with one of the results of observation.

Here are the five types of reasoning with a biblical example of human intuition.

## 1. Observation and Intuition

Observation, The First Way to Human Reasoning[4] (5.3)

Observation is the first and primary way human beings gather information. From observation, hopefully, correct facts are established. We start by sourcing facts. Like fake news, we can have fake or distorted facts. Our source AND the interpretation of what we observe must be reliable.

In the Bible, we have one of the clearest examples of reasoning with Eve. First, God gave her facts; then, the Serpent fed her fake facts. Finally, she made a fatally wrong decision based on intuition.

> **Genesis 3:2-6**
>
> 2 And the woman said to the serpent, We may eat of the fruit of the trees of the garden:
>
> 3 But of the fruit of the tree which is in the midst of the garden, God has said, You shall not eat of it, neither shall you touch it, lest you die (Sam: True fact, she quotes the Source).

---

2. https://www.psychologytoday.com/us/basics/intuition

3. https://www.merriam-webster.com/dictionary/intuition

4. https://theexplanation.com/observation-first-way-human-reasoning/

4 And the serpent said to the woman, You shall not surely die (Sam: Fake news, notice the source):

5 For God does know that in the day you eat thereof, then your eyes shall be opened, and you shall be as gods, knowing good and evil (Sam: Fake news, what propaganda).

6 And when the woman saw that the tree was good for food, and that it was pleasant to the eyes, and a tree to be desired to make one wise, she took of the fruit thereof, and did eat, and gave also to her husband with her; and he did eat.

Eve *saw;* she observed, listened to the fake news, and intuitively made a terribly wrong decision. She was deceived (1 Timothy 2:14), a victim of her intuition.

How many of us read the Source, the Bible, even quote what *God said* (like Eve) and then intuitively decide what is right and wrong?

## 2. Philosophy

The second of the five types of reasoning.

- Philosophy, the Love of Wisdom. Whose Wisdom?[5] (5.4)
  Philosophy asks questions about the interconnection of the universe, the world, and humankind. The wisdom of the meaning of life is the conclusion of human thought. They think they can answer what the purpose of life is. Why are we here?
- Spiritual Philosophy. Wisdom and Spirituality[6] (5.5)

---

5. https://theexplanation.com/philosophy-love-wisdom-whose-wisdom/

The love of wisdom with an additional ingredient. The human being with spiritual enlightenment.
- Eastern Philosophy. Not a Religion, It's a Way[7] (5.6)
- Paranormal. Real Activity Beyond Physical Explanation[8] (5.7)

## 3. Science

The third type of reasoning.

- Science, Our World's Savior. This is Human Reasoning[9] (5.8)
  Our World's Savior. Human reasoning sees science and technology solving world ills. Today, most Western civilization tends to believe and reason this way.
- Science Facts or Fiction, Vital For Human Reasoning[10] (5.9)
- Quantum fields in Sensory Science. A Very Brief History[11] (5.10)
- Extrasensory Fields in Spiritual Science. A Brief History[12] (5.11)
- Limits of Science. Origin of the Universe and Mind?[13] (5.12)

## 4. Religion

---

6. https://theexplanation.com/spiritual-philosophy-wisdom-spirituality/

7. https://theexplanation.com/eastern-philosophy-not-religion-a-way/

8. https://theexplanation.com/paranormal-activity-beyond-physical-explanation/

9. https://theexplanation.com/science-world-savior-human-reasoning/

10. https://theexplanation.com/science-facts-fiction-vital-human-reasoning/

11. https://theexplanation.com/quantum-fields-a-very-brief-history/

12. https://theexplanation.com/extrasensory-fields-spiritual-science-brief-history/

13. https://theexplanation.com/limits-science-origin-universe-mind/

The fourth of the five types of reasoning.

- Religion—Is it the Solution to World Peace?[14] (5.13)
  Although fractioned into tens of thousands of beliefs, religion is believed in or practiced by 85% of the world's population. Despite the rise of science, the metaphysical runs off as the winner of human minds.
- God or gods. The Foundation of Religion[15] (5.14)
- Religious Belief is a Mighty Motor of Human Reasoning[16] (5.15)
- Religions, All Types: Bible Quoters, Pseudo, Secular[17] (5.16)
- Religious Experiences. Fact But Inexplicable[18] (5.17)

## 5. Theology

The vast majority frown on the fifth of the five types of reasoning in ethics, science, and other fields.

- Deity and Sound, Reasoned Words are the Crux of Theology[19] (Origin of the Universe 1.2)
  Theology is the God-intended meaning of Scripture. What does God have to say? What is His reasoning?
- Godview. You can't build a savvy worldview on intuitive opinions[20] (Evidence for Bible Wisdom 1.1)

---

14. https://theexplanation.com/religion-solution-world-peace/

15. https://theexplanation.com/god-or-gods-foundation-religion/

16. https://theexplanation.com/religious-belief-mighty-motor-human-reasoning/

17. https://theexplanation.com/religions-all-types-bible-quoters-pseudo-secular/

18. https://theexplanation.com/religious-experiences-fact-inexplicable/

19. https://theexplanation.com/deity-and-sound-reasoned-words-are-the-crux-of-theology/

20. https://theexplanation.com/can-you-build-true-worldview-on-savvy-opinions-experience/

The majority say the Bible is not adapted to the 21st century; myths and antiquated bedtime stories like Noah's flood are foolish; they have nothing to offer in an era of technology and information. So science searches for consciousness in every nook, cranny, and neuron of the body and comes up with no evidence; yet, they intuitively agree that consciousness arises from the material world.

Moses foretold this problem "Beware, lest your hearts be deceived and you turn away and serve other gods and worship them" (Deut. 11:16). Intuitive thinking got Eve into deep trouble, and that dilemma continues to this day. That's why the first four types of reasoning (other gods) cannot solve the mind-body and societal problems. The extent of human reason cannot reach into godly theology, which sums it up with a principle from the time of Noah that describes our age (Matthew 24:37-39).

### Genesis 6:5

> And GOD saw that the wickedness of man was great in the earth, and that every *imagination* (H3336) of the *thoughts* (H4284) of his heart was only evil continually.

This *imagination* results from the four types of reasoning, the 5th characteristic of neshama, consciousness. Check the Biblical Hebrew below; both *imagination* and *thoughts* imply and are translated by *purpose*, which is the 1st characteristic of neshama[21], consciousness. Sound theology reveals that humans are using their *dual* human nature[22] (Tree of *Good* and *Evil*) to choose *evil continually*. as Genesis 6:5 states.

---

21. https://theexplanation.com/what-purpose-of-life-why-humans-crave-an-answer/

22. https://theexplanation.com/human-nature-how-humans-worldwide-should-work/

Humankind is confined to human types of reasoning. That is the cause of the woes and anxiety of human society. Our *imagination* runs wild with human opinions, speculations, and solutions, and we bear the fruit of the seed we've sown. Human consciousness reasons wrongly.

*Imagination* (H3336) and *thoughts* (H4284) can bear thorns or fruit depending on whether they are human or godly. So we have the choice; that's our dual nature, the first characteristic of how humans function[23].

### H3336

יֵצֶר yêtser yay'-tser; from H3335 (יָצַר); a form; figuratively, conception (i.e. purpose):

KJV - frame, thing framed, imagination, mind, work.

### H4284

מַחֲשָׁבָה machăshâbâh makh-ash-aw-baw'; or מַחֲשֶׁבֶת; from H2803 (חָשַׁב); a contrivance, i.e. (concretely) a texture, machine, or (abstractly) intention, plan (whether bad, a plot; or good, advice):

KJV - cunning (work), curious work, device(-sed), imagination, invented, means, purpose, thought.

Theological reasoning should be the basis of real education[24]. Please be careful with what I'm saying here. Not religion (the 4th of the five types of reasoning, and it's incorrect) but respect for God and His wisdom, as Proverbs tells us.

---

23. https://theexplanation.com/human-nature-how-humans-worldwide-should-work/

24. https://theexplanation.com/definition-of-education-teach-learn-wisdom/

**Proverbs 9:10**

> The fear of the LORD is the beginning of wisdom: and the knowledge of the holy is *understanding* (H998 from H995).

*Knowledge of the holy* is proper theology, the 5th of the five types of reasoning. That's adequate *understanding* from the Tree of Good to grasp the importance and relevance of the book of Proverbs in the 21st century. Yes, today, we have access to God's psychological way for humankind, but only very few follow the godly type of reasoning, theology. On the other hand, the Bible talks about human construction of their multiple differing worldviews based on the four types of reasoning: intuition, science, philosophy, and religion.

**Isaiah 45:9, 29:15-16**

> 9 Woe to him that strives with his Maker! Let the potsherd strive with the potsherds of the earth. Shall the clay say to him that fashions it, What make you? or your work, He has no hands?
>
> 29:15 Woe to them that seek deep to hide their counsel from the LORD, and their works are in the dark, and they say, Who sees us? and who knows us?
>
> 16 Surely your turning of things upside down shall be esteemed as the potter's clay: for shall the work say of him that made it, He made me not? or shall the thing framed say of him that framed it, He had no *understanding*? (H995).

Read those verses closely. Isa. 45:9 says let the potsherd strive with the potsherds of the earth. It describes human potsherds' bickering debates in politics, government, science, philosophy, and religion. Each person or author thinking they're right, "be admonished: of making many books there is no end; and much study is a weariness of the flesh" (Ecclesiastes 12:12). Above, Isaiah says, "their works are in the dark, they've turned things upside down." The four authors mentioned in the last chapter, giving the rules of life, have no basis for the why, what, and how of consciousness. Their reasoning is misguided and defective.

Whether people talk about or omit God, they've removed all trace of Him from the very foundation of their worldview. God is just another one of those million pieces of facts and fiction, maybe a little more important, but certainly not the foundation. That's the meaning of *He has no hands* in Isa. 45:9. We humans think we're here with consciousness, and there was no Creator!

Come to your senses. In Isa. 29:16, we must realize 100% He, God, has *understanding* (H995); He is neshama, the ultimate Consciousness and Foundation. He's embedded a portion of His neshama in each one of us. That consciousness endows you and me with a purpose in life, human functions, social relationships, and reasoning powers. We must learn not to reason according to our imagination but according to the knowledge of the holy, the most fitting of the five types of reasoning.

# 20. What it Means to be Human. The Astonishing Ultimate Meaning

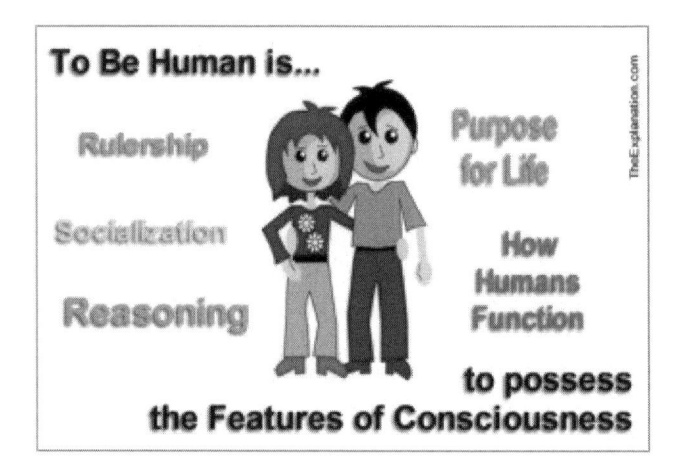

**To Be Human is...**
Rulership
Socialization
Reasoning
Purpose for Life
How Humans Function
**to possess the Features of Consciousness**

**The meaning of being human is to possess the five features of consciousness. It is a psychological and biblical definition.**

*The Explanation* has solved the first part of the mind-body problem. To be human signifies being endowed with consciousness, which confers five characteristics: how humans function, reasoning, socialization, rulership, and purpose for life.

These defining traits are what God bestowed on the first human He created in His image. God has these traits; hence humans acquired them. We see their manifestation in Genesis 1-3 immediately after the Creation.

1. How humans function: They could choose from the two Trees; their dual nature resulted in bad behavior (Genesis

3) and disobedience to God's ethics; justice was served in ousting them from the Garden. Humans are in a period of self-reflection; most will return to God and be forgiven. This is God's plan for the first humans and their descendants; it plays out over thousands of years.
2. Reasoning: Immediately on Creation, God asked the first human to name the animals. The man did this and reasoned he had no partner (Gen. 2:20).
3. Socialization: God blessed the couple and told them to multiply, build a family, and replenish the Earth (Gen. 1:28).
4. Rulership: God gave them dominion and told them to subdue the Earth (Gen. 1:28).
5. Purpose for Life: God told the first human to dress and keep the Garden. The deep meaning of this poor translation is to serve and worship God[1] (Gen. 2:15).

The above course of action can only be activated because God ingrained those characteristics in the first human and each descendant of the first couple. All five of these traits are intimately related to the ultimate purpose for which God created humans. Just like a jet pilot must be fitted with health, weather, navigation, flight control, and plane engineering to accomplish their purpose, similar to humans for their eternal purpose.

## Mind-Body Problem. First Part Solved

Here's how Wikipedia defines the mind-body problem[2].

> The mind–body problem is a debate concerning the relationship between thought and consciousness in the

---

1. https://theexplanation.com/dress-keep-garden-of-eden-man-destined-to-be-a-gardener/
2. https://en.wikipedia.org/wiki/Mind%E2%80%93body_problem

human mind, and the brain as part of the physical body. It is larger than, and goes beyond, just the question of how mind and body function chemically and physiologically (for example, the neural correlates of consciousness), as that question presupposes an interactionist account of mind–body relations. This question arises when mind and body are considered as distinct, based on the premise that the mind and the body are fundamentally different in nature.

We have solved a portion of the first part of the problem. I say a piece because I have purposely NOT used the term *mind* to this point in the book. *The Explanation* has limited the discussion to neshama - consciousness, to show what it is to be human.

The aspect of the mind-body problem we've solved so far is body and consciousness are definitely different in nature. The body is dust, and consciousness is God's neshama, the divine essence of non-material origin; this is the profound meaning of Genesis 2:7.

We still have much more to discover. For example, the nature of mind, what is mind? How it correlates with consciousness and the dust brain (part of the body). And particularly the interactions between the material body and non-material consciousness and mind. The rest of the book answers all those questions and takes you even further.

The Bible shows us why God endowed us with both consciousness and mind and how we must prepare them now before we can jump into the cockpit seat and be at the command of one of the most powerful pieces of equipment humans have created. Imagine what would happen if you had your hands on the throttle and controls if you weren't prepared. There's nothing worthwhile you can do well without preparation and training. It takes time, and you require physical, social, and mental prerequisites for most specific careers. Consciousness, with its five characteristics, is a prerequisite to being human.

## Psychology and Being Human

Abraham Maslow, a psychologist, established the hierarchy of the five human needs in the 1940s. Starting with the most basic, they are psychological, safety, love/belonging, esteem, and self-actualization. It includes many elements we've witnessed in what it is to be human but falls short of a complete picture. And especially the correct order of human needs. Obviously, we require enough for physical survival, but beyond that, we need direction about life (how humans function and proper reasoning); this is clearly seen in an affluent society shackled with a lack of future perspective, anxiety, and crime.

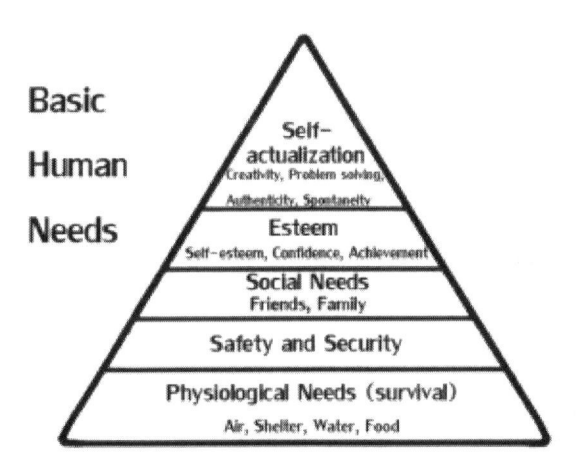

Figure 9. Maslow's hierarchy of human needs

Understanding consciousness and its five characteristics is grasping the real fundamental needs of ALL humans. They are within the scope of psychology worldwide. They should be the basis of education, starting with parents and all people responsible for modeling and training young people today to be the adults of tomorrow. To be human means to possess consciousness, illustrated below by an image summarizing how we need to cater to those needs.

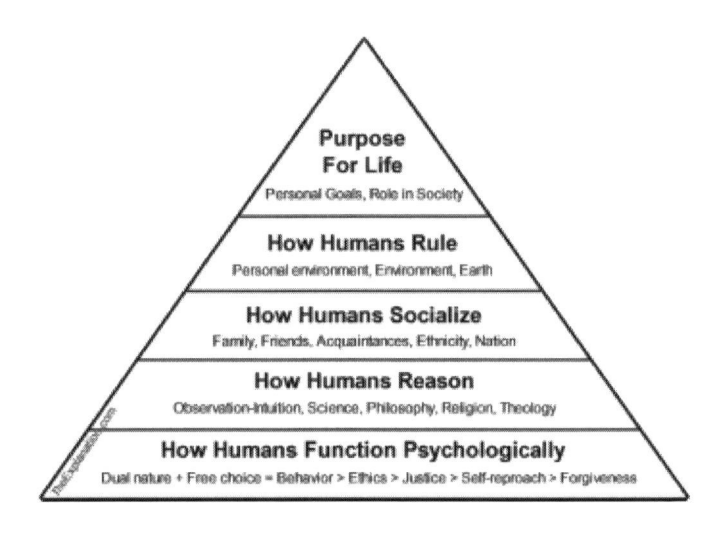

Figure 10. Pyramid of human consciousness

## 1. How humans function

The foundation is how humans function because that is the first item on the menu for toddlers. Every infant displays their dual nature by doing things they shouldn't, like sticking their finger in an electric socket or climbing up on an open window ledge. They choose to disobey their parents' directives to stop screaming or pick up their toys. Have parents taught them these ethics and set the bounds with justice? Are the children learning to obey (self-reproach or self-control)? Finally, are children receiving forgiveness (after correcting a wrong choice), love, praise, and encouragement when they make the right choices? This approach is valid for all ages and all people planetwide.

## 2. How humans reason

The rules for psychologically stable children and adults are in the Bible. Detractors focus on the hard questions of capital punishment and sacrifices (which can be answered) to the detriment of solid living principles provided by God in the book of Proverbs[3]. Everyone should meditate on those words (Psa. 1:2). They are the basis of ethical reasoning, without which it's impossible to lead an abundant life in this world today.

## 3. How humans socialize

Socialization is where Western civilization has jumped the track. It has nothing to do with spirituality or theology. Socialization means raising children with love and respect to be an integral part of society. Psychology deals with dysfunctional children and adults caused by a breakdown in the socialization chain of upbringing. The more broken homes, the more anti-social behavior we'll have. Socialization is in dire need of parental education. But even upstream from that, we need homes with two loving male and female parents. Society goes the way of parenting.

## 4. How humans rule

To rule is to manage, starting with toys and the spoon that brings food to our mouth, not all over the place. As we grow, our rulership extends outwardly and upwardly with more and more responsibility. It includes our time, TV, reading, social media, and

---

3. https://theexplanation.com/rules-for-life-wisdom-for-living-abundantly-in-the-world/

bigger and more powerful things, like a car or a gun. If we can't rule life responsibly[4], how can we be expected to rule weapons or anything else we're given to govern?

## 5. Purpose for life

In an ideal world, unfortunately not ours, people should receive opportunities to see and experience various activities as they grow. As they develop their talents, skills, and tastes, they will narrow their choices and focus on their calling in life. Whether it's to be a plumber or a pilot, a bricklayer or a beautician, a teacher or a politician, all trades and professions are needed. Thankfully, we're all different, and together, each one's purpose in life covers the gamut of human needs.

In summary, what it is to be human, these five characteristics of consciousness are biblical, but they apply to every single human who has ever walked the face of this Earth. God set in motion the basis for abundant life for humanity. Of course, it is better to believe in God. Still, even without such belief, a fulfilled life and a stable society are achievable if we fulfill these principle requirements of consciousness.

## Spirituality, Christianity, Theology, and Being Human

God created humans, including the body, consciousness, and mind, so the questions arise, how do these elements interconnect? How does God interact with each of those entities? *The Explanation* will answer those questions, one by one, in due time. But, for now, God's Creation looks like this graphic, establishing what it is to be human. God's Creation: Physical, Flora, Fauna, Humankind

---

4. https://theexplanation.com/rule-life-responsibly-the-key-human-singularity/

composed of Dust and Neshama, which are Body and Consciousness.

```
              God's Creation
            /    |     |    \
      Physical Flora Fauna Humankind
                            ∧
                       Dust + Neshama
                         |        |
                       Body + Consciousness
```

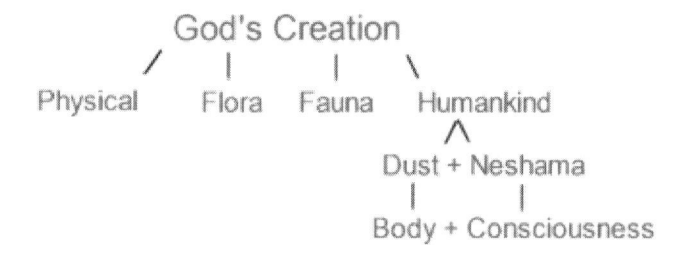

Figure 11. God's Creation

The same five characteristics of consciousness apply to worshippers of God. Although this is obviously on another level, and God does not expect non-believers to be at this stage, the above steps apply to them. To each his own in God's time.

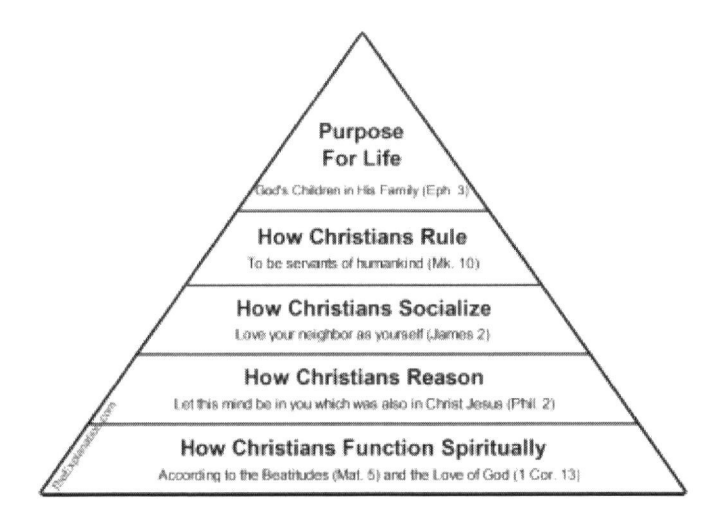

```
                    /\
                   /  \
                  / Purpose \
                 / For Life  \
                /God's Children in His Family (Eph. 3)\
               /──────────────────────\
              /   How Christians Rule   \
             /  To be servants of humankind (Mk. 10) \
            /──────────────────────────\
           /   How Christians Socialize   \
          /  Love your neighbor as yourself (James 2) \
         /──────────────────────────────\
        /     How Christians Reason       \
       / Let this mind be in you which was also in Christ Jesus (Phil. 2) \
      /──────────────────────────────────\
     /  How Christians Function Spiritually  \
    / According to the Beatitudes (Mat. 5) and the Love of God (1 Cor. 13) \
   /──────────────────────────────────────\
```

Figure 12. Pyramid of biblical consciousness

## 1. How God's people function

For those animated by God and His Spirit, our respect for Him and our neighbor (the two Great Commandments) are the prime motivators. The spiritual application of God's way of life involves the Beatitudes: poor in spirit, mourn, meek, merciful, hunger and thirst for righteousness, pure in heart, peacemakers (Matthew 5), and God's definition of love (1 Corinthians 13).

## 2. How God's people reason

In the last chapter, we saw five reasoning options[5], of which only one is a valid basis in God's eyes, theology, not intuition, science, philosophy, or religion.

I've put reasoning second in the hierarchy of what it takes to be human. However, in biblical terms, it comes first. The Apostle Paul sums it up well, "Let this mind be in you, which was also in Christ Jesus (Philippians 2:5). That is the practical application of true theology.

## 3. How God's people socialize

God's goal in granting the aspect of socialization as part of consciousness is because He is a Family[6] that will be parenting His children as more and more enter His Family. That's another exciting story, but God's Family functions in a specific way (Love for Father (God) and love for brothers and sisters (neighbor)); this is social relations.

God created humans in His image. Likewise, we are one human family, and each belongs to their smaller family and functions in a

---

5. https://theexplanation.com/5-types-of-reasoning-life-hangs-ultimate-choice/

6. https://theexplanation.com/human-family-elohim-god-works-both-create-rule/

specific way (love the head of the family, father, mother, and our brothers, sisters, and neighbors). Our human family is training for our spiritual family.

## 4. How God's people rule

Christ gave us the principle in Mark 10:42-44 "But Jesus called them [the disciples] to him, and said to them, You know that they which are accounted to *rule* over the Gentiles exercise lordship over them; and their great ones exercise authority on them. But so shall it not be among you: but whosoever will be great among you, shall be your minister: And whosoever of you will be the chiefest, shall be servant of all." Christian rulership is service to all our neighbors.

Proverbs 25:28 applies to all humans, as I wrote above, but even more so to people who are converted, "He (or she) that has no rule over his own spirit is like a city that is broken down, and without walls." We will discuss this *spirit* but suffice it to say; a Christian has self-control.

## 5. Purpose for life

God has an incredible, out-of-this-world purpose for life. So he implanted His Neshama, our consciousness, in each of us to accomplish that purpose; to become His Sons and Daughters in His Family and reign for all eternity.

Salvation is a free gift of God, but He offers it to those who use their consciousness to glorify Him according to His purpose. Therefore, the way humans function, their reasoning power, socialization, rulership, and purpose are now in training, preparing for the time God will accomplish His plan.

# IV. Ruach - The Power of Life and Mind

The activator and motor of consciousness.

# 21. Spirit in the Bible is Very Controversial and Misunderstood

**The word *spirit* in the Bible is sometimes mistranslated and often misinterpreted. It's time for scriptural enlightenment.**

What does spirit in the Bible refer to? How does spirit in the Bible relate to neshama? "Study to show yourself approved to God, a workman that needs not to be ashamed, rightly dividing the word of truth" (2 Timothy 2:15).

So far, we have focused on neshama and established the following biblical facts.

- In Genesis 2:7 neshama is translated *breath* of life[1]
- Neshama comes from God (Job 32:8[2])

---

1. https://theexplanation.com/breath-of-life-unique-possessors-neshama-earth/

2. https://theexplanation.com/5-types-of-reasoning-life-hangs-ultimate-choice/

- God gave a part of His own neshama to humans (Job 32:8[3])
- Humans alone (not animals) possess neshama (Joshua 11:14[4])
- Job 32:8 reveals the neshama confers inspiration which gives understanding
- *The Explanation* equates neshama with consciousness which automatically confers five qualities on all humans: purpose, function, socialization, rulership, and reasoning

This divine essence is the distinguishing mark of humans. From the example of Nebuchadnezzar[5], we saw that, without neshama, he lost all five of the above capacities; he was reduced to the state of an animal.

Notice that as an animal, Nebuchadnezzar could still fulfill animal needs like foraging for food, which is their primary occupation, followed by sleeping and mating. Some animals also take care of their young for a limited period of time. Considering they do NOT have neshama, we shall see what animals DO possess that confers on them the variety of behaviors that characterize their hunting, mating, migration, and other activities. But when Nebuchadnezzar regained his reason (Daniel 4:34-36), it was accompanied by reinstating all five qualities.

The rest of this book focuses on *spirit* in all its types and strengths. There are many more than you realize. This spirit in the Bible relates to animals, humans, spirit beings, and God. Spirit poses some of the most difficult theological problems. Materialists, who don't believe in spirit, explain the Universe in purely material ways.

---

3. https://theexplanation.com/5-types-of-reasoning-life-hangs-ultimate-choice/

4. https://theexplanation.com/breath-of-life-unique-possessors-neshama-earth/

5. https://theexplanation.com/neshama-inspiration-discover-the-deeper-meaning/

# MIND-BODY PROBLEM SOLVED

For believers, there's spirit and Spirit, with few knowing their relationship. Furthermore, in the Bible, and especially religion, in its holy state, as the Holy Spirit, many believe it is a Person, a member of the Trinity, while others reject this teaching.

## Breath of Life

We will start with a look at Biblical Hebrew and translations to show just how delicate this subject is. At UnlockBibleMeaning.com[6], search for *breath of life*. Switch to Strong's Concordance and check the Strong's number following the word *breath*.

> **Genesis 2:7** And the LORD God formed man of the dust of the ground, and breathed into his nostrils the *breath* (H5397) of life; and man became a living soul.
>
> **Genesis 6:17** And, behold, I, even I, do bring a flood of waters upon the Earth, to destroy all flesh, wherein is the *breath* (H7307) of life, from under heaven; and every thing that is in the Earth shall die.
>
> **Genesis 7:15** And they went in unto Noah into the ark, two and two of all flesh, wherein is the *breath* (H7307) of life.
>
> **Genesis 7:22** All in whose nostrils was the *breath* (H7307 of H5397) life, of all that was in the dry land, died.

Here's the confirmation in the King James Version and Strong's Concordance. You can also look at each verse in the Interlinear to verify the Hebrew word.

---
6. https://unlockbiblemeaning.com

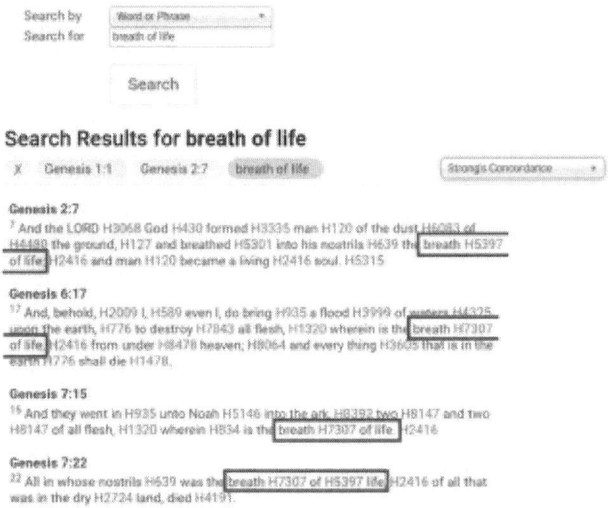

Figure 13. Search results for *breath of life*

Translations are helpful but not always dependable; this is a prime example. The identical term in English (*breath* of life) comes from two unrelated Hebrew words: *ruach* (H7307) and *neshama* (H5397). Considering the fact these four phrases are within five chapters, one has to wonder what the translators were thinking. However, we've spent eight chapters examining Gen. 2:7, H5397, and neshama, so we're clear on that.

The three other verses have H7307, *ruach*. Many know *ruach* is Biblical Hebrew for *spirit* in the Bible.

### H7307

רוּחַ rûwach roo'-akh; from H7306 (רוּחַ); wind; by resemblance breath, i.e. a sensible (or even violent) exhalation; figuratively, life, anger, unsubstantiality; by extension, a region of the sky; by resemblance spirit, but only of a rational being (including its expression and functions):

KJV - air, anger, blast, breath, × cool, courage, mind, × quarter, × side, spirit(-ual), tempest, × vain, (whirl-) wind(-y).

H7306

רוּחַ rûwach roo'-akh; a primitive root; properly, to blow, i.e. breathe; only (literally) to smell or (by implication, perceive (figuratively, to anticipate, enjoy):

KJV - accept, smell, × touch, make of quick understanding.

Ruach appears about 380 times in Biblical Hebrew, of which about 235 are translated as *spirit* in the Bible, 100 with *wind*, and 30 with *breath*. *Wind* and *breath* are often used figuratively to mean spirit; this fits Step 2 to master Biblical Hebrew[7]. *Spirit* in the Bible will be our focus; there is much to study and discover. Simply by reading the above translations and the Strong annotations, we can see its similarity to *neshama* with reference to *immaterial* and *understanding*. Similitude, yes, identical, in no way.

## Spirit in the Bible

We know humans possess ruach, *spirit* in the Bible, so I always wondered why Genesis doesn't discuss *ruach* associated with neshama and nefesh (soul) and humans in Genesis 2:7 at Creation. So let me offer two points.

---

7. https://theexplanation.com/fastest-bible-study-method-god-intended-meaning/

1. When God created the first human, *ruach* was already present in the animals! This is clear from Genesis 7:15, "they [the animals] went in unto Noah into the ark, two and two of all flesh, wherein is the *breath* (H7307) of life." Animals, including birds, fish, and the creeping things were created on Days 5 and 6, PRIOR to humans.
2. Since ruach was already present in the living animal kingdom, highlighting neshama only in Gen. 2:7 confirms humans alone possess it; animals did not receive it and do not possess it, as the episode in Joshua 11:14 aptly demonstrated.

In Chapter 13, I showed you the Interlinear image for Genesis 7:22 with both words, neshama and ruach, side by side and remarked, "you have to ask yourself why the KJV translators left out one of these two words (spirit). I will explain this, but not now," Well, now that we're broaching spirit in the Bible, it's time for an answer.

For neshama, the KJV translators rendered *breath*, *soul*, and *spirit* for their translations. Unfortunately, these exact translations are used for other Biblical Hebrew words, which we will see below; this adds to the confusion of comprehension of what this first human, representing all humans, is.

**Genesis 7:20-22**

20 Fifteen cubits upward did the waters prevail; and the mountains were covered.

21 And all flesh died that moved upon the Earth, both of fowl, and of cattle, and of beast, and of every creeping thing that creep upon the Earth, and every man:

# MIND-BODY PROBLEM SOLVED

22 All in whose nostrils was the *breath* (H5397) of life, of all that was in the dry land, died.

Here's an image of verses 21-22 from the Interlinear Bible, revealing a huge problem the KJV translators missed and didn't know what to do about it. Unfortunately, you can NOT see this in English.

```
Ge 7:21
    H776      H5921    H7430        H1320    H3605      H1478
    hā·'ā·reṣ, 'al-    hā·rō·mêś   bā·śār    kāl        way·yiḡ·wa'
    הָאָרֶץ    עַל־    הָרֹמֵשׂ    ׀ בָּשָׂר  כָּל־      וַיִּגְוַע
    the earth  on      that moved   flesh     all        And died

               H3605         H2416              H929          H5775
               ū·ḇə·ḵāl      ū·ḇa·ḥay·yāh,     ū·ḇab·bə·hê·māh bā·'ō·wp̄
               וּבְכָל־      וּבַחַיָּה         וּבַבְּהֵמָה   בָּעוֹף
               and of every  and of beast       and of livestock both of birds

               H3605     H776      H5921     H8317          H8318
               wə·ḵōl    hā·'ā·reṣ, 'al-     haš·šō·rêś     haš·šō·rêṣ
               וְכָל     הָאָרֶץ    עַל־     הַשֹּׁרֵץ      הַשֶּׁרֶץ
               and every the earth on        that creeps    creeping thing

                                                            H120
                                                            hā·'ā·ḏām.
                                                            הָאָדָם׃
                                                            man

Ge 7:22
         H2416       H7307        H5397         H834      H3605
         ḥay·yîm     rū·aḥ        niš·maṯ-     'ă·šer     kōl
         חַיִּים     רוּחַ        נִשְׁמַת־    אֲשֶׁר     כֹּל
         of life     of the spirit the breath   that [had] all

    H4191     H2724           H834  H3605        H639
    mêṯ.      be·ḥā·rā·ḇāh    'ă·šer mik·kōl     bə·'ap·pāw,
    מֵת׃      בֶּחָרָבָה     אֲשֶׁר מִכֹּל      בְּאַפָּיו
    died      in the dry [land] that [was] of all in the nostrils
```

Figure 14. Genesis 7:22, the breath of the spirit

In Genesis 7:21-22, notice the two Biblical Hebrew words *nishmat* (neshama - the breath) and *ruach* (of the spirit). You don't see this in most English translations, as I explained in Chapter 13[8]. There, I also pointed out why this passage refers to humans.

Here, we want to emphasize the presence of this couple, *neshama* and *ruach,* associated with humans. A better rendering of the Biblical Hebrew in Genesis 7:22 is;

"and every man, all in whose nostrils was the *breath* (H5397 – neshama) of the *spirit* (H7307 – ruach) of life."

Quite a difference. Humans (*every man*, in the above verse) absolutely do possess both *neshama* and *ruach*, *spirit* in the Bible. Genesis 2:7, the Creation of the first human, makes no mention of ruach, but it is 100% sure God infused this spirit with the neshama. Spirit is not mentioned there because it was already present in the animals, and God wanted to draw our attention to the distinctive mark of humans, *neshama*. But the biblical fact is that neshama and ruach are inseparable.

Let's do another exercise; transpose this Biblical Hebrew phrase into 21st century scientific jargon. "And every man, all in whose nostrils was the *breath* (H5397 – neshama) of the *spirit* (H7307 – ruach) of life."

We've already established the significance of *neshama* as *consciousness*. And the KJV translators rendered *ruach* (H7307 above), among other words, with *mind*. So, in contemporary terms, Genesis 7:22 reads like this:

> And every human, all in whose nostrils was *consciousness* with the *mind* of life.

---

8. https://theexplanation.com/breath-of-life-unique-possessors-neshama-earth/

They are two separate but complementary elements, *neshama* and *ruach*, *consciousness* and *mind*. *The Explanation* will elaborate on exactly what the mind is in relation to consciousness, and what it allows humans to accomplish. And remember, animals possess this ruach as well, so we shall also see what exactly it equips them to perform.

I do not intend to explain the motivations of the 17th century King James Version translators concerning the absence of the word *ruach* in Genesis 7:22. We run into the same problem with the *breath of life*, translated from both *neshama* and *ruach*. And we are going to run into the mistranslations of nefesh-soul as well. All I will say is these unfortunate renderings have left us with a trail of confusion, false interpretation, and worse, false doctrine. This controversy and misunderstanding of the term *ruach-spirit* in the Bible is the reason *The Explanation* must venture into the Biblical Hebrew to solve the mind-body problem.

Understanding the companionship of neshama and ruach, consciousness and mind is a good start.

# 22. Neshama and Ruach, the Ultimate Backbone of Humans

**Neshama and ruach are the two components possessed by every single human being. Together they confer humanity on humankind.**

Neshama and Ruach are the essential constituents that endow humans with their humanity. This chapter aims to show the reality and inseparability of this spirit duo. We will discuss the exact role of *ruach* later.

We're focusing on the creation of humans. Specifically, what makes humans human. The Bible presents the neshama and the ruach as imparted by God to humans. The following chapters about *ruach* cast the base of spirituality (obviously, Christ is the Foundation) and psychology. *The Explanation* will show you why each human possesses ruach and how to use it advantageously, both spiritually and secularly.

# MIND-BODY PROBLEM SOLVED 211

We'll start by seeing this association of neshama and ruach as an indivisible twosome. We saw this next verse in the last chapter, but it is the first time the duo is joined; therefore, it is crucial to see it again. Unfortunately, the KJV translators omitted the translation for one of the Hebrew words; in Biblical Hebrew, you can see BOTH ruach and neshama appear, and they are BOTH associated with humans.

```
Ge 7:22
H2416      H7307         H5397        H834       H3605
hay·yim    rū·ah         niš·mat-     'ă·šer     kōl
חַיִּים    רוּחַ         נִשְׁמַת־    אֲשֶׁר     כֹּל
of life    of the spirit the breath   that [had] all

H4191      H2724         H834         H3605      H639
mē·tū.     be·ḥā·rā·bāh  'ă·šer       mik·kōl    be·'ap·pāw,
מֵתוּ׃     בֶּחָרָבָה    אֲשֶׁר       מִכֹּל     בְּאַפָּיו
died       in the dry [land] that [was] of all   in the nostrils
```

figure 15. Genesis 7:22 Notice the two Biblical Hebrew words *nishmat ruach* (breath of the spirit). You don't see this in most English translations.

### Genesis 7:22 (KJV)

All [humans] in whose nostrils was the breath (H7307 of H5397) life, of all that was in the dry land, died.

The New King James Version has "All in whose nostrils was the breath of the spirit of life, all that was on the dry land, died."

Straight away, we see a significant issue that will confront us throughout our study of *ruach*, its translation. In Gen 6:17, *ruach* chayim (רוּחַ חַיִּים) is translated *breath of life*. In Gen. 2:7, *nishmat* chayim (נִשְׁמַת חַיִּים) is ALSO translated identically in English *breath of life*. You cannot translate two different Hebrew words with the same English word. In English, it is impossible to see this and correctly understand what the Word of God is telling us. Verify it yourself at UnlockBibleMeaning.com[1].

The KJV translators did not understand, as with most people today, the role of the ruach. Similarly, they didn't understand that of the neshama, either. And to top it off, who understands the relationship between ruach and neshama? In Genesis 7:22, the ruach and neshama are side-by-side. They are different, and at the same time, both are interconnected and directly involved with human life.

This association is so essential for comprehension that we will look at all ten verses where we find this twosome. There are only 24 verses with *neshama* (H5397) in the Old Testament, of which a whopping ten include *ruach*. I dare say that very few Bible readers know the relationship between neshama and ruach. Even fewer are likely to know there are numerous critical biblical references to this duo. We'll see them in Bible book order.

### 2 Samuel 22:16

> And the channels of the sea appeared, the foundations of the world were discovered, at the rebuking of the LORD, at the *blast* (H5397 – neshama) of the *breath* (H7307 – ruach) of his nostrils.

As we go through these verses:

1. See who possesses neshama and ruach. In this case, God.
2. See for what and how God uses neshama and ruach. In this case, literally, to shake Earth to protect His servant

---

1. https://unlockbiblemeaning.com

> David. They emanate from God's nostrils, so it's fitting He blew the neshama into the first human's nostrils (Gen. 2:7).

## Job 4:9

> By the *blast* (H5397 – neshama) of God they perish, and by the *breath* (H7307 – ruach) of his nostrils are they consumed.

Eliphaz, Job's friend, reminds him how these godly attributes put down enemies. Both terms can have both a positive and negative effect, depending on the context; this is the 1$^{st}$ Step to Master Biblical Hebrew[2]. God gives and takes life (Deut. 32:39). This is an essential concept for modern liberal Christians who see God only as a do-gooder, loving God. God is love (1 John 4:8), but it also includes His wisdom of knowing when and how to take life. Keep in mind that the same instruments (neshama and ruach) that give life can also take it away; this is the paradox of God, particularly for those who don't understand God's purpose for humankind[3].

## Job 27:3

> All the while my [Job] *breath* (H5397 – neshama) is in me, and the *spirit* (H7307 – ruach) of God is in my nostrils;

Job, during his ordeal, confirms he still possesses neshama and ruach. He knew the difference between these two elements and that he, a human being, like all other humans, retains both.

---

2. https://theexplanation.com/each-biblical-hebrew-word-is-a-precious-jewel-to-be-discovered/

3. https://theexplanation.com/all-time-hidden-truth-elohim-god-is-a-family/

### Job 32:8

> But there is a *spirit* (H7307 – ruach) in man: and the *inspiration* (H5397 – neshama) of the Almighty gives them understanding.

Humans possess the ruach. It is a human component. This is the spirit, translated *mind*, among other words, by the KJV translators; I will expand on this correct translation in the following chapters. You will see why, in humans, the spirit cannot work without the neshama and vice versa. Both essences must be possessed to be *human*. Neshama, given by God as we saw in Gen. 2:7[4], is directly related to the ability to understand; this is consciousness that confers the human qualities of purpose, function, socialization, rulership, and reasoning on humans. Ruach acts on these five attributes, and this God-given duo makes humans who they are.

### Job 33:4

> The *Spirit* (H7307 – ruach) of God has made me, and the *breath* (H5397 – neshama) of the Almighty has given me life.

Important verse; this is parallel to Genesis 2:7. There we saw *God formed* (yatsar), and here we see *God's Spirit made*. This is additional, complementary information. Job points out God's attribute of using the Ruach (with a capital *S*) to CREATE and the Neshama to GIVE LIFE.

### Job 34:14

---

4. https://theexplanation.com/neshama-humankinds-relationship-god/

> If he [God] set his heart upon man, if he gather unto himself his *spirit* (H7307 – ruach) and his *breath* (H5397 – neshama).

If, or rather when a human dies, God collects each human's ruach and neshama. The neshama, our ability to understand, our intellect (Job 32:8 above), AND the spirit that animated us RETURN TO GOD on our death. God gave them to us to live our life; they return to Him on death. Why? We shall see, but for now, retain that both neshama and ruach return to God, not just the ruach, which is what most Bible readers know.

Secondarily, as we go through this duo of neshama and ruach with a focus on the latter, notice man's spirit (small *s*) as in Job 34:14 and God's Spirit (capital *S*) as in Job 33:4. The same essence, *spirit*, but two very different states.

### Psalm 18:15

> Then the channels of waters were seen, and the foundations of the world were discovered at your rebuke, O LORD, at the *blast* (H5397 – neshama) of the *breath* (H7307 – ruach) of your nostrils.

This verse is similar to 2 Samuel 22:16 above about how God can deal with enemies.

### Isaiah 42:5

> Thus says God the LORD, he that created the heavens, and stretched them out; he that spread forth the Earth, and that which comes out of it; he that gives *breath* (H5397 – neshama) to the people upon it, and *spirit* (H7307 – ruach) to them that walk therein:

God is the Creator of Earth, flora, and fauna (what comes out of it), and at the pinnacle, he gives both neshama and ruach to humans. This verse is clear that ALL human beings receive neshama and ruach. Nowhere does it say animals receive BOTH these components. *The Explanation* has elaborated on how the Bible shows neshama is for humans alone[5]. While animals do possess ruach alone, as we saw in Genesis 7:15.[6]

**Isaiah 57:16**

> For I [God] will not contend for ever, neither will I be always wroth: for the *spirit* (H7307 – ruach) should fail before me, and the *souls* (H5397 – neshama) which I have made.

God will not be upset with humankind continually. He's angry because humankind is MISusing the neshama and ruach God has given them. In other words, humans are not using their God-given components to rule for peace and prosperity. But God says, in this verse and context, that He will straighten this situation out. He will not continue in His wrath; this is the last verse with neshama and ruach together and is the fabulous faith we can have in God for the future of humankind.

Notice how, throughout these passages, the translations of neshama and ruach continually change and sometimes switch from one to the other. Note the translation of this last *neshama* is *soul*, the same as *nefesh*. Indeed, the KJV translators were at a loss with these Biblical Hebrew words. And, in all translations, it is impossible to understand what's going on.

---

5. https://theexplanation.com/breath-of-life-unique-possessors-neshama-earth/

6. https://theexplanation.com/spirit-in-the-bible-controversial-misunderstood/

Remember, we're explaining a fundamental component of each human being worldwide. Yet, readers and scholars don't comprehend it. We don't understand what a human being really is. Amazing. But you are learning the answer to this enigma from *The Explanation*.

From these verses, we can understand at least four essential points about the components of each and every human being;

1. Neshama and ruach, the latter in particular, include *breath* (breathing), but both represent something much deeper than that.
2. Since God possesses them, we shall see, in one way or another, they can NOT BE PHYSICAL. Neshama and ruach have immaterial counterparts with humans. Therefore humans possess intangible components.
3. Since neshama and ruach, being metaphysical, are *invisible* to and *unmeasurable* by any physical devices, this means they are inaccessible to science. So we're into the realm of the meeting of theology and science, even if science doesn't know it. Neshama and, especially, ruach are the missing links between these two disciplines. Stay with *The Explanation* because *ruach* has much to do with science.
4. These initial conclusions about neshama and ruach describe the immaterial components of each human. They are the solution to the mind-body problem. The mind and body are two totally separate entities, one (composed of the two spirits) is transcendent and intangible, while the second, the body, is material and physical.

The title of this book, *Mind-Body Problem Solved*, is not in vain. But we will discover much more, HOW the immaterial components in all humans work and WHY we possess them. We will also reveal how to maximize their secular and spiritual use for peace and prosperity.

God possesses ruach; it is, therefore, clearly more than the physical breath that humans AND animals have. When the ruach is associated with the neshama, this is reserved solely for humans. Combined, they endow each human being with their spiritual component, which differentiates and places them mountains above animals.

In the next chapter, we'll home in on ruach and see precisely what it is and what it accomplishes.

## 23. The Bible Definition of Spirit, the Ruach, in One Word is... Power

**One of the biggest mistruths in religion is the Bible definition of spirit, whether with a small s or a capital S. In both cases, it is *power*.**

We have established the biblical fact that God breathed neshama into the first human (Genesis 2:7). This neshama is God's *inspiration*[1] (Job 32:8), endowing humans with *understanding* (Job 32:8 - H995) or, from H995, a *mark of discernment or perception*. *The Explanation* transposes this meaning into modern terminology: *consciousness*. God infused neshama - consciousness into the first and subsequent humans, conferring on them the five attributes that make them human: function[2], socialization[3], rulership[4], reasoning[5], and purpose[6].

---

1. https://theexplanation.com/neshama-inspiration-discover-the-deeper-meaning/

2. https://theexplanation.com/human-nature-how-humans-worldwide-should-work/

3. https://theexplanation.com/social-relationships-puzzling-humans-love-hate/

This is clearly indicated by the goals God set for humans in Genesis 1-3[7]. He equipped humans with the five qualities to achieve His purpose for His Creation. Those five characteristics are not a biological DNA imprint; they are a non-material psychological design. The human singularity is at birth. Each of us is automatically endowed with the potential to perform those five prerogatives.

*The Explanation* revealed WHY humans accomplish these five specific tasks; because God performs these identical functions[8]. Humans are of the God kind[9], training in these five domains to join the God Family. Humans have a unique and indelible relational link with their Creator through the neshama that implants these five characteristics. But there's still one significant missing dimension: the ruach.

Let's go straight to the crux of the matter regarding the Bible definition of spirit. *Spirit*, maybe because of its metaphysical nature, is possibly the most twisted term in the Bible. Here are some verses that establish the basis of the Bible definition of spirit. They reveal:

- The relationship of God's Spirit to human spirit
- The nature of God's Spirit
- The nature of human spirit

## The Relationship of God's Spirit to Human Spirit

---

4. https://theexplanation.com/human-rulership-responsibility-people-resources/

5. https://theexplanation.com/5-types-of-reasoning-life-hangs-ultimate-choice/

6. https://theexplanation.com/what-purpose-of-life-why-humans-crave-an-answer/

7. https://theexplanation.com/astonishing-meaning-what-it-means-to-be-human/

8. https://theexplanation.com/astonishing-meaning-what-it-means-to-be-human/

9. https://theexplanation.com/all-time-hidden-truth-elohim-god-is-a-family/

# MIND-BODY PROBLEM SOLVED

God's Spirit and human spirit are separate, but they can interconnect. The following verses convey the vital teaching of becoming a part of God's Family[10]. However, to focus, we will only look for the Bible definition of spirit.

**Rom 8:14-16**

> 14 For as many as are led by the Spirit of God, they are the sons of God.
>
> 15 For you have not received the spirit of bondage again to fear; but you have received the Spirit of adoption, whereby we cry, Abba, Father.
>
> 16 The Spirit itself bears witness with our spirit, that we are the children of God:

There are TWO distinct spirits, God's Spirit (capital *S*) and human spirit (small *s*). But verse 16 shows they are intimately bound; TOGETHER, they reveal we are part of God's Family. There's a close-knit functioning relationship between human spirit and God's Spirit. Verse 15 calls this connection the *Spirit of adoption*, allowing us to recognize God as our Father. This translation is correct, but Paul, the author, is inspired to add the Hebrew word *Abba*.

Allow me a brief story. I took Hebrew lessons when I was ten years old. At age 16, I went to Israel and stayed in a hotel with a swimming pool, and 60 years later, I still remember hearing this kiddie voice crying out *abba* to his dad standing beside the pool. This wasn't the formal *father* but the loving cry of "*dad*, look what I can do." The words *bears witness with* mean *corroborate* or *testify together* (see G4828 at UnlockBibleMeaning.com[11]). Words fail to

---

10. https://theexplanation.com/all-time-hidden-truth-elohim-god-is-a-family/

express this intimate union of a parent-child relationship. When connected to God's Spirit, the human spirit undergoes a vibrant change in its approach.

## The Coupling of God's Spirit and Human Spirit

Humans are born with human spirit but not God's Spirit. There is a specific moment when this deep connection occurs. Christ told the disciples to prepare for that instant.

> **Luke 24:49**
>
> And, behold, I send the promise of my Father upon you: but tarry you in the city of Jerusalem, until you be endued with *power* (G1411) from on high.

That power is the Holy Spirit, given to the Apostles on the day of Pentecost.

> **Acts 1:8**
>
> But you shall receive *power* (G1411), after that the Holy Ghost (God's Spirit G4151-pneuma) is come upon you: and you shall be witnesses to me both in Jerusalem, and in all Judaea, and in Samaria, and to the uttermost part of the Earth.

God's Spirit confers power on humans. These verses are corroborated by hundreds of other contexts in both the Old and New Testaments. The spirit in man and God's Spirit are two fundamental givens that are unchangeable throughout the history of humankind, starting with the first human in Gen. 2:7 on Earth. This *power* is the Bible definition of spirit.

---

11. https://unlockbiblemeaning.com

### G1411

δύναμις dunamis doo'-nam-is; From G1410; force (literally or figuratively); specifically miraculous power (usually by implication a miracle itself):

KJV - ability abundance meaning might (-ily -y -y deed) (worker of) miracle (-s) power strength violence mighty (wonderful) work.

### G1410

δύναμαι dunamai doo'-nam-ahee; Of uncertain affinity; to be able or possible:

KJV- be able can (do + -not) could may might be possible be of power.

From the Greek *dunamis,* we have the English words *dynamo, dynamic,* and *dynamite.* I believe they speak for themselves and their relationship to *power.* Let's see how the Old Testament uses the word *power* for God's Spirit.

## Power - The Nature of God's Spirit

Note the interchangeability of power and God's Spirit. If there's one word for the Bible definition of spirit, it is *power.*

### Micah 3:8

But truly I am full of *power* (H3581) by the *spirit* (H7307) of the LORD, and of judgment, and of might, to declare to Jacob his transgression, and to Israel his sin.

In the Bible definition of spirit we see the word *power* literally substituted for *God's Spirit*. In the first verse below, God's Spirit is the vector of Creation; subsequently, it's His Power.

### Psalm 104:30

You send forth your *spirit*, (H7307) they are created: and you renew the face of the Earth.

### Jeremiah 27:5, 32:17

I have made the Earth, the man and the beast that are upon the ground, by my great *power* (H3581) and by my outstretched arm, and have given it to whom it seemed meet to me.

32:17 Ah Lord GOD! behold, you have made the heaven and the Earth by your great *power* (H3581) and stretched out arm, and there is nothing too hard for you:

*Man*, *beast*, *Earth*, and *heavens*; God made, He created them all by His Spirit, which is His Power. The underlying essence of the Bible definition of spirit is *power*. In the Old Testament, the Biblical Hebrew word *koach* (H3581) is similar to the Greek *dunamis* (G1411), as both represent power. Please compare the translations of both of them.

### H3581

כֹּחַ kôach ko'-akh; or (Daniel 11:6) כּוֹחַ; from an unused root meaning to be firm; vigor, literally (force, in a good or a bad sense) or figuratively (capacity, means, produce); also (from its hardiness) a large lizard:

KJV - ability, able, chameleon, force, fruits, might, power(-ful), strength, substance, wealth.

## God's Power and Human Power

You know Jesus was both man (by His virgin birth) and God (The *Holy Spirit* shall come upon you, and the *power* (G1411) of the Highest shall overshadow you (Luke 1:35)). The power of the Holy Spirit conceived Christ and to accomplish His life and ministry the Father gave Him the Holy Spirit without limit. When you study the Bible, notice how many times the Bible definition of Spirit is *power*.

### John 3:34

For he [Christ] whom God has sent speaks the words of God: for God gives not the Spirit by measure to him.

### Luke 4:14

And Jesus returned in the *power* (G1411) of the Spirit into Galilee: and there went out a fame of him through all the region round about.

### Mark 5:30

And Jesus, immediately knowing in himself that *virtue* (G1411) had gone out of him, turned him about in the press, and said, Who touched my clothes?

Note that in English, this power representing the Holy Spirit can be translated otherwise; in the above verse, *virtue*. Elsewhere *dunamis* refers to Christ's mighty works and miracles. Therefore, this Bible definition of spirit also includes the spirit's accomplishments. Hence we see the *spirit of love* (2 Tim. 1:7); here, the understanding is that the Spirit gives us the power to transform our human love into godly love.

## Servants of God Animated by the Power of God's Spirit

It's not only Christ Who was animated by the power of the Spirit, but all God's servants have this additional *dunamis* to perform God's purpose in their personal lives and in the work God has called them to do.

> **1 Corinthians 2:4**
>
> And my speech and my preaching was not with enticing words of man's wisdom, but in demonstration of the Spirit and of *power* (G1411).

> **2 Timothy 1:7**
>
> For God has not given us the spirit of fear; but of *power* (G1411), and of love, and of a sound mind.

Note a crucial point in Paul's message to Timothy; the power of the Spirit confers a sound mind. We shall return to this point when discussing psychology and especially Christian conversion. The mind is the *spirit in man,* both alone and coupled with the *Holy Spirit:* a sound mind is central to life itself.

## Ability - The Nature of Human Spirit

Finally, but essential as an integral part of the Bible definition of spirit, we must broach a concept that may be new to you; this has to do with the *spirit in man*. Remember, every human has neshama and *ruach*[12]; the *ruach* is the spirit in (hu)man(s). Therefore this concerns all humans and has nothing to do with Christianity, religion, or race.

We saw *ability* in the KJV translations for both H3581 (koach) and G1411 (dunamis). Every person worldwide has their personal *power* or *ability*. And the basis of G1411, dunamai (G1410), reveals the translations *be able* and *can do*. Those are common words to describe any activity we undertake. Whatever you are *able to do*, everything you accomplish daily, monthly, and yearly for your entire life.

All these accomplishments, from brushing our teeth to writing a note, from turning on our computer to flying to the moon, humans are *able to do* them because of the power, the strength of the spirit we all possess. This is the Bible definition of spirit for all humans and is, therefore, directly related to psychology. These Bible verses confirm all humans have the power to be *able to do*.

> **Daniel 1:4** Children in whom was no blemish, but well favoured, and skilful in all wisdom, and cunning in knowledge, and understanding science, and such as had *ability* (H3581) in them to stand in the king's palace, and whom they might teach the learning and the tongue of the Chaldeans.

> **Matthew 25:15** And to one he gave five talents, to another two, and to another one; to every man according to his several *ability* (G1411); and straightway took his journey.

---

12. https://theexplanation.com/human-mind-mind-power-neshama-ruach/

**Acts 11:29** Then the disciples, every man according to his *ability* (G1411), determined to send relief to the brethren which dwelt in Judaea:

**Matthew 6:24** No man *can* (G1410) serve two masters:

**Matthew 6:27** Which of you by taking thought *can* (G1410) add one cubit to his stature?

The two last verses clearly refer to every human being. We *CAN DO* or CAN NOT DO those mental activities because we have the power of the spirit in man in us. That's our mind, the psychological, immaterial spirit that animates us.

In the next chapter, we will see the exact relationship between the neshama and the ruach, the consciousness, and this spirit that powers and energizes us and is synonymous with the mind.

# 24. The Amazing Role of the Ruach, Spirit, in Living Beings. Part 1

**The Biblical Role of the Ruach**

**Software of Living Beings**

The role of the ruach, curiously, can be compared to the use of computer software. There are all types of software, as there are numerous types of spirit.

All humans and all animals possess ruach (Eccl. 3:19 ...all have one breath (ruach)). You can only understand why living beings are the way they are if you grasp the role of the ruach. This is fundamental knowledge for psychology and spirituality.

God breathed neshama-consciousness into Adam's nostrils[1]; this is human awareness of their potential, their sensitivity to what they are; their five psychological characteristics that make them human[2], and the underlying basis of the mind; making them fundamentally different from animal-kind.

---

1. https://theexplanation.com/neshama-humankinds-relationship-god/

2. https://theexplanation.com/read-content-audit-universe-online/

Coupled with the neshama comes the spirit in humans[3]; the role of the ruach[4] is a second spiritual component furnishing power and ability to grow mentally and skillfully; this is the mind-power enabling humans to learn, enact, and progress throughout their lives.

Today, we will venture into the analogy of comparing the mind to computer software; this is risky, and I will lay down my rules for doing this. But first, why use the mind-software metaphor? Because humans have ruach AND animals have ruach[5]. One could erroneously conclude that humans are animals, even if we often act that way. Today, science and psychology do a lot to show how animals have human characteristics and the continuity between the two.

The ground rules are humans are not animals, and animals are not humans. There are some similarities, granted, but humans are humans, and animals are animals, and never the twain shall meet. It is fundamental knowledge with Bible corroboration.

The Bible evidence reveals humans have neshama and animals don't. This is why humans would run off with all the Nobel prizes in a competition, but animals with all the Olympic medals.

# Role of the ruach and Software

## Rule number one:

The Bible tells us that two human components are spiritual: neshama[6] and ruach[7]. In our analogy, both mind (consciousness &

---

3. https://theexplanation.com/spirit-in-the-bible-controversial-misunderstood/

4. https://theexplanation.com/spirit-in-the-bible-controversial-misunderstood/

5. https://theexplanation.com/gods-spirit-ruach-animates-living-beings/

mind-power as a whole, neshama & ruach) AND software will be considered NON-material. In other words, we can consider them as NOT being an intrinsic part of the computer, which is hardware; without software, it's like the inert dust of Adam's body AND brain before God breathed the neshama into it (Gen. 2:7).

Likewise, with any animal! They have a body and brain PLUS something that confers on each fauna species its characteristics and within each species individual traits. So what makes some dogs droop their head and put their tail between their hind legs when scolded? They know they've done wrong and show it. How can a dog act that way?

Remember, it's an analogy. I'm using software analogous to the spiritual human mind. Hardware, a computer or other device, is comparable to the human brain. Similarly, we'll use software and hardware for animal capability and brains.

Here's the definition of software: *the intangible part of a computer*[8].

Various biblical verses corroborate this concept; James 2:26 says the body without the spirit is dead. If the spirit is absent, the device won't run. The human spirit runs the human brain just as animal instinct runs animal brains.

Now, we need to briefly discuss how software works with computers and devices. I'm going to use the first sentences from Wikipedia.

1. **BIOS**[9] (Basic Input/Output System) is non-volatile

---

6. https://theexplanation.com/neshama-inspiration-discover-the-deeper-meaning/

7. https://theexplanation.com/spirit-in-the-bible-controversial-misunderstood/

8. *https://www.bing.com/search?q=software+definition*

9. https://en.wikipedia.org/wiki/BIOS

firmware used to perform hardware initialization during the booting process and to provide runtime services for operating systems and programs. The BIOS firmware comes pre-installed on a personal computer's system board, and it is the **first software to** run when powered up.
2. **Firmware**: In electronic systems and computing, firmware[10] is a specific class of computer software that provides the low-level control for the device's specific hardware. For less complicated devices, firmware acts as the device's complete operating system, performing all control, monitoring, and data manipulation functions. Typical examples of **devices containing firmware** are consumer appliances and computer peripherals, like a printer or mouse. Almost all electronic devices beyond the simplest include some firmware.
3. In the next chapter, we'll discuss operating systems and programs with regard to humans and the role of the ruach.

## Animals

The first level of software (combining BIOS and firmware) is the most basic and always pre-installed. Another way of putting this is embedded[11]; this is software that is specific to only one type of device. Firmware is everywhere: telephones, robots, appliances like microwaves, cookware, toys, pacemakers, security systems, televisions, and digital watches. It can get very sophisticated, such as for the International Space Station or sending humans to Mars.

An unfortunate example of firmware is the Boeing 737 MAX. The Maneuvering Characteristics Augmentation System (MCAS)

---

10. https://en.wikipedia.org/wiki/Firmware

11. https://en.wikipedia.org/wiki/Embedded_software

# MIND-BODY PROBLEM SOLVED

is firmware explicitly designed to handle the aircraft at slow speeds by controlling its angle (up, down) or direction. Unfortunately, because this firmware is probably faulty, authorities grounded these planes, and the company must rewrite the software.

The unique characteristic of firmware is that each software is specific to one device. MCAS is only for the maneuverability of aircraft. Pacemaker firmware will not work in your television and vice versa.

That's precisely the way animal instinct works. Instinct is distinct for each animal, and it is not interchangeable. As each device has software specific to its hardware, **each animal has instincts specific to its brain and body**.

In Genesis 1, we saw God created fish, fowl, and animals[12], and I Corinthians 15:38-39 says there's a different flesh for fish, fowl, and animals.

### 1 Corinthians 15:38-39

38 But God gives it a body as it has pleased him, and to every seed his own body.

39 All flesh is not the same flesh: but there is one kind of flesh of men, another flesh of beasts, another of fishes, and another of birds.

Likewise, each species and subspecies have different firmware and different instincts. God created this instinct; this is the specific firmware, the role of the ruach for each particular animal. He embedded it in every individual type of fish, fowl, and animal; this is God's hand, His magnificent design on nature. This is the

---

12. https://theexplanation.com/creation-day-5-and-6-god-created-fish-fowl-and-fauna/

meaning of Romans 1:20 "For the invisible things (Sam: the role of the ruach) of him [God] from the creation of the world are clearly seen, being understood by the things that are made, (Sam: the animals, their instinct and habits correspond to the functioning of their bodies. Perfect correlation) even his eternal power and Godhead; so that they are without excuse."

Biologists are amazed at the bodies and instincts of specific animals. Just like you and I are surprised at a vacuum robot that automatically goes across every inch of a floor, picking up the dirt and then heading back to its home station, emptying the garbage, and recharging. The firmware perfectly matches the animal or device it guides and animates. God created each instinct the same way programmers create each distinct firmware.

This instinct, similar to the firmware, cannot be modified. You might be able to enhance it a little by paying for an upgrade, but the ability and capacity of that firmware are limited to a specific device. Identical with instinct. Animals have a little leeway. You can train a lion, dolphin, or chimp to do a few tricks and upgrade its instinct, so to speak. But, you hit a brick wall at a given point, and the animal will not respond to any enhancement. Firmware has limited adaptability. Animals have ruach, they have set embedded instinct[13], innate abilities designed for them to accomplish incredible feats[14], but beyond that, there is no or minimal variation.

## Prehistoric Beings

We must take the time here to differentiate between prehistoric beings and humans. *The Explanation* cannot refer to them as

---

13. https://theexplanation.com/innate-capabilities-animals-leave-human-swimmers-their-wake/

14. https://theexplanation.com/animal-abilities-animal-communication/

*prehistoric* The Bible states that Adam was the first man, the *first* human. Adam and Eve are the parents of ALL humans.

**1 Corinthians 15:47**

The first man is of the Earth, earthy: the second man is the Lord from heaven.

**Genesis 3:20**

And Adam called his wife's name Eve; because she was the mother of all living.

*The Explanation* considers this correct; the story of humans and prehistory on Earth is not the subject. However, paleontologists have discovered prehistoric beings, including erectus, habilis, neanderthal, and dinosaurs, that need a clear explanation. These creatures existed BEFORE the creation of our world, which started with *let there be light* in Gen 1:3, and Adam and Eve (Gen 2.7 and onward).

We have to be very careful with our use of paleontological terms. For instance, *homo*[15] is Latin for *human,* and *homo sapiens* (*wise*) refers to modern humans. However, *homo* erectus, *homo* habilis, and all the other *homos* are misnomers. We cannot call prehistoric beings *homo*, humans. Modern humankind ALONE is in the genus *Homo* if we want to use that classification.

Since Adam and Eve and their descendants are humans, what were Erectus, Habilis, Neanderthal, and all the other similar species? They were beings with more complex firmware. Just like animals, the role of the ruach of prehistoric beings was more developed, as seen by their accomplishments[16]. It is probable, but I have not

---

15. https://en.m.wikipedia.org/wiki/Homo

studied this, that successive prehistoric beings had more and more developed ruach (firmware, software).

We have evidence that through the role of the ruach, they could manufacture rudimentary tools, bury their dead, and live in communities. As advanced and impressive as these accomplishments may be, this does not qualify them as humans (the next chapter explains *humans*). Watch this Ted Talk[17] to see that Genevieve von Petzinger, in her thorough study of cave art throughout Europe, found only 32 symbols. With that in mind, as intricate as it may be, can you present prehistoric cave art as human? It is undoubtedly more advanced because of the role of the ruach than any animal species could accomplish. But it is a very far cry from what defines humans.

In light of the Bible telling us Adam was the first (hu)man, I submit to you that all prehistoric beings were not human. They had specific body characteristics of humans that are undeniable, but mentally, they were far, far short of the human mind. *The Explanation* is the role of the ruach was more developed with firmware explicitly designed for them, giving them more capacity than animals. They were indeed on a level above their surroundings, but with only 32 symbols over thousands of years, they were incapable of going beyond their embedded firmware, the limits of the role of their ruach.

In the next chapter, we will see how the software operating systems and programs, neshama, AND the role of the ruach define humans.

---

16. https://genographic.nationalgeographic.com/early-human-milestones/

17. https://youtu.be/hJnEQCMA5Sg

*Notes:*

# 25 Ruach in the Bible Part 2. Creates Amazing Human Superiority

**Ruach in the Bible, when coupled with neshama, generates the most dominant species on Earth, Humankind.**

Spirit, ruach in the Bible parallels *power* and *ability to do*[1]. We saw ALL living beings are so endowed[2]. However, as with software, there are various levels. BIOS and firmware are the minimum requirements, and they animate all animals with their diverse instincts.

The critical feature of firmware is its design to do ONLY ONE specific task. For example, firmware for a wristwatch can NOT run cookware and, of course, vice versa. Such software is beneficial for

---

1. https://theexplanation.com/bible-definition-of-spirit-in-one-word-is-power/
2. https://theexplanation.com/the-role-of-the-ruach-spirit-in-living-beings/

# MIND-BODY PROBLEM SOLVED

one particular assignment but stops there; it is constrained with practically no modification of its essential functions.

1. BIOS[3] (Basic Input/Output System) performs hardware initialization.
2. Firmware[4] provides low-level control for a device's specific hardware.

Now, let's see the higher levels of software that are open to unlimited exploitation. This software is head and shoulders above the capacities of BIOS and firmware. Of course, that is a manner of speaking, but we must realize the vast chasm separating these two types of software just as the abyss separates animals from humans.

## Human *Software*

1. An **operating system**[5] (**OS**) is system software that **manages computer hardware and software resources** and provides standard **services for computer programs**. You have at least one of the three on your computer, Windows, Linux, and Mac OS. Mobile phones have Android and IOS (Apple).
2. A **computer program**[6] is a collection of instructions that performs a specific task when executed by a computer, which requires programs to function. The best known are Microsoft Office and Apple iWork. They include word processors, game programs, spreadsheets, database systems, graphics programs, and web browsers.

---

3. https://theexplanation.com/the-role-of-the-ruach-spirit-in-living-beings/
4. https://theexplanation.com/the-role-of-the-ruach-spirit-in-living-beings/
**5. https://en.wikipedia.org/wiki/Operating_system**
**6. https://en.wikipedia.org/wiki/Computer_program**

Figure 16. Computer programs

## Neshama - Human Operating System Software

Now, we come to you and me. Not only do we have more than 32 symbols of prehistoric beings[7], but we have language(s) to make words, sentences, paragraphs, chapters, books, series, and encyclopedias. Considering the subjects humans have researched, learned, and written about, it is safe to say humans are limitless in their mental capacities. I'm not saying humans can do anything and everything, but they're unlimited in their imagination to do anything and everything.

**What confers on human beings this limitless imagination?**

Humans have a different Operating System than any other beings, including prehistoric beings that have walked this planet. God breathed this human operating system into Adam's nostrils in Genesis 2:7. It is the neshama. Never before and never since has any other type of physical being been endowed with neshama, contrary to ruach, which animated prehistoric beings and now energizes

---
7. https://theexplanation.com/the-role-of-the-ruach-spirit-in-living-beings/

animals. That's why it's the neshama, and NOT the ruach, God breathes into Adam's nostrils as indicated in Genesis 2:7; this is a preeminently historic moment.

Adam is the first (hu)man, the precursor of the Second man, Jesus Christ Himself. Breathing neshama into Adam's nostrils is a unique, awe-inspiring moment that initiated the Plan of God and the Story of Humankind.

The neshama, the human consciousness, confers on each human being born into this world HUMAN SINGULARITIES. *The Explanation* defined those five fundamental characteristics[8] of purpose[9], function[10], socialization[11], rulership[12], and reasoning[13]; this is the operating system that God breathed into Adam.

When comparing software to consciousness and mind, there are rules. In the last chapter, we saw rule one: Both mind (consciousness & mind-power as a whole, neshama & ruach) AND software will be considered NON-material.

## Rule Number 2:

Regarding software, we must make a crucial distinction between computer software and human neshama. Computer software is mechanistic[14]. (Read Andrei Sorin's information[15], it is vital to understand the fundamental limitations of computers). It is

---

8. https://theexplanation.com/read-content-audit-universe-online/
9. https://theexplanation.com/what-purpose-of-life-why-humans-crave-an-answer/
10. https://theexplanation.com/human-nature-how-humans-worldwide-should-work/
11. https://theexplanation.com/social-relationships-puzzling-humans-love-hate/
12. https://theexplanation.com/human-rulership-responsibility-people-resources/
13. https://theexplanation.com/5-types-of-reasoning-life-hangs-ultimate-choice/
14. http://www.softwareandmind.com/articles/frauds.html
15. http://www.softwareandmind.com/articles/frauds.html

limited to mechanically calculating possibilities and combinations based on data that has been input into that machine. Of course, you can stuff, even force-feed a computer with data. Its own sensors can gather information, but the device is ONLY capable of handling that data, which it can do very well, even better than humans. But they are LIMITED to mechanically managing that acquired data.

On the contrary, humans have limitless imagination. Data input does not limit humans. I'm not talking about memory or the capacity to retain and recall encyclopedic facts and figures; I'm talking about the human ability to add data to their ruach, their minds, by themselves. To innovate, find new solutions, invent, and create. That is the prerogative of the human mind and only the human mind. That is the open-source operating system God breathed into Adam.

The firmware that endows all NON-human beings can only activate their possessor to that software's specific and distinct level. That firmware cannot be inserted in any other device and cannot transmit its capacities to any other firmware/device. Each non-human species/being that possesses ruach in the Bible is a unique species/being, and they cannot go beyond the instinct or capacity conferred on them via their ruach.

Humans are a different and unique species. They alone have neshama, analogous to an OPEN-SOURCE operating system characterized by imagination and creativity. Humans can write the computer code, the firmware, to send a human into space. They can install the code on a dedicated computer and use it to send Neil Armstrong to the moon. In a billion years, a computer could never write the code; this is the difference between possessing neshama, open-source operating systems, and simple firmware-ruach.

The human neshama, an open-source operating system, is the five fundamental characteristics of:

- Purpose
- Function
- Socialization
- Rulership
- Reasoning

At birth, each human is endowed with *unlimited* bounds in these areas. Unlimited is *tongue in cheek* because, of course, we're limited by our nature and nurture, our genetics and environment-education. We shall see this aspect, but the fact is ALL types of rulership operate[16], revealing this open-source diversity.

## Ruach - Human Computer Programs

For humans, it doesn't stop with an open-source operating system; that's just the starting point. That's why I refer to it as consciousness. Just like a computer, an OS manages the computer itself and provides standard services for the various computer programs you upload to the machine.

But the breakdown is multitudinous, and hundreds of thousands of computer applications are on the market today. I have developed a specific one for the internet, a Bible Concordance that you can find at UnlockBibleMeaning.com[17]. Human ruach, the mind, can access, choose, and download/acquire any of these ruach-programs into their compatible ruach-mind through learning and practice.

---

16. https://theexplanation.com/human-government-personal-world-peace/
17. http://unlockbiblemeaning.com

The OS and programs work together. One is of no real practical value without the other. Similarly, in humans, neshama and ruach combine, consciousness and mind work in cohorts. Everyone has the five capacities of purpose, function, socialization, rulership, and reasoning conferred by the neshama. We then individualize and personally weave each of those characteristics with a choice of ruach-programs we add and develop as part of our minds; that's the ruach in the Bible for all humans.

A baby is born with consciousness, but it has no skills, no competencies, and no capabilities. Yes, it has genetic nature passed on via its parental genealogy. As the baby grows, progressing through critical learning periods[18], the parents and the nurture upload programs which work in conjunction with the neshama, the toddler's consciousness. Those programs express themselves through the brain, sending signals to the rest of the body. So, for example, there's a program for learning about sights and sounds, feeling mom's skin, and relishing dad's care (there are physical and mental programs).

Later there are applications of how to eat, walk, and speak. No two babies receive the same education or the same programs; this explains why each human being is an individual with their particular ruach-applications.

All human beings have neshama, consciousness, an open-source operating system PLUS ruach, their mind and mind-power to choose and activate countless learning, skill, social, art, professional, life, and other ruach-programs. The knowledge and skills each of us uploads into our minds become part of our individual nature and nurture. Add, mix, and stir all these components together, and you have a distinctive human being;

---

18. https://theexplanation.com/critical-periods-when-babies-and-children-learn/

the ruach in the Bible refers to this individuality when it relates, "...every (hu)man according to *his several ability*." Therefore, we have a unique mixture of various levels and abilities.

**Matthew 25:14-15**

> 14 For the kingdom of heaven is as a man travelling into a far country, who called his own servants, and delivered to them his goods.
>
> 15 And to one he gave five talents, to another two, and to another one; to every man according to *his several ability*; and straightway took his journey.

Later in life, or rather, more than ever, quite early in life, the child begins to upload its OWN programs (hence the need for parental control). Youngsters, teenagers, and adults have likes and dislikes, talents and aptitudes. Each, in function of their physical and mental makeup, will be drawn to particular experiences, studies, and professions.

There is a choice of hundreds of thousands, even millions of ruach-programs. Some humans will even create new ones. Human ruach in the Bible is manifold. They'll discover, design, or invent something no one has ever done before. That's the open-source neshama with open-source ruach-programs producing unique individuals, which we all are. But some are more outstanding than others—different abilities.

We will continue to build out the relationship between God, humans, animals, neshama, and ruach in the Bible. Here is a diagram with consciousness, mind, instinct, and human software. It will be modified and added to; for instance, we need to include the role of the brain and body.

**God's Creation of the Universe**

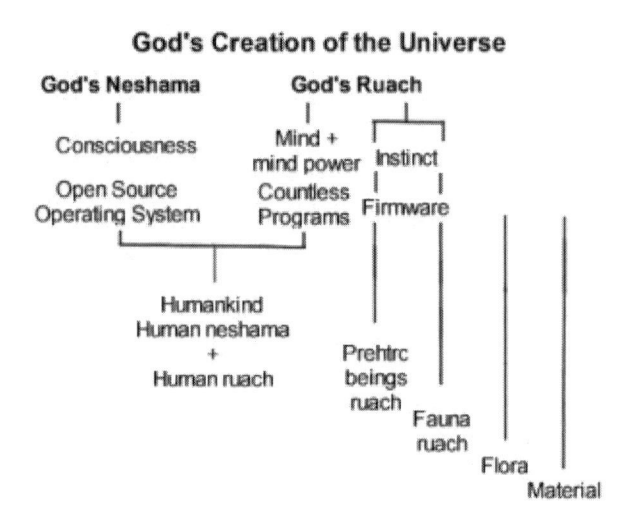

```
God's Neshama              God's Ruach
     |                          |
 Consciousness          Mind +        |
                       mind power   Instinct
 Open Source            Countless     |
Operating System        Programs   Firmware

        Humankind
      Human neshama              
            +                 Prehtrc
       Human ruach             beings
                                ruach
                                       Fauna
                                       ruach
                                              Flora
                                                   Material
```

Figure 17. God's Creation. Neshama and Ruach

In Genesis 2:7, God breathed neshama into Adam and formed the spirit in him, launching the story of humankind. Human imagination, creativity, purpose, behavior, socialization, rulership, and reasoning are open source. We shall forever be amazed at what human beings can and will do. Both good and evil. Humans have free choice to conceive and upload any ruach-program they want. Their imagination is limitless. The question is, where is this heading? *The Explanation* narrates this story of humankind, the profound story of ruach in the Bible.

# 26. Living Soul. The Fascinating Bible Meaning for Humans & Animals

**A Living Soul. The definitive definition. According to the Bible, both humans and animals are living souls. So what's the vital difference between them?**

If you can NOT answer the question, you do NOT know who you are, nor how you differ from an animal or a worm; this is fundamental spiritual and psychological understanding, so let's get it right. In Genesis 2:7, the phrase *nefesh chaya* translated *living soul* in the King James Bible, occupies center stage in the entire Bible story.

Most Bible readers do not realize that Genesis 1 includes *nefesh chaya* no less than FOUR times, all referring to animals. That's right, animals AND humans are *nefesh chaya*, living souls, if we use the Genesis 2:7 translation.

In Genesis 1, the word *nefesh* (H5315) appears four times in verses 20, 21, 24, and 30, where it's translated *creature* and *life*. It refers to fish, beast, fowl, and everything that creeps on Earth. In other words, nefesh refers to every single living creature God created up until the first human.

Likewise, Genesis 1 uses the word *chai, chaya* (H2416) eight times in verses 20, 21, 24, 25, 28, and 30. It also refers to every living thing created by God before the first human.

Please verify this at UnlockBibleMeaning.com[1], where you'll find an Interlinear and Strong's numbers. It is so important that I've also included an image of both the Interlinear and KJV translations. Both these words, *nefesh* and *chaya*, are present. They are used together as *nesfesh chaya* in verse 30, translated in the Interlinear, "in which *life is living*." (reading Hebrew right to left). Whereas in the KJV, the translators omitted a word with "wherein *is life*."

---

1. https://unlockbiblemeaning.com

# MIND-BODY PROBLEM SOLVED

Figure 18. Genesis 1:30, in which life is living

Please grasp the vital difference between the Hebrew and KJV translation. The Hebrew says in every beast is a *living life*. The KJV says in every beast is *life*. The implication from the Hebrew is there is a life happening inside the living beast. What is that life animating the animal kingdom?

The Bible says it is the *ruach*. This life-giving spirit confers on beasts, fish, fowl, and crawlers their instinct and unique traits[2] for sleeping, hunting, eating, and reproducing. The specific survival qualities each species demonstrates and has always displayed since their creation.

---

2. https://theexplanation.com/the-role-of-the-ruach-spirit-in-living-beings/

God's ruach (careful, this has a small *r*, not the capital *R* associated with the Holy Spirit) animates every living animal, as we saw two chapters ago.

### Ecclesiastes 3:19-21

19 For that which befalls the sons of men befalls beasts; even one thing befalls them: as the one dies, so dies the other; yea, they have all one *breath* (H7307 - ruach); so that a man has no preeminence above a beast: for all is vanity. (Sam: when it comes to breathing, humans and animals are identical)

20 All go to one place; all are of the dust, and all turn to dust again. (Sam: God created animals and humans from the Earth, dust, and that's where their bodies return)

21 Who knows the *spirit* (H7307 - ruach) of man that goes upward, and the *spirit* (H7307 - ruach) of the beast that goes downward to the Earth? (Sam: in addition to *breathe*, ruach means *spirit*. Here there's an enormous difference between animals whose spirit follows the body. But the spirit of humans returns to God who gave it. Read Eccl. 12:7)

The proper translation of Genesis 1:30 tells us there is an essence, something living within a live, breathing animal. This essence is the ruach, the spirit; this is the first error of science - it doesn't believe there's a non-material essence. From this point on, there's irreconcilable understanding.

But that's not the only comprehension problem. The ruach, the essence animating animals, emanates from God, that's clear, but more precisely from God's Ruach, the Holy Spirit. The Bible point, here and elsewhere, is that the Holy Spirit is an Essence, the Essence of God. Why can *The Explanation* affirm this? Because of

**Psalm 33:6**

By the word of the Lord were the heavens made; and all the host of them by the *breath* (H7307) of his mouth.

**Psalm 104:30**

You send forth your *spirit* (H7307), they are created: and you renew the face of the Earth.

God's *breath* (H7307) and His *Spirit* (H7307) are the same creative Essence; this is the first error of traditional Christian religion; it doesn't believe the Holy Spirit is an Essence. So from this point on, there's irreconcilable understanding.

## Humans and Nefesh Chaya

It was about animals multiplying and eating until mid-Day 6 of Creation (Gen. 1:25, 30). In a word, animals survive as *nefesh chaya,* the identical phrase we see in Gen. 2:7. From this point forward; it's about humans and how they thrive.

**Genesis 2:7**

And the LORD God formed *man* (adam) of the dust of the ground, and breathed into his nostrils the breath of life; and man became a *living soul* (nefesh chaya).

Genesis 2:7 refers to *nefesh chaya* as the moment of creation of the first human. What is essential to understand is this is NOT the same *nefesh chaya* as in Gen. 1:30. How can *The Explanation* affirm this?

God breathed the *neshama chayim* (*nishmat chayim* in Hebrew) into the human's nostrils. There's no such reference to animals. Gen. 2:7 is the very first mention of neshama.

The *nefesh chaya* in Gen. 2:7 for humans includes three elements;

1. The body made from *dust*.
2. The *ruach* is a similar essence but different in nature from animals.
3. The *neshama chayim*, which no other physical living being than humans possesses[3].

The *nefesh chaya* in Genesis 1:30, referring to animals, ONLY has the ruach; there's no neshama; this puts humans in a category of their own – the human species, the human race. So, in biblical terms, following on from the vocabulary used in Genesis 1, *after their kind*[4], we can say, "And God made humans from the dust after their kind."

**And the human kind is heavily related to God because only God and humans possess neshama! That's the meaning of "God created humans in His Image after His Likeness."**

Genesis 2:7 tells us there is a material body + the immaterial ruach + the immaterial neshama. ALL three together make up the *nefesh,* for which the KJV translators used one word, *soul*. Science and

---

3. https://theexplanation.com/breath-of-life-unique-possessors-neshama-earth/

4. https://theexplanation.com/all-time-hidden-truth-elohim-god-is-a-family/

religion are at loggerheads internally and with each other, each lacking comprehension of this primary subject.

The entire Bible is the story of humankind, of billions of *nefesh chaya*, and neither science nor religion understands what a *human being* is. So how can they get the story right if we don't know to what or whom we're referring?

The last two chapters showed the chasmic difference between devices with firmware and those with an operating system and computer programs. The first is limited to ONE task; the second is analogous to humans with unlimited imagination. It's identical to the animal living soul and the human living soul.

The animal living soul is a body with ruach, instinct allowing its possessor to live one life trajectory. It could be a beaver, a flamingo, an orca, or a cheetah. But it will always be what the ruach that animates it designates it to be. It can never develop its talents beyond the limits set by its ruach. It can never change its *animal status* and evolve into a higher or any other species. However, the number of variations within the limits of its ruach is unlimited, explaining multiple breeds and diversity within the same species.

On the other hand, the human living soul possesses neshama and consciousness, conferring the five traits of purpose, function, socialization, rulership, and reasoning[5]. On that base, each human living soul can build their own dream by adding and developing their choice of ruach-programs. They can become a scientist, sportsperson, author, cook, caretaker, or a million other things.

## The Chasm Between Animal Living Soul and Human Living Soul

---

5. https://theexplanation.com/astonishing-meaning-what-it-means-to-be-human/

This chapter is devoted to *ruach the animator of living souls*. Of course, we must respect all life, but all life is NOT equal. There's animal life solely animated by ruach, then far-and-away superior; there's human life animated by neshama and ruach.

The chasm between an animal living soul and a human living soul is impassable. Humans are not animals, and they did NOT evolve from fauna. Humans are humans because God breathed *neshama* into the nostrils of the first human and gave him *ruach*, setting the stage for the story of humankind.

To be straightforward with you, if we don't integrate this Bible wisdom, we cannot understand what it is to be human, the story of humankind, or the Bible.

We'll end this chapter with a brief reference to the last chapters of the book *Inventory of the Universe*, entitled *The Human/Animal Dilemma*. I wrote this book to address the common sense of readers who do not believe in a Higher Power. Therefore, not once in this book is there any reference to a Superior Being.

However, the idea is to reveal how there are so many *coincidences and interdependent just-in-time systems* in our Universe that there is no way they all *just happened*. Animals are predictable; humans are unpredictable. You can always know what a young lion will turn out to be, but you can never know what a young child will grow up to be.

Here's a summary of the insurmountable distinctions between animal living souls and contrasting human living souls.

## 10 The Human/Animal Dilemma

- The Human/Animal Dilemma[6] (10.1)

# MIND-BODY PROBLEM SOLVED 255

Humankind sits at the Pinnacle of the Amazing Life Chain. Why?

- Amazing Animals and Less Amazing Humans[7]
  Animals and humanity cohabit but live in two separate worlds.
- Animal Senses[8]
  Light-years beyond what Humankind is Capable of. Why?
- Animal Bodies[9]
  Animals exist with or without every single organ. For example, Jellyfish don't have a heart, blood, brain, or any other organs.
- Animal Movement and Survival in Extreme Conditions[10]
  Animal lifestyle allows them to do things humans cannot do: burrow, hibernate, go without sleep, and live without food or water for days and months, but humans adapt to their resources.
- Animal Stages of Life and Sociability[11]
  Animals do not perform wanton, wholesale destruction, nor do they kill for fun, but they have no role in establishing peace on Earth.
- Animal Accomplishments[12]

---

6. https://theexplanation.com/mankind-sits-at-the-pinnacle-of-the-life-chain-why/

7. https://theexplanation.com/amazing-animals-less-amazing-humans-they-are-separated-by-a-gulf/

8. https://theexplanation.com/animal-senses-light-years-beyond-what-mankind-is-capable-of-why/

9. https://theexplanation.com/animal-bodies-all-shapes-sizes-forms-and-characteristics/

10. https://theexplanation.com/animal-survival-and-movement-capabilities-far-outshine-those-of-mankind/

11. https://theexplanation.com/animal-and-human-stages-of-life-and-sociability-what-do-they-tell-us/

No animals take the initiative to make any improvement to their lifestyles. They are immune to imagination.
- Animal and Human Intelligence[13]
Humans have a mind to formulate and hands with manipulative dexterity to fabricate whatever they imagine. They have vocal cords and the written word to communicate, exchange ideas, and interact socially.
- What Is an Animal? What Is a Human?[14]
Animals, with all their intelligence, emotions, and behavior, have had no impact on this planet's forward march; only humans have.
- Final Notions, Concepts, and Ideas for Thought[15]
Humankind's combination of neshama and ruach is the gulf separating them from animals. Their consciousness and mind capacities don't give them an edge; they are universes apart in their accomplishments.

Humans and animals, biblically, are both living souls. However, only the spiritual components, neshama and ruach, reveal the vast abyss between them. In animals, ruach is their instinct; in humans, their mind and ability. But ruach has many other mysteries we'll unravel.

---

12. https://theexplanation.com/animal-accomplishments-are-zero-compared-to-human-accomplishments/

13. https://theexplanation.com/animal-instinct-and-human-intelligence-the-insurmountable-gulf/

14. https://theexplanation.com/what-is-animal-intelligence-what-is-human-intelligence-do-they-compare/

15. https://theexplanation.com/mankinds-mind-the-key-to-final-notions-and-ideas-for-thought/

# 27. Mental Mind. The Extraordinary Activity of Consciousness

**The mental mind and its power identify and animate only human beings; it is the essence of ruach**

### Neshama - Consciousness

Consciousness, neshama, and the mental mind, ruach, are the fundamental components of each human being. They confer on us all the qualities that make us human. Therefore, grasping these basics is paramount to understanding the story of humankind.

*The Explanation* elaborates on the most critical aspect of the entire Universe. The epitome of the creation in Genesis 2:7. Not just the creation of the first human being. But, in particular, what differentiates a human from any other life on Earth and, indeed, the rest of the physical Universe. We can affirm this because *adam* is the specific description of the father of all humanity (Gen. 5:1).

The particularity that characterizes humans, and only humans, is neshama. Getting that first piece of the human puzzle wrong will distort the rest of the human picture. And indeed, in psychology and the humanities, confusion reigns as to what consciousness and mind are. Neshama is the base layer of two layers of human mental capacity. Using God's Word, *The Explanation* identifies this with consciousness. The Merriam-Webster Dictionary[1] furnishes seven definitions, but we will go with the first:

> The quality or state of being aware, especially of something within oneself.

Humans are aware of five fundamental qualities they possess. We could call them the features that characterized the first human. The features of consciousness have sub-features. These are all distinctive attributes of humans. These traits mark every human being who has walked the face of the Earth.

1. **Purpose**[2]: Human nature, space time, creativity, imagination, learning, choices, growth, challenges, and ruling life.
2. **Function**[3]: Recognizing one's dual nature, free choice, behavior, ethics, justice, self-reproach, and forgiveness.
3. **Relationships**[4]: With self, gender, dating, marriage, parenting, friendships, and outlook on people and the world.

---

1. https://www.merriam-webster.com/dictionary/consciousness
2. https://theexplanation.com/what-purpose-of-life-why-humans-crave-an-answer/
3. https://theexplanation.com/human-nature-how-humans-worldwide-should-work/
4. https://theexplanation.com/social-relationships-puzzling-humans-love-hate/

4. **Rulership**[5]: Government at all levels, respect for individual and collective rights, reach peace and prosperity for all peoples.
5. **Reasoning**[6]: Based on observation-intuition, philosophy, religion, science, and theology.

Features are nice, but what they are used for is the key. The benefits are in their effectiveness. So here's the second layer of mentality.

## Ruach - Mind

Whereas neshama is more of a static spirit, like a feature or a blueprint defining a human, the ruach is the dynamic, dunamis[7], active spirit. It is the force that energizes the neshama. By definition, being endowed with neshama, a human can learn. The process of learning is accomplished by utilizing ruach. Every human is born with cognition. Wikipedia explains cognition[8] this way:

> Cognition is "the mental action or process of acquiring knowledge and understanding through thought, experience, and the senses." Cognition encompasses many aspects of intellectual functions and processes such as attention, the formation of knowledge, memory and working memory, judgment and evaluation, reasoning and computation, problem-solving and decision making, comprehension and production of language. *Cognitive processes use existing knowledge and generate new knowledge.*

---

5. https://theexplanation.com/human-rulership-responsibility-people-resources/
6. https://theexplanation.com/5-types-of-reasoning-life-hangs-ultimate-choice/
7. https://theexplanation.com/bible-definition-of-spirit-in-one-word-is-power/
8. https://en.wikipedia.org/wiki/Cognition

I italicized *Cognitive processes use existing knowledge and generate new knowledge* for a reason. Generating new knowledge is a lifelong, ongoing, never-ending experience that only characterizes human beings and their mental minds. Animals do not accumulate knowledge. Even computers only manipulate knowledge into new patterns and spit out new results, but this is not new knowledge per se; it is merely old knowledge in a new format.

Ruach-mind is the activity of consciousness. Consciousness is a quality you possess at birth. Mind is all the activity, attitudes, moods, mindsets, feelings, emotions, sensations, thinking, and cognition, the active processes associated with these five qualities.

These ongoing cognitive procedures that characterize humans result from ruach, the second layer of divine essence, the mental mind. The *spirit* that God has given to each human being. It is this spirit, working intricately with the neshama, that allows the cognitive mind to develop over its entire lifespan.

### Job 32:8

But there is a *spirit* (ruach - H7307) in man: and the *inspiration* (neshama) of the Almighty gives them understanding.

### Job 34:14

If he [God] set his heart upon man, if he gather to himself his *spirit* (ruach - H7307) and his *breath* (neshama);

This last verse is vital in understanding these two spiritual elements that have animated every mental mind of every deceased human being and all living human beings. Upon death, God gathers the neshama and the ruach, and together they represent the imprint, the memory, the life, and every recorded instant of each human being. I don't want to elaborate here, but it is the neshama and ruach at the moment of resurrection, and only at that moment, that confer the specific personalization on the resurrected being. After Christ's resurrection, He was a Spirit, but the Apostles and others who knew Him recognized His personality and character.

These two interlaced God-given spiritual components, neshama and ruach, interconnect and impart the intellect to each human being. Together, consciousness and mind-power compose the mental mind. By the way, I'm not calling it the *human mind* because that's a pleonasm. Why? Because human ruach is different from animal ruach[9], the first is *mind*; the second is *instinct*; only humans possess *mind*.

Put it this way; the ruach motorizes the neshama. The ruach is the imaginative, creative, animating power or dynamic force that solely endows human beings. The neshama is like having an entire electrical circuit for city housing, shops, factories, public buildings, street lighting, and hospitals. Neshama is a unique framework and channel. But without ruach, electricity, it's useless. Likewise, electricity without the framework is futile. The circuit and electricity work together. The neshama and the ruach work hand-in-hand.

### H7307

> רוּחַ rûwach roo'-akh; from H7306 (רוּחַ); wind; by resemblance breath, i.e. a sensible (or even violent) exhalation; figuratively, life, anger, unsubstantiality; by extension, a region of the sky; by resemblance spirit, but

---

9. https://theexplanation.com/the-role-of-the-ruach-spirit-in-living-beings/

only of a rational being (including its expression and functions):

KJV - air, anger, blast, breath, × cool, courage, *mind*, × quarter, × side, spirit(-ual), tempest, × vain, (whirl-) wind(-y).

We've seen this Strong's definition on numerous occasions for different reasons. Ruach is the basis for understanding the mental mind. Notice that King James translators rendered *ruach* with *mind*. This mind equates to the stillness of *air* and the violence of a *whirlwind*. This mind oscillates in its intensity. It is an aspect of the plasticity of the mind; this is the invisible (unsubstantiality[10] - without material substance) spirit. It is what powers our consciousness.

I can't emphasize enough how important this most basic understanding is. The mind-body, spirit-material controversy[11] has been going on for over 400 years and still rages on today. Philosophy and science cannot solve this issue. Philosophy can only speculate about the non-material; science cannot measure and rejects the non-material. Religion has been misled and stammers around, muddled and confused.

True theology and proper comprehension of Genesis 2:7 give the limpid answer. Humans are *formed dust*, the body, into which God infused the *neshama*, consciousness, and *ruach*, the mind. These elements, the material and the non-material, the physical body plus the spiritual consciousness and mind, compose a human being.

---

10. https://www.dictionary.com/browse/unsubstantial

11. https://theexplanation.com/the-mind-body-dilemma-400-years-old-and-still-unsolved-why/

The Bible alone has the correct answer. Proper theology alone can unlock and reveal coherent completeness.

Check Strong's concordance[12] for associated Biblical Hebrew words for ruach (H7307). For instance, H7306 includes a KJV translation, *quick understanding*, H7304 is translated *be refreshed* and *large*. H7305 has the same notion of *enlargement*. The idea is the spirit can be revived; it can be enlarged for understanding; this is the powerful cognition of the mental mind.

The above paragraphs concerning who and what a human being is are the most critical in this entire book. Deforming or missing this one piece of the puzzle falsifies comprehension of the rest of the story of humankind.

King David of Israel knew he had a spirit, and as we'd say, the spirit in him, his mind had ups and downs, good and bad phases. Humans are not robots; we're subject to all sorts of positive and negative experiences and influences around us. Our spirits can be on a yoyo emotional, interrogative ride.

### Psalm 51:10

> Create in me a clean heart, O God; and renew a right *spirit* (H7307 - ruach) within me.

In another example, Hannah was the mother of the prophet Samuel. It was a long time before she became pregnant, and that caused her some mindful despair. She talks about how her *spirit* was affected.

### 1 Samuel 1:15

---

12. https://unlockbiblemeaning.com

> And Hannah answered and said, No, my lord [Eli, the Priest], I am a woman of a sorrowful *spirit* (H7307 - ruach): I have drunk neither wine nor strong drink, but have poured out my soul before the LORD.

Here's a third example of a vigorously turbulent mind. During Job's troubles, there was a lengthy discussion with three of his closest friends and peers. A fourth, younger individual, Elihu, was also present, but he kept quiet, not having the same experience and stature as the three others. As the exchanges boiled on and each side maintained its stance, Elihu became increasingly upset. He knew both parties were off-subject. Finally, he could no longer hold back and burst into the conversation.

Job 32:18

> For I [Elihu] am full of matter, the *spirit* (H7307 - ruach) within me constrains me.

His ruach was like the *whirlwind* definition. Poetically, Elihu begins to dispense sounder wisdom to these older men (read verses 19-20). He used his consciousness and mind power, neshama and ruach, to reason soundly. The ensuing exposé is of utmost importance by its content and impact.

This chapter simply shows you what the Bible says about how the minds of all men and women function. Every day, minute-by-minute activity takes place in your mental mind. Not in the brain. These are workings taking place at the *neshama* and *ruach* level. They fit tightly together like protons and neutrons in the nucleus of an atom, inseparable and fundamental particles of each human.

We will return to the role of the mental mind in psychology and spiritual conversion. It is the central piece of the puzzle generally unknown to decision-makers and influencers in both world and spiritual leadership roles. Yet, this is the number one reason for the state of worldwide mental health and spiritual turmoil in many religious organizations.

So what role does the physical brain play with these two spiritual essences? That's for the next chapter.

# 28. The Human Brain. Its Surprising Agile Role in Body and Mind

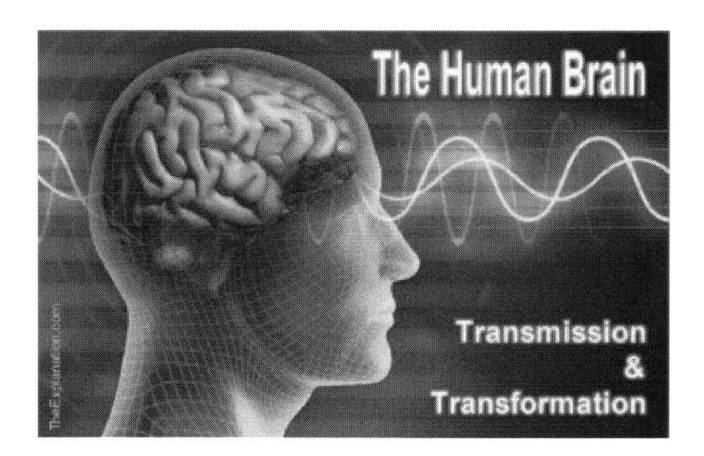

**The human brain is the focal point of the mind-body problem. It's the primary transmission and transformation organ of information.**

This chapter connects the dots between neshama, ruach, and the human brain. It is the continuity of the understanding of neshama[1] (Genesis 2:7) and ruach[2] (Zechariah 12:1).

God formed the first human from the material *dust of the ground* and the immaterial *breath of life, neshama, consciousness*, the seat of the *mind*. The human brain is a physical organ; it is dust, a part of the human body involved in two essential functions. The first is *transmission* which I'll illustrate with the *drilling of the Channel*

---

1. https://theexplanation.com/neshama-inspiration-discover-the-deeper-meaning/

2. https://theexplanation.com/ruach-in-the-bible-creates-human-superiority/

*Tunnel*. The second is *transformation* demonstrated by a *phone*. These two analogies reveal how to understand the mind-body issue.

## Breakthrough and Transmission in the Channel Tunnel

The 50,45 km Channel Tunnel[3] was drilled deep below the seabed of the English Channel between Folkstone, (Dover) UK, and Coquelles, (Calais) France. Drilling started simultaneously at both ends and met near the middle. This video[4] shows the breakthrough; the French climbing through to the English side and the English climbing through to the French side. But, of course, once they enlarged the hole, there were no *sides*. It was all *one conduit for transmission*.

The tunnel breakthrough allows for a free-flow transmission of two different nations, French and English, exchange of different flags and languages. Of course, all other nations can travel BOTH ways through the Chunnel. With mind and body, there's a free-flow transmission of information between different entities; *neshama/ruach* (immaterial) and *dust* (material).

Genesis 2:7 is the junction of mind and body. At this point, God made the breakthrough and launched the free-flow transmission of information between spirit, neshama consciousness, and the physical, dust brain.

These two different essences, or substances, work seamlessly together—billions of physical cells of the dust-body work intricately with the complexity of human thought. There is the transmission of information from mind to body. An author can imagine a story in their mind and write it down with their body

---

3. https://en.wikipedia.org/wiki/Channel_Tunnel

4. https://youtu.be/SGikebYtAZc

(fingers with a pen or keyboard). The ideas transit smoothly from the neshama/ruach via the body to paper.

The inverse itinerary is just as effortless. You read a literary description with your physical eyes, and then you can picture the scene in your mind. We transport physical and sensory information to our immaterial minds. The diagram below enumerates this neshama/ruach-dust two-way transmission of information between mind and body.

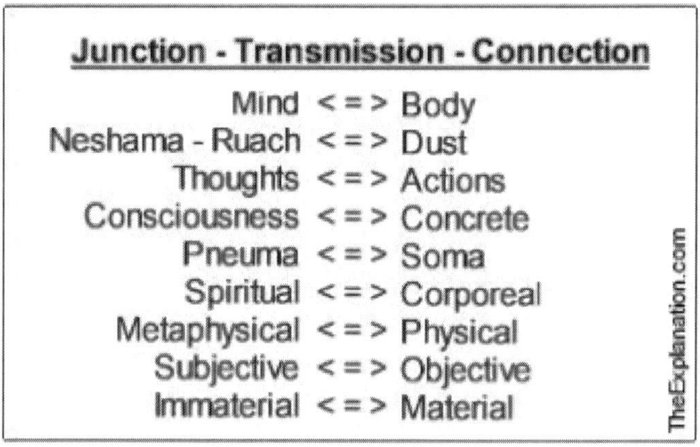

### Junction - Transmission - Connection

| | | |
|---:|:---:|:---|
| Mind | < = > | Body |
| Neshama - Ruach | < = > | Dust |
| Thoughts | < = > | Actions |
| Consciousness | < = > | Concrete |
| Pneuma | < = > | Soma |
| Spiritual | < = > | Corporeal |
| Metaphysical | < = > | Physical |
| Subjective | < = > | Objective |
| Immaterial | < = > | Material |

TheExplanation.com

Figure 19. Junction, transmission, connection

The Channel tunnel connection is baby stuff compared to the junction between the invisible and the visible. There are two separate tunnels, each for one-way-only traffic. The train schedule leaves enough space between the trains for safety reasons. There are two control centers; in France and the UK. Each can take control of the entire system if required.

The human brain is the intersection where information transits. It's a multi-directional thoroughfare between mind and body,

# MIND-BODY PROBLEM SOLVED

thoughts and actions. The human brain is the conduit through which the spiritual and the material freely flow. The neshama-consciousness and the ruach-mind transit from the spiritual to the physical—the corporeal chemical and electrical impulses transit from the sensory body organs to the spirit mind. There's an intricate meshing and working together to accomplish each individual's goals. That's where the dissimilar essences, the spiritual and the physical, meet.

The first step is this instantaneous multi-directional junction and transmission of information between the mind and the body—transport of two distinct *substances* (spirit ruach and material chemical and electrical impulses). Secondly, there's the instant transformation of each substance into the other.

## Transformation of Images and Sound in a Phone Modem

A newscast takes place in a studio. The camera and microphone are transducers that transform, *MO*DULATE the scene into waves and transport them to your television or smartphone, where transducers transform, *DEM*ODULATE the waves into electrical pulses that activate your screen and speakers. Objects and voices convert into *invisible* waves that reconvert to *visible* images and sounds.

Figure 20. Modem

For a video call, each party has a MODEM, from *mo*dulator, *dem*odulator; there's an instantaneous transformation and transmission of images and sound to electromagnetic waves and vice versa so you can talk and listen, see, and be seen.

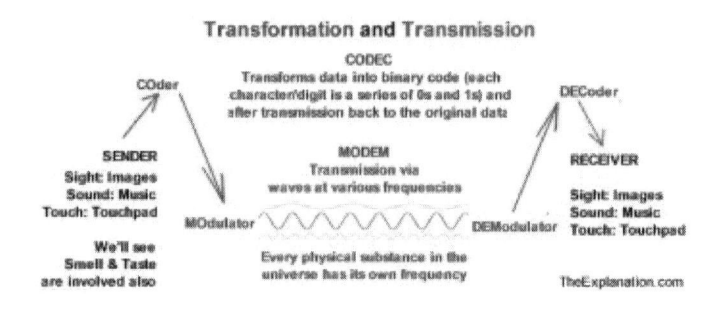

Figure 21. Transformation and transmission

## Codec

There is also another type of remarkable transformation taking place in your TV, smartphone, and computer. How do images and text get faithfully transported via electricity? Each color spot of an image and each letter transforms into binary code. Read this for details[5]; each item translates into a corresponding series of **0**s and **1**s[6]. To do this translation, you need a codec (*co*der-*dec*oder), a device, or a computer program for encoding and decoding digital signals.

Physical, visible information (images, sound, text) has to be transformed (*co*ded) into identifiable immaterial electromagnetic waves to transport it from its source to its destination. There, it is once again transformed (*dec*oded) into physical information that our human body sensors can capture.

The coding, decoding, modulation, and demodulation from information to energy and back again in your electronic devices have to function as an automatic, instantaneous combination.

# The Human Brain

## Modem and Codec

The brain, via its circuitry, is the body's codec and modem. As a codec *(co*der-*dec*oder), it transforms material information (body code) into immaterial code that impacts our mind and vice-versa. As a modem (*mo*dulator-*dem*odulator), it converts material energy (electrical or chemical impulses in the body) to immaterial impulses in the mind-ruach/consciousness-neshama and vice-versa.

---

5. https://www.bbc.com/bitesize/guides/zpfdwmn/revision/2

6. https://en.wikipedia.org/wiki/Digital_signal

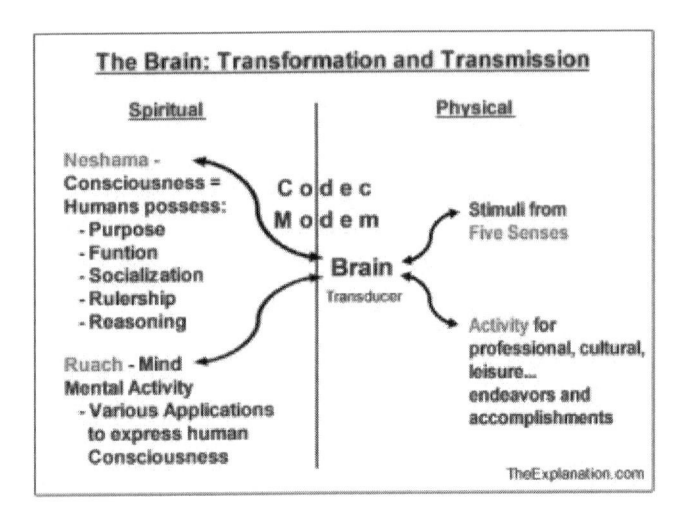

```
The Brain: Transformation and Transmission

         Spiritual              |          Physical

Neshama -                       |
Consciousness =      C o d e c  |
Humans possess:      M o d e m  →  Stimuli from
  - Purpose                     |   Five Senses
  - Funtion                     |
  - Socialization      Brain    |
  - Rulership         Transducer|
  - Reasoning                   →  Activity for
                                |   professional, cultural,
Ruach - Mind                    |   leisure...
Mental Activity                 |   endeavors and
  - Various Applications        |   accomplishments
    to express human            |
    Consciousness               |
                                |            TheExplanation.com
```

Figure 22. Codec, modem. Brain, transducer

Think of the human brain managing breathing or blood flow. The body replaces 50-70 BILLION cells every single day. Each operation involves chromosomes, genes, proteins, DNA, four bases, and their chemicals. ALL this information is managed by the cells in conjunction with the brain. As you know, if there are aches and pains, it goes directly to your mind. Brain codec and modem are in action 24/7/365.

Considering the quantity of information that passes through our minds and bodies, you can imagine (that's an activity of the neshama-ruach) the enormous amount of data that flows and transforms in the conduit.

Don't get lost in the computer internet jargon. Those are all analogies. They are very sophisticated communication tools that need bona fide software and firmware to function optimally. That's the neshama operating system and ruach software[7] God uploaded

---
7. https://theexplanation.com/ruach-in-the-bible-creates-human-superiority/

## MIND-BODY PROBLEM SOLVED

to Adam. That's the consciousness that endows the five human features on each one of us[8]. Humans are God's crowning creation. That's why so much space, indeed the entire Bible, is devoted to that creation.

The neshama does not end there; that's only the beginning. Your TV and computer have many, many other uses. For example, let's discuss interactive gaming. Or rather, Massively Multiplayer Online Game[9] (MMOG). Players congregate worldwide on their devices and compete with each other. We're talking about tens of thousands of simultaneous electronic devices intricately intertwined via ONE platform. Connections and exchanges of information are real-time.

That's how the flow, in ALL directions worldwide, has to be. The central computers continuously receive, interpret, and send signals to all the players. The system treats the virtual information and resends it for transformation into high-speed reality images (bullets in war games) and sounds.

Imagine the incoming waves and their changeover to electrical impulses; imagine the transformation of piloting a joystick into moving images; imagine the continuously modifying high-speed scenes on each player's screen. The codecs and modems are working at maximum capacity to update the game's parameters in real-time; this is what your brain does precisely. It monitors the massive flow and transformation of information that comes from and leads to instant-by-instant NEW situations. That is the plasticity of the immaterial mind and material brain.

That is the ruach establishing the most efficient pathways for the flow and transformation of information. The human brain is the

---

8. https://theexplanation.com/mental-mind-fabulous-activity-of-consciousness/

9. https://en.wikipedia.org/wiki/Massively_multiplayer_online_game

## THE EXPLANATION

hardware, but the ruach is the software. Remember, Who breathed the neshama and gave the ruach to humans. Also, remind yourself this is the conduit that allows communication between the spirit world and humans.

On top of the neshama, we can upload further passions[10], imaginations, inventions, skills, languages, and sports. These programs allow each of us to possess, acquire, and develop whatever skills we want. We have personal likes and dislikes according to our nature and nurture, our culture and experience, our education, and our activities.

Figure 23. Computer programs

Above is a screenshot of part of my computer screen displaying an Apple computer. Along the bottom of both the Mac and my computer are the icons of programs we've uploaded according to our needs and likes. Then, using each of these applications, we create data and information which is stored in memory.

---

10. https://theexplanation.com/human-software-god-breathed-neshama-adam/

This action parallels the ruach[11], allowing us to add whatever skills, learning, and aptitudes we might want to use and develop. These are akin to software programs our parents upload during child-rearing. Then, at a very early age, we begin, with the help of our parents, to upload our own software; this is the time of critical periods[12] starting with language, geometry (shapes, sizes, relative space), and a library of knowledge and games. There are also life values programs like obedience, initiative, sociability, work ethics, and honesty; this latter endeavor is the customized activation of the neshama, consciousness.

Schooling, social environment, social networks, and media also play an essential role in this personalization. All influences and influencers that impact the neshama and ruach, the consciousness and mind of human beings, play a role in a person's development.

There are all-around responsibilities and obligations which we shall also discuss. As youngsters progress to adulthood, they go on to sexual identity, gender relationships, sports, a profession, leisure activities, and many other programs that can be uploaded and updated throughout life. That's human plasticity, which the combination of neshama and ruach confer on humans alone.

Here's an updated graphic with the human brain, the immaterial, and the material.

---

11. https://theexplanation.com/the-role-of-the-ruach-spirit-in-living-beings/

12. https://theexplanation.com/critical-periods-when-a-child-s-brain-accelerates-its-development/

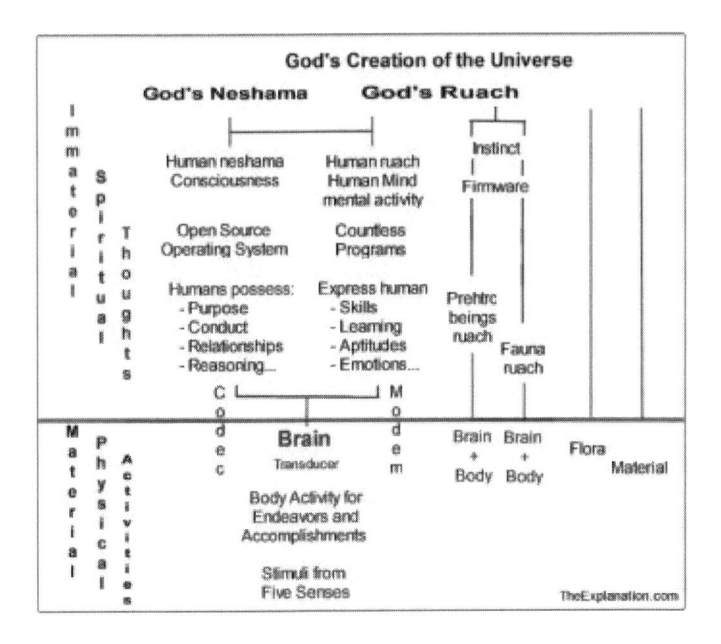

Figure 24. Immaterial consciousness, mind, and material brain

The brain is the most complex material device in the Universe. Physically, the human brain resembles the most prominent animal brain[13]. Yet, human mental capacity and accomplishments are light-years above any other life form.

As vital and complex as the human brain is, that's not the answer. It is in Genesis 2:7 when God breathed the neshama into the dust body, the brain. The spirit neshama and ruach confer on humankind their humanity; the brain is the transducer, the junction between the immaterial neshama, ruach, and the material body. This is basic knowledge from God's Word, the Bible. It is only on this basis that we can understand the rest of the story of humankind.

---

13. https://www.scientificamerican.com/article/what-makes-our-brains-special/?redirect=1

# V. Ruach and the Creation of Everything

Another major scientific enigma related to ruach.

# 29. Quantum Physics & Spirit of God Moved. Strange Encounters

**SPIRIT of God MOVED over the water and Quantum Physics?!**

**Quantum physics. What is it? What could its relationship be with the Spirit of God that MOVED over the waters in Genesis?**

Quantum physics seems light years away from the Spirit of God *moving* over the waters according to Genesis, but curiously there's an interconnection. In English, to *move* has various meanings like move forward, move house, moved by emotion, and various other understandings. So why focus on God's Spirit, and what exactly is the Biblical Hebrew meaning of the common word *move* in Genesis 1:2?

In the last chapter, we saw the interconnection between the immaterial world of the neshama-ruach and the material brain-body of humankind on Earth. The Creation story of the first human clearly defines both the spirit and physical environments

# MIND-BODY PROBLEM SOLVED

and the relationship between the two. The spirit acts on the material; this is the process of the mind acting on the brain.

I have no idea how this works, but it is clear that the spirit impacts the physical. In Genesis 2:7, the emphasis is on neshama because only humans possess it[1]. There are twenty-four references in the Bible referring to God and humans with *breath* and *inspiration.* I do not want to be disrespectful by diminishing its role, but despite that, other verses clearly show God also endowed the first and subsequent humans with ruach. Of the twenty-four neshama verses, ten include ruach, and the latter is found about three hundred and eight times in the Old Testament, far more than neshama.

So, what's so important about ruach? This Section is entitled *Ruach and the Creation of Everything,* and we are about to plunge into unchartered waters. Ruach is much more profound than you can imagine. It plays a central role, one of the fullest and least understood in God's purpose. In fact, it is paramount to quantum physics. Theology and science mesh together wonderfully.

## Why Refer to Quantum Physics?

Allow me to introduce this subject with a little historic build-up. When I started this writing project, leading to this commentary of Genesis, I knew what I had in mind, but I had no idea it would lead to what I'm about to explain. I started *The Explanation* blog in May 2014, but the notes, outlining, and writing of *Inventory of the Universe*[2], my first book, began in 2010. This was a couple of years before the 4th of July 2012. Why that date? Because that's the date

---

1. https://theexplanation.com/breath-of-life-unique-possessors-neshama-earth/

2. *https://theexplanation.com/inventory/read-all-the-content-of-inventory-of-the-universe-online/*

the Higgs Boson was discovered and witnessed for the first time by the Large Hadron Collider in Geneva, Switzerland.

You might not see the relationship between the Higgs Boson fundamental quantum particle and my writing, but I assure you there is one. Here's an article from June 2014 discussing the Higgs Boson[3]. Of course, I don't expect you to understand the scientific jargon; I don't fully grasp it myself! But I would like you to see some vocabulary used to describe what's happening in the quantum physics Universe.

> To *shake* around, new *energy* space, this *bent,* and *squeezed* space-time, creating *ripples* known as gravitational *waves* that also *twisted* the radiation that passed through the universe. Background *microwave* radiation, characteristic *twisted* or *curled waves* called the B-mode pattern—an intense *jittering* in the *energy field.*

In the following few chapters, we'll see how quantum physics revolutionized scientific thinking in the five years following the discovery of the Higgs Boson. How elementary particles such as quarks are no longer considered elementary. How the concepts of waves (immaterial) and particles (material) have given way to *fields*. Now, the focus of fundamental science is on quantum fields.

## Moved Over the Waters

As we saw above, these quantum fields use descriptive terminology like shake, energy, bent, squeezed, ripples, waves, twisted, microwaves, curled waves, jittering, and energy fields. Keep these descriptive terms in mind as we look at the meaning of the Spirit of God MOVED on the face of the waters.

---

3. https://www.livescience.com/46478-universe-should-have-collapsed.html

## Genesis 1:1-3

> 1 In the beginning God created the heaven and the earth.
>
> 2 And the earth was without form, and void; and darkness was upon the face of the deep. And the Spirit of God *moved* (H7363) upon the face of the waters.
>
> 3 And God said, Let there be light: and there was light.

These two verses are capital because they set the stage. In verse 2, we have the presence of the Spirit, and in verse 3, the Creation of light. The Spirit is implicated in Creation in a much deeper way than you can envision. But the first point to realize is that there's a junction between the invisible Spirit and the visible light, similar to invisible neshama and visible body-brain. You've possibly never thought about it, but God transforms spirit into physical, and there's a definite interconnection between the two. Science thinks something can come from nothing. The Bible reveals that behind the visible world is the invisible Spirit.

These introductory verses present all the essential elements, bar the humans and their environment. The main stage is our Earth. A secondary stage is heaven. The producer of this production is God. Remember, this is Elohim[4], plural, composed of God the Father and God, the Word[5]. And the final all-important presence is the Spirit of God**,** which is *moving* over the water-inundated planet. What is the Biblical Hebrew *move*?

### H7363

---

4. https://theexplanation.com/all-time-hidden-truth-elohim-god-is-a-family/

5. https://theexplanation.com/does-god-exist-yes-higher-power-yhvh-elohim/

רָחַף râchaph raw-khaf'; a primitive root; to brood; by implication, to be relaxed:

KJV - flutter, move, shake.

*Move* is *rachaph,* a primitive root meaning it is the most basic form of a Hebrew word composed of the three-letter root; this is Step 3 of the 4-Step Biblical Hebrew Word Mastery method[6]. This word, *rachaph*, has no other derivative words and appears only three times in the entire Old Testament. The above is the first time. Here are the other two.

### Deuteronomy 32:11

As an eagle stirs up her nest, *flutters* (H7363) over her young, spreads abroad her wings, takes them, bears them on her wings:

### Jeremiah 23:9

My heart within me is broken because of the prophets; all my bones *shake* (H7363); I am like a drunken man, and like a man whom wine has overcome, because of the LORD, and because of the words of his holiness.

I'm using the first and fourth Steps to master Biblical Hebrew words here. The fact is the King James translators used various words to translate the same Biblical Hebrew word[7]; all these translations are interconnected and tell a story[8]. This story uses three analogies.

---

6. https://theexplanation.com/fastest-bible-study-method-god-intended-meaning/

7. https://theexplanation.com/fastest-bible-study-method-god-intended-meaning/

8. https://theexplanation.com/biblical-hebrew-roots-to-anchor-your-bible-comprehension/

1. The first is the **fluttering wings** of an eagle caring for her eaglets. I've pictured this in the feature image above, although showing fluttering wings in a two-dimensional way is challenging.
2. The second analogy refers to Jeremiah, who is **shaking down to his bones** because of the nonsense expounded by false prophets in the name of God (read the context).

Figure 25. Shaking down to his bones

1. The third analogy is the comparison with a **drunken man**. The most straightforward test to see if a driver is drunk is to get them to walk a straight line. You know what happens; they weave and wave to the left and right of the line.

There's one Biblical Hebrew word (rachaph - H7363) for three translations (move, flutter, shake) and three analogies (fluttering wings, shaking bones, drunken man). I believe it is reasonable to conclude that the Spirit of God was moving over the water with a wavy up and down, in and out, side-to-side type of motion. You might think this is imaginative or unimportant. Well, I'd say that the first few verses and chapters of Genesis are paramount for capturing the essence of the Bible narrative.

Compare the movement of the Spirit of God to the quantum fields article: shake, energy, bent, squeezed, ripples, waves, twisted, microwaves, curled waves, jittering, and energy fields. Those are the descriptions of quantum fields we saw above. It sounds a lot like fluttering and shaking. *Shake* is used both in the Bible and in the quantum fields article.

Please understand that we're at the beginning of this expose. Understand what I'm NOT saying. The Spirit of God is certainly NOT a quantum field. That's ridiculous. Neither the Large Hadron Collider nor any other human-devised instrument can measure the Spirit of God. That, too, would be ludicrous.

What I am doing is taking you into unknown territory. Genesis 1:2 juxtaposes two very different phenomena that we don't contemplate. On the one hand, you have the Spirit of God, which, by any definition, is an immense SPIRITUAL power. But, on the other hand, you have planet Earth covered with water, which is a PHYSICAL entity. So you have two wholly opposed essences or substances.

We also know the relationship between the Spirit of God and the physical creation. Job 26:13 says, "By His Spirit, He [God] garnished the heavens." Psalm 104:30 reiterates, "You send forth your spirit, they are created: and you renew the face of the earth." From these verses, we know the Spirit of God is the Power, the Force used to create the material universe. YHVH, Christ, the Word is the Creator[9]. He uses the Spirit of God that moves in a fluttering, shaking motion to create quantum fields that react like ripples, twisted microwaves, curled waves, and jittering energy fields.

---

9. https://theexplanation.com/yahweh-yahveh-meaning-identity-gods-name/

## God's Spirit Oversees the Physical-Quantum Physics

I'd simply like you to realize that the Spiritual gives rise to the material; that the invisible gives rise to the visible. That God gives rise to the creation. The Spirit of God gives rise to the light, the reconditioning of Earth, flora, and fauna. It endows humankind with their mind and mind power, including diverse ways of reasoning.

There is a continuity between God's spiritual environment and our human physical world. We see it in Genesis 1:2 with the Spirit of God moving, fluttering, and shaking on the face of the waters. We now see this same shaking in quantum fields at the very basis of our material world.

Has scientific research discovered the ultimate step in quantum physics? Or should we say the first measurable step in the origin of our physical universe? The shaking, energy, bent, squeezed, ripples, waves, twisted, microwaves, curled waves, jittering, and energy fields? Those are the descriptions for quantum fields. It corresponds perfectly with the moving, fluttering, and shaking of the Spirit that brought the physical universe into existence.

Is science meeting God? That's a big question. We're just starting with this subject. But we are headed for some answers that will astound you. *The Explanation* is beginning to bring science and theology, material knowledge, and spiritual understanding into coherent completeness.

# 30. The Meaning of Ruach is Dazzling. Sure, Almost Unbelievable

**Meaning of Ruach**

Junction between the invisible and the visible

**The genuine meaning of ruach, spirit, will blow you away. Its omnipresence links the material and immaterial worlds.**

The meaning of ruach has everything to do with God. Likewise, the meaning of ruach impacts our physical world much more than you'd ever believe. Spirit God created the physical universe and oversees it. To exercise His creative and transformative power, there has to be a juncture or intersection where they both meet. But where?

This chapter is both a continuation of the creation of the first human, Adam, and a transition reported in Genesis 2:7. Even though it doesn't mention God's Spirit explicitly, it is inherent to the verse, being inseparable from the neshama and being the essential link between God and humans (Romans 8:14-16). Hence the need to discuss the Spirit of God; this has a capital S and is akin to the Holy Spirit.

**Matthew 12:31-32**

31 Wherefore I [Jesus] say to you [Pharisees, religious leaders], All manner of sin and blasphemy shall be forgiven to men: but the blasphemy against the Holy Ghost [Spirit] shall not be forgiven to men.

32 And whosoever speaks a word against the Son of man, it shall be forgiven him: but whosoever speaks against the Holy Ghost, it shall not be forgiven him, neither in this world, neither in the world to come.

This intervention by Christ places the importance of the Holy Spirit ABOVE Himself. Very unusual. He says this concerns ALL humans, every single one of us. Very unusual. And it's not only in our world today, but Christ says there's a world to come. Very unusual. It's clear the Holy Spirit has a preponderant role in God's purpose.

Here are the first words in Genesis (1:2) and the last words in Revelation (22:17) referring to the role of the Spirit. They are significant in revealing the meaning of ruach within the purpose of God's Creation.

**Genesis 1:2-3**

2 And the earth was without form, and void; and darkness was upon the face of the deep. And the *Spirit* (H7307) of God moved upon the face of the waters.

3 And God said, Let there be light: and there was light.

As the Bible opens with Spirit, so it closes with Spirit.

> **Revelation 22:17**
>
> And the *Spirit* (G4151) and the bride say, Come. And let him that hears say, Come. And let him that is athirst come. And whosoever will, let him take the water of life freely.

This last verse describes the only way to spiritual conversion, the goal of God for all humankind through the Holy Spirit, which we'll discuss in the seventh and final Section of this book. However, the meaning of ruach, spirit, with a small s, which is associated with and a derivative of the Holy Spirit, is the theme of this, and the following Section devoted to psychology. *The Explanation* will answer the questions posed by the conversation between Jesus and the Pharisees. In the meantime, the quick answer is at the beginning, the meaning of Ruach is the Creation of everything physical (Gen. 1:2). Ultimately, the primary meaning of Ruach is spiritual Creation (Rev. 22:17).

## Ruach: Visible and Invisible

The Bible opens with a clear meaning of Ruach, the spiritual and physical environments, and the relationship between the two. The Spirit acts on the material; this is the process of creative transformation of the physical by the Spirit of God. Genesis 1:2, *the Spirit moving on the face of the waters*, is an incredible statement when we stop to meditate on it. With that in mind, we have the first appearance of the Biblical Hebrew word *ruach, spirit*. Let's see another unsuspected meaning of ruach.

H7307

רוּחַ rûwach roo'-akh; from H7306 (רוּחַ); wind; by resemblance breath, i.e. a sensible (or even violent) exhalation; figuratively, life, anger, unsubstantiality; by extension, a region of the sky; by resemblance spirit, but only of a rational being (including its expression and functions):

KJV - air, anger, blast, breath, × cool, courage, mind, × quarter, × side, spirit(-ual), tempest, × vain, (whirl-) wind(-y).

Strong's resume indicates this dichotomy of the meaning of ruach.

- **Visibility**: wind, breath
- **Invisibility**: unsubstantiality, spirit

The KJV translators do the same. *Air, breath,* and *wind* portray visibility, while the *spirit* represents invisibility.

The point is the concept of the invisible combined with and wholly connected to the visible is a given in the Bible: Strong and the translators recognize this foundation. Some Bible scholars or theologians look for physical phenomena to explain the effects of the ruach. In other words, they're searching for physical explanations for spiritual miracles. An eclipse to resolve Joshua's long day. A shooting star to describe the star that led the wise men to Christ or a hurricane to part the sea for Moses and the Israelites to cross.

Such surmisings deny the ruach, the spiritual intervention to transform the physical universe. Miracles are just that, the spirit acting on the material. Don't look for some physical explanation when Christ changed the water to wine. The spirit turned the physical water into physical wine. Only God knows how this works, and yes, it takes faith to believe, but that's what Scripture proclaims.

The spirit creates and transforms the physical in Genesis 1 and is the basis for understanding the rest of the Bible. Readers either incorporate or not this concept into their comprehension. Further reading of Genesis and the rest of the Bible depends on this fundamental fact. Yes, it's not an exaggeration to call it a fact; it's biblical reality. One is free to accept or reject this fact, just like any other.

Realize, however, that this fact is a piece of our puzzle. The rest of the picture will be askew if the piece is rejected, altered, or placed in the wrong position. Right from Genesis 1:2 and the meaning of Spirit, most Bible readers begin to blur the accurate puzzle, and it gets blurrier and blurrier from there. No wonder there's so much confusion when it comes to Bible understanding.

Back to the Spirit of God, the Ruach. The invisible and its relation to the visible creation. In the last chapter[1], *The Explanation* developed the meaning of the Biblical Hebrew word *move*. It is to *flutter* and *shake*, akin to wave, jitter, ripples, and other such descriptions of quantum fields. Yes, God's Spirit is spirit. Yes, quantum fields, although invisible, are physical. They are two totally different environments. But like Genesis 1:2, where the Spirit moves over the waters, there's a connection between the two environments.

I suggest to you that the SAME SHAKING MOTION of God's Spirit is connected to SHAKING QUANTUM FIELDS via creation and transformation.

---

1. https://theexplanation.com/quantum-physics-spirit-of-god-moved-strange/

This concept may be new ground for you; the coherent completeness of the SPIRITUAL and the PHYSICAL. God connects with the physical, and you and I, as physical beings, can connect with God. Theology means God's logos, which is His logical word. The Greek term *logos* is at the origin of both *logic* and *word*; this is the junction between the spiritual (God) and the physical (His Word, Scripture).

When we believe in the Bible, we believe in SPIRIT. We're here on Earth, and we believe in the PHYSICAL. Rationally, there must be a conjunction between the two. Science and theology must meet and be in accordance. That is precisely what we're dealing with in Genesis 1-2 with God's Spirit and physical creation.

A SPIRIT God creating a PHYSICAL Universe. The Spirit interacts with the physical.

Here's where this reasoning is leading. God's Spirit FLUTTERS and SHAKES. At the minutest level of the physical universe are quanta[2], the minimum amount of any physical entity involved in an interaction. The tiniest form of electromagnetic waves in a field has the specific quality of SHAKING and, in so doing, emitting energy. These minute shakers are known as energy fields[3].

So *The Explanation* continues to develop this fascinating subject; the key to remember is the shaking or the VIBRATIONS of Spirit in God's realm and the shaking or VIBRATIONS of quanta fields in our universal realm.

## Spirit = Smell

---

2. https://en.wikipedia.org/wiki/Quantum

3. https://theexplanation.com/spirit-of-god-moved-face-waters-meaning/

Here's just one interesting and exciting example that is scientific and, as you will see, has biblical backup. It's about **our sense of SMELL**. Smelling involves the nose taking in a breath of air, which includes the fragrance emitted by the substance smelled.

What science has come to realize is that **SMELLING is akin to HEARING**. Yes, when I heard that, I was skeptical too. However, they are both the result of VIBRATING substances. Watch this video[4]; it'll start just before the section about *smell* and explain the relationship between smell and vibrating material.

Here are a couple of verses that include God *smelling* the sweet savor of sacrifices. That is the Old Testament counterpart of *hearing* our prayers (Revelation 5:8). The Bible assimilates *smelling* and *hearing*.

### Numbers 15:13

> All that are born of the country shall do these things after this manner, in offering an offering made by fire, of a sweet *savour* (H7381) to the LORD.

### Ezekiel 20:41

> I will accept you with your sweet *savour* (H7381), when I bring you out from the people, and gather you out of the countries wherein you have been scattered; and I will be sanctified in you before the heathen.

Now for the kicker, the Biblical Hebrew for *savor*. Look at the following three references in Strong's Concordance. Figure out the Biblical Hebrew relationship, showing the interconnection

---

4. https://youtu.be/q4ONRJ1kTdA?t=860

# MIND-BODY PROBLEM SOLVED

between what is SPIRIT and what is PHYSICAL. Realize that seeing this in English or any other translation is impossible.

## H7381

רֵיחַ rêyach ray'-akh; **from H7306** (רוּחַ); odor (as if blown):

KJV - savour, scent, **smell**.

## H7306

רוּחַ rûwach roo'-akh; a primitive root; properly, to blow, i.e. breathe; only (literally) to smell or (by implication, perceive (figuratively, to anticipate, enjoy):

KJV - accept, **smell**, × touch, make of **quick understanding**.

## H7307

רוּחַ rûwach roo'-akh; **from H7306**[5] (רוּחַ); wind; by resemblance breath, i.e. a sensible (or even violent) exhalation; figuratively, life, anger, unsubstantiality; by extension, a region of the sky; by resemblance spirit, but only of a rational being (including its expression and functions):

KJV - air, anger, blast, breath, × cool, courage, mind, × quarter, × side, spirit(-ual), tempest, × vain, (whirl-) wind(-y).

This chapter started with H7307, the meaning of ruach, revealing the interconnection of the material *breath* to the immaterial *spirit*.

---
5. http://www.unlockbiblemeaning.com/browse/

Notice that both H7307-ruach and H7381-rayach come from H7306. The point is SMELL and SPIRIT have the same Biblical Hebrew root. Also note that H7306 has a physical translation, *smell,* and a mental one, *quick understanding*; the same Hebrew word has material and immaterial meanings and is related to frequency and vibrations. Finally, even if you can't read Hebrew, you can see that all three words have identical 1st and 3rd letters, *raish* ( ר ) and *chet* ( ח ). The middle *vav* ( ו ) and *yod* ( ׳ ) are vowels and can be interchanged.

We know that two of our human senses, sound and sight, have to do with vibrating energy waves. We now see a third sense, smell[6], resulting from shaking quantum fields pictured in the featured image above, as well as aromatherapy[7] which activates frequency receptors in your nose. Read these articles about taste[8], which detects flavor at 1-4 Hz, and touch[9]; human skin is sensitive[10] to spatial differences at the frequency bands of 1-3 Hz and 18-32 Hz). Realize that ALL our human senses are directly related to vibrating energy packets, electromagnetic waves.

The Biblical Hebrew words ruach (spirit, breath) and rayach (smell) show this tightly knit relationship between the spirit and the physical; smelling is intimately tied to breathing, and they are related to the spirit. So the meaning of ruach is the connection between the spirit realm and the physical realm. We are just getting started; *The Explanation* will show you HOW they're interconnected.

---

6. https://www.biorxiv.org/content/10.1101/300194v1.full

7. https://scholar.google.fr/
   scholar?q=aromatherapy+and+vibrations&hl=en&as_sdt=0&as_vis=1&oi=scholart

8. https://www.biorxiv.org/content/10.1101/300194v1.full

9. https://www.sciencedaily.com/releases/2012/12/121211154437.htm

10. https://ieeexplore.ieee.org/document/1406920

# 31. Fluctuations of S/spirit. Astonishing: Vibrations & Frequency

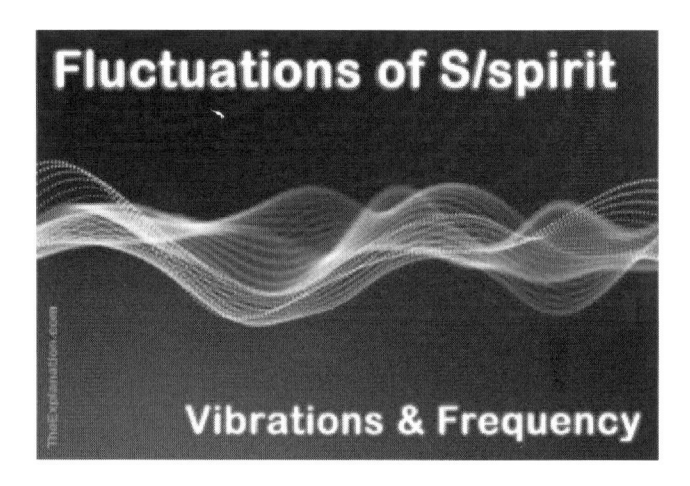

**Fluctuations of the power of the Spirit of God and the spirit of humans and the Universe are Bible reality. Here's why.**

We've discussed how God's Spirit moved on the face of the waters[1]. There's an interface between the spiritual world of God (His Spirit) and the physical world of humankind on Earth. In other words, between God's Spirit, quantum energy packets, and the spirit in humans (Job 32:8). According to the Bible, two different but related phenomena are real and interactive. We've established the following regarding *spirit:*

1. The Holy Spirit and spirit in (hu)man(s) are interconnected[2] (Romans 8:16).

---

1. https://theexplanation.com/spirit-of-god-moved-face-waters-meaning/

2. The Holy Spirit is God's Power[3].
3. Spirit flutters[4], shakes (Holy Spirit), ripples, and waves (physical quantum fields).
4. The Hebrew word ruach is visible (breath, smell) and invisible (spirit)[5].

Ruach, Strong's H7307, starting in Genesis by moving over physical water and ending in Revelation as the Power of spiritual conversion[6], sets the stage for the whole story of the Spiritual working with the physical.

Now for an additional contour in the shape of the *ruach* puzzle piece. The fluctuations of the spirit. How its power changes; turning it up and down, as we'd do with a dimmer switch on a light. Yes, this sounds strange, but let's take a look.

### H7307

רוּחַ rûwach roo'-akh; from H7306 (רוּחַ); wind; by resemblance breath, i.e. a sensible (or even violent) exhalation; figuratively, life, anger, unsubstantiality; by extension, a region of the sky; by resemblance spirit, but only of a rational being (including its expression and functions):

KJV - air, anger, blast, breath, × cool, courage, mind, × quarter, × side, spirit(-ual), tempest, × vain, (whirl-) wind(-y).

---

2. https://theexplanation.com/the-meaning-of-ruach-is-dazzling-unbelievable/

3. https://theexplanation.com/bible-definition-of-spirit-in-one-word-is-power/

4. https://theexplanation.com/quantum-physics-spirit-of-god-moved-strange/

5. https://theexplanation.com/the-meaning-of-ruach-is-dazzling-unbelievable/

6. https://theexplanation.com/quantum-physics-spirit-of-god-moved-strange/

Notice the fluctuating nature of R/ruach. God can modulate its power. The translations used for *ruach* indicate this: air, breath, wind, windy, blast, tempest, whirlwind. That list of modulations reaches a climax. Once again, this is not Sam Kneller's idea. All I've done is take the KJV translations we find for Strong's H7307 and placed them in ascending, rather than alphabetical, order which is what Strong does.

From air to whirlwind, with increasing speed and directional movement. From the stillness of air to the tourbillon of a tornado or hurricane. From the silence and tranquility of the eye of a cyclone to the din and uproar of its outer towering thunderstorms. Notice also that wind and breath (unless in icy cold conditions) are invisible, while a whirlwind is visible to the naked eye. Now that you know this Bible fact of fluctuations of the Spirit of God, you will see it in your study.

Here are a few verses that refer to the Spirit, even if they don't all directly use that word. Search for others at UnlockBibleMeaning.com[7]

### Judges 14:6, 19

> The Spirit of the LORD came upon him [Samson] mightily, so that he tore him [a lion] as one tears a young goat though he had nothing in his hand...

An ordinary man can't rip up a lion. However, this becomes possible with the additional power of a certain amount of the Spirit.

### Zechariah 4:6

---

[7]. https://unlockbiblemeaning.com

> Then he [God] said to me [the prophet Zechariah], This is the word of the LORD to Zerubbabel saying, 'Not by might nor by power, but by My Spirit,' says the LORD of hosts.

Not by human power, but by God's Power. This phrase reminds us of Mark 5:30, where Jesus immediately recognizes that some of His spiritual Power transferred to a woman with an issue of blood and healed this physical problem instantaneously. Christ's Power diminishes, transferred to transforming the physical. This variation of the Power of the Spirit of God and its impact on the material is a reality. Through God's Spiritual Power, Zerubbabel rebuilt the Temple in Jerusalem following the return from the Babylonian exile.

In Mark 9:28-29, the disciples could not cast out a powerful demon (even demons have authority). "And when he [Jesus] was come into the house, his disciples asked him privately, Why could not we cast him [the powerful demon] out? And he said to them, This kind can come forth by nothing, but by prayer and fasting." The implication is the disciples did not have enough spiritual power. One way to receive more of God's Spirit power is through prayer and fasting.

Here is another example of fluctuations with the added solution of maintaining, stabilizing, and increasing the power of God's Spirit.

Christ was brimful with the Power of the Spirit, as John 3:34 tells us, "For he whom God has sent speaks the words of God: for God gives not the Spirit by measure to him." This is the fullness of the Holy Spirit, also referred to in Acts 10:38 "You know of Jesus of Nazareth, how God anointed Him with the Holy Spirit and with power, and how He went about doing good and healing all who were oppressed by the Devil, for God was with Him."

This power is the means whereby the spiritual acts on the physical. It is what makes miracles miraculous. Human beings can receive this same Power of the Spirit in proportion to the role God calls them to accomplish. Some receive more, some less; these are the fluctuations.

**1 Corinthians 12:4-11**

> 4 Now there are diversities of gifts, but the same Spirit.
>
> 7 But the manifestation of the Spirit is given to every man to profit withal.
>
> 8 For to one is given by the Spirit the word of wisdom; to another the word of knowledge by the same Spirit;
>
> 9 To another faith by the same Spirit; to another the gifts of healing by the same Spirit;
>
> 10 To another the working of miracles; to another prophecy; to another discerning of spirits; to another divers kinds of tongues; to another the interpretation of tongues:
>
> 11 But all these work that one and the selfsame Spirit, dividing to every man severally as he will.

The Apostles received enough power to witness Christ worldwide. The disciples in Rome received the joy, peace, belief, and hope from God's Spirit's power. Of course, the Apostles had these qualities too. And obviously, the disciples in Rome witnessed it very locally. But the takeaway is that the Apostles and disciples had different functions and different amounts of the Holy Spirit to accomplish their given tasks.

In chapter 23, We discussed the *ability*[8], *dunamis*, and *power* that every human possesses because of the *spirit* in humans.

**Matthew 25:15**

> And to one he gave five talents, to another two, and to another one; to every man according to his several *ability* (G1411); and straightway took his journey.

Do you see the modulation of human spirit and God's Spirit? The different levels of power or energy needed for the following results: various abilities, skills, talents, and mighty works?

**1 Thessalonians 1:5**

> For our gospel came not to you in word only, but also in power, and in the Holy Ghost, and in much assurance; as you know what manner of men we were among you for your sake.

The Apostle Paul spoke those words in Thessalonica. And, through the power of the Spirit, he did much more than that. He had the assurance to speak boldly despite persecution (1 Thes. 2:2). Paul referred to the possibility of quenching (lowered fluctuations) of the Spirit (2 Thes. 5:19). He noted that there is also the improper use of this spiritual power (2 Thes. 2:9 - G1411), talking about a false prophet with all power and signs and lying wonders. Someone filled with much more negative power (this power is not from God but instead from Satan) than others in their entourage.

The Biblical Hebrew word *ruach* represents both the spiritual and the physical. It represents power or energy that fluctuates, flutters,

---

8. https://theexplanation.com/bible-definition-of-spirit-in-one-word-is-power/

and shakes[9]. On the physical level, how can we express this? I'd suggest:

## Fluctuations of Waves or Frequencies

Sound, light, movement, sea waves, heartbeats, breathing, a pneumatic drill, and a mixer all have cycles or frequencies and waves. They have regular motion. We can feel the recurring pulse of a heartbeat and see the wave pattern at the seaside. Other systematic movements, like a swing, pendulum, and printer head, take longer. Light oscillations are so rapid and short-lived that it is impossible to see the individual waves; we see them as a beam or stream. This short video is a practical example of wave fluctuations[10].

Let's realize that all this oscillating movement (vibrations) is because more or less energy is involved. More varieties and quantities of fluctuating vibrations are going on in your TV than in your light bulb. Expressed another way, we could also talk in terms of vibrations and frequencies. That's where it begins to get intricate. To keep it simple, running a TV takes more power and different circuits than a light bulb.

The fluctuations of the ruach are characterized by breath, wind, windy, blast, tempest, and whirlwind. The fluttering or, dare I say, the vibrations of the ruach, God's Spirit, as well as the spirit He's given humans,[11] is characterized by the flapping wings of an eagle[12]

---

9. https://theexplanation.com/spirit-of-god-moved-face-waters-meaning/

10. https://youtu.be/X5Uy7MhFiWA

11. https://theexplanation.com/two-spirits-gods-spirit-spirit-in-humans/

12. https://theexplanation.com/fluctuation-frequency-power-spirit/

and bones shaking[13]. The ruach refers to the spiritual and the physical.

The characteristic of power fluctuations and frequencies (vibrations) applies to both the spiritual and physical. The spiritual vibrates. The physical vibrates. Fluctuations, vibrations, and oscillations are the heart and core of the spiritual and physical environments.

They are two different environments, but the key is to see a continuity between them. Spiritual God created physical Earth; God's Spirit moved on the waters. That Spirit flutters and fluctuates from the transformation of Earth to the healing of a woman with an issue of blood, to distributing joy and hope, just as waters can be still, rippled, or tumultuous with waves depending on the energy deployed. So, Earth is transformed, or healing is accomplished depending on the amount of Spirit deployed.

This video will give you some idea of the intricacies of frequencies and fluctuations[14] and the vibrations behind the energy of our physical world.

The spirit realm consists of an unbelievable variety of power that goes far beyond our imagination and descriptive abilities. Similarly, the physical realm is also an incredible variety of energy that goes far beyond what we imagined. For example, the image of a black hole in outer space has been published, an astonishing feat due partly to the energy of gravitational waves that bend light. It is another testimony to the immense power of the physical universe.

Vibrations and fluctuations of energy and power are the reality of the spiritual and physical realms. The Spirit of God moved

---

13. https://theexplanation.com/fluctuation-frequency-power-spirit/

14. https://youtu.be/cfXzwh3KadE

(fluttered, vibrated) on the waters. Light and heat vibrate to illuminate Earth. Quantum fluctuations make possible the material universe. *The Explanation* is bringing the spiritual and the physical into coherent completeness.

# 32. Energy, the Astounding Origin of Our Material World

**Energy spheres are the source of our material world. Our solid physical foundation isn't solid at all; its composition is so tiny that it will always be invisible.**

How real are the spiritual and physical realms to you? Do you believe the physical world comes from the spiritual? Do you believe the physical can become spiritual and then physical, over and over, at will? Or are you a doubting Thomas?

**John 20:24-31**

24 But Thomas, one of the twelve, called Didymus, was not with them when Jesus came.

25 The other disciples therefore said to him, We have seen the Lord. But he said to them, Except I shall see in his hands the print of the nails, and put my finger into

the print of the nails, and thrust my hand into his side, I will not believe.

26 And after eight days again his disciples were within, and Thomas with them: then came Jesus, the doors being shut, and stood in the midst, and said, Peace be unto you.

27 Then said he to Thomas, Reach hither your finger, and behold my hands; and reach hither your hand, and thrust it into my side: and be not faithless, but believing.

28 And Thomas answered and said to him, My Lord and my God.

29 Jesus said to him, Thomas, because you have seen me, you have believed: blessed are they that have not seen, and yet have believed.

30 And many other signs truly did Jesus in the presence of his disciples, which are not written in this book:

31 But these are written, that you might believe that Jesus is the Christ, the Son of God; and that believing you might have life through his name.

The above example is a biblical spiritual and physical reality. Christ's physical body was put in a burial cavern, He rose as God, a Spirit Being, and entered rooms with closed doors. He appeared and *disappeared*, transforming from one state to another at will.

There has to be an interconnection between the spirit and the physical realms. The ruach-spirit occupies that role. In our physical world, this has a small *s*. The Power of God's Holy Spirit produces the invisible spirit, which takes on two forms:

1. Invisible as the instinct in animals and the spirit in humans, which is the human mind[1].
2. Visible as quanta, the minutest form of energy.

This diagram helps focus on this setup.

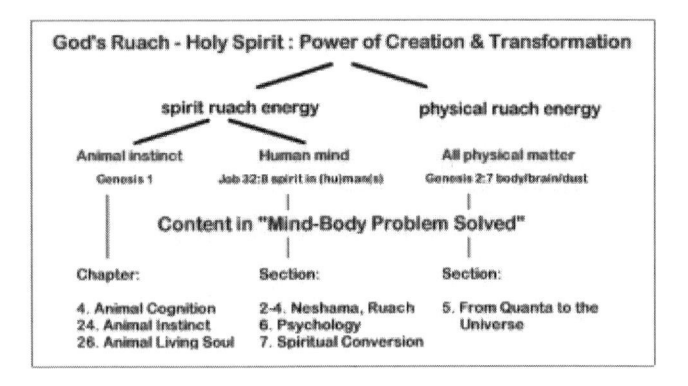

Figure 26. God's Ruach – Holy Spirit: Power of Creation & Transformation

## The Material World from Nothing or What?

Science cannot answer this question but recognizes a significant problem in not answering it. This quote comes from Wikipedia[2]. Some people don't appreciate Wikipedia, especially on such profound scientific issues. However, it is *layman's science*, and I'm using it to make this information as accessible as possible:

---

1. https://theexplanation.com/ruach-in-the-bible-creates-human-superiority/
2. https://en.wikipedia.org/wiki/Quantum_fluctuation

> Vacuum fluctuations appear as virtual particles, which are always created in particle-antiparticle pairs. Since they are created spontaneously, without a source of energy, vacuum fluctuations and virtual particles are said to violate the *conservation of energy*. This is theoretically allowable because the particles annihilate each other within a time limit determined by the uncertainty principle so they are not directly observable.

The law of conservation of energy[3], first proposed and tested by Émilie du Châtelet, means that energy can neither be created nor destroyed; rather, it can only be transformed or transferred from one form to another.

As expounded by the above quote, the theory says that vacuum fluctuations (the minutest form of energy) are created spontaneously, without a source of energy, leading to the often-heard conclusion - *something from nothing*. If you are interested in this debate, do an internet search for *something from nothing in science*.

Ruach solves both these fundamental problems; Spirit energy gives rise to quantum fluctuations: something from something. It is Spiritual energy converted to physical energy, thus respecting the law of conservation of energy.

## The Nature of the Minutest Form of Energy, Quantum Fluctuations

I'm going to try to do something. I don't know how exact this is scientifically, and I don't know if I can make it understandable for readers. Consider it a draft that will need revisions and editing.

---

3. https://en.wikipedia.org/wiki/Conservation_of_energy

Here's a layman's explanation of quantum physics. No equations, just concepts to understand how the physical world is constructed.

The same Wikipedia article[4] above starts with this phrase: Please forget about all the jargon.

> In quantum physics, a quantum fluctuation (also known as a vacuum state fluctuation or vacuum fluctuation) is the temporary random change in the amount of energy in a point in space.

Focus on *point in space*, our first concept. In my opinion, understanding starts with grasping what this *point* or *pinpoint* is. It's the SMALLEST possible space. This point is impossible to calculate[5]. The shortest length so far is the Planck length of $1.6 \times 10^{-35}$ meters (the number 16 preceded by 34 zeroes and a decimal point). This length is used in various aspects of physics, and the point is tiny, tiny, tiny. So, how many points are there in the universe?

This brings us to the second concept—the q*uantum field*. When we use the term field, we conjure up a two-dimensional image, like a soccer field; this is further lodged into our minds by two-dimensional graphics of magnetic fields. Science, though, describes a quantum field as a *fluid*. In other words, something that completely fills any container. It's everywhere at the same time; it's THREE-dimensional. Now, try to get your head around this. All those Planck length points from our first concept fully occupy the three-dimensional space. That's a lot of points, whatever the space! Imagine the entire Universe filled with these tiny points; that's the quantum field.

---

4. https://en.wikipedia.org/wiki/Quantum_fluctuation

5. https://www.bbc.com/news/science-environment-19434856

# MIND-BODY PROBLEM SOLVED

The third concept is *Quantum fluctuations*. The quote above explains what this is, *random change in the amount of energy in a point*. So, EACH of those minuscule points is emitting energy. Let's pause here and consider what's happening. What does a point emitting energy look like?

Any point emitting energy resembles a firecracker exploding or the tip of an antenna emitting waves.

Figure 27. Point emitting energy resembles an exploding firecracker

Remember, this image is two-dimensional (width and height). But, in reality, the explosion is three-dimensional (including depth). Think about what it means when you throw a pebble into a pond; you see TWO-dimensional ripples spreading out from the *point* of impact, but the reality is, the ripples ALSO spread out in the water BELOW and in the air ABOVE; we just don't see them. So it's really THREE-dimensional ripples. Even the word *ripples* is misleading because of its two-dimensional implication.

Often, here's the way these points are presented graphically as a quantum field. It is TWO-dimensional.

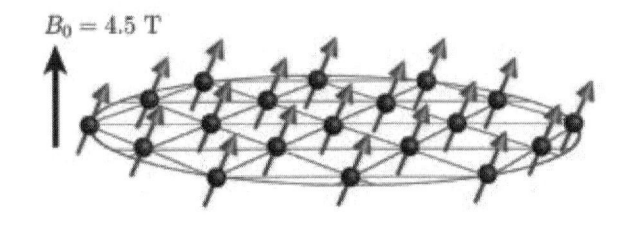

$B_0 = 4.5\ T$

Figure 28. Presentation of a two-dimensional quantum field

Graphic presentations have limitations; therefore, the uninitiated in this complex dimension can have misinformed ideas. Thus, similar to the fields, waves are often present in TWO-dimensions. For example, the feature images of smell in Chapter 30 and fluctuating, vibrating waves in Chapter 31 are presented this way. But it is vital to realize that, in reality, this is not the case. Points of energy and waves are up-down, right-left, and everywhere in-between.

Therefore I'm going to coin a couple of terms here to help us grasp what I'm trying to show. *Energy spheres* (what science calls *energy packets, particle-like packets*) and *sphering*. Every single one of those minuscule points is a quantum sphere, emitting energy in ALL directions, like blowing up a balloon. It expands in a spherical shape. Hence the term *sphering energy*.

Here's an excellent summary from physicist Jim Al-Khalili:

> A quantum wave *smearing* itself out across the cell. The energy doesn't simply move from A to B, it heads in every direction at the same time. It's *spreading itself out*

as a wave so that it can *explore all possible routes simultaneously*. This strikes at the very heart of what's so strange about quantum mechanics. The *wave is following all paths at the same time,* that's what gives it such incredible efficiency. It's trying *every route to the reaction center at once;* it's bound to find the fastest possible way to deliver its energy.

This video will start with the above concept[6], but I suggest you watch the entire video to understand quantum physics in everyday life better.

To describe this movement of energy, science uses terms like *fluctuations, ripples, smearing, spreading itself out,* and *all possible routes simultaneously.* The only way this can happen is by what I call *sphering.* The energy expands like the explosion of a firecracker covering all space in every direction.

Here's one of the reasons why I'm explaining this. Once you grasp the concept of *sphering,* you immediately understand that each INDIVIDUAL point sphere intersects and interacts with every other sphere! This sphering energy is in the form of waves.

Now I want to take your imagination to the nth level. Imagine that each sphering point can emit energy on EVERY FREQUENCY, from the lowest to the highest. All the waves are superimposed, one on the other, filling the Universe.

---

6. https://youtu.be/bKa3ZNgBxVs?t=2150

Figure 29. Superimposed sphering points

As the energy spheres intersect, they INTERACT (see the image), bringing into existence all the MATTER and ENERGY in the Universe. Included in this are dark matter (27%) and dark energy (68%), which we know exist because that's what fuels the accelerating expansion of the Universe. Together they represent 95% of all energy in the Universe. On the other hand, the visible matter created from the remaining energy represents only 5% of the total sphering energy.

Science has revealed the smallest of small. We can't see it, but we know it's there. There's no such thing as *a space with nothing*. Today we recognize a vacuum (an item from which all air has been removed) is not empty.

In quantum physics, a quantum fluctuation (also known as a vacuum state fluctuation or vacuum fluctuation) is the temporary random change in the amount of energy in a point in space.

# MIND-BODY PROBLEM SOLVED

Figure 30. Quantum (vacuum) fluctuation

In the accompanying image, we visualize the physical fluctuations in a vacuum, the sphering of all those points that constitute the quantum field. Please note this animation is within a cube, so we picture the visible physical fluctuations/vibrations hitting the side. In reality, SPACE has no sides; these *fluctuations* continue on their way, ad infinitum, filling the entire Universe.

We have already established the *fluctuations* of spirit ruach[7]. I want you to realize that there's an interface between the energy of the fluctuating SPIRIT energy of God and the fluctuating PHYSICAL sphering energy of the Universe. The invisible meets the visible, and the following Bible verse should take on a new light.

**Romans 1:20**

> For the invisible things of him from the creation of the world are clearly seen, being understood by the things that are made (Sam: the visible things), even his eternal power and Godhead; so that they are without excuse:

---

7. https://theexplanation.com/fluctuations-spirit-vibrations-frequency/

The visible comes from the invisible; something comes from something. Physical sphering energy comes from spirit ruach energy. Our visible Universe comes from an invisible Creator God.

# 33. Vibrations. A Troubled Mind Pounding with Throbbing Temples

**Vibrations are the surprising common denominator of everything that exists. Both visible and invisible. Here's the impressive evidence.**

Vibrations are like the regular beating of a drum, the pounding surf on a seashore, or a throbbing headache. When you feel your heartbeat, you're in touch with a pulsating vein and can measure so many beats per minute. In fact, every atom and electron of your body is in continual movement. So is your mind.

Louis Victor de Broglie[1] introduced the idea of vibrations and energy fields some 100 years ago, in 1924.

> We proceed in this work from the assumption of the existence of a certain periodic phenomenon of a yet to

---
1. https://en.wikipedia.org/wiki/History_of_quantum_field_theory

be determined character, which is to be attributed to each and every isolated energy parcel.

Science has come a long way since then. We now know that our quantum-sphering material and immaterial world is likewise constituted of energy or vibration packets.

## Vibrations of the spirit in (hu)man(s)

From a biblical point of view, The Creation in Genesis 1:1-2 reveals the relationship of the spiritual (God) to the material world. We saw that the ruach moves, flutters, and shakes from the Biblical Hebrew[2]. *The Explanation* associates this with vibrations and frequency. What about the *spirit in humans*, the mind, that INVISIBLE element that science can neither see nor measure? Does other Biblical Hebrew vocabulary confirm its vibrational nature? Yes.

### Genesis 41:8

> And it came to pass in the morning that his *spirit* (H7307 - ruach) was *troubled* (H6470); and he sent and called for all the magicians of Egypt, and all the wise men thereof: and Pharaoh told them his dream; but there was none that could interpret them to Pharaoh.

Pharoah had two strange dreams (about the seven years of plenty followed by seven years of famine). When he awoke, he was perturbed. Genesis says his *spirit was troubled*. Put that in modern language, and you get *his mind was racing*. Dreams take place at the consciousness level, and our minds react accordingly. So what does the Biblical Hebrew *troubled* mean?

---

2. https://theexplanation.com/spirit-of-god-moved-face-waters-meaning/

### H6470

פָּעַם pâ'am paw-am'; a primitive root; to tap, i.e. beat regularly; hence (generally) to impel or agitate:

KJV - move, trouble.

### H6471

פַּעַם pa'am pah'-am; or (feminine) פַּעֲמָה; from H6470 (פָּעַם); a stroke, literally or figuratively (in various applications, as follow):

KJV - anvil, corner, foot(-step), going, (hundred-) fold, × now, (this) + once, order, rank, step, + thrice, (often-), second, this, two) time(-s), twice, wheel.

### H6472

פַּעֲמֹן pa'ămôn pah-am-one'; from H6471 (פַּעַם); a bell (as struck):

KJV - bell.

Note the rhythmic pattern of H6470. The dreams were causing Pharaoh's mind to *pound*. He possibly had a throbbing headache where you can literally feel your temples beating or your ears ringing, specifically referring to vibrations. We can almost say his mind was pulsating. But, of course, from a purely logical point of view, that is nonsense: the mind is invisible, and we cannot attribute a visible phenomenon like *pulsating* to an immaterial essence.

But the Bible does! Pharoah's spirit moved in a beating regular, *order*ly (H6471 translation) way, like a *bell* (H6472 translation).

I've put Strong's numbers and the KJV translations to emphasize this is not Sam Kneller's interpretation; this is what Biblical Hebrew tells us.

This pounding, throbbing, troubled mind, with the same H6470, *paam*, also refers to Nebuchadnezzar (Dan. 2:1).

## Frequency and Vibration of God's Holy Spirit

The same word, *paam*, used to describe the spirit in man, explains how God's Spirit can move people. This associates *Spirit* (God's) and *spirit* (human).

> **Judges 13:25**
>
> And the Spirit of the LORD began to *move him* [Samson] *at times* (H6470) in the camp of Dan between Zorah and Eshtaol.

You know the story of Samson and how God used him to battle the Philistines. From time to time, the Spirit had him accomplish feats.

God's Spirit *moving* Samson refers to regular intervention. Strong expressed it wonderfully in H6470 with *beat regularly*; this is picked up notably in H6471 with the notion of *time* and its *repetition*, *twice*, *thrice*, and *steps*. When we walk, we do so with a regular gait. A *bell* (H6470) doesn't have to be *struck regularly* but often is when used to tell *time*. *Paam* (H6470) is also used in Psalm 77:4 when David prays to God, "You hold my eyes waking: I am so *troubled* (H6470) that I cannot speak." When troubled, we often have spasmodic breathing and a marked beating of the heart. Again, the concept of increased and more amplified frequency.

There are many ways to express the idea of *move* (push, budge, propel, advance). The Biblical Hebrew has not just used ONE verb, but TWO. I think it is safe to say God's Spirit and the human spirit advance in such a way. I believe that biblically, we can attribute this characteristic to S/spirit in the spiritual world.

## Material World

Now let's examine the material world. What is the fundamental nature of the material Creation?

The answer is *quantum fields*, discussed in the last chapter[3]. Sphering energy pinpoints fill every nook and cranny of the Universe, emitting waves on all possible frequencies. God's Spirit is obviously NOT a quantum field, that's absurd, but there is communal ground between the spiritual and the physical. I am saying that scientists are dumbfounded to realize the material world is composed of energy packets. What we call electrons, quarks, leptons, and consider to be particles are ALL packets of immaterial energy. They move around via the fields with which they're associated[4].

The material world is composed of energy packets that are in continual movement in the form of waves[5]. For example, when you sing in the shower, the air vibrates over your vocal cords, and you produce sound waves. If you're good enough, your song vibrations will be heard via sound waves emitted as radio waves. Keep in mind that these are all regular beats. We've all played with magnetic waves and used electricity in the form of electromagnetic waves. The air is filled with light, TV, radio, Wi-Fi, microwaves, mobile phone, and other waves.

---

3. https://theexplanation.com/energy-invisible-origin-of-our-material-world/

4. https://en.wikipedia.org/wiki/Quantum_field_theory

5. http://scienceprimer.com/types-of-waves

We sense different colors and the gamut of sounds because the waves vibrate at different speeds and have different amplitudes. As you know, this refers to the frequency, calculated as vibrations per second. One vibration per second equals 1 Hertz (Hz). Below you can see that we humans have a hearing range of about 20 Hz-20 kHz. The diagram shows that 7 Hz and below are annoying and even dangerous. Brainwaves are about 0.5 Hz to 42 Hz, so those infrasounds we can't hear are within the range of our brainwaves and can still hurt us.

Notice that a dog whistle is in the 23-54 kHz frequency range, and we can't hear that. Where wind turbine noise is below our hearing frequency, dog whistles are above our capacity. A lot of animals have a much broader range than humans.

## Sound Waves

|  | No Effective Shielding | Easily Shielded |  |
|---|---|---|---|
|  | Infrasound (inaudible) | Audible Sound (to humans) | Ultrasound (inaudible) |

0 Hz     15 Hz                               20,000 Hz
Noise Frequency ~ cycles per second, or Hertz (Hz)

Highest Danger (7 Hz)

Example: Wind Turbine Noise

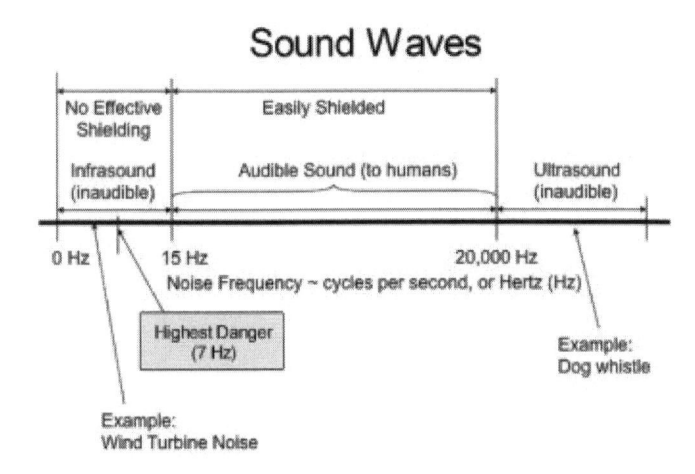

Example: Dog whistle

Figure 31. Sound waves

We're indirectly discussing sound waves because that is how our human senses capture information. We like to say we humans are stardust. Now we must realize that dust is energy packets moving

## MIND-BODY PROBLEM SOLVED

on quantum fields. Humans are waves, and we capture information via waves. God's Spirit moves like waves, and He breathed the neshama[6] in the first human and formed the spirit[7] in him as well.

I submit to you that there's a relationship between the spiritual world and the material world, the Spirit's movement and human movement in the largest sense of the term. We are waves, and as humans, we exchange waves of different frequencies with each other and the universe. So when we pray to God, whether vocally or in our minds, there's a definite exchange between the human and the Spiritual.

Here's another diagram with a much more extensive range of frequencies showing the shortest and longest that involve us. Notice that although we're affected by all these frequencies, there are only two groups indicated on the graph that we *sense* - we *hear* radio waves and *see* visible light waves. The fact is, even within the useable range of frequencies, human senses capture just a tiny portion of the wavelengths and frequencies.

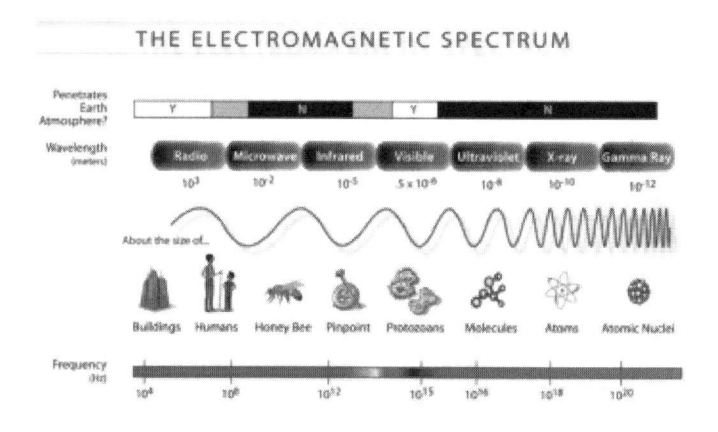

Figure 32. The Electromagnetic spectrum

---

6. https://theexplanation.com/neshama-inspiration-discover-the-deeper-meaning/

7. https://theexplanation.com/ruach-in-the-bible-creates-human-superiority/

The movement of God's Spirit represents the spiritual world. We now recognize the material world isn't as material as we thought. The movement of waves characterizes our world, and we are composed of trillions of packets of energy, each vibrating at a particular wavelength. As a result, our earthly world is much more spiritual than we ever realized.

I want to leave you with one thought. Notice the Frequency bar at the bottom of the above image; these frequencies concern humans. On the left, from lower than 10 to the power of 4 Hz, 10000 cycles per second, to the right end with more than ten followed by 20 zeros. From an extremely low frequency to an immensely high frequency.

On the above electromagnetic spectrum, human senses only occupy the radio (hearing) and visible (seeing) frequencies and wavelengths. But here's the point. That bar, with even lower and higher frequencies, is without limit at both ends! So there can be both higher and lower frequencies ad infinitum.

I want to be careful how I say this because God and His Spirit are in the spiritual world and are not concerned, in that sense, with the electromagnetic spectrum. But the Spirit flutters, shakes and beats regularly. Does that sound like some sort of vibrational frequency? Humans are made in the image of God. So there's a definite relationship, some *meeting of frequencies*, between the spiritual and physical worlds.

God's Spirit *paamed,* moving Samson at regular times, and Pharaoh's mind *paamed*, was troubled, pounding with questions. Quantum sphering emits periodic vibrations; we could easily use the verb *paam*, orderly movement, or regular agitation beats to describe it accurately. God's Holy Spirit (with a capital *S*), the human mind, the human spirit (with a small *s*), and our entire

## MIND-BODY PROBLEM SOLVED

physical Universe are characterized by vibrations, frequencies, and wavelengths. We are bringing the Spiritual, the spiritual, and the material worlds into coherent completeness.

**Additional Thoughts on Frequencies and Vibrations**

### Emotional frequency, real or not? Can you raise or lower the vibrations of emotions?

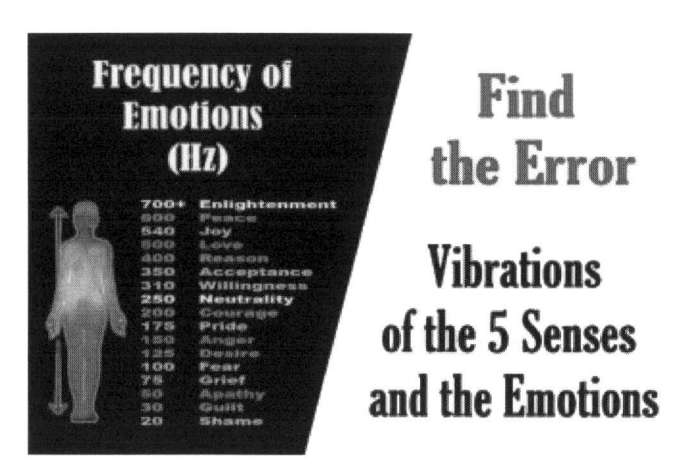

**Frequency of Emotions (Hz)**

| Hz | Emotion |
|---|---|
| 700+ | Enlightenment |
| 600 | Peace |
| 540 | Joy |
| 500 | Love |
| 400 | Reason |
| 350 | Acceptance |
| 310 | Willingness |
| 250 | Neutrality |
| 200 | Courage |
| 175 | Pride |
| 150 | Anger |
| 125 | Desire |
| 100 | Fear |
| 75 | Grief |
| 50 | Apathy |
| 30 | Guilt |
| 20 | Shame |

**Find the Error**

**Vibrations of the 5 Senses and the Emotions**

Emotional vibrations refer to the energy or vibrations associated with different emotional states. Terms like *good vibes* invoke such sensations. The featured image above refers to such frequencies. The word emotion comes from the French émouvoir, meaning *to move*. Indeed we are moved in two ways,

1. By a conscious mental reaction like love or hate
2. By a physiological change, what we call body language

These are two distinct aspects.

1. A non-material feeling of sadness, happiness, etc.
2. A material bodily reaction such as changes in heart rate,

blood pressure, and muscle tension

Science and its instruments can only measure the latter; body, heart, etc. But, regarding feelings and emotions like fear, anger, and euphoria, we can only measure brainwaves corresponding to these excitation states.

That's the error in the feature image; there is no such thing as frequency, in hertz, of shame, pride, joy, love, or enlightenment. They do reveal changes in brainwaves which science has measured. But these are in the gamma frequency range of 30-150 Hertz. They have nothing to do with the supposed frequencies of the image above.

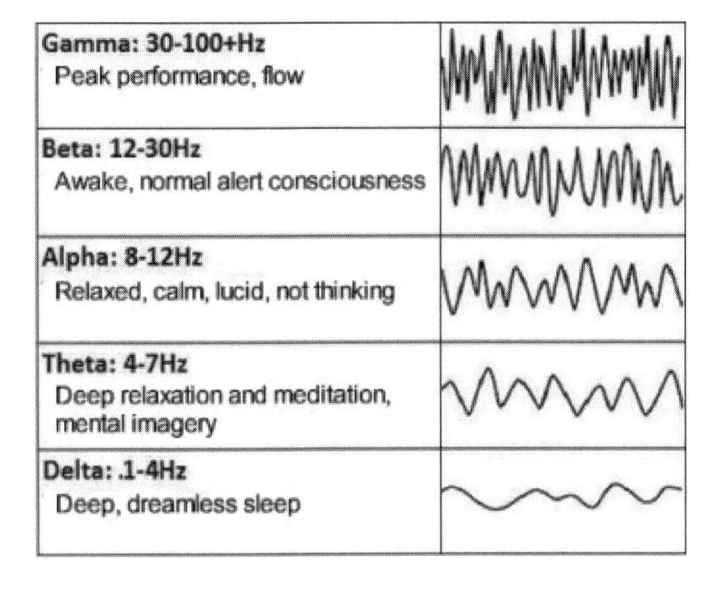

| | |
|---|---|
| **Gamma: 30-100+Hz**<br>Peak performance, flow | |
| **Beta: 12-30Hz**<br>Awake, normal alert consciousness | |
| **Alpha: 8-12Hz**<br>Relaxed, calm, lucid, not thinking | |
| **Theta: 4-7Hz**<br>Deep relaxation and meditation, mental imagery | |
| **Delta: .1-4Hz**<br>Deep, dreamless sleep | |

Figure 33. Brainwave frequencies

So where did such frequencies and ideas come from? It is an arbitrary scale[8] created by Dr. David Hawkins, a psychologist, in his book Force vs. Power. How did he get there?

It's an extended mixture of solfeggio[9] dating from ancient Western Gregorian and Eastern Sanskrit chants believed to affect and heal the conscious and subconscious mind. Today, solfege is a seven-tone scale (do, re, mi, fa, sol, la, si) corresponding to specific frequencies[10] said to have therapeutic powers. These frequencies are in tandem with chakras[11] that originated in Buddhist and Hindu practices about 1500 BC and are energy centers (hence vibrational) along the spine that supposedly affect emotional moods.

The scientist, Isaac Newton, associated the solfeggio frequencies with colors[12] surmising they had the same vibrational qualities, which they don't. Likewise, the Western chakra system[13] gave rise to psychological and other attributes, rainbow colors, and a wide range of supposed correspondences with other methods such as alchemy, astrology, gemstones, homeopathy, Kabbalah, and Tarot.

---

8. https://www.westlamensretreat.org/wp-content/uploads/2017/04/David-Hawkins-Power-vs-Force-Energy-Grid.pdf
9. https://www.bettersleep.com/blog/science-behind-solfeggio-frequencies
10. https://skeptoid.com/episodes/4474
11. https://en.wikipedia.org/wiki/Chakra
12. https://en.wikipedia.org/wiki/Solf%C3%A8ge
13. https://en.wikipedia.org/wiki/Chakra

| Emotional | | Solfège | | Chakras | | Color | |
|---|---|---|---|---|---|---|---|
| | Frequency Hz | | Frequency Hz | | Frequency Hz | | Frequency $10^{14}$ Hz |
| Enlightenment | 700+ | ti/si | 987 | Crown | 963 | violet | 7.50 |
| Love | 500 | la | 880 | 3rd Eye | 852 | blue | 6.66 |
| Willingness | 310 | sol | 783 | Throat | 741 | cyan | 5.99 |
| Courage | 200 | fa | 698 | Heart | 639 | green | 5.45 |
| Desire | 150 | mi | 659 | Solar Plexus | 528 | yellow | 5.16 |
| Grief | 75 | re | 587 | Sacral | 417 | orange | 5.00 |
| Shame | 20 | do | 523 | Root | 285/396 | red | 4.62 |

Figure 34. Emotional, solfège, chakras, color frequencies

The lower frequencies relate to negative emotions like shame, with the positive emotions (love) attached to higher frequencies. This combination amalgamates musical tones with colors to improve health and mental states. Thus, we arrive at Dr. David Hawkins's research and his Map of Consciousness (the above image is a concise representation), a scale he created for the hidden determinants of human behavior.

*The Explanation* believes the Bible refers to music having a soothing and spiritual effect. David played the lyre for King Saul (1 Samuel 16), and music accompanies the Psalms for worshipping God.

On the other hand, monotones, from which we derive the word *monotonous*, are single frequencies played continuously and are not considered music. Research shows that such monotony can, in fact, adversely affect mood changes[14] and could lead to the development of depression-like traits.

---

14. https://www.psychologytoday.com/us/blog/understand-other-people/201503/too-many-dull-moments

On a material scale, there's no such thing as *emotional frequency*; the best we can do is measure brainwaves (about 1-150 Hz) that correspond to emotions.

# 34. The Spirit Power of Creation is the Theory of Everything

*Mind-Body Problem Solved* reveals the answer to a much deeper question. Spirit power, human spirit power, and material energy power. Here's the theory of everything.

*Ruach and the Creation of Everything* is the title of this Section of the book *Mind-Body Problem Solved*. It is fitting to conclude with God's Spirit Power because it characterizes the *Theory of Everything*. That's the pot of gold scientists wish to find. I won't give you the mathematical equations; I don't have a clue. But, if we want a Theory of literally everything, then we must consider the spiritual world, which Science, of course, can't do.

From the Bible, *The Explanation* has revealed the following.

1. God's Holy **Spirit Power** flutters and shakes.

# MIND-BODY PROBLEM SOLVED

2. God infused all humans with **spirit power** through neshama and ruach[1], consciousness, and mind[2]. They are, therefore, outside of the body[3], non-material, and hence, invisible to science.
3. Our physical world, the interest of science, consists of **material energy** packets. All the solid and invisible particles from the most giant celestial phenomena to the minutest invisible Higgs Boson particle, including Dark Matter and Energy, are, in fact, quantum fluctuations, or as I've dubbed them, sphering pinpoints of energy waves.

These three elements define the focus of the Bible story, humans, as summarized in Genesis 2:7.

1. God formed the first human through the *Holy Spirit Power.*
2. God breathed the neshama (also the *spirit power in (hu)man(s)*, Job 32:8), the identifier of humans.
3. *Dust is the physical body, the material energy,* including the flesh, brain, cortex, and synapses.

I'm going to make a rather provocative statement because of its importance. Your *life,* now and in the future, depends on your belief in the above three elements.

- NOW, every human's peace and prosperity depend on how they treat their mind and body. The next Section of this book on *psychology* will expand on this.
- In the FUTURE, every human's eternal peace and

---

1. https://theexplanation.com/neshama-ruach-make-humans-human/
2. https://theexplanation.com/consciousness-and-human-mind-you-cant-have-one-without-the-other/
3. https://theexplanation.com/human-brain-role-consciousness-mind/

prosperity will depend on how they work with the Holy Spirit, spirit mind, and the material body. The final Section on *spiritual conversion* will expand on this.

**1 Peter 3:18**

For Christ also has once suffered for sins, the just for the unjust, that he might bring us to God, being put to death in the flesh, but *quickened* (G2227) by the Spirit:

The Holy Spirit *quickens*. See UnlockBibleMeaning.com[4] for the meaning of *quicken*.

**G2227**

ζωοποιέω zōopoieō dzo-op-oy-eh'-o; From the same as G2226 and G4160; to (re-) vitalize (literally or figuratively):

KJV - make alive, give life, quicken.

Christ's body died (3rd element), but He was given back spiritual and spirit life by the Spirit (1). Just like His earthly life and ministry were by the Spirit. Mary was found with child of the *Holy Spirit* (Mat. 1:18), and God gave Christ the *Spirit* without measure (John 3:34). The Spirit (1) gives physical life (3 body and the Universe), the Spirit gives spiritual life (2), and the Spirit (1) raises from the dead (3) and gives Eternal Life.

How the Holy Spirit (1) works with human spirit (2) and material energy (3) is fundamental to understanding and faith. This *equation* includes EVERYTHING.

---

4. https://unlockbiblemeaning.com

**Romans 8:16, 11**

> 16 The Spirit (1) itself bears witness with our *spirit* (2), that we are the children of God:

> 11 But if the *Spirit* (1) of him that raised up Jesus from the dead dwell in you, he that raised up Christ from the dead shall also *quicken* (G2227) your mortal *bodies* (3) by his *Spirit* (1) that dwells in you.

These three elements, God's Spirit, human spirit, and material energy, represent the sum total of EVERYTHING. God's realm, consciousness, mind, and our material world are fully interconnected.

This final chapter in the Section *Ruach and the Creation of Everything* proposes an alternative way of establishing the Theory of Everything, including both the entire physical Universe with its matter and the spirit power domain with neshama and ruach. *The Explanation* will go a step further and include the Holy Spirit (Ruach), which is part of God's spiritual realm.

We have Bible evidence the Holy Spirit, the spirit in (hu)man(s), and the material energy all flutter, shake, beat in rhythm, and vibrate on specific frequencies. For the physical world, we can calculate them; we cannot for the invisible spirit world; all we know is there's no limit to the range of frequencies in the spirit realm.

Here's the diagram for the Theory of Everything. The Holy Spirit powers what is inside the green (outer) rectangle, the spirit in (hu)man(s) powers what is inside the gold (bottom right) rectangle, and sphering energy packets power what is inside the red (inner) rectangle.

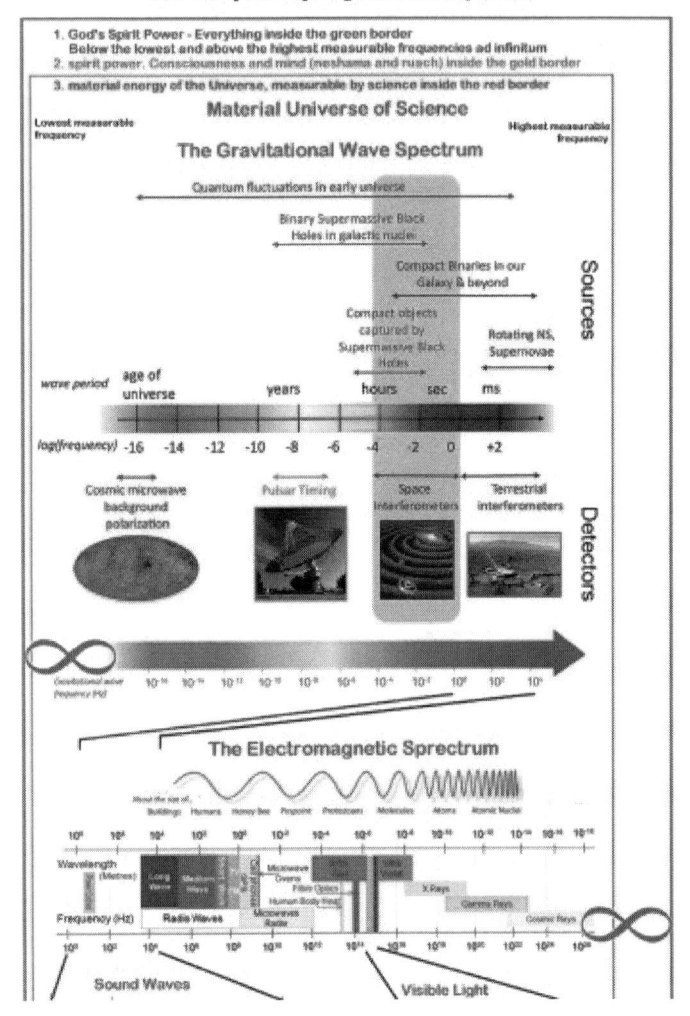

Figure 35a. Theory of everything based on frequencies

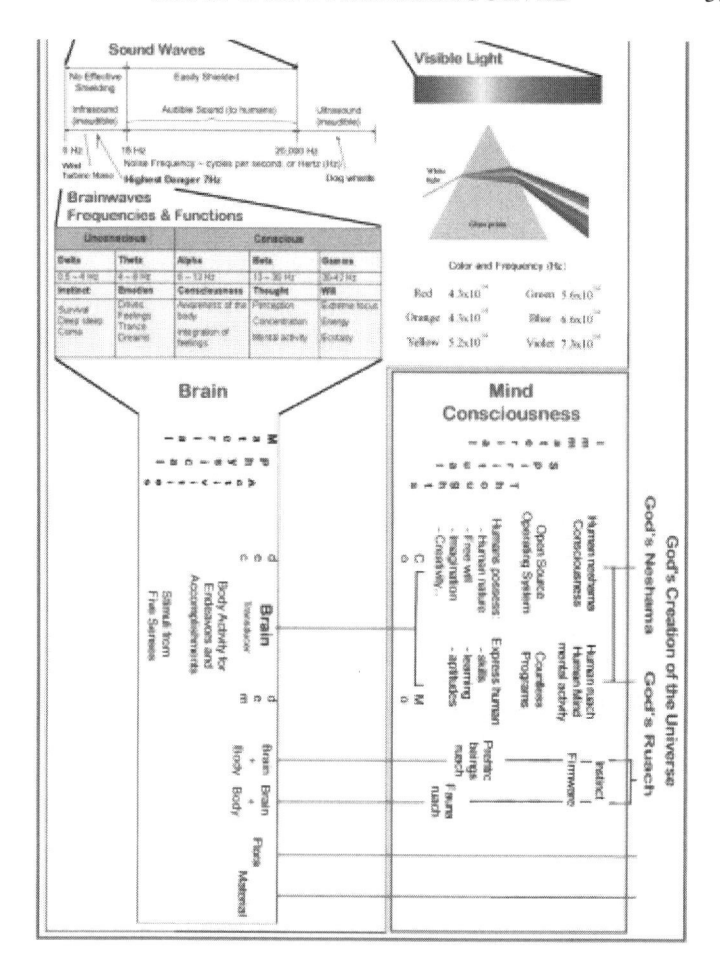

Figure 35b. Theory of everything based on frequencies

I'm not expecting you to understand all of this. We're simply showing the relationship between the spiritual and the physical, that it has to do with energy waves in the form of frequencies.

The dust, neshama, and ruach of Genesis 2:7 have a minimal presence in the entire electromagnetic spectrum. But we function perfectly within that tiny range. God spoke at the original creation in Genesis 1:1[5] and during re-creation week[6] in the rest of Genesis

1, and the Spirit Power fluttered His sayings into existence. It energized and restored the physical energy packages that gave rise to all the inanimate objects and living beings on Earth through animated quarks, atoms, molecules, and cells.

The fluttering Spirit Power created energy packages of vibrating matter. Do you see the connection between *fluttering* and *vibrating*? That's the common denominator of the Theory of Everything.

In Genesis 2:7, God breathed neshama into a dust body. Our mind's immaterial thought-frequencies work with our human material body and senses' frequencies. The transducer work of the brain[7] perfectly coordinates this activity. Humans, through their neshama, are on the same frequency as all other humans with whom they can exchange, reason, and communicate.

Likewise, through our neshama, we can be on the same frequency with God and exchange and communicate with Him. I'm calling them *thought-frequencies* because psychology talks about *brainwaves,* but biblically, *The Explanation* has demonstrated that thoughts are mind-based[8], not brain-based. Therefore, we can refer to mind-waves and mind-frequency. Of course, I don't know what that frequency is, it's spiritual, but it's real. The consciousness and mind-waves communicate with the brainwaves, which liaison with the frequencies of our physical senses; they, in turn, connect with the frequencies of the material and immaterial world around us; this is the Theory of Everything.

---

5. http://theexplanation.com/genesis-creation-starts-off-with-a-surprise-how-about-a-big-bang/

6. http://theexplanation.com/8-1-preparing-for-man/

7. https://theexplanation.com/the-human-brain-role-in-consciousness-and-mind/

8. https://theexplanation.com/human-brain-role-consciousness-mind/

Look at the diagram with the range of frequencies, from the lowest ($10^{-16}$ Hz), represented by the most significant distance in the Universe, its diameter, to the highest ($10^{35}$ Hz), represented by the tiny, smallest distance, something like a quark or maybe the composition of Dark Energy or Dark Matter. We can't grasp the extensiveness and tininess of the dimensions and frequencies discussed here.

Realize that BOTH ENDS of this graph REMAIN OPEN. Humanly, we've reached the absolute limit of what we can investigate, both the immensity and the minuteness. A good portion of this is mathematically established theory, which we are not even in a position to verify.

The open-endedness extends from gargantuan enormousness to infinitesimal smallness. For humans, it is beyond our scope; for God, it is child's play. From what science gathers physically, we've reached the edge of the known Universe, the lowest frequencies. At the other end of the frequency spectrum, we've also peered into the highest frequencies, but we don't know what those minutest of minute elementary particles are. We do know they represent large packages of energy. However, unlike the edge of the Universe, we don't know where the physical Universe starts on the high-frequency, minute-sphering, energy packet side of the spectrum.

But I know that at both ends of this frequency spectrum, there's a spiritual spectrum where the Holy Spirit carries on at lower and higher frequencies. The Holy Spirit is the Spirit Power, Energy God used to create and transform the physical Universe. It is the Spiritual Force that encompasses the entire physical energy of which the Universe is composed. It is also the ultimate Force working with the spirit in humans. That's what God told Job. God's Energy is behind physical and spirit energy.

**Job 38:31-36**

31 Can you [Job] bind the sweet influences of Pleiades, or loose the bands of Orion?

32 Can you bring forth Mazzaroth in his season? or can you guide Arcturus with his sons?

33 Know you the ordinances of heaven? can you set the dominion thereof in the earth?

34 Can you lift up your voice to the clouds, that abundance of waters may cover you?

35 Can you send lightnings, that they may go, and say to you, Here we are?

36 Who has put wisdom in the inward parts? or who has given understanding to the heart?

All those questions reiterate what God accomplished through His Spirit Power in Genesis 1. And verse 36; *Who has put wisdom in the inward parts? or who has given understanding to the heart?* refers specifically to Genesis 2:7, breathing the spiritual neshama-consciousness and attributing ruach-mind that confer wisdom and understanding on humans. The physical and the spiritual are joined together by and with ONE Creator. There is the *Theory of Everything*. The Energy of God assembles the energies that make the Universe and Humankind function fantastically.

# MIND-BODY PROBLEM SOLVED

What is puny man that you, God, should consider him? Asked the psalmist.

**Psalm 8:3-4**

3 When I consider your heavens, the work of your fingers, the moon and the stars, which you have ordained;

4 What is man, that you are mindful of him? and the son of man, that you visit him?

Yes, what is that minute range of frequencies? Well, God has given humans dominion over the entirety of the rest of the range of frequencies (read the rest of Psalm 8). Not only that, but God gives humans the opportunity to join His Kind and put on His image and likeness (Genesis 1:28, 1 Corinthians 15:50-53).

**I Corinthians 15:45, 49**

45 And so it is written, The first man Adam was made a *living soul* (Sam: material body and spiritual neshama and ruach); the last Adam was made a *quickening spirit* (Sam: Neshama and Holy Spirit).

49 And as we have borne the image of the *earthy* (Sam: material), we shall also bear the image of the *heavenly* (Sam: pure Spirit).

God's Holy Spirit Power, with spirit neshama and ruach on the human plane, and all material animate and inanimate entities have a common denominator - fluctuating energy packages. Regarding the physical Universe, we express this in terms of *frequencies*. God has endowed humankind and the Universe with many of His capacities on a much lower human level, as Psalm 8 tells us. Nonetheless, this interrelationship of the spirit and the material, the animate and inanimate, our present and future states fit wholly and neatly into the Theory of Everything.

# VI. Psychology of the Neshama and Ruach

Biblical psychology for stable mental health for everyone worldwide.

# 35. Psychology, what is it? The Best Bible Definition for Humans

**Psychology, what it's all about. Here's the ultimate definition related to human beings.**

We've solved the mind-body problem. Consciousness is neshama[1], and mind is ruach[2], the two spiritual components God gives (Genesis 2:7) that make each human unique[3]. Humans are in contact with both the physical world, the energy packets around them, AND God through the Holy Spirit in due time.

Two Greek words compose psychology; *psyche,* meaning *mind*, and *logos,* meaning *study*. In English, we use *psyche* with other significations like *spirit* and *soul*. *The Explanation* has already

---

1. https://theexplanation.com/neshama-inspiration-discover-the-deeper-meaning/

2. https://theexplanation.com/read-content-of-mind-body-problem-solved-online/

3. https://theexplanation.com/neshama-ruach-make-humans-human/

# MIND-BODY PROBLEM SOLVED

clarified that the mind is ruach[4], the spirit in (hu)man(s) (Job 32:8) placed there by God. So, if we want to use the term spirit, no problem, just so long as we realize it comes from God and relates to the Holy Spirit in that we can communicate with each other and with Him (Romans 2:8 God's Spirit witnesses WITH our spirit...).

We have also established that this R/ruach (whether it be God's or humans') is a P/power[5]. This P/power can activate, mobilize, trigger, switch on, call on, and stimulate; specifically, the spirit in humans energizes our consciousness, the neshama.

The mind is spirit; hence, it is invisible and outside the material body. The physical brain is the transducer[6] that converts mind waves to brainwaves and vice-versa. It allows our mind to interact with our body to transmit our physical sensations (from our five senses) to our non-physical thoughts and vice versa.

## Consciousness

At the base of the mind is consciousness. As defined by Genesis 2:7, this is the neshama, the understanding and awareness that God places in each human being. Consciousness is there from birth and is the fundamental makeup of every human. Neshama identifies what a human is[7].

When I wrote those consciousness chapters in Section III, I put them in a pyramid because of Maslov's pyramid of human needs. At the time, I fought with what should be at the base and summit and the order of the five elements. In the pyramid, they are, from

---

4. https://theexplanation.com/mental-mind-fabulous-activity-of-consciousness/

5. https://theexplanation.com/bible-definition-of-spirit-in-one-word-is-power/

6. https://theexplanation.com/the-human-brain-role-in-consciousness-and-mind/

7. https://theexplanation.com/astonishing-meaning-what-it-means-to-be-human/

bottom to top: *functions, reasoning, socialization, rulership,* and *purpose.*

As the book developed, I realized that order did not make sense, and now it's time to correct it. But I've decided to leave the former chapters with the pyramidal diagrams as they are, simply to show the original idea and how we can be wrong when reasoning based on previous work and accepted assumptions.

These five elements must be placed in a circle where neither is above any other. All five elements are present in each human, and the interaction is permanent and continuous right from the start of life and throughout it to the end. Therefore, I want to portray it as a circle.

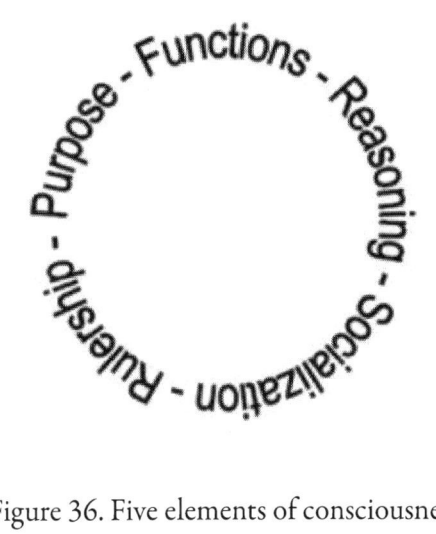

Figure 36. Five elements of consciousness

## Mind

This circle is encompassed on all sides by the mind, the spirit, the ruach. I've represented it in the diagram with a circle associated with the five areas of consciousness. The reason is that neshama and ruach are inseparable. The mind is continuously active around something to do with consciousness. Psychology involves both working together.

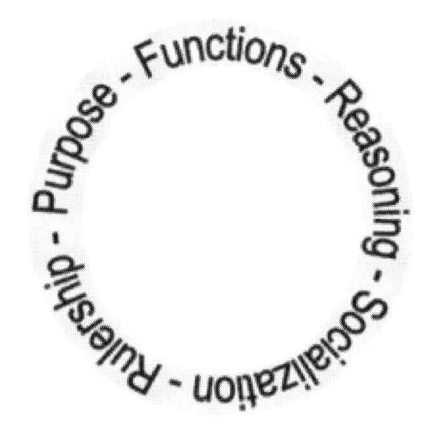

Figure 37. Consciousness and mind

Everything the mind does, thinking mentally or accomplishing physically, is associated with the five elements of consciousness. For instance, take *purpose*. Each person thinks about their purpose in life; some, even many, depending on culture and other circumstances, have no say in their life destiny. Others may follow their whims. Many might not know and take time to figure it out. But, on the other hand, based on their talents and likes, some might know at an early age what they want to accomplish and set a plan in motion to reach that goal.

All the thinking, hesitation, fortitude, planning, effort, or not to do something with one's life is mind activity around the conscious concept that humans have a *purpose*.

## Internal Influences

Our consciousness and minds are subject to every influence around us. So these effects need to be added to the definition of the psychology diagram. Each person has intuition, personal experiences, subconscious activity, dreams, emotions, and feelings to different degrees. These are immensely powerful because they are vivid personal events we have lived in our minds and bodies. They are genuine and authentic. There's no point denying them or trying to convince someone of their non-existence.

Figure 38. Consciousness and mind, internal & external influences

We shall devote an entire chapter to these inner events and impulses.

## External Influences

These are events over which we have no or little control. We are born into conditions, including our upbringing, beyond our power or the lack thereof.

In my initial pyramidal approach to consciousness, I put *how humans function* at the base. However, the first influence we undergo is socialization. Do parents, our mother and father, cuddle us? Does Mom breastfeed us? Is Dad present, and does he play with us? Simple questions but lasting effects on babies to be, children to be, adults to be, and the next generation of leaders responsible for the generation of babies after us. And the circle goes round and round.

This is the nurture aspect of human disposition each of us bears and, in adolescence and adulthood, injects into our decisions, relationships, and way of life. These influences can be negative, neutral, or positive. We all have a unique mixture of these traits representing our personality and character. This whole combination of components makes us an individual like no other on this planet.

Let's look at the meaning of the two Greek words that compose psychology, *psycho* and *logos*.

## Psyche

The number of translations in Hebrew and Greek reveals the difficulty with the concepts of *spirit* and *mind*.

In Hebrew, *mind* is translated by the words: zimma (plan - H2154), yetzer (purpose - H3336), lev (heart - H3820), nefesh (soul - H5315), peh (mouth - H6264), and ruach (spirit - H7307).

There are 15 Greek words rendered *mind* or derivatives like *bring to mind*. The principal words are *noos* (understanding - G3563) and *phroneo* (understanding - G5426). The primary Greek word is *psuche* (G5990), from which we get *psycho*, the first part of *psycho*logy. It appears 109 times and is rendered *mind* a mere 3x, *life* 40x, and *soul* 58x.

### G5590

> ψυχή psuchē psoo-khay'; From G5594; breath that is (by implication) spirit abstractly or concretely (the animal sentient principle only; thus distinguished on the one hand from G4151 which is the rational and immortal soul; and on the other from G2222 which is mere vitality even of plants: these terms thus exactly correspond respectively to the Hebrew [H5315] [H7307] and [H2416]:
>
> KJV – heart (+ -ily), life, mind, soul + us + you.

Here's what Wikipedia says about *psyche*[8], the basis of the word, and discipline *psychology*.

> In psychology, the psyche is the totality of the human mind, conscious and unconscious... The basic meaning of the Greek word ψυχή (psyche) was "life," although unsupported, some have claimed it is derived from the verb ψύχω (psycho, "to blow"). Derived meanings included "spirit", "soul", "ghost", and ultimately "self" in the sense of "conscious personality" or "psyche".

Regarding the word's origins, Wikipedia (unsupported derivation from *to blow*) is opposed to Strong (from G5594; *breath*). *The Explanation* simply states that biblically, both *ruach* and *neshama* imply *breath* (breath of life - Gen. 2:7).

---
8. https://en.wikipedia.org/wiki/Psyche_(psychology)

Also, regarding the word *neshama*, the Hebrew translations have a dilemma. Even more so, bringing the concept of neshama into the New Testament. Most readers are unaware of neshama in the Old Testament and certainly not in the New Testament.

The crux is this, neshama and ruach, consciousness and mind, are indissociable. They are two peas in a pod, so the *psyche* in *psychology* must include both elements. Look at this verse.

> **Philippians 1:27**
>
> Only let your conversation be as it becomes the gospel of Christ: that whether I come and see you, or else be absent, I may hear of your affairs, that you stand fast in one *spirit* (G4151 pneuma), with one *mind* (G5590 psuche) striving together for the faith of the gospel;

We have no difficulty understanding the English translations *spirit* and *mind*. However, I would offer you a possible alternative; *ruach* (pneuma - spirit) and *neshama* (psuche - consciousness). I did say *possible alternative*, my verdict is still out, but do you see how *neshama* and *ruach*, *consciousness*, and *mind* assemble together? We will conclude by saying the psuche/psyche in the word *psychology* involves the immaterial components of humans, the neshama and ruach.

## Logos

In dictionary terms, *logos, the logy* of psycho*logy,* means a *study* or [9]*research* of the mind. So that you understand the confusion that reigns in the *study* and *research* of the mind, I suggest you peruse this article[10]. I leave you with a partial quote, "...there is still a lot of

---
9. https://en.wikipedia.org/wiki/Psychology#Etymology_and_definitions

10. https://en.wikipedia.org/wiki/Mind

difference of opinion concerning what the exact nature of mind is, and various competing definitions have been proposed." That says it all.

*Logos* presents us with other meanings like *logic* or *reasoned discourse*, as well as *logo*, identifying signs of companies and organizations we see around us all the time. In biblical terms, Logos is of the utmost importance, translated *Word* and used as the name of God (Revelation 19:13) and Scripture (Luke 8:11).

*Logos* means sound reasoning; proper science deals with the rules and processes used in accurate thinking and reasoning. The logic, reflection, and meditation that comes from God's Word. So, the definition of *psychology* is NOT about *humankind's research of the psyche*; it's the neshama and ruach (psyche) according to God's Word (logos).

> The ultimate definition of *psychology*: **God's Word applied to the neshama and ruach.**

In summary, below are the five fundamental aspects of *consciousness* and the subsequent detailed practical everyday application by the *mind*.

The diagram below reveals the *psyche* under the benevolent umbrella of God's *Logos*: practical, efficient, godly psychology.

Figure 39. Consciousness and mind guarded by God's Word

Here are the five areas of each person's consciousness with the steps and procedures their mind activates to reach these goals (see details at the links).

## 1. The Purpose of Life[11] (Chapter 15)

- Nature of Humans, Consciousness & Mind[12]
- Space Time[13]
- Creativity[14]

---

11. https://theexplanation.com/what-purpose-of-life-why-humans-crave-an-answer/

12. https://theexplanation.com/nature-of-humans-consciousness-mind-reveal-adroit-humans/

13. https://theexplanation.com/space-time-is-not-only-scientific-theory-its-also-a-human-singularity/

14. https://theexplanation.com/creativity-sets-humankind-apart-from-and-above-all-other-life-on-earth/

- Imagination[15]
- Learning[16]
- Choices[17]
- Growth Mindset[18]
- Facing Challenges[19]
- Rule Life Responsibly[20]

## 2. How Humans Function[21] (16)

- Two-faced Humanity[22]
- Free Will[23]
- Behavior[24]
- Ethics[25]
- Justice[26]
- Self-Reproach[27]

---

15. https://theexplanation.com/imagination-another-singularity-of-humankind-in-your-mind/
16. https://theexplanation.com/bears-dont-learn-to-ride-bicycles-humans-learn-that-and-much-more/
17. https://theexplanation.com/your-choices-tell-us-who-you-are-in-fact-they-identify-you/
18. https://theexplanation.com/growth-mindset-unique-humankind/
19. https://theexplanation.com/challenge-accompanied-courage-needed-face-new-struggles-another-human-singularity/
20. https://theexplanation.com/rule-life-responsibly-the-key-human-singularity/
21. **https://theexplanation.com/human-nature-how-humans-worldwide-should-work/**
22. https://theexplanation.com/two-faced-humanity-depraved-priests-and-kind-criminals/
23. https://theexplanation.com/free-will-we-all-possess-it-but-we-cant-always-utilize-it/
24. https://theexplanation.com/human-behavior-is-the-expression-of-human-nature-and-free-will/
25. https://theexplanation.com/ethics-are-the-blueprint-for-behavior-how-humanity-should-function/
26. https://theexplanation.com/justice-goes-hand-in-hand-with-ethics-to-obtain-peace

- Forgiveness[28]

## 3. Social Relationships[29] (17)

- Human Society[30]
- Unique Individuals[31]
- Gender Equality[32]
- Bride and Groom[33]
- Couple Relationship[34]
- Marriage[35]
- Family[36]
- Parenting[37]
- Extended family[38]
- Ethnicity[39]
- Nations[40]

---

27. https://theexplanation.com/self-reproach-the-essential-beginning-step-toward-real-peace/

28. https://theexplanation.com/forgiveness-the-healing-bond-for-humans-to-function-peacefully/

29. **https://theexplanation.com/social-relationships-puzzling-humans-love-hate/**

30. https://theexplanation.com/human-society-the-only-global-social-species/

31. https://theexplanation.com/you-are-a-unique-individual-among-7-billion-on-earth/

32. https://theexplanation.com/gender-equality-gender-inequality-or-gender-compatibility/

33. https://theexplanation.com/bride-and-groom-is-a-cross-cultural-worldwide-phenomenon/

34. https://theexplanation.com/couple-relationship-binding-husband-and-wife-in-marriage/

35. https://theexplanation.com/healthy-marriage-a-happy-twosome-with-abundant-benefits/

36. https://theexplanation.com/family-the-cornerstone-of-human-society/

37. https://theexplanation.com/parenting-father-mother-have-essential-complementary-roles/

38. https://theexplanation.com/extended-family-many-generations-world-population/

39. https://theexplanation.com/ethnicity-clans-tribes-where-did-they-all-come-from/

40. https://theexplanation.com/nations-identified-by-their-own-patriotic-ethnic-culture/

- Languages[41]
- Globalization[42]

## 4. Human Rulership[43] (18)

- Human Government[44]
- Governance Structure[45]
- Government for the People[46]
- Human Needs[47]
- Inner Peace[48]
- Peace of Mind[49]
- National and Individual Prosperity[50]
- History of Individuals and Nations[51]
- Individual Rights vs. Collective Rights[52]
- Peace[53]
- Government Organization[54]
- Best Form of Government[55]

---

41. https://theexplanation.com/origin-of-language-an-unsolvable-scientific-mystery

42. https://theexplanation.com/globalization-integration-segregation/

43. **https://theexplanation.com/human-rulership-responsibility-people-resources/**

44. https://theexplanation.com/human-government-personal-world-peace/

45. https://theexplanation.com/governance-structure-important-role-in-rulership/

46. https://theexplanation.com/government-for-people-concern-for-poor/

47. https://theexplanation.com/human-needs-basics-person-expect/

48. https://theexplanation.com/inner-peace-citizen-goal-government/

49. https://theexplanation.com/peace-mind-tranquil-result-leadership/

50. https://theexplanation.com/prosperity-nation-prosperity-citizen/

51. https://theexplanation.com/history-of-individuals-and-nations-practical-bible-wisdom

52. https://theexplanation.com/individual-rights-vs-collective-rights-the-bible-balance/

53. https://theexplanation.com/peace-national-international-government-concern/

54. https://theexplanation.com/government-2-choices-bottom-up-top-down/

55. https://theexplanation.com/best-form-government-aiming-common-good/

## 5. Reasoning[56] (19)

- Observation and Intuition[57]
- Philosophy[58]
- Science[59]
- Religion[60]
- Theology[61]

Psychology is the five properties of neshama activated by the ruach, the fundamental elements of our consciousness developed by our mind power in accord with God's Word. That's wonderful for people who might believe in God's Word, but what about all the others? Is God interested in all individuals' well-being, regardless of their belief in Him? In other words, can modern psychology apply principles from the Bible to establish, improve, and maintain the mental health of all people, regardless of culture and beliefs? We shall see this in the next chapter.

---

56. https://theexplanation.com/5-types-of-reasoning-life-hangs-ultimate-choice/

57. https://theexplanation.com/observation-first-way-human-reasoning/

58. https://theexplanation.com/philosophy-love-wisdom-whose-wisdom/

59. https://theexplanation.com/science-world-savior-human-reasoning/

60. https://theexplanation.com/religion-solution-world-peace/

61. https://theexplanation.com/deity-and-sound-reasoned-words-are-the-crux-of-theology/

# 36. Human Reasoning Annihilates God's Desire of Good for All People

**Human reasoning is poisoning humanity's well-being. Is God the God of chosen individuals, or is He interested in all humans reaching a level of accord and well-being?**

From a psychological point of view, this is a fundamental issue related to God. Does God play favorites? Why are some seemingly blessed while others wallow in misfortune? Why is mental wellness at the top of our health issues?

These might sound like philosophical questions, but they are primary when understanding how God deals with all humans. In the last chapter, we defined psychology[1] as the *neshama and ruach, the consciousness and mind influenced by our life's internal and external circumstances.* Did God even initiate a positive set of

---
1. https://theexplanation.com/psychology-best-bible-definition-for-humans/

influences that would put humanity on the right track to favorable goals? What does the Bible say? Let's call this Godly psychology in contrast to the human reasoning of classic psychology.

Let's return to the first humans in the Garden of Eden. The context occurs immediately after eating from the prohibited tree. Let's follow the events that are not easily understandable through translations.

**Genesis 3:6-8**

> 6 And when the woman saw that the tree was good for food, and that it was pleasant to the eyes, and a tree to be desired to make one wise, she took of the fruit thereof, and did eat, and gave also to her husband with her; and he did eat.
>
> 7 And the eyes of them both were opened, and they knew that they were naked; and they sewed fig leaves together, and made themselves *aprons* (H2290).
>
> 8 And they heard the voice of the LORD God walking in the garden in the *cool* (H7307) of the *day* (H3117): and Adam and his wife *hid* (H2244) themselves from the presence of the LORD God amongst the *trees* (H6086) of the garden.

First, let's focus on verse 8. There's a vital contrast present here but obscured. It was a big enigma for me, *cool of the day*. In such a delicate moment, not to say a historic turning point, why are we talking about the weather? Let's look at the Hebrew for *cool of the day*.

# Cool of the Day

### H7307

רוּחַ rûwach roo'-akh; from H7306 (רוּחַ); wind; by resemblance breath, i.e. a sensible (or even violent) exhalation; figuratively, life, anger, unsubstantiality; by extension, a region of the sky; by resemblance spirit, but only of a rational being (including its expression and functions):

KJV – air, anger, blast, breath, × cool, courage, mind, × quarter, × side, spirit(-ual), tempest, × vain, (whirl-) wind(-y).

Do you recognize the Hebrew for *cool*? Sure you do; it's ruach, which we've associated with *spirit, power,* and *mind*[2]. This is its second appearance after Genesis 1:2, *the Spirit of God moved*. In Gen. 3:8, *cool of the day* describes the garden, the atmosphere that reigns in God's presence. It is not about the weather; that's secondary; look at the meaning of *day* in Biblical Hebrew and note the third step to master Biblical Hebrew[3]: figurative meaning.

### H3117

יוֹם yôwm yome; from an unused root meaning to be hot; a day (as the warm hours), whether literal (from sunrise to sunset, or from one sunset to the next), or figurative (a space of time defined by an associated term), (often used adverb):

KJV – **age**, + always, + chronicals, continually(-ance), daily, ((birth-), each, to) day, (now a, two) days (agone), + elder, × end, + evening, + (for) ever(-lasting, -more),

---

2. https://theexplanation.com/bible-definition-of-spirit-in-one-word-is-power/

3. https://theexplanation.com/fastest-bible-study-method-god-intended-meaning/

✕ full, **life**, as (so) long as (… live), (even) now, + old, + outlived, + perpetually, presently, + remaineth, ✕ required, season, ✕ since, **space**, then, **(process of) time**, + as at other times, + in trouble, weather, (as) when, (a, the, within a) while (that), ✕ whole ([phrase] age), (full) year( ly), + younger.

Figuratively, *day* refers to *space*, *time* (*age*), and *life*[4]. Remember, step 4 to mastering Biblical Hebrew[5] is all the meanings tell one story. The narrative is that the *Garden of Eden is a spiritual place and time where life exists*. Frankly, once you understand the meaning of the words, I know you see the relationship to God's eternal abode.

However, we're not just deciphering Biblical Hebrew to understand words. The goal is always to unlock Bible meaning. Psychology means God's Word governs one's consciousness and mind[6]. God's Garden of Eden is the epitome of this. Occupants of the Garden (exterior influences) have their interior influences (the spirit of life (the Tree of Life)) governed by God's Word, His way of life. That is the Godly psychology of the ones who enter and abide in God's presence, as described by the term *cool of the day*, the Spirit of Eternal Life in God's Garden, His Eden.

## Hid in the Trees

Now for the amazing contrast, human reasoning. Adam and Eve *hid* among the *trees*. So what is the deeper Biblical Hebrew meaning?

### H2244

---

4. https://theexplanation.com/evening-morning-day-powerful-abstract-meaning/

5. https://theexplanation.com/fastest-bible-study-method-god-intended-meaning/

6. https://theexplanation.com/psychology-best-bible-definition-for-humans/

חָבָא châbâ' khaw-baw'; a primitive root (compare H2245 (חָבַב)); to secrete:

KJV - × held, hide (self), do secretly.

## H2245

חָבַב châbab khaw-bab'; a primitive root (compare H2244 (חָבָא), H2247 (חָבָה)); properly, to hide (as in the bosom), i.e. to cherish (with affection):

KJV – love.

*Hide* means to do secretly and love it. Adam and Eve were enthralled by being in the secrecy of the grove of trees. So much could be said here, but space doesn't permit it. Think of secret societies that love to think their knowledge and wisdom can solve our problems. Here's the origin of such wishful human reasoning, reflected in the meaning of *tree*.

## H6086

עֵץ 'êts ates; from H6095 (עָצָה); a tree (from its firmness); hence, wood (plural sticks):

KJV - + carpenter, gallows, helve, + pine, plank, staff, stalk, stick, stock, timber, tree, wood.

## H6095

עָצָה 'âtsâh aw-tsaw'; a primitive root; properly, to fasten (or make firm), i.e. to close (the eyes):

KJV – shut

# MIND-BODY PROBLEM SOLVED

Trees represent, among other things, *gallows* and look at the root meaning: *shut eyes*. So instead of being in the *spirit of life* that characterizes God's Garden, Adam and Eve loved the secrecy of having their eyes, figuratively, their minds shut up, prepared to go to the gallows of death.

Eating from the restricted tree transformed Adam and Eve's psychological makeup. Their inside influences were loving their shut eyes to God's Word; that's human reasoning, hiding in the trees (the Tree of Knowledge of good and evil that leads to death (gallows)) away from the Spirit of the Garden. Their frame of mind did a flip and was no longer in line with the mindset of God's Garden. Do you see the contrast and why God had to remove them? It all comes down to their wrong psychological approach.

Genesis 3:8 reveals the results of the first INSIDE and OUTSIDE INFLUENCES on the human condition and our psychological state. Our human reasoning is hiding us from God's benevolence. Not only that, but we've taken measures to try to solve our own problems. Adam and Eve *sewed fig leaves together and made themselves aprons.*

Read this chapter from *Agony of Humankind and the Antidote*[7] to grasp the meaning of fig leaves[8]. In a nutshell, it's a temporary fix that's a poor solution; fig leaves have a short lifespan once removed from the tree, and you can't tailor them. It's solving problems with human reasoning instead of God's solutions. Here's the meaning of *apron*.

## H2290

---

7. https://theexplanation.com/read-all-the-content-of-agony-of-humankind-online/
8. https://theexplanation.com/fig-leaves-or-clothing-tinker-or-build-practical-bible-wisdom/

חָגוֹר chăgôwr khag-ore'; or חֲגֹר; and (feminine) חֲגוֹרָה; or חֲגֹרָה; from H2296 (חָגַר); a belt (for the waist):

KJV – apron, armour, gird(-le).

## H2296

חָגַר châgar khaw-gar'; a primitive root; to gird on (as a belt, armor, etc.) :

KJV – be able to put on, be afraid, appointed, gird, restrain, × on every side.

Adam and Eve became *restrained* by their human reasoning, causing them to *be afraid*. It sounds just like anxiety and depression caused by outside oppression so many suffer from today. Human reasoning can lead to inextricable constraints and despair. God could've left them in this precarious position. He didn't.

## God Clothed Them Despite Their Sin

Adam's and Eve's minds were no longer in harmony with the Spirit of the Garden. They'd switched to human reasoning. Now, God clothes them according to their new degraded mindset; but He doesn't abandon them. Look at the meaning of *clothed* in verse 21 "to Adam also and to his wife did the LORD God make *coats* (H3801) of skins, and *clothed* (H3847) them."

## H3847

לָבַשׁ lâbash law-bash'; or לָבֵשׁ; a primitive root; properly, wrap around, i.e. (by implication) to put on a garment or clothe (oneself, or another), literally or figuratively:

KJV – (in) apparel, arm, array (self), clothe (self), come upon, put (on, upon), wear.

The average Bible reader focuses on *nakedness* and *fig leaves*. They are missing the critical point; the *figurative* reference to *clothing*. That's Step 2 in mastering Biblical Hebrew[9]. At the beginning of *Agony of Humankind,* we discuss clothing in the context of the man's and the woman's nakedness[10]. Please revise the information at the link. To summarize, dirty and clean clothing represent sinful and righteous living. That is the figurative usage of clothing.

You can study this fascinating subject at UnlockBibleMeaning.com[11]. For instance, look at all the verses which include H3847. In Leviticus, you'll see the sumptuous garments God ordered for the High Priest, His spiritual representative here on Earth. That Priest prefigured Jesus Christ, Who is *clothed* with righteousness.

Figuratively, clothing, like nakedness, points us to a *frame of mind*, a way of critical thinking coupled with a way of acting. In short, behavior. God made Adam and Eve *coats* (H3801). Something to envelop them, to protect and fit them.

## H3801

כְּתֹנֶת k$^e$thôneth keth-o'-neth; or כֻּתֹּנֶת; from an unused root meaning to cover (compare H3802 (כָּתֵף)); a shirt:

KJV – coat, garment, robe.

---

9. https://theexplanation.com/each-biblical-hebrew-word-is-a-precious-jewel-to-be-discovered/

10. https://theexplanation.com/adam-and-eve-naked-possessing-spiritual-wisdom/

11. https://unlockbiblemeaning.com/

### H3802

כָּתֵף kâthêph kaw-thafe'; from an unused root meaning to clothe; the shoulder (proper, i.e. upper end of the arm; as being the spot where the garments hang); figuratively, side-piece or lateral projection of anything:

KJV – arm, corner, shoulder(-piece), side, undersetter.

In the New Testament, the Apostle Paul talks about the upper clothing, "Stand therefore, having your loins girt about with truth, and having on the breastplate of righteousness;" (Ephesians 6:14). God dressed Adam and Eve with the necessary garments to thrive in their new life. Look at the meaning of these clothes of *skins*.

### H5785

עוֹר 'ôwr ore; from H5783 (עוּר); skin (as naked); by implication, hide, leather:

KJV – hide, leather, skin.

### H5783

עוּר 'ûwr oor; a primitive root; to (be) bare:

KJV – be made naked.

Go to the links at *Agony of Humankind and the Antidote* for the full explanation. Originally, Adam and Eve were naked[12], representing their pureness of mind related to the way of life in the Garden of Eden. After their demise, they clothed themselves with temporary *fig leaves*, and God immediately dressed them in clothes of *skins*[13].

---

12. https://theexplanation.com/adam-and-eve-naked-possessing-spiritual-wisdom/

13. https://theexplanation.com/critical-thinking-antidote-to-the-agony-of-humankind/

The meaning is *nakedness* (H5783); the NEW coats and skins represent the new rules of life. However, the Bible doesn't use the term rules. Instead, we find vocabulary like laws, commandments, judgments, and statutes.

## God Cares for the Converted AND UNconverted

Despite Adam and Eve's adoption of human reasoning, God still dresses, cares, and equips them with everything necessary for their new life, despite their transformed frame of mind. From this point on in the history of humankind, God works with UNconverted people using human reasoning to solve their problems.

The primary example is the nation of Israel God brought out of Egypt. They were His people, BUT they were UNconverted. The Ten Commandments and all the laws were given to people who used human reasoning to solve their problems. They did not put on God's clothes of skins. However, look what happens when UNconverted people dress in God's clothing[14].

> **Deuteronomy 4:5-6**
>
> 5 Behold, I have taught you statutes and judgments, even as the LORD my God commanded me, that you should do so in the land where you go to possess it.
>
> 6 Keep therefore and do them; for this is your wisdom and your understanding in the sight of the nations, which shall hear all these statutes, and say, Surely this great nation is a wise and understanding people.

The commandments, statutes, and judgments God clothed Israel with are their wisdom and understanding. And they can be the

---
14. https://theexplanation.com/critical-thinking-antidote-to-the-agony-of-humankind/

same for ALL nations who clothe themselves that way. That's what these verses are telling us.

Instead, Israel dressed in fig leaves and obstinately rejected God's ways (Deuteronomy 12:8, 29:19, 4). The clothes God gave Adam and Eve and the nation of Israel are for spiritually BLINDED people who are DISobedient and who do what is right in their OWN EYES (the cause of psychological disorders). God clothes the UNconverted with RULES they CAN and SHOULD follow (Godly psychology leading to peace and calmness). That's ALL God expects of them.

Deuteronomy 7:13 indicates that God will oversee all His creation when it simply follows that code of ethics. God set in motion appropriate psychology for all humanity, His ways to be practiced by each human's neshama and ruach, body, brain, consciousness, and mind.

# 37. Morality. The Universal Code Defines Good and Bad Behavior

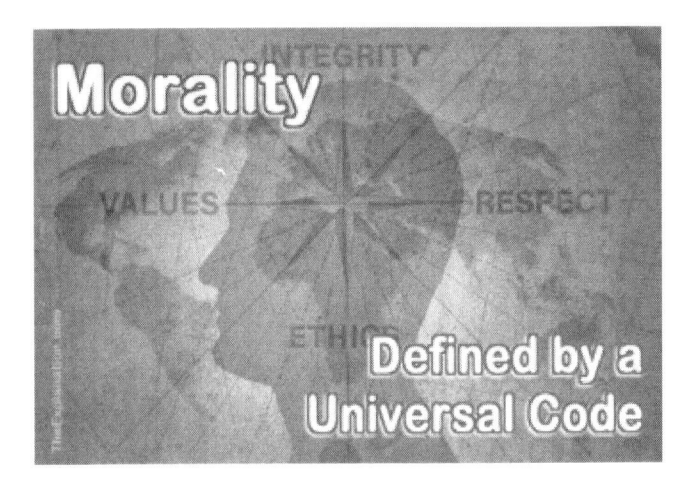

The title about morality immediately poses three questions. First, can or should we define good and bad behavior? Second, do morality and behavior matter in human affairs? Third, can there be one worldwide code of ethics to establish a basis for well-being?

This chapter will answer those questions. The context is practical psychology, the internal and external influences on all humans, our consciousnesses and minds. Should this impact from all sides be regulated? For example, I just got a new phone with the heading Digital Wellbeing and Parental Controls in the settings. It includes sections like supervising this phone remotely, monitoring screen time, setting limits as needed, and adding restrictions to services like app approvals or content filters.

First, we have the very deliberate word *control*. It's giving parents the authority to manage content accessible to their children. In biblical terms, it's like saying *have dominion over* (Genesis 1:29). This means parents are responsible for supervising and setting *limits* for what their children see, hear, and do with their phones. Put another way; parents govern what influences impact their children's minds. That's practical psychology and applies to all parents and children worldwide.

Since, not if parents manage what goes into their children's minds, WHO and WHAT supervises what goes into parents' or adults' minds? What control is there over influences and forces that affect the population? In other words, is there a universal code to define good and bad behavior?

*The Explanation* has developed the five areas of consciousness (purpose[1], function[2], socialization[3], rulership[4], and reasoning[5]). How humans function[6] includes seven steps, the fourth of which is *ethics;* they define acceptable behavior (3rd component of how humans function) and are guaranteed by equitable justice (5th component). Common sense, terms and conditions of use (which govern everything we come in contact with), and the Bible indicate, without hesitation, that morality and ethics are essential for societal relations to run smoothly. That's the answer to questions 1 and 2 above.

## A Worldwide Code of Ethics

1. https://theexplanation.com/what-purpose-of-life-why-humans-crave-an-answer/
2. https://theexplanation.com/human-nature-how-humans-worldwide-should-work/
3. https://theexplanation.com/social-relationships-puzzling-humans-love-hate/
4. https://theexplanation.com/human-rulership-responsibility-people-resources/
5. https://theexplanation.com/5-types-of-reasoning-life-hangs-ultimate-choice/
6. https://theexplanation.com/human-nature-how-humans-worldwide-should-work/

The definition of Godly psychology[7] is *Scripture, as it influences human consciousness and mind*. In the last chapter, we saw God *clothed* disobedient Adam and Eve, the parents of humankind. I wrote *figuratively; clothing, like nakedness, points us to a frame of mind, a way of critical thinking coupled with a way of acting, in short, behavior*[8]. Clothing for undisciplined human beings represents God's code of morality. Despite Adam and Eve's rejection of God, He clothed them, expressing His desire for human well-being via a code of ethics. We've just answered the third question.

Furthermore, God told Adam and Eve (humankind) to govern the world (Genesis 1:28). He told them their purpose. So it follows that He also gave them a code of HOW TO GOVERN themselves, how to socialize, and how to rule to reach peace and prosperity for all.

The only question is, what is this universal code?

As we examine the theological answer to this all-important question, please realize why we're doing this. We want good mental health for all humans. Psychologically we must have the RIGHT INTERIOR AND EXTERIOR INFLUENCES ON people's CONSCIOUSNESSES AND MINDS to reach that goal. The universal code of morality represents those influences. That's practical psychology. So, while we establish the theological answer, we are designating the foundation for mental health. God's morality and ethics, His universal code that governs all human behavior, is the road to humanity's well-being.

We're talking theology, but we're tackling applicable psychology. I use the word tackle because of its meaning; determined efforts to deal with a difficult task. The Apostle Peter describes Paul's epistles;

---

7. https://theexplanation.com/psychology-best-bible-definition-for-humans/

8. *https://theexplanation.com/human-reasoning-crushes-gods-good-for-people/*

*some things hard to be understood, which they that are unlearned and unstable wrest, as they do also the other scriptures* (2 Peter 3:15).

We are going to discuss Paul's writings on *morality* and *ethics* briefly. Those terms are not in the Bible; Paul uses the expression *law* instead. And so, all sorts of questions arise as to what law? The Ten Commandments, civil, moral, or ceremonial law? Then there's the law of Moses and the law of Christ. So, yes, we have to talk about law, but it must apply to influences on humans.

Here's the context. The Apostle Paul is writing to a group of converted Christians in Galatia, the area of Ankara, Turkey, today. He describes the spiritual state of all human beings before and after a specific event, the death of Jesus Christ. That death took place about 2000 years ago. But Christ's death applies to an individual human being, you and me, only when it's accepted in one's personal life. Paul accepted Christ on the road to Damascus a few years after Christ's death and the Galatians a few years later when Paul preached to them; I accepted Christ some 50 years ago.

Understanding this timeframe distinction is vital because Christ ushered in the New Covenant, but an individual person is only part of this New Covenant when they sign it; in other words, when they accept Christ, repent, are baptized, and receive the Holy Spirit, which is the seal of the New Covenant (Ephesians 1:13 ...In whom also after that you believed, you were sealed with that holy Spirit of promise). For those converted Christians, we shall discuss Christian psychology in Section VII, the next, and the last one of this book.

Paul is writing to converted Galatians and explaining their and his spiritual state BEFORE and AFTER this crucial turning point in their individual lives. This Sixth Section of *Mind-Body Problem Solved* refers to all people worldwide BEFORE they accept the death of Christ for the forgiveness of their sins in their lives. Section VI addresses UNcoverted people worldwide and what should influence their psychological makeup so they and all humankind can benefit from good mental health. The worldwide code of ethics applies to them.

**Galatians 3:22-26**

22 But the **scripture has concluded all under sin** (Sam: every human being who has ever lived), that the promise by faith of Jesus Christ might be given to them that believe (Sam: at the time each person accepts Christ).

23 But before faith came, **we were kept under the law**, shut up to the faith which should afterwards be revealed. (Sam: this is the before and after. Paul and the Christians in Galatia and elsewhere are after, but all other humans are before; hence they are still *under the law*. We shall see what that means)

24 Wherefore **the law was our schoolmaster to bring us to Christ**, that we might be justified by faith. (Sam: the law leads people to Christ).

25 But after that faith is come, we are no longer under a schoolmaster. (Sam: Christians are no longer under the law, but all others are still under the law. Their schooling under the law will be over when they meet/accept Christ).

26 For you are all the children of God by faith in Christ Jesus (Sam: those who have repented, been baptized, and received the seal of the Holy Spirit).

From these verses, five points are clear.

1. *All under sin* means every human being. Past, present, and future. We are ALL sinners.
2. The law was a schoolmaster, and schoolmasters are a good thing.
3. The law teaches us what sin is. It instructs us what to do and what NOT to do. It reveals right and wrong, good and bad.
4. People are no longer under a schoolmaster when they accept faith in Christ, are baptized, and receive the Holy Spirit.
5. Summary: ALL are sinners, ALL are under the law, and all need and are under this schoolmaster, except Holy Spirit-led Christians.

Continue your study of this subject at UnlockBibleMeaning.com[9]

## The Ten Commandments

What is this schoolmaster law? Paul tells us in Gal. 3:16-17, "the law that came 430 years after the promises... made to Abraham." That's the Ten Commandments, the law God gave after the Exodus to the descendants of Abraham, Isaac, and Jacob, including the mixed multitude (non-Israelites, representing the Gentiles) who exited with them (Ex. 12:38). This is a primary issue. ALL (Israelites and Gentiles) people, past, present, and future, are sinners and, therefore, under the schoolmaster law, now defined as the Ten Commandments. We will discuss ceremonial, moral, and civil law; for now, at a minimum, ALL people are UNDER the Ten Commandments.

---

9. https://unlockbiblemeaning.com

That's the theology; now apply it to practical psychology; the interior and exterior influences each person should practice and submit to are the Ten Commandments. For now, let's just take the last six Commandments.

5. You shall honor your father and mother.

6. You shall not murder.

7. You shall not commit adultery.

8. You shall not steal.

9. You shall not lie.

10. You shall not covet.

We'll discuss the first four Commandments later. Just imagine the psychological effect on people if all of society, the WHOLE world, applied just those six laws. What if coaches, teachers, and those with responsibilities to manage other people had a curriculum for adults and children that, at a minimum, revolves around those six rules; quite a difference that would make. In the last chapter, God clothed Adam and Eve, parents of all humankind, with *coats of skin representing* the *right way of life in the world* outside the Garden. At a minimum, the above six commandments should clothe ALL humans.

This morality and ethics are the fundamentals of practical psychology. Do you see how this application would increase mental health if you knew your neighbor and children would abide by these rules? I realize this is hypothetical, but God clothed all humans with the potential to reach this goal. Not to get ahead of the story, but the Bible reveals there will be a Godly society of UNconverted inhabitants on Earth governed by the Ten Commandments that will have psychological peace. See Micah 4:4

"But they shall sit every man under his vine and under his fig tree; and none shall make them afraid." That's physical prosperity and psychological peace for EVERY human.

Paul continues this theme of being *under the law* into the next chapter of Galatians.

### Galatians 4:1-5

> 1 Now I say, That the heir, as long as he is a child, differs nothing from a servant, though he be lord of all;
>
> 2 But is **under tutors and governors** until the time appointed of the father.
>
> 3 Even so we, when we were children, were in bondage **under the elements of the world**: (under sin)
>
> 4 But when the fulness of the time was come, God sent forth his Son, made of a woman, made **under the law**,
>
> 5 To redeem them that were **under the law**, that we might receive the adoption of sons.

I've used bold font to enhance four phrases that begin with the word *under*. Verses 2, 3, 4, and 5. All people, past, present, and future, are under tutors, the law, and sin... UNTIL the time appointed of the Father. Yes, Christ came at the appointed time, about 2000 years ago. BUT, and I repeat, a person only receives the adoption as a child of God when God the Father calls them at His appointed time. John 6:44, "No man can come to me, except the Father which has sent me draw him: and I will raise him up at the last day."

Here's an analogy to clarify how God works with humans. God has a signed contract, with the blood of Jesus Christ, to forgive sin. That contract is ready for anyone God calls. But that contract, like any contract, is only valid when the second party's signature is affixed to it. The person must accept the conditions, the blood of Christ, for the forgiveness of their sins. Only then are they no longer under the schoolmaster of the law, but they do have other obligations, which we will discuss in the last Section of this book.

The point of this chapter is that until a person signs the contract with God, they are under the schoolmaster, under the law. And the basis of that law is the Ten Commandments. Is that a good or bad situation for those under the law? To have a schoolmaster?

**Romans 7:10-14**

10 And the commandment, which was ordained to life (Sam: positive influence on the neshama-ruach), I found to be unto death (When Paul *signed the contract*).

11 For sin, taking occasion by the commandment, deceived me, and by it slew me (Sam: the law is the tutor explaining/defining what sin is).

12 Wherefore the law is holy, and the commandment holy, and just, and good. (Sam: these are the Ten Commandments that are the foundation of morality).

13 Was then that which is good made death unto me? (Sam: Paul is asking, "Is the law bad?") God forbid (No). But sin, that it might appear sin (the commandments tutor us about sin), working death in me by that which is good; that sin by the commandment might become exceeding sinful.

14 For we know that the law is spiritual: but I am carnal, sold under sin. (Sam: the Ten Commandments define the code of morality, it is this spiritual law that should impact the neshama-ruach of all humans; this is God's law impacting the mind, appropriate psychology leading to good mental health).

God's Word establishes that the Ten Commandments teach us what sin is and, therefore, what morality is. They show us what our thoughts, free choices, and behavior should be, what should influence each human being's consciousness and mind, and what should not. It is positive and negative psychology. Over the following chapters, we shall show the extent of these fundamental rules for life; morality and its favorable impact on mental health.

# 38. Here are Godly Ethics Approved in the Bible for All Humankind

**Godly ethics, one code from a higher source than humans, should be our guide for appropriate behavior. That blueprint exists, but unfortunately, humans are not receptive.**

God clothed Adam and Eve with a way of life to live outside the Garden of Eden in psychological harmony. Each of their descendants is *under the law*[1], defined, at minimum, as the Ten Commandments[2], Godly ethics, until the appointed time of their calling by the Father. In this chapter, we continue to define that *law*. Regarding psychology, in 2023, the *law* refers to the morality or ethics encompassing our behavior, the good and bad actions that

---

1. https://theexplanation.com/morality-universal-code-defines-good-behavior/

2. https://theexplanation.com/morality-universal-code-defines-good-behavior/

govern our interrelationship with the world, the material resources at our disposal, and the people in our sphere of influence.

## Godly Ethics and Psychology

This image incorporates the Ten Commandments into psychology. They surround our exterior influences, like a guardrail we grip so we don't tumble off the edge. The Ten Commandments stop us from falling into bad behavior and plunging into suffering.

Figure 40. Godly ethics and psychology

Notice eight of the ten commandments are in red; these are the *do-nots*. Only two are in green; these are the *dos*. Again, the emphasis is on the *do-nots*; otherwise, you will topple over the brim into physical and mental ill-health.

A guardrail also keeps you on the right path of good corporal and emotional health. That's the role of remembering the Sabbath (which I cannot elaborate on here, read this chapter[3] in *Evidence for Bible Wisdom*). I hope the importance of honoring your father and mother is evident to you; unfortunately, this is no longer the case in many circles. We've fallen off the edge, and sadly, our kids are paying a heavy mental health penalty, as are parents, because we're not following God's ethics.

One might ask, are humans capable of applying the Ten Commandments? Of course, nobody can do that perfectly, but could humans tend in that direction and stay more within the bounds of the guardrails?

In the image, note the yellow background behind the Ten Commandments; it represents the spirit in (hu)man(s) we discussed in Chapter 25. God provides each human with the spirit (with a small *s*) to accomplish the duties He's assigned to them. "For what man knows the things of a man, save the spirit of man which is in him?" (1 Corinthians 2:11, I will quote the rest of the verse in Section VII). The spirit of man is the mind power we possess to accomplish the five aspects of consciousness, one of which is how humans function (see image above).

God gave us the spirit-power and the method, the Ten Commandments, to reach well-being, including mental stability, through the application of Godly ethics.

God's standards, the Commandments, as established by His Word for the well-being of all people, guide the five areas of human

---

3. https://theexplanation.com/meaning-of-the-sabbath-day-god-rested-we-rest/

consciousness, our life here and now. Those five areas are why God created Earth and placed humans here. As much as we align these guidelines with our principles, we benefit, individually and collectively, from mental health and prosperity in our lives and community.

The Creator knows how His Creation functions best; He provided the instruction manual. For example, a car owner cannot decide how to do maintenance on the vehicle; if they don't follow manufacturer instructions sooner or later, they'll run into problems. With humans, this does not mean a total absence of setbacks; it does ensure a stable society. Wouldn't we enjoy that?

The Bible states that life's results correlate to how we live our lives. "Be not deceived; God is not mocked: for whatsoever a man sows, that shall he also reap" (Galatians 6:7). It's our choice to live positively (put on God's clothing) or negatively (put on fig leaves). Psychology exists to help babies, children, and adolescents put on God's clothing from the start of their lives. On the other hand, remedial psychology helps those who, for whatever reason, have wrapped themselves in fig leaves, in negative worldly influences, take off such dirty clothing and don clean clothes instead.

Let me add a corollary here. If psychologists or instructors are themselves wearing fig leaves, that's the blind leading the blind, and both will tumble off the cliff. "Let them alone: they be blind leaders of the blind. And if the blind lead the blind, both shall fall into the ditch" (Matthew 15:14). If science and psychology don't know what the mind is, how can they treat it? Could this situation be the cause of our mental health state today?

## Adam and Eve, Natural Law, and Old Testament Godly Ethics

# MIND-BODY PROBLEM SOLVED

Adam and Eve needed the know-how, Godly ethics, and rules to play and win at relationships and rulership in their new location, Eden. So God clothed Adam and Eve. In addition, He gave them *physical* protection. Figuratively, we see this as the instruction *to correctly reason and lead their lives on a physical plain in the new world*[4]. *The Explanation* aims to elucidate the difference between human and God's ways through God's Word. Humans have figured out a few of these Godly ethics through observation and intuition.

### Romans 2:14-15

14 For when the Gentiles, which have not the law, do by nature the things contained in the law (Sam: The Old Testament Godly ethics), these, having not the law, are a law unto themselves:

15 Which shew the work of the law written in their hearts, their conscience also bearing witness, and their thoughts the mean while accusing or else excusing one another.

Natural law is a theory in ethics[5] and philosophy that says humans possess intrinsic values that govern their reasoning and behavior. If any person, family, or nation applies Godly ethics, they will be blessed physically. Of course, there will be sorrow, but with that sorrow will also come benefits. God wants His and all UNconverted nations to maintain balanced physical and mental lives.

Here's a quick summary of laws and statutes; you can read more details here[6]. We can call them anything we want, rules, ways, and

---

4. https://theexplanation.com/morality-universal-code-defines-good-behavior/

5. https://www.investopedia.com/terms/n/natural-law.asp#toc-examples-of-natural-law

6. https://theexplanation.com/critical-thinking-antidote-to-the-agony-of-humankind/

ethics; this chapter calls them Godly ethics. It's basic; there are many other references to these vast subjects. The idea here is to realize that God expects us, individuals and nations, to follow law and order. These Godly ethics relate to two of the five characteristics of our consciousness.

## Relational Laws

- Deuteronomy 15:7-11 How to help the poor. 24:14 Respect of servants and poor
- 24:19 At harvest: leaving a portion for the stranger (foreigner), fatherless, widow (23:24)
- 24:6, 10 Making loans to the poor
- 21:10 Dating
- 21:15 Marriage
- 21:18 Parenting
- 22:13 Men/women relations: adultery (verse 22), rape (25), divorce (24:1)

## Rulership Laws

- Deuteronomy 17:13 How a King should rule. His responsibilities
- 19 Justice in the Community
- 19:2 How to handle different types of murderers (21:1)
- 19:14 Respect of property (21:22)
- 19:15 The role of witnesses in Justice
- 19:22 Capital punishment[7] (a vast subject to be understood in the context of what death is[8])
- 24:7 Slavery[9] (another contentious issue to be understood

---

7. https://theexplanation.com/true-justice-in-old-testament-savage-or-salutary-evidence/

8. https://theexplanation.com/what-is-death-rest-in-peace-or-dust-which-why/

9. https://theexplanation.com/slavery-labor-working-conditions-practical-bible-wisdom/

- in that context)
- 24:14 Employee relations
- 24:8 Contagious diseases. Directives on how to handle Coronavirus
- 25 Justice includes measured punishment, retribution, and rehabilitation, but there's no reference to prison
- 25:4 Treatment of animals (22:1-6)

Do a detailed study to see that each judgment can be judiciously adapted and applied to contemporary cases. All aspects of life are covered here. Do not denigrate the laws in the Old Testament. The Apostle Paul knew them intimately and gave recommendations about their application. Retain his inspired evaluation of these laws. We'll see more in the next chapter.

**2 Corinthians 3:7**

> But if the ministration of death, written and engraven in stones, was glorious, so that the children of Israel could not stedfastly behold the face of Moses for the glory of his countenance; which glory was to be done away:

Punishment, and even punishment by death, are necessary elements of Justice to maintain law and order. Paul states Godly ethics; the law is GLORIOUS. Many focus on the end of this verse, "which glory was to be done away." YES, done away for repentant believers in Christ, those in the Church, no longer under the law[10], to whom Paul is writing—a small minority. But the key is that these glorious Godly ethics would bring peace and prosperity to all people worldwide. Here's the implication.

---

10. https://theexplanation.com/morality-universal-code-defines-good-behavior/

God did not give this glorious code of ethics just for Israel's sake. It was for the whole world. Meditate on the following passage. Generally overlooked, but a key to understanding God and how He works with the UNconverted worldwide. Israel was to be a beacon nation. The light shining in the dark, projecting Godly ethics, His statutes, judgments, and law (see verse 8 below). Israel and ALL nations can and should recognize GOD as *the* God and His moral code as the one leading to harmony.

**Deuteronomy 4:5-9**

5 Behold, I have taught you statutes and judgments, even as the LORD my God commanded me, that you should do so in the land whither you go to possess it.

6 Keep therefore and do them; for this is your wisdom and your understanding in the sight of the nations, which shall hear all these statutes, and say, Surely this great nation is a wise and understanding people.

7 For what nation is there so great, who has God so nigh to them, as the LORD our God is in all things that we call upon him for?

8 And what nation is there so great, that has statutes and judgments so righteous as all this law, which I set before you this day?

9 Only take heed to yourself, and keep your soul diligently, lest you forget the things which your eyes have seen, and lest they depart from your heart all the days of your life: but teach them your sons, and your sons' sons; (Sam: down through the generations)

Only when a nation is ready to accept these Godly ethics, adjusted for modern living, will God intervene to bless that nation. Study the examples of Jonah sent to Nineveh (Book of Jonah) or King Josiah (2 Kings 22-23). God did NOT ask for their spiritual conversion. Even Nineveh, not an Israelite nation, benefited from the blessings of the glorious law engraved in stones, as Paul put it.

Adam and Eve ate from the forbidden Tree. They warranted *death*. But always keep in mind God wants *life* to prevail, "Say to them, As I live, says the Lord GOD, I have no pleasure in the death of the wicked; but that the wicked turn from his way and live: turn you, turn you from your evil ways; for why will you die, O house of Israel?" (Ezekiel 33:11).

It was valid for Israel and Nineveh and is just as accurate for individuals and any nation today. Turning from evil ways to God's ethics is part of the answer to many of the world's problems and would undoubtedly be beneficial to mental health.

# 39. Bible Proverbs, the Guiding Rules for Life in the 21st Century

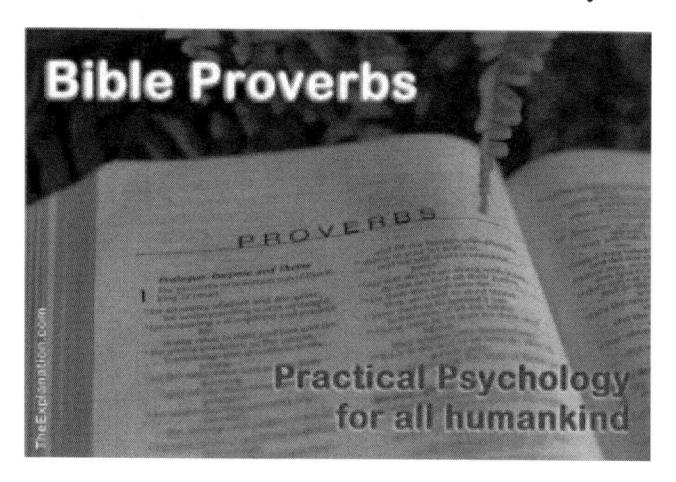

**Bible Proverbs are the world's compass to living physically and mentally healthy lives in our contemporary world.**

Why Bible Proverbs and not Deuteronomy? The latter gave the basis for national law as Israel entered a new country. National or civil laws covered all aspects of life; judges administered laws regarding land, crime, commerce, property, and relationships. In addition, there was a whole tribe and Priesthood to oversee worship and education. In a national setting with UNconverted citizens, these glorious, righteous laws are the best recipe for peace and prosperity for the entire population[1].

On the other hand, Proverbs addresses morality given from a father to his son. These are rules (call them whatever you want) each person can take to heart to govern their own life. These principles

---

1. https://theexplanation.com/godly-ethics-approved-bible-for-all-humankind/

apply the Ten Commandments on a personal level in the 21st century. Here's a national law in Deuteronomy that sounds immoral; however, if you consider this son as a thug terrorizing women or a hoodlum pushing drugs on adolescents, who won't listen to reason, an incorrigible, entrenched in their own ways, it takes on a different light.

**Deuteronomy 21:18-21**

18 If a man have a stubborn and rebellious son, which will not obey the voice of his father, or the voice of his mother, and that, when they have chastened him, will not hearken to them:

19 Then shall his father and his mother lay hold on him, and bring him out to the elders of his city, and to the gate of his place;

20 And they shall say to the elders of his city, This our son is stubborn and rebellious, he will not obey our voice; he is a glutton, and a drunkard.

21 And all the men of his city shall stone him with stones, that he die: so shall you put evil away from among you; and all Israel shall hear, and fear.

In Deuteronomy, the nation and the community take precedence over the individual[2]. Preserving the well-being of women and adolescents has priority over the crime of one individual. In Bible Proverbs, the emphasis is on prevention. We find a different, more modern approach to a severe individual problem.

---

2. https://theexplanation.com/individual-rights-vs-collective-rights-the-bible-balance/

**Proverbs 13:24** He that spares his *rod* (H7626) hates his son: but he that loves him *chastens* (H4148) him betimes.

**Proverbs 22:15** Foolishness is bound in the heart of a child; but the *rod* (H7626) of *correction* (H4148) shall drive it far from him.

**Proverbs 29:15** The *rod* (H7626) and *reproof* (H8433) give wisdom: but a child left to himself brings his mother to shame.

Before we become indignant at corporal punishment (which was not the case in 1600 when the translators used the term *rod*), let's see the meanings of this Biblical Hebrew word, as well as *correction* (H4148) and *reproof* (H8433).

## H7626

שֵׁבֶט shêbeṭ shay'-bet; from an unused root probably meaning to branch off; a scion, i.e. (literally) a stick (for punishing, writing, fighting, ruling, walking, etc.) or (figuratively) a clan:

KJV - × correction, dart, rod, sceptre, staff, tribe.

## H4148

מוּסָר mûwçâr moo-sawr'; from H3256 (יָסַר); properly, chastisement; figuratively, reproof, warning or instruction; also restraint:

KJV - bond, chastening(-eth), chastisement, check, correction, discipline, doctrine, instruction, rebuke.

H8433

תּוֹכֵחָה tôwkêchâh to-kay-khaw'; and תּוֹכַחַת; from H3198 (יָכַח); chastisement; figuratively (by words) correction, refutation, proof (even in defence):

KJV - argument, × chastened, correction, reasoning, rebuke, reproof, × be (often) reproved.

There's chastisement, but note how it's kept in *check* and includes *discipline*, *doctrine*, *instruction*, *reasoning*, and the like. This is not punishment for punishment's sake; it involves remedial direction to transform the individual's behavior. As I pointed out in the last chapter[3], "I have no pleasure in the death of the wicked; but that the wicked turn from his way and live:" (Ezekiel 33:11). That is the goal of the father and mother of this son.

The application of Bible Proverbs is practical psychology[4]. It opens the way to physical and mental health, a more level-headed society.

In one sense, if this child had been raised according to the principles in Proverbs, s/he would not be in this position of requiring remedial psychology. But, unfortunately, we don't live in a perfect world with perfect parents or children. Restoring physical and mental health with doctors and psychologists is part of life, but it would be infinitely better if done in God's way.

## Bible Proverbs

The rules for life are concentrated in one book. Bible Proverbs. Therein we find ALL the basics covering mainly INDIVIDUAL laws but also broaching NATIONAL and WORSHIP laws. The

---

3. https://theexplanation.com/godly-ethics-approved-bible-for-all-humankind/

4. https://theexplanation.com/rules-for-life-wisdom-for-living-abundantly-in-the-world/

study of Proverbs should be a daily exercise. Imagine if we practiced it at home and in school. We desperately need an essential Code of Ethics in a secular society. Bible Proverbs puts God first, where He should be. But, even if you take God out of the picture, the Proverbs contain sufficient advice to establish balanced individual citizens in a peaceful nation.

Proverbs Chapter 1 sets the stage, with the preface including the most vital points to keep in mind.

**Instruction**: 1:2 The proverbs of Solomon the son of David, king of Israel; To know wisdom and instruction; to perceive the words of understanding; (Sam: In every aspect of our lives, this yields mental peace).

**Fear of the Lord**: 1:7 The fear of the LORD is the beginning of knowledge: but fools despise wisdom and instruction.

This proverb is where it all starts. It has nothing to do with *The Explanation* or *Sam Kneller*. Right at the outset, the first five minutes of the play, as I've said, the book of Proverbs makes it clear. The respect and reverence of God are where wisdom and the rules of life begin; this summarizes the first four of the Ten Commandments. Bible Proverbs expands all Ten in practical psychological terms for all humankind in our society today.

**Listen**: 1:8 My son, hear the instruction of your father, and forsake not the law of your mother: (Sam: Are we teaching young people, who become parents, the Bible Proverbs on a family, national, and international level?)

**Wisdom**: 1:20 Wisdom cries without; she utters her voice in the streets:

Bible Proverbs has been around and available for thousands of years. It's even published separately and is possibly the most prolific book in the world. It is the book of practical wisdom.

## Consciousness, Mind, and Bible Proverbs.

Below are the five areas of human consciousness[5] coupled with a few Bible Proverbs to get you started. This study is lengthy but practical and rewarding. Each Proverb can be associated with one or more of the Ten Commandments and fits into one or more areas influencing and affecting our mental health. Their study, meditation, and application[6] would go a long way to improving our quality of life.

## Purpose - Goals

- **Professional goals** Proverbs 12:11 He that tills his land shall be satisfied with bread: but he that follows vain persons is void of understanding
- **Personal growth** 3:13 Happy is the man that finds wisdom, and the man that gets understanding
- **Health** 3:7-8 Do not be wise in your own eyes; fear the Lord and shun evil. This will bring health to your body and nourishment to your bones
- **Family** 22:6 Train up a child in the way he should go: and when he is old, he will not depart from it

## How Humans Function

- **Anger** 14:17 He that is soon angry deals foolishly: and a man of wicked devices is hated

---

5. https://theexplanation.com/psychology-best-bible-definition-for-humans/
6. https://unlockbiblemeaning.com

- **Integrity** 11:3 The integrity of the upright shall guide them: but the perverseness of transgressors shall destroy them. (We need more honesty today)
- **Thoughts** 12:5 The thoughts of the righteous are right: but the counsels of the wicked are deceit. (We need more upright thinking. We're not teaching people How To Think[7])

## How Humans Socialize (Relationships)

- **Parents** 1:8 My son, hear the instruction of your father, and forsake not the law of your mother: (Family, father, mother, and children with proper parental guidance)
- **Children** 17:25 A foolish son is a grief to his father, and bitterness to her that bare him. (Often the result of poor parenting. Not always, for sure. But parents must invest in the correct raising of their children)
- **Husband** 31:23 Her husband is known in the gates, when he sits among the elders of the land
- **Wife** 14:1 Every wise woman builds her house: but the foolish plucks it down with her hands
- **Friendship** 18:24 A man that has friends must shew himself friendly: and there is a friend that sticks closer than a brother. (True friendship is a necessary part of life)

## How Humans Rule (Rulership)

- **Counsel** 11:14 Where no counsel is, the people fall: but in the multitude of counselors there is safety. (This can refer to competent leadership and government)
- **Righteous-wicked** 10:16 The labour of the righteous

---

7. https://theexplanation.com/5-types-of-reasoning-life-hangs-ultimate-choice/

tends to life: the fruit of the wicked to sin
- **Lies** 19:5 A false witness shall not be unpunished, and he that speaks lies shall not escape. (the antidote to fake news)
- **Ruler** 29:4 The king by judgment establishes the land: but he that receives gifts overthrows it. (Bribes and bad influence. Read chapter 29, all about national leadership for ALL countries)

## How Humans Reason

- **Arrogance** 16:25 There is a way that seems right to a man, but the end thereof are the ways of death
- **Contempt** 15:32, 18:3 He that refuses instruction despises his own soul: but he that hears reproof gets understanding
- **Reflection** 2:11 Discretion (or *thought*) shall preserve you, understanding shall keep you: (Proper examination of a subject. how about critical thinking to reason correctly)

Bible Proverbs cover all the bases for a balanced and sane life. We could modernize the language into a *How To Live* book. I'd be glad to hear from you if anyone is interested in such a project.

You'll notice that there's not much about worship. Not because we shouldn't worship God. The book is clear that all starts with God, but this book is designed for all UNconverted people. It lays bare the fundamentals for ALL populations, everywhere, throughout history, regarding how to live a decent life. That said, there is enough about God to know His plan is being accomplished, and the wise person is aware of the existence of God.

- **God's presence** 17:3 The fining pot is for silver, and the furnace for gold: but the LORD tries the hearts. (The discerning student of Proverbs knows that God oversees the world)
- **God's plans** 19:21 There are many devices in a man's heart; nevertheless the counsel of the LORD, that shall stand
- **God's knowledge** 22:12 The eyes of the LORD preserve knowledge, and he overthrows the words of the transgressor. (God will have the upper hand. It's worthwhile taking a closer look at His ways)

God clothed Adam and Eve with these rules for life. He clothed humankind down through the centuries, including you and me today, with these rules; this is the basis for society, whether they believe in God or not. Authors like Jordan Peterson, Yuval Harari, and others include some secular principles elaborated in Bible Proverbs. But they are short on the Godly-oriented preface and even God Himself. It's only when nations and their citizens, collectively and individually, apply this to the best of their mental capacity that we'll harvest the blessings God promised to pour out on those that look to Him and lead a decent way of life.

At the beginning of Deuteronomy, that Old Testament law for Israel and all nations, God inspired this passage about passing the information down through the generations.

### Deuteronomy 6:5-7

5 And you shall love the LORD your God with all your heart, and with all your soul, and with all your might.

6 And these words, which I command you this day, shall be in your heart:

7 And you shall teach them diligently to your children, and shall talk of them when you sit in your house, and when you walk by the way, and when you lie down, and when you rise up.

Isn't that clear enough?

The New Testament corroborates this impregnation of God's rules for life, "Be mindFUL of the words which were spoken before by the holy prophets..." (2 Peter 3:2). This is true mindFULness that we hear so much about. We are to fill our minds, not empty them, brimFUL of Bible Proverbs, the rules for life. God's ways, elaborated in His manual, are practical psychology, representing the way to physical and mental health for all humankind.

# 40. Warring Proverbs. Is Each of Us Fighting the Good Fight?

**Warring Proverbs. We read the Proverbs for their good intentions. But do we pay attention to their red-light warnings?**

Is all wisdom valid wisdom? Warring Proverbs slam dunks an astounding NO. There is positive and negative wisdom, and all humans have a choice.

God gave us the book of Proverbs as the practical expression of the Ten Commandments[1]. It is the clothing of Adam and Eve's descendants[2] so they could live appropriately through history and into the 21st century. The Proverbs are guidelines to keep us from going over the edge of the negative influences all humans are subject to.

---

1. https://theexplanation.com/bible-proverbs-rules-for-life-in-21st-century/

2. https://theexplanation.com/human-reasoning-crushes-gods-good-for-people/

Psychologically, our minds can be swayed into good or bad knowledge and understanding; this is the warring wisdom to which each human is exposed. Proverbs is designed to keep the world population on the straight and narrow.

### Proverbs 8:1, 35

> 1 Does not wisdom cry? and understanding put forth her voice?
>
> 35 For *whoso finds me* finds life, and shall obtain *favour of the LORD*.

Note *whoso finds me*... the wisdom in Proverbs is accessible to everyone worldwide. It opens the way to *favor from God*. This wisdom is the spiritual Prozac that beats all anti-depressants and anxiety drugs; It's all here in this book, free for worldwide consumption.

## Warring Proverbs, Anti-Proverbs

In contrast to God's wisdom, there's *human wisdom* or anti-wisdom because humankind thinks it can do it better than its Creator. So humans continue to dress in fig leaves and reject God's clothing[3].

### Proverbs 21:30

> There is no wisdom nor understanding nor counsel against the LORD.

Here's a straightforward fundamental statement when evaluating arguments about God and the Bible. The intelligentsia of this world has far more degrees, education, facts, and knowledge than

---

3. https://theexplanation.com/godly-ethics-approved-bible-for-all-humankind/

most of the readers of this book, myself included. The subject has nothing to do with people's qualifications; it has to do with wisdom in conformity with, and not warring against, God's wisdom.

Here are a few of what I call *anti-proverbs*. The guardrail Proverbs are there to keep us from falling into these damaging practices. Anti-proverbs (red, underlined) are the abyss and mental turmoil we topple into.

> **Proverbs 1:7** The *fear of the LORD* is the beginning of knowledge: but fools despise wisdom and instruction.
>
> **Pro. 12:24** The hand of the *diligent* shall bear rule: but the slothful shall be under tribute.
>
> **Pro. 15:32** He that refuses instruction despises his own soul: but he that *hears reproof* gets understanding.
>
> **Pro. 18:21** Death and *life* are in the power of the tongue: and they that love it shall eat the fruit thereof.
>
> **Pro. 20:3** It is an honour for a man to *cease from strife*: but every fool will be meddling.
>
> **Pro. 21:2** Every way of a man is right in his own eyes: but the LORD ponders the hearts.

Personal wisdom *is right in his/her own eyes*; it's the counsel against the LORD (Pro. 21:30). There's no remedy, and that's why there's no use getting into debates with people who have no intention of being reasonable. Pro. 23:9 "Speak not in the ears of a fool: for he will despise the wisdom of your words."

We can add a further three circles to explain human behavior. Proverbs (inner green circle); God's psychological guardrail protects human consciousness and mind. Anti-proverbs (outer red circle); human reasoning and behavior that exposes and harms consciousness and mind. The few verses above represent these opposing green and red circles. In between (blue circle) are our warring minds (the red and green arrows) being pulled to the proverbs, the anti-proverbs, the wisdom or the anti-wisdom. Human functioning, purpose, reasoning, socialization, and rulership pay a stiff penalty in anxiety and depression when we make wrong choices.

Figure 41. Wisdom and anti-wisdom in Proverbs

## Wisdom and Anti-Wisdom in Proverbs, Two Warring Women

In Proverbs, two women personify *wisdom*. The words *wisdom* or *wise* appear over 115 times in Proverbs; in fact, wisdom is mentioned in every chapter of this book.

Both women have positive points, but one also has negative characteristics. Similar to the forbidden fruit that looked attractive but had disastrous results that weren't evident from the outside.

Why does a woman portray both types of wisdom in Proverbs? The book is about a father addressing his son with rules for life. And one of the most important principles is choosing that one and only partner, his future wife. It is, therefore, fitting that the book ends with an entire chapter devoted to what we call the virtuous woman[4]. It's the summary of the choice of a very wise woman, the appropriate wisdom each person should determine.

Between chapters one and thirty-one, the father expands on all types of women, from the best to the worst, warring against each other. They are warnings and encouragements.

## The *Good Woman-Godly Wisdom*

> **Proverbs 1:20** Wisdom cries without; she utters her voice in the streets:
>
> **2:2** So that you incline your ear to wisdom, and apply your heart to understanding;
>
> **2:6** For the LORD gives wisdom: out of his mouth comes knowledge and understanding.
>
> **2:10** When wisdom enters into your heart, and knowledge is pleasant to your soul;

---

4. https://theexplanation.com/proverbs-31-feminism-and-womens-rights-what-mix/

**3:13** Happy is the man that finds wisdom, and the man that gets understanding.

We can't look at all the verses here; go to UnlockBibleMeaning.com[5]. Search for and study all the verses with *wisdom* and *wise* in Proverbs; this is the way to psychological health. From a stable, loving marriage perspective, a wise man should search for this in a partner.

## The <u>Bad Woman-Human Wisdom</u>

### Proverbs 5:1-8

1 My son, attend to my wisdom, and bow your ear to my understanding:

2 That you may regard discretion, and that your lips may keep knowledge.

3 For the lips of a strange woman drop as an honeycomb, and her mouth is smoother than oil:

4 But her end is bitter as wormwood, sharp as a twoedged sword.

5 Her feet go down to death; her steps take hold on hell.

6 Lest you should ponder the path of life, her ways are *moveable* (fugitive), that you can not know them.

7 Hear me now therefore, O you children, and depart not from the words of my mouth.

---

5. https://unlockbiblemeaning.com

8 Remove your way far from her, and come not nigh the door of her house:

Do you see how God refers to this warring between the two wisdoms and His urging to choose the right one while still leaving us the choice? You can't see this in English, but *moveable* in verse 6 is the same Hebrew as Cain the *fugitive* in Genesis 4:12, 14. This nasty woman is a fugitive; you cannot know her character unless you follow God's wisdom.

**Proverbs 7:7-14, 27**

7 And beheld among the simple ones, I discerned among the youths, a young man void of understanding,

8 Passing through the street near her corner; and he went the way to her house,

9 In the twilight, in the evening, in the black and dark night (Sam: like Adam and Eve who hid in the forest[6]):

10 And, behold, there met him a woman with the attire of an *harlot*, and *subtil* of heart (Sam: clever and intelligent)

11 (She is loud and stubborn; her feet abide not in her house:

12 Now is she without, now in the streets, and lies in wait at every corner.) (Sam: negative wisdom perseveres, that's why continuous warring against it is vital)

---

6. https://theexplanation.com/human-reasoning-crushes-gods-good-for-people/

13 So she caught him, and kissed him, and with an impudent face said to him,

14 I have peace offerings with me; this day have *I payed my vows*. (Sam: presents herself as religious, but it's all a facade)

27 Her house is the way to hell, going down to the chambers of death.

## Excellent Godly Wisdom: Chochma (H2451)

Proverbs is the book of Godly wisdom warring against human wisdom. This concept of one wisdom leading to death and the other to life can be challenging to assimilate. Wouldn't all wisdom lead to life? No, says God's Word. Let's compare them.

### Ezekiel 28:12

Son of man, take up a lamentation upon the king of Tyrus, and say to him, Thus says the Lord God; You sealed up the sum, full of *wisdom* (H2451), and perfect in beauty.

The King of Tyrus symbolizes one of the highest angels in God's realm, Lucifer. No man can have full wisdom (other than Jesus Christ) and beauty; Lucifer did[7]. Here's Strong's annotation for this top-of-the-class wisdom, the summum of Godly wisdom which characterized this angel, Lucifer, excellent wisdom the father admonishes his son to obtain in Proverbs.

### H2451

---

7. https://theexplanation.com/fallen-from-heaven-the-fate-of-lucifer/

חָכְמָה chokmâh khok-maw'; from H2449 (חָכַם); wisdom (in a good sense):

KJV – skilful, wisdom, wisely, wit.

It is a unique type of superior wisdom. You're probably familiar with this word if you've been around the Jewish community. When their Rabbis and scholars evoke a wise saying or draw a wise lesson from the Torah or Gemara, they earn the epitaph, *chacham*. Chacham is a derivative of H2451 (chochma), indicating the highest possible wisdom, God's wisdom. In the New Testament, we find the Pharisees, Sadducees, and Scribes parading around as the *chachams* of the religious world.

## Human Wisdom, *Good* but Very Fallible: Sakal (H7919)

In Genesis 3.6, when Eve, under the influence of the Serpent, contemplates the tree of knowledge of good and evil and sees "a tree to be desired to make one *wise* (H7919)," a totally different Biblical Hebrew word is used here. It's a translation shortcoming; this is definitely wisdom, but there's a distinct difference from *chochma*.

Here, it is *sakal* wisdom. It includes both *good qualities when humans use correct reasoning* and a bad side because it is devoid of Godly wisdom. This sakal wisdom is the characteristic of the Tree of *GOOD* and EVIL; even sound human wisdom ultimately leads to death. We need Godly wisdom.

### H7919

שָׂכַל sâkal saw-kal'; a primitive root; to be (causatively, make or act) circumspect and hence, intelligent:

> KJV – consider, expert, instruct, prosper, (deal) prudent(-ly), (give) skill(-ful), have good success, teach, (have, make to) understand(-ing), wisdom, (be, behave self, consider, make) wise(-ly), guide wittingly.

Reading the above annotation and translations, everything looks dandy; I'd dare say that's the kind of *sakal* wisdom we'd all like. Yes and no. This wisdom (H7919) includes many excellent attributes, but *sakal* wisdom differs from *chacham* wisdom. If we want to understand the contours of these puzzle pieces fully, it is essential to comprehend the difference between these two types of *wisdoms*[8] because the contrast is night and day.

To comprehend the pseudo wisdom Eve saw in the Tree of Knowledge of Good and Evil, which leads to death, study this chapter[9] in the book *Agony of Humankind and the Antidote* to grasp the difference between chacham and sakal wisdom. Let's illustrate it with a New Testament passage.

### 1 Corinthians 2:11-14

> 11 For what man knows the things of a man, save the spirit of man which is in him (SAKAL things)? even so the things of God knows no man, but the Spirit of God (CHOCHMA things).

> 12 Now we have received, not the spirit of the world (SAKAL), but the spirit which is of God (CHOCHMA); that we might know the things that are freely given to us of God.

---

8. https://theexplanation.com/fallen-from-heaven-the-fate-of-lucifer/

9. https://theexplanation.com/wisdom-of-god-or-the-serpent-which-one-roused-eve/

13 Which things also we speak, not in the words which man's wisdom teaches (SAKAL wisdom), but which the Holy Ghost teacheth; comparing spiritual things with spiritual (CHOCHMA wisdom).

14 But the natural man receive not the things of the Spirit of God: for they are foolishness unto him: neither can he know them, because they are spiritually discerned.

Wisdom is ONE word in English, but it covers TWO very different concepts; this is a major piece of the puzzle, and we must have the correct contours if we hope to understand the psychology of humankind. Why the world is in its present state, and the kind of wisdom it will take to move it to real peace and prosperity.

Section VI of *Mind-Body Problem Solved* addresses the masses of humans devoid of chochma wisdom; God only expects all humans to apply the GOOD part of SAKAL wisdom; that's setting our consciousness on the right track regarding learning how to function with a dual nature and choose the correct behavior. We are all in a warring posture for our own and others' minds and well-being: having a life purpose, integrating into our family and society, ruling our responsibilities correctly, and reasoning sanely.

That's the primary role of parents in preventive psychology and psychologists in remedial practice. Children, adolescents, and adults of all ages and backgrounds cannot make giant leaps at solving their psychological dramas, but the goal is to help them accomplish one little step at a time. Point them and accompany them in the right direction using the Proverbs guidelines.

# 41. Can Satan Influence and even Corrupt a Human Mind? Yes.

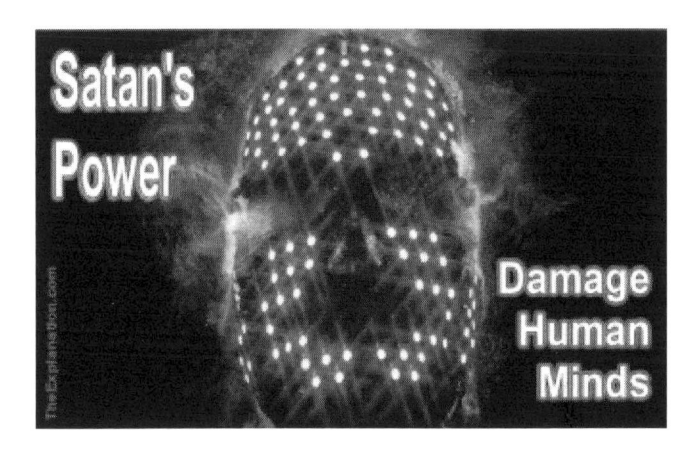

**Psychology is about influences on our consciousness and mind. Satan the Devil labors at that to damage humans to their utmost.**

The Serpent aims to weaken, break, and rip apart the link between humans and God. Let's be brutally honest; it has done an excellent job! That's not my evaluation; the Bible tells us this. We have to broach a challenging but necessary subject. Our mental stability depends on it. In the last chapter, we discussed warring Proverbs. It is war, and there's a serious fight going on, and most are not even aware of it.

Psychology doesn't know what the mind is nor what the battle for human minds is. It's spiritual warfare. The Apostle Paul, inspired by God, writes, "For we wrestle not against flesh and blood, but against principalities, against *powers*, against the rulers of the *darkness of this world*, against *spiritual wickedness in high places"* (Ephesians 6:12).

Scripture is point blank about the origin of the powerful evil influences all humans are subject to. They are spiritual, just like the mind and consciousness. It's not a question of maybe; this is reality. Unfortunately, such affirmations are considered nonsense in many, probably most circles. You're at a terrible disadvantage if you don't even identify your opponent and know what weapons they're wielding. That's the general case today and a primary reason for our degrading mental health. Paul is explicit in designating the enemy.

Satan uses obscure observation, phony philosophy, distorted science, and irreverent religion to bewilder the minds of humans. This Section about practical psychology would be amiss not to address this phenomenon. The third Section of the book *Agony of Humankind and the Antidote*[1] on *Serpent Influence* elaborates on all these areas. This chapter drives this point home. *The Serpent is out for mind control*[2].

It is pulling out all the stops to inflict as much harm as possible. The Apostle Paul warns the Church in Ephesia about this phenomenon. The following verses contain essential principles about the Serpent and its combat against humankind. Given the available space, we can only peek into its depth. I invite you to deepen your understanding using the Bible study tools at UnlockBibleMeaning.com[3].

In Ephesians 2, we find the Serpent's rulership (*prince*) and authority (*power*) to assume its role. Next, we see the means (*spirit*) by which Satan accomplishes its task and the medium (*air*) where

---

1. https://theexplanation.com/category/read-agony-oh-online/3-serpent-influence/

2. *https://theexplanation.com/mind-control-the-serpents-number-one-goal/*

3. https://unlockbiblemeaning.com

it functions. We also witness the specific areas of humankind Satan targets (*flesh*, *mind*) and, finally, its worldwide influence (*nature*, *children of disobedience*, *wrath*).

**Ephesians 2:2-3**

2 Wherein in time past you walked according to the course of this world, according to the *prince* (G758) of the *power* (G1849) of the *air* (G109), the *spirit* (G4151) that now works in the children of *disobedience* (G543):

3 Among whom also we all had our conversation in times past in the lusts of our *flesh* (G4561), fulfilling the desires of the *flesh* (G4561) and of the *mind* (G1271); and were by *nature* (G5449) the children of *wrath* (G3709), even as others.

There is much to meditate on here. It's interesting to look at the root meaning of words. For instance, *disobedience* (G543) includes *unbelief*, which describes many people. Check the basis of *wrath*; you'll find it's *orgy*. Unfortunately, that covers extensive territory, including pornography, pedophilia, illicit sex, stalking, and gawking.

**G758 - Prince**

ἄρχων archōn ar'-khone; Present participle of G757; a first (in rank or power):

KJV - chief (ruler) magistrate, prince, ruler.

**G1849 - Power**

ἐξουσία exousia ex-oo-see'-ah; From G1832 (in the sense of ability); privilege that is (subjectively) force capacity, competency freedom or (objectively) mastery (concretely magistrate superhuman potentate token of control) delegated influence:

KJV- authority, jurisdiction, liberty, power, right, strength.

## G109 - Air

ἀήρ aēr ah-ayr'; From ἄημι aēmi (to breathe unconsciously that is respire; by analogy to blow); air (as naturally circumambient):

KJV - air. Compare G5594.

## G4151 - Spirit

πνεῦμα pneuma pnyoo'-mah; From G4154; a current of air that is breath (blast) or a breeze; by analogy or figuratively a spirit that is (human) the rational soul (by implication) vital principle mental disposition etc. or (superhuman) an angel daemon or (divine) God Christ's spirit the Holy spirit :

KJV - ghost, life, spirit (-ual -ually), mind. Compare G5590.

## G4561 - Flesh

σάρξ sarx sarx; Probably from the base of G4563; flesh (as stripped of the skin) that is (strictly) the meat of an animal (as food) or (by extension) the body (as opposed to the soul (or spirit) or as the symbol of what is external or as the means of kindred or (by implication) human nature (with its frailties (physically or morally) and passions) or (specifically) a human being (as such):

KJV - carnal (-ly + -ly minded), flesh ([-ly]).

## G1271 - Mind

διάνοια dianoia dee-an'-oy-ah; From G1223 and G3563; deep thought properly the faculty (mind or its disposition) by implication its exercise:

KJV - imagination, mind, understanding.

## G5449 - Nature

φύσις phusis foo'-sis; From G5453; growth (by germination or expansion) that is (by implication) natural production (lineal descent); by extension a genus or sort; figuratively native disposition constitution or usage:

KJV - ([man-]) kind, nature ([-al]).

## G3709 - Wrath

ὀργή orgē or-gay'; From G3713; properly desire (as a reaching forth or excitement of the mind) that is (by analogy) violent passion (ire or [justifiable] abhorrence); by implication punishment:

KJV - anger, indignation, vengeance, wrath.

The Serpent occupies the position of a prince, 1st rank on Earth. Lucifer was a top-ranking archangel until its fall[4]. Satan has the power, competency, authority, privileges, and jurisdiction, among other things, over the air. The air refers to Earth's atmosphere. Satan uses the power of its toxic spirit carried through the air. Paul is talking spiritually, but technically this is how the Serpent works. It transmits its influence via AIRwaves.

You might think this is ridiculous, but *The Explanation* spent a lot of time, in the context of the human mind, expounding the nature of God's Holy Spirit[5], what ruach is, and how it functions. The fluttering, moving, shaking[6] fluctuations of waves and frequencies[7]. Now we see the Serpent is *Master of the Air*. Satan also has its frequencies. It broadcasts directly to the human *mind* (G1271), where the imagination is. It incites the *flesh* (G4561), as discussed in *Agony* regarding UNethical behavior[8]. Through their susceptible human nature (G5449), people everywhere are pulled down by convincing publicity and other harmful influences and end up following their basic instincts, their *passions* (G3709).

These two verses express the *Agony of Humankind*. Please don't get me wrong. We can NOT blame Satan for all of our wrongdoing. Why? Because we possess free will. As such, we can and should make the right decisions to WITHSTAND these temptations. But we are weak flesh, and more often than not, we succumb to these passions.

---

4. https://theexplanation.com/fallen-from-heaven-the-fate-of-lucifer/

5. https://theexplanation.com/gods-spirit-ruach-animates-living-beings/

6. https://theexplanation.com/spirit-of-god-moved-face-waters-meaning/

7. https://theexplanation.com/fluctuation-frequency-power-spirit/

8. https://theexplanation.com/ethical-behavior-break-the-rules-heres-the-outcome/

Pliable power, spirit airwaves, free will, decisions, disposition, ALL these traits are part of the MIND and nothing else. Did you see Strong's annotation for *wrath* (G3709)? *reaching forth or excitement of the mind*. I realize Strong is not scripture, but he hit the nail on the head. *Wrath,* from the Greek word *orgy,* is the excitement of the mind. This provocation is not limited to sexual deviance. We all have our minds stimulated and incited by the wrong purposes for immoral reasons. It is how humans reason[9]: observation, philosophy, science, and, yes, religion.

Do you think *The Explanation* exaggerates when it says Satan has mind control worldwide? Reread verse 3, "Among whom also *we all* had our conversation (an old English word for *behavior*) ... and were by nature the children of wrath, even as others." Paul includes himself (we) and says, *we ALL*, ending the verse with *as others*. Those *others* were *ALL* people not associated with God's Church, of which Paul was an Apostle. In other words, everyone worldwide. Numerous other verses, including verse 2, *according to the course of this world*, corroborate this. I invite you to search them out and study them.

## The Spirit World Exists and Manifests Itself

Whether you believe the Bible or not, Satan and its shenanigans are part and parcel of the package. The spirit world exists. Satan is real; it rebelled against God[10], Who cast it and its cohort to Earth, where they continue their malicious work.

### 2 Corinthians 4:3-4

3 But if our gospel be hid, it is hid to them that are lost:

---

9. https://theexplanation.com/observation-first-way-human-reasoning/
10. https://theexplanation.com/fallen-from-heaven-the-fate-of-lucifer/

> 4 In whom the god of this world has **blinded the minds** of them which believe not, lest the light of the glorious gospel of Christ, who is the image of God, should shine unto them.

You can't get much more precise than that. The Serpent is the god of this entire world; Satan has blinded the MINDS of those who don't believe. Today, fewer and fewer believe, and even among those who do, what do they believe? The Serpent has got the upper hand through mind control. Here are some of its methods. There's no space to go into a lot of detail. There are links to further information, but I insist, do NOT get involved in these activities. There are some amazing testimonials about what Satan can do; this is real, BUT to be avoided.

## Genius

You don't have to be a Bible believer or reader to know such spirit phenomena exist. Elizabeth Gilbert investigated this and gave a TED talk[11] with over 21 million views. Ruth Stone also knows there's something to the spirit world; these are two rational human beings.

## Evil Spirit Beings

In New York, in 1976, there was a spree of murders. Police apprehended a man going by the name *Son of Sam*. He was convicted and sentenced to life imprisonment, where he still is today. In prison, over the years, he got his life together. I debated whether to include one of his testimonial videos[12] and decided to

---

11. https://www.ted.com/talks/elizabeth_gilbert_your_elusive_creative_genius

12. https://youtu.be/RdJJUcTGGVc

do so. Today, David Berkovitch, his real name, is very lucid and open about his horrific experience. Here are a few quotes.

> My life and personality were coming apart, disintegrating, being controlled by other entities that I opened myself up for. I had a propensity for that, all my life, because of the experiences I had in childhood. The trauma and everything. It opened up the door to demonic strongholds being set up in my life.

Both these videos are eloquent in the admission of a spirit world. Furthermore, it is evident; they target mind control. People should avoid such activities no matter who they are or where they are. Again, the Apostle Paul said in 1 Corinthians 14:32, "And the spirits of the prophets are subject to the prophets." Be it prophets or you and me, we are to be in control of our spirit, our mind at all times. Our mental health stands on that foundation. The next chapter will give the foundation for wholesome mental health.

# Other Malevolent Phenomena to Avoid

## Hypnotism and Medical Experiences

- Regressive therapy
- After-death experiences (Death is reality[13] and part of the *Agony of Humankind*)
- Former lives, distant, past experiences (before you were born)
- Multiple personalities

## Church and Spiritual Practices

---

13. https://theexplanation.com/what-is-death-rest-in-peace-or-dust-which-why/

- Speaking in tongues. It has biblical overtones, but don't practice it when you cannot control what happens to you, like falling down backward or being unable to react normally
- Reincarnation
- Calling on the defunct, ouija boards
- Satanic sects
- Activities in the dark, like groves and forests
- Casting out demons. Invoking the spirits. Dangerous
- Shamanism involving trances, meditation, potions, spells
- Unicult: a communal framework for promoting joy[14]. I'll let you look into this but stay away
- You will be able to gain a direct experience of your Timeless and Eternal Self rapidly—Read this for an enlightened opinion[15]

## Practices That Invoke Potent Forces From the Earth

- Ley lines
- Dowsing rods
- Feng Shui (radio and other wave frequencies can be nauseous, you should avoid them when you can, but certain practices go much further with *waves*)
- Automatic writing and drawing
- Ghosts and related paranormal activities[16]
- Haunted or enchanted places

---

14. https://theexplanation.com/mind-control-the-serpents-number-one-goal/

15. https://www.theguardian.com/world/2020/jan/09/strange-hypnotic-world-millennial-guru-bentinho-massaro-youtube

16. https://theexplanation.com/paranormal-activity-beyond-physical-explanation/

# MIND-BODY PROBLEM SOLVED

We can add two more circles with Satan's influence on our consciousness and mind diagram, including Satan's "*spirit* that now works in the children of disobedience" (Eph. 2:2), illustrated by the pink background (gray, depending on the publication).

Figure 42. Satan's influence on our consciousness and mind

Other areas, too vast to mention, make people susceptible to mind attacks by Satan, like violent music, festivals, weird diets, purges, abstinence[17], and spiritual[18] Eastern philosophies[19] revolving around awareness and enlightenment. It has multiplied the

---

17. https://theexplanation.com/mind-control-the-serpents-number-one-goal/

18. https://theexplanation.com/spiritual-philosophy-wisdom-spirituality/

19. https://theexplanation.com/eastern-philosophy-not-religion-a-way/

practices and methods. There's one for every type of the 8 billion minds on Earth today. And, unbeknown to most, the ways it uses look like legitimate remedies and authentic help. So the Apostle John warns us.

**1 John 4:1**

> Beloved, believe not every spirit, but try the spirits whether they are of God: because many false prophets are gone out into the world.

Be wise; Satan seeks whom it might devour, and its main line of attack is the mind. God gave us the human mind, so we look outward and upward toward Him. We DO NOT relinquish our minds to any external control under any circumstances—more on preserving the mind in the next chapter.

# 42. Everyday Psychology for Everybody. Healthy Mental Vision

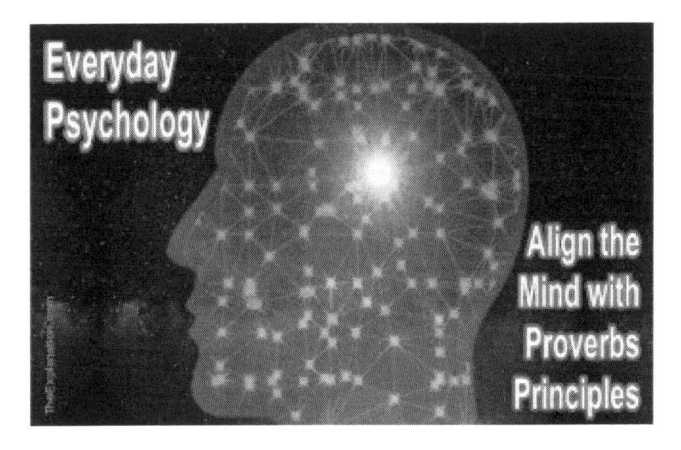

**Everyday psychology for all involves preserving a positive mental framework. Here's the basis for better mental health.**

This chapter closes this sixth Section on the psychology of the neshama and ruach. We've solved the mind-body problem[1] and established the full composition of a human being[2], a dust body with the neshama consciousness and the ruach mind. We know that we're dealing with the *spiritual*, and this Section is for everyday psychology for everyone; how to establish, develop, and maintain mental health for the vast majority of people who don't believe in God and Scripture.

We have seen that people are blinded to God's Word, but God still clothed them. God set in motion the human mentality and the guardrails to keep humanity on the straight and narrow. All the

---

1. https://theexplanation.com/mental-mind-fabulous-activity-of-consciousness/
2. https://theexplanation.com/living-soul-fascinating-meaning-man-and-animal/

instruction has always been present, symbolized by God clothing Adam and Eve with skin coats[3], but God has also given humans free choice. Human freedom has led them to imagine every possible way to live their own lives, moving further and further away from God's path. Some have plunged over the precipice; most have strayed, many far into the forest of darkness, despair, and anxiety[4].

This final chapter summarizes everyday psychology or how to preserve human consciousness and mind intact, despite the 21st century consequences we're subject to. Is it even imaginable to think the world can have good mental health? Yes, peace of mind will be a worldwide phenomenon.

What if you could walk the streets and paths, even in the forest, day or night, and know that no one would harass you, let alone attack you? What if ladies could take public transport with no lascivious looks and gestures from male travelers? What if children weren't the brunt of fatherly mistreating or parent squabbling?

What if you knew nobody would lie about you but rather respect your competency at work? What if you didn't have to worry about drunkenness, drugs, or insults when driving? That's a lot of *what-ifs*, but how much would that lower your anxiety and give you peace of mind?

**Disclaimer**: I am not a psychologist or competent to prescribe mental health advice. This biblical explanation of preventive means will lessen anxiety and enhance mental health. It is not a magic wand, a five-minute solution. Still, it reveals the root causes and demonstrates how to fertilize them appropriately to grow a vibrant, stable society where individuals function with healthy bodies and wholesome minds.

---

3. https://theexplanation.com/morality-universal-code-defines-good-behavior/

4. https://theexplanation.com/can-satan-influence-corrupt-a-human-mind-yes/

The above scenario is, unfortunately, illusory in today's society; that's why mental health will remain in a state of flux, if not worsen.

But there are personal solutions and hope for the more or less distant future. The Bible relays this *expectancy* and the *causes* for these favorable *circumstances*. In opposition to the illusory tableau I painted above, this will be a reality in the community, nations, and worldwide.

**Micah 4:2-4**

2 And many nations shall come, and say, Come, and let us go up to the mountain of the LORD, and to the house of the God of Jacob; and he will teach us of his ways, and we will walk in his paths: for the law shall go forth of Zion, and the word of the LORD from Jerusalem.

3 And he shall judge among many people, and rebuke strong nations afar off; and they shall beat their swords into plowshares, and their spears into pruninghooks: nation shall not lift up a sword against nation, neither shall they learn war any more.

4 But they shall sit every man under his vine and under his fig tree; and none shall make them *afraid* (H2729): for the mouth of the LORD of hosts has spoken it.

This Bible prophecy telescopes us into a future world. I do not have space to explain the *what* and *when*, but it's when housing, rurality, consumption, health, and families will be in harmony. The result is the absence of people and events that scar our mental health today; this is positive everyday psychology for everybody, "none shall make them *afraid*" (H2729).

### H2729

חָרַד chârad khaw-rad'; a primitive root; to shudder with terror; hence, to fear; also to hasten (with anxiety):

KJV - be (make) afraid, be careful, discomfit, fray (away), quake, tremble.

No more *discomfort* or *trembling* when you're alone. Note Strong's use of *anxiety*; that will be an obsolete sentiment. Yes, unreal now, maybe even a joke for most, but that's what Scripture tells us, and it portrays a world we can only dream of today. But the factors that make this fantasy come true are in verse 2.

> He [God] will teach us of his ways, and we will walk in his paths: for the *law* (H8451) shall go forth of Zion, and the *word* (H1697) of the LORD from Jerusalem.

The *law* is *torah* (H8451), the first five books of the Bible, and *word* is *dabar* (H1697), the same Hebrew word used for the Ten Commandments in Exodus 34:28. Verify this at UnlockBibleMeaning.com[5].

This worldwide free-will choice of people to follow God's Law and His Word will be closely coupled with a second principle.

### Isaiah 30:21

> And your ears shall hear a word behind you, saying, This is the way, walk you in it, when you turn to the right hand, and when you turn to the left.

---

5. https://unlockbiblemeaning.com

The right teachers with the proper subject matter are the recipe for appeasing mental health. In other words, the level of psychological well-being in a country and the world reveals the state of WHO is teaching and WHAT is being taught.

The Bible denounces those teaching, coaching, or in leadership responsibilities who wrongly impact the minds of children, youth, or adults. "To the law and to the testimony: if they speak not according to this word, it is because there is no light in them" (Isaiah 8:20). Note that this verse points us right back to the law, God's way, even for people who don't believe in God and Scripture.

Let's be open and upfront. If society could seriously diminish or come close to eliminating *divorce, child abuse, murder, illicit sex, adultery, theft,* and *lying,* imagine what kind of society we'd have. Talk about everyday psychology and peace of mind; That list in italics is none other than the last six of the Ten Commandments. That's the law in Micah 2:2 for teachers in Isa. 30:21. Parents (nurturing, preventive psychology), teachers, and psychologists (healing, remedial psychology) have a solid basis for working with those they counsel.

I'm not saying it's easy; in fact, it's downright hard because you're bucking the trajectory of society. But that's part of the recipe for mental wellness with real-world reality. So let's look at this in the overall picture.

## How Humans Function

Figure 43. Five elements of consciousness

Consciousness consists of five main areas: How humans function[6], reason[7], socialize[8], and rule[9], and their purpose in life[10]. The above points: law, rules or ethics, and teachers, whether parents or psychologists, affect the most personal aspect of consciousness: how you and I function. If you have a complex machine, like a printing press, and you don't know how it works, it's of little value.

Read this chapter for details of how humans function[11]. The seven primary phases are dual nature, free choice, behavior, ethics, justice, self-reproach, and forgiveness. Everyday psychology helps people see their dual nature, the good and evil (yes, there is right and wrong), and make wise choices based on solid ethics, which results in appropriate behavior. In addition, by avoiding wrongdoing,

---

6. https://theexplanation.com/human-nature-how-humans-worldwide-should-work/

7. https://theexplanation.com/5-types-of-reasoning-life-hangs-ultimate-choice/

8. https://theexplanation.com/social-relationships-puzzling-humans-love-hate/

9. https://theexplanation.com/human-rulership-responsibility-people-resources/

10. https://theexplanation.com/what-purpose-of-life-why-humans-crave-an-answer/

11. https://theexplanation.com/human-nature-how-humans-worldwide-should-work/

people will immediately have a load lifted from their shoulders: less anxiety and more peace of mind.

Teaching how to function as a human being, for oneself, and in the presence of other people is everyday psychology, and it is the primary role of parents. When young children enter school, this suitable functioning should already be inculcated within each child. Imagine what that would do for the atmosphere in a class. Teaching a child how to function is not the role of a kindergarten, preschool, or any school teacher.

Figure 44. Consciousness and mind, internal & external influences

All of the influences (inner and outer circles) exercised by the mind (beige background) on the consciousness are part of life. Therefore, parenting means applying preventive psychology when a child is in the malleable, critical periods[12] of the first years of their life.

---

12. https://theexplanation.com/critical-periods-when-babies-and-children-learn/

Everyday psychology by professional psychologists straightens out and remedies these interior and exterior influences of their patients.

The key to preventive and remedial psychology is *the way*. Remember Micah 2:2, "He will teach us His way," and Isaiah 30:21, "This is the way, walk you in it."

Even non-believing psychologists should know and help patients practice not killing, lying, stealing, and the thoughts and actions associated with the last six of the ten commandments. I realize this is extremely difficult with media, TV, streaming services, cartoons, gaming, real-life violence, and drama having a daily effect on our minds, but that's our role to the best of our abilities.

## Positive and Negative Influences are a Daily Combat

We have let immorality seep into our society[13] insidiously, and we are well nigh going under. Yet, despite that, through appropriately aware and prepared parents, teachers, coaches, and psychologists, everyday psychology can make a difference. The whole program is represented by the green (two inner) and red (two exterior) circles, the positive and negative ethics we instill in people.

---

13. https://theexplanation.com/ethical-behavior-break-the-rules-heres-the-outcome/

# MIND-BODY PROBLEM SOLVED

Figure 45. Consciousness and mind, positive & negative influences

Which will it be? The Ten Commandments or the Ten Anti-Commandments? The warring Proverbs[14] or the sound Proverbs? This is the continual *fight, the good fight* each of us faces in our personal lives and with those we are responsible for.

How humans function is the starting point for mental health but not sufficient without the other four aspects of consciousness.

## Socialize, Rule, Reason, and Purpose

I believe you understand how our personal mode of psychological functioning will affect our **socialization** and management (**rulership**) of that for which we have a responsibility. I refer you to

---

14. https://theexplanation.com/warring-proverbs-each-fighting-the-good-fight/

Sections 3[15] and 4[16] of *Audit of Humankind* for detailed workings and applications for these aspects of consciousness.

**Reasoning** is a major subject we cannot delve into here. But, in the context of everyday psychology for everyone, I'd point you to a Bible principle. Our world is eating from the Tree of knowledge of good and evil[17]. That's a choice made, for whatever reason, by those apart from God. Psychologists and all teachers should teach the *good* of the Tree. That good is represented by organizations and millions of individuals worldwide volunteering and accomplishing many encouraging and edifying projects. Let accurate reasoning encourage us to do secular good works.

With how humans function, I believe **purpose** plays a crucial role in mental health. Too many people, especially the younger generations, are lost. They have valid queries: I don't know who I am, where I came from, or where I'm going. They're unsettled about their future and don't see much meaning in their present lives. That's the formula for despair and hopelessness.

We must help people establish short and long-term goals for their education, skills, recreation, professions, careers, and future. Parents and counselors have a debilitating tendency to say *don't do this or that*. Of course, we should avoid dangers, but we must replace them with safe substitutes. And they become the practical purposes people strive for and reach.

There's nothing like the feeling of success to replace despair. There's nothing like attaining a recreational or professional goal to boost one's mental health. That's beneficial for everyday psychology.

---

15. https://theexplanation.com/human-society-the-only-global-social-species/

16. https://theexplanation.com/human-government-personal-world-peace/

17. https://theexplanation.com/human-reasoning-crushes-gods-good-for-people/

Consciousness and mind, neshama and ruach, are spiritual components of each human being. They are the most important and precious elements we possess. Therefore, it behooves those in all leadership and influential roles to practice everyday psychology in an uplifting way to bring about wholesome mental health.

# VII. Spiritual Conversion

When God becomes real, His Word becomes real, and the Holy Spirit witnesses with your spirit when you're called. Then you can believe, repent and become a son or daughter of God.

# 43. Spiritual Conversion. From Human Filth to Godly Purity

**Spiritual Conversion is the transformation of human filth and fighting into Godly purity and peace.**

The seventh and final Section of *Mind-Body Problem Solved* is devoted to spiritual conversion. We have established that neshama-consciousness[1] and ruach-mind[2] are spiritual elements God breathed into each human. It gave them physical and mental life. We've seen that in Genesis 2:7, *breath* refers to *neshama; however, life* is in the plural, *chayim; it* is *nishmat chayim*, the *breath of lives*. Why is it plural? What are these multiple lives?

## All is Packets of Energy and Spirit

---

1. https://theexplanation.com/neshama-inspiration-discover-the-deeper-meaning/

2. https://theexplanation.com/ruach-in-the-bible-creates-human-superiority/

And even more profoundly, why did God, who alone possesses neshama, breathe this life-giving element into lowly humans? We've seen God *yatsar-formed*[3] humans; why? Was it only to live out 70 years of physical life on Earth and die? And that's it? So many questions that science, philosophy, and, yes, religion do not answer.

Here's another aspect of these same questions. We've established that the common denominator of the Theory of Everything is energy packets. The mind extends into the spiritual realm because it is the spirit in humans; it powers our neshama-consciousness[4]. We also saw that the Holy Spirit is God's Power that creates and transforms[5]. The spirit animates our human world, and the Holy Spirit animates God's spiritual domain.

Is there a relationship between the spirit in humans and God's Holy Spirit that ties these two realms together? If so, what is it, and how does it function?

It all comes down to why God created humankind with free will and let them become obnoxious warring beings when He is pure and peaceful. When you think about it, it sounds like the opposite of *let's make humans in our image* Genesis 1:26. Humans are corrupt while God is pristine.

What's going on here?

That's where spiritual conversion comes fully into play. There are two clear aspects here.

# 1. *Spiritual* in Spiritual Conversion

---

3. https://theexplanation.com/human-family-elohim-god-works-both-create-rule/

4. https://theexplanation.com/neshamah-and-ruach-ultimate-backbone-of-humans/

5. https://theexplanation.com/spirit-power-and-creation-theory-of-everything/

Spiritual as opposed to physical; this is not a body or clothing makeover; this tells us the focus is on the spiritual change of mind. This verse is crucial in grasping spiritual conversion; "let this mind be in you, which was also in Christ Jesus" (Philippians 2:5). Why spiritual? Because the Theory Of Everything is all about spirit, and God is all about Spirit. Christ and His mind are Spirit.

The Bible shows us that spiritual conversion is God's process of taking the spirit in humans and slowly transforming it, molding it into the Spirit of God.

Look at what has happened to the spirit in humans, the mind, and where it's taken humanity. The book of Romans is that of spiritual conversion. It gives us the entire process, starting with the state of humankind, and it's not bright.

### Romans 1:19-31

19 Because that which may be known of God is manifest in them; for God has shewed it to them.

20 For the invisible things of him from the creation of the world are clearly seen, being understood by the things that are made, even his eternal power and Godhead; so that they are without excuse: (Sam: It is clear that there are too many coincidences in nature for the Creation to be a hazard[6]. See Section I of *Mind-Body Problem solved*).

21 Because that, when they knew God, they glorified him not as God, neither were thankful; but became vain in their imaginations, and their foolish heart was darkened. (Sam: note the initial problem is with

---

6. https://theexplanation.com/did-a-fine-tuned-universe-give-rise-to-earth/

humans; they distanced themselves from God, just like Adam and Eve hid from God in the trees[7]. In Job 15:2, 16:3, a translation of ruach, רוּחַ, is *vain*, fitting for *vain imaginations* of humans).

22 Professing themselves to be wise, they became fools (Sam: Remember the emphasis on warring Proverbs between wisdom and foolishness[8]. Human wisdom, their ideas of spirituality, is their foolishness).

23 And changed the glory of the uncorruptible God into an image made like to corruptible man, and to birds, and fourfooted beasts, and creeping things. (Sam: This is the transgression of the first four of the Ten Commandments).

24 Wherefore God also gave them up to uncleanness through the lusts of their own hearts, to dishonour their own bodies between themselves:

25 Who changed the truth of God into a lie, and worshipped and served the creature more than the Creator, who is blessed for ever. Amen.

28 And even as they did not like to retain God in their knowledge, God *gave* them *over* (G3860) to a reprobate mind, to do those things which are not convenient; (Sam: Understand, God did not change human minds. Humans rejected God and transformed themselves into reprobates; God decided to leave them in that state, for the time being).

---

7. https://theexplanation.com/human-reasoning-crushes-gods-good-for-people/

8. https://theexplanation.com/warring-proverbs-each-fighting-the-good-fight/

Humans have betrayed God and imprisoned their minds in foolishness. Here are alternate translations of *give over*. Check the deeper meaning of *reprobate* at UnlockBibleMeaning.com[9]; you'll see the renderings *castaway* and *rejected*. Humans have thrown themselves on the rocks and are shipwrecked, yet they don't know it.

**G3860**

> παραδίδωμι paradidōmi par-ad-id'-o-mee; From G3844 and G1325; to surrender that is yield up intrust transmit:

> KJV - betray, bring forth, cast, commit, deliver (up), give (over up), hazard, put in prison, recommend.

God Himself allowed humans to retain their *reprobate minds*. Strange, this seems counter-productive. Why didn't He wave a magic wand and make all humans pure and pristine? Because He has an excellent reason for doing it His way.

## 2. *Conversion* in Spiritual Conversion

Conversion means moving from point A to point Z. However, it is not an instant, ah-ha moment. One moment I'm not spiritual, and the next, I am; I'm saved. Conversion means starting at point A and proceeding to B, then C, then D, and through all the steps until you reach the final stage, point Z.

Spiritual conversion is not human ingenuity. Why do I say this? How many gurus offer 5-minute solutions? You've just got to master this, or that technique, and you'll reach spirituality. We are in an age of spirituality[10], spiritual conversion, nature retreats,

---

9. https://unlockbiblemeaning.com

music, mind transformation, meditation, mindfulness, awakening, awareness, Eastern philosophy, healing, connection with nature, hugging trees, near-death experiences, and drug tripping; it's endless. There are more teachers, trainers, pastors, and coaches in this area, each with their method of spirituality, than ever before. But are these human methods based on God's Word?

Godly transformation takes time. A child doesn't become an adult in five minutes; it's a many-year process, like spiritual conversion.

## The Gulf Humans Must Breach to Reach Spiritual Conversion

In this chapter, let's see the gaping crevice humans must cross to reach a fuller image of God. Study the contrasting examples of light and darkness, day and night, serving and being served, and the warring Proverbs[11]. There is a distinct gaping hole between these opposites. Humans, with spirit in man, cannot span this gap. We will see how God helps us reach spiritual conversion.

## 1. Realize the gulf between human ways and God's ways

Some may think that the term I used in the title, *humans are filth*, is outrageously overly exaggerated. Look at this verse.

### Isaiah 64:4, 6-8

4 For since the beginning of the world men have not heard, nor perceived by the ear, neither has the eye seen, O God, beside you, what he has prepared for him that waits for him.

---

10. https://theexplanation.com/i-am-gods-name-or-deep-human-spirituality-which/

11. https://theexplanation.com/warring-proverbs-each-fighting-the-good-fight/

6 But we are all as an unclean thing, and all our righteousnesses are as filthy rags; and we all do fade as a leaf; and our iniquities, like the wind, have taken us away. (Sam: quite an indictment against humans).

7 And there is none that calls upon your name, that stirs up himself to take hold of you: for you have hid your face from us, and have consumed us, because of our iniquities.

8 But now, O LORD, you are our father; we are the clay, and you our potter; and we all are the work of your hand.

The prophet Isaiah, inspired by God, uses the term *filthy* to describe human righteousness; that's the gulf between God and humans. Our hope and sure promise are knowing that God is our potter, the same Biblical Hebrew word as *formed*, *yatsar*, in Genesis 2:7. As Christ said in John 5:17, "My Father works hitherto, and I work." They work at bridging the gulf between sin and righteousness; we'll see the *how* and *why* later.

We discussed the Ten Commandments God gave the ancient Israelites. Let's understand the nature of this episode.

The nation was reprobate. Despite the miracles of the Exodus, they were rebellious against God. Just like Adam and Eve, after they'd received God's instruction (Ten Commandments), "they said to Moses, let not God speak with us, lest we die, and the people stood afar off" (Exodus 20:19-21). If there would've been trees, they'd have hidden among them. Instead, they withdrew themselves from God.

God gave the Ten Commandments to an unmanageable nation that did not follow Him. Even if some did keep them, this is not considered spiritual conversion. Look at our red (2 outer) and green (2 inner) *circles of psychology*™ of humans, the minimum requirement for humankind to maintain a semblance of peace.

Figure 46. Psychological requirements to maintain peace

Adherence to this moral code means doing the *good* and avoiding the *bad* of the Tree of the Knowledge of good and evil. There is no spiritual conversion in this compliance. There is recognition and obedience, but remember, our righteousness is as filthy rags.

Spiritual conversion is not how well we apply traditions like frequency of Church attendance, how long we pray, or how many times we fast. It is not niggling over what we eat, how we keep the day of rest, or how we dress. Or debates about law and grace, once saved forever saved, or degrees of application of the law. Of course, all those points play a part, but as Christ said, "cleanse first that which is within the cup and platter, that the outside of them may be clean also" (Matthew 23:26).

## 2. Realize that only God's Holy Spirit can help you make that leap

In Genesis 1, the Holy Spirit moved over the physical waters of tohu and bohu, confusion and emptiness[12], filth and fighting. It transformed them into the luscious landscape of a home for humankind. So likewise, the Spirit must do the same spiritually for each of us. It is the essential missing ingredient humans are unaware of, but they will be. Here's our hope expressed by King David.

> **Psalm 51:1-19**
>
> 1. Have mercy on me, O God, according to your lovingkindness: according to the multitude of your tender mercies blot out my transgressions (Sam: David knew he was filthy).
>
> 3 For I acknowledge my transgressions: and my sin is ever before me (Sam: self-reproach, recognition of the gulf, necessary repentance, which we'll discuss).
>
> 10 Create in me a clean heart, O God; and renew a right spirit within me. (Sam: this is God's work and help in the process of spiritual conversion).
>
> 11 Cast me not away from your presence; and take not your holy spirit from me. (Sam: there's the ingredient.

---

12. https://theexplanation.com/tohu-va-bohu-signifies-confusion-and-void-a-horrible-state-to-be-in/

Spiritual conversion only happens when the Holy Spirit is present).

David understood the Apostle John's inspired definition of spiritual conversion, "God is a Spirit: and they that worship him must worship him in spirit and in truth" (John 4:24).

Worshipping God in spirit with the power of the Holy Spirit is how we exercise our minds to apply God's **purpose** in our lives and **reason** according to His Word (love God, the first four of the Ten Commandments). How we transform our minds to apply God's way of **socialization** and **rulership** (love neighbor, the last six of the Ten Commandments), and how we **function** (repentance and personal spiritual transformation in truth). Those are the five elements of consciousness. Spiritual conversion is putting on Christ's mind to exercise our consciousness in conformity with His Word.

David recognized the gulf between his filthy transgressions and a clean heart. He desired to apply his mind to the Godly enactment of the five aspects of consciousness. He also knew that spiritual conversion starts with and entails the Holy Spirit.

# 44. Spiritual Calling, Definition, Revealing The Bible Meaning

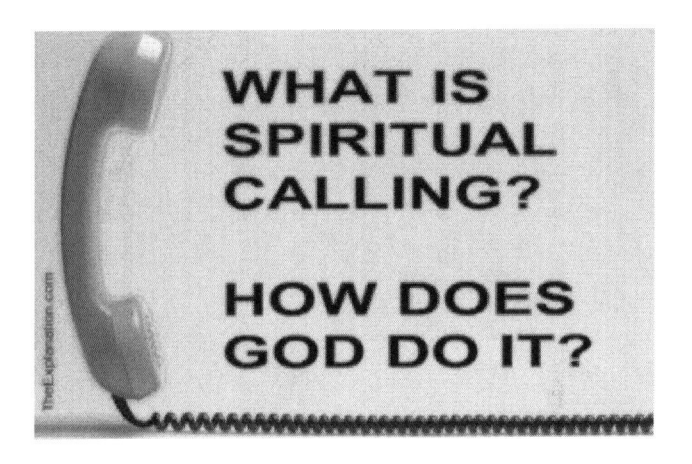

**Spiritual calling is the first event on the way to spiritual conversion. Precisely what is it, and how does it work? How emotional is it?**

On the one hand, people are leaving the classical Church[1] in droves, and on the other, they're searching for spirituality. A paradox, to say the least, because they're not finding it in Church. What leads to spiritual calling? How do you know if it's a real spiritual calling? How do you respond to spiritual calling?

Here's a Bible conundrum. Christ the Messiah, the Son of God, performed miracles without number and preached the Gospel day and night for three and a half years, and the meager results were 12 Apostles and 70 disciples. It sounds like a failed mission, but it

---

1. https://news.gallup.com/poll/341963/church-membership-falls-below-majority-first-time.aspx

wasn't. The Apostles picked up where Christ left off, and whether it was in the areas near or far, even to Rome, the converts were few and far between. Why not much more spiritual calling and conversion? It was always a tiny minority of Christians in a sea of unbelievers.

## The Gulf Between the Called and Not Called

Human beings, whoever they are, do not initiate spiritual calling. No one can work it up; we can seek, but ultimately, it is the Father Who calls. Many times, we don't seek, and yet, He still calls. Christ's Words are significant in this respect.

### John 6:44

No man can come to me, except the Father which has sent me draw him: and I will raise him up at the last day.

## What is the Evidence of Spiritual Calling?

Spiritual calling can be a controversial subject. Many equate it with feeling an emotion, like ecstasy from a high, whatever its cause, or witnessing an event like a near-death experience. It's where emotions like joy and illumination come into play. I'm not saying sentiments don't have their role, but is that the definition of a spiritual calling? No. Christ gave much teaching on this point.

### Matthew 13:15-23

15 For this people's heart is waxed gross, and their ears are dull of hearing, and their eyes they have closed; lest at any time they should see with their eyes, and hear with their ears, and should understand with their heart, and should be converted, and I should heal them. (Sam:

this appears counter-productive but isn't. People have hidden themselves from God, and He's left them with their reprobate minds[2]).

16 But blessed are your eyes, for they see: and your ears, for they hear.

17 For verily I say to you, That many prophets and righteous men have desired to see those things which you see, and have not seen them; and to hear those things which you hear, and have not heard them.

18 Hear you therefore the parable of the sower.

19 When any one hears the word of the kingdom, and understands it not, then comes the wicked one, and catches away that which was sown in his heart. This is he which received seed by the way side.

20 But he that received the seed into stony places, the same is he that hears the word, and anon (truly, quickly) with joy receives it; (Sam: Joy accompanies the hearing the Word, but the latter is what's significant).

21 Yet has he not root in himself, but dures for a while: for when tribulation or persecution arises because of the word, by and by he is offended.

22 He also that received seed among the thorns is he that hears the word; and the care of this world, and the deceitfulness of riches, choke the word, and he becomes unfruitful.

---

2. https://theexplanation.com/spiritual-conversion-human-filth-godly-purity/

> 23 But he that received seed into the good ground is he that hears the word, and understands it; which also bears fruit, and brings forth, some an hundredfold, some sixty, some thirty.

This meaning of spiritual calling is fundamental and vital. The key is to *hear the word*. So let me make the most important statement in this book.

> Spiritual calling is the reason God gave each human being neshama-consciousness and ruach-mind.

All five elements of consciousness are wrapped up in *hearing the word*. First, God exposes His *purpose* in Scripture. Second, the Word explains how humans *function*. Third, the Father calls sons and daughters into a *relationship* with Him. Fourth, verse 19 says *word of the kingdom*; that's the calling to participate in *rulership*, and finally, fifth, the Word has everything to do with *reasoning*. Spiritual calling is, above all, rational, not emotional.

God gave humans neshama, a part of Himself so that we can understand Him. That understanding starts with the calling to His Terms and Conditions expressed in His Word, Scripture. Some two thousand years ago, Christ came to die for our sins; of course, I do not want to diminish that act in any manner, but it happened in one day, a few hours; why did His Ministry last three and a half years? Because He was teaching and preaching the Word of God. Hearing the Word is the initial part of spiritual calling but not the only ingredient.

## How Calling and Growing Seeds Take Place

There are numerous parables involving planting and growing seeds. They all explain spiritual calling and growth. However, there's only one way this spiritual process can occur: with the Holy Spirit.

**1 Corinthians 2:9-13**

> 9 But as it is written, Eye has not seen, nor ear heard, neither have entered into the heart of man, the things which God has prepared for them that love him. (Sam: Humans, by themselves, cannot understand God)

> 10 But God has revealed them to us by his Spirit: for the Spirit searches all things, yea, the deep things of God. (Sam: the Spirit is the critical Element)

> 11 For what man knows the things of a man, save the spirit of man which is in him? even so the things of God knows no man, but the Spirit of God.

> 12 Now we have received, not the spirit of the world, but the spirit which is of God; that we might know the things that are freely given to us of God.

> 13 Which things also we speak, not in the words which man's wisdom teaches, but which the Holy Ghost teaches; comparing spiritual things with spiritual.

Solely, by and with the Holy Spirit, can we grasp the *things of God*. And those *things* are in His *Word*. Note verse 13, the Holy Spirit teaches; some think it's between them and the Holy Spirit. No, Paul, teachers, preachers, and God's Church have a vital role here. Christ did the teaching during His Ministry with the help of the Holy Spirit.

**444**  **THE EXPLANATION**

So far, our circles of the psychology of humans only include the *things of man*. It's time to add the *things of God*. And the first is the Holy Spirit, represented by the inner green background circle; it alone opens spiritual calling when God sows the seed; it allows humans to hear and act on God's Word.

Figure 47. Circles of psychology with the things of God

Here's an enigmatic but significant context that occurred at a specific moment, shortly after Christ's Resurrection. Why this gesture at this moment?

**John 20:20-23**

20 And when he [Christ] had so said, he shewed to them his hands and his side. Then were the disciples glad, when they saw the Lord.

21 Then said Jesus to them again, Peace be to you: as my Father has sent me, even so send I you.

22 And when he had said this, he *breathed* (G1720) on them, and said to them, Receive you the Holy Ghost:

23 Whose soever sins you remit, they are remitted to them; and whose soever sins you retain, they are retained.

Breathed (ἐμφυσάω emphusaō) appears only once in the New Testament. It is the counterpart of Yahveh Elohim blowing the *breath* of life into the first human in Genesis 2:7. The neshama-consciousness is the basis of humankind, coupled with the spirit-mind in hu(man)s[3] that God also infused in that first human at that moment (Job 32:8). With those elements, humans begin to accomplish mental activities related to their physical life's purposes.

Look what the Holy Spirit helps accomplish; verse 23, remittance and retention of people's sins. Christ specifically addressed the Apostles. *Forgiving sins* is not given to everyone; the point to make is that blowing the Holy Spirit on them gives spiritual prerogatives and purpose to their lives.

This *breathing* begins their spiritual calling to accomplish spiritual activities related to their life's divine purposes. Do you see the perfect parallel here? Adam was the first (human) man prefiguring Christ, the second (spiritual) man (1 Corinthians 15:45, 47). So

---

3. https://theexplanation.com/neshamah-and-ruach-ultimate-backbone-of-humans/

likewise, Adam's earthy descendants prefigure Christ's spiritual descendants. The Apostle's public and visible reception of the Holy Spirit happened a few weeks later at Pentecost (Acts 2).

A point to retain here is the progressive reception of the power of the Holy Spirit. The Apostles were still growing; even after the Death and Resurrection of Jesus, the disciples hesitated greatly in their belief.

## How Does This Calling Work in Practical Terms?

The first evidence of spiritual calling is understanding God's Word.

> **Luke 24:27-49**
>
> 27 And beginning at Moses and all the prophets, he [Jesus] expounded to them in all the scriptures the things concerning himself.
>
> 44 And he said to them, These are the words which I spake to you, while I was yet with you, that all things must be fulfilled, which were written in the law of Moses, and in the prophets, and in the psalms, concerning me.
>
> 45 Then opened he their understanding, that they might understand the scriptures,
>
> 49 And, behold, I send the promise of my Father upon you: but tarry you in the city of Jerusalem, until you be endued with power from on high.

It comes down to understanding Scripture. Why? Everything has to do with God's purpose, function, relationship, rulership, and reasoning; the basis of neshama-consciousness is God's Word.

The Holy Spirit will lead you into all truth, but the Word must be taught and preached.

**Romans 10:13-17**

13 For whosoever shall call upon the name of the Lord shall be saved.

14 How then shall they call on him in whom they have not believed? and how shall they believe in him of whom they have not heard? and how shall they hear without a preacher?

15 And how shall they preach, except they be sent? as it is written, How beautiful are the feet of them that preach the gospel of peace, and bring glad tidings of good things! (Sam: do you see the progressive process of spiritual calling?)

16 But they have not all obeyed the gospel. For Esaias says, Lord, who has believed our report?

17 So then faith comes by hearing, and hearing by the word of God.

Many leave the Church or don't believe because of teaching a false gospel of peace. They know the Word is not preached to them; they know something is wrong. People are looking for answers, but they're not getting fed.

Read the account of Philip teaching the eunuch from Ethiopia in Acts 8. The eunuch couldn't understand a prophetic passage in Isaiah. He knew he needed *some man to guide him*. "Then Philip opened his mouth, and began at the same scripture, and preached to him Jesus" (vs. 35). The eunuch believed in Jesus and was baptized.

When you meet someone or something new, the only way to get to know them is by speaking or reading about them. That exchange of words is the precursor of developing trust and confidence in that person or item. It's based on an interaction of dialogue. That's identical to a spiritual calling. God gives us a small portion of the Holy Spirit to begin understanding His Word. We thus become acquainted with God and His purpose. What we do with that seed depends on us. Many have a spiritual calling, but few bear fruit (Matthew 22:14); many are called, but few are chosen.

# 45. Not in The World = Decisive Makeover of Our Neshama & Ruach

**Spiritual conversion is our presence in the world but not being of the world—total redirection of our consciousness and mind.**

Let's recapitulate. *Mind-Body Problem Solved* reveals the mind is a spiritual entity[1], by definition, separate from the physical body-brain. The Bible affirms that the ruach-mind is inseparable from a second spiritual entity, the neshama[2], which we've defined as consciousness[3]. Every human being is endowed with both neshama-ruach, consciousness-mind. Another given is we all live IN the world.

---

1. https://theexplanation.com/brain-to-mind-can-material-create-immaterial/

2. https://theexplanation.com/neshama-ruach-make-humans-human/

3. https://theexplanation.com/where-full-definition-mind-body-consciousness/

When we come to spiritual conversion, the subject of this final Section of the book, the Bible states;

**John 17:11, 14**

11 And now I [Christ just before His Crucifixion] am no more in the world, but these [Christ's disciples] are **in the world**, and I come to you. Holy Father, keep through your own name those whom you have given me, that they may be one, as we are.

14 I have given them your word; and the world has hated them, because they are **not of the world, even as I am not of the world**.

That is one of the most straightforward definitions of spiritual conversion. The question is, how did this come about for the Apostles and disciples? And how does God perform spiritual conversion now by taking people *in the world* and making them *not of the world*? Here are three images to illustrate what *in the world* means in practical terms. The first is the spiritual makeup of all humans: consciousness-mind, neshama-ruach; briefly, the five elements of purpose, function, socialization, rulership, and reasoning, all coupled with the ruach-mind-power to develop and grow these qualities. The second comprises the interior-exterior influences each human is subject to via their heredity and environment, the nature-nurture equation.

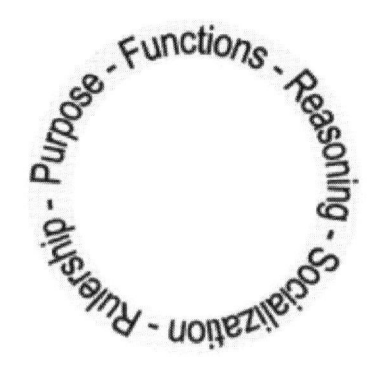

Figure 48. Consciousness and mind

Figure 49. Consciousness and mind, internal & external influences

The third is the battle each person fights daily between the good and bad pulls and pushes within us and in society. This latter image summarizes *in the world*. For example, in chapter 36, *Human Reasoning*, we discussed Genesis 3, when Adam and Eve made themselves aprons of fig leaves (Genesis 3:7), and God dressed them in coats of skins (Genesis 3:21). The former represents humans making their own makeshift decisions in contrast to God giving them a stable plan for living *in the world* outside of the Garden of Eden.

Humans have been torn between the fig leaves and the coats of skins ever since. But, unfortunately, humankind has donned more fig leaves; that's *in the world*. And with open eyes, we should see the state of our world today.

Figure 50. Consciousness and mind in the world

In this state of human depravation, the Father performs spiritual calling[4]. He does it by planting and watering seeds, giving access to His Word, the Scriptures, and a little portion of the Holy Spirit. The goal is spiritual understanding.

---

4. https://theexplanation.com/spiritual-calling-definition-bible-meaning/

After spiritual calling by the Father, someone hears the Word and either responds or not. "But he that received seed into the good ground is he that hears the word, and understands it; which also bears fruit, and brings forth, some an hundredfold, some sixty, some thirty" (Mat. 13:23).

What is *bears fruit*? What is God's Word, coupled with the Holy Spirit, supposed to help to *understand*? Here are the first Words of Christ in Mark.

> **Mark 1:14-15**
>
> 14 Jesus came into Galilee, preaching the gospel of the kingdom of God,
>
> 15 And saying, The time is fulfilled, and the kingdom of God is at hand (Sam: this is *hear the Word*): *repent* (G3340) you, and *believe* (G4100) the gospel.

To *bear fruit* is to *believe* and *repent*. Those are specific actions that a person God calls must understand. Believe what? Repent from what? What is the relationship between *believe* and *repent*? And, in particular, how does this move you from *in the world* to *not of the world*?

## Believe

Fundamentally the existence of an all-powerful being and its coming to Earth to pay for humanity's sins is somewhat crazy. Fiction tells stories of heroes who die to save others, but not for everyone, and not for their sins so that they can live forever. We have to admit the Bible account is rather bizarre and outlandish. Yet, it's real, and there must be substantial belief to accept these facts.

**Romans 10:8, 9, 17**

8 But what says it? The word is near you, even in your mouth, and in your heart: that is, the word of *faith* (G4102), which we preach;

9 That if you shall confess with your mouth the Lord Jesus, and shall *believe* (G4100) in your heart that God hath raised him from the dead, you shall be saved.

17 So then *faith* (G4102) comes by hearing, and hearing by the word of God.

Note the relationship between *belief* and *faith*. In English, *faith* appears firmer; the reality is they are both about *conviction,* and they're of equal importance.

**G4100**

πιστεύω pisteuō pist-yoo'-o; From G4102; to have faith (in upon or with respect to a person or thing) that is credit; by implication to entrust (especially one's spiritual well being to Christ):

KJV - believe (-r), commit, (to trust), put in trust with.

**G4102**

πίστις pistis pis'-tis; From G3982; persuasion that is credence; moral conviction (of religious truth or the truthfulness of God or a religious teacher) especially reliance upon Christ for salvation; abstractly constancy in such profession; by extension the system of religious (Gospel) truth itself:

KJV - assurance, belief, believe, faith, fidelity.

There are dozens of verses with *believe* and *faith*; study them at UnlockBibleMeaning.com[5]. Strong's emphasis of reliance on Christ for all matters of salvation is correct.

**John 17:20-21; 20:31**

John 17:20 Neither pray I for these alone, but for them also which shall *believe* (G4100) on me through their word;

21 That they all may be one; as you, Father, are in me, and I in you, that they also may be one in us: that the world may *believe* (G4100) that you have sent me.

John 20:31 But these signs and miracles are written, that you might *believe* (G4100) that Jesus is the Christ, the Son of God; and that *believing* (G4100) you might have life through his name.

*May have life through His name.* During Christ's signs and miracles, those disciples, like us, already have life; this is an additional life. Remember, God breathed the breath of liveS on the first human (Genesis 2:7). This is why *neshama* has multiple liveS. It's only because God endowed us with this element; now He's showing us how to access this new life through Christ's name, not in the world. The first step is to believe and have faith in Christ and all that He represents.

Now we come to the second directive by Christ as reported in Mark 1.

---

5. https://unlockbiblemeaning.com

## Repent

Repentance is much more than feeling sorry for our wrongdoing.

> **Romans 2:4**
>
> Or despise you the riches of his goodness and forbearance and longsuffering; not knowing that the goodness of God leads you to *repentance*? (G3341)

That's God's calling; His goodness in leading us individually to this turning point in our lives. So let's meditate on the depth of the Greek meaning, which like Hebrew, reveals more than the translation.

> **G3341**
>
> μετάνοια metanoia met-an'-oy-ah; From G3340; (subjectively) compunction (for guilt including reformation); by implication reversal (of [another's] decision):
>
> KJV - repentance.
>
> **G3340**
>
> μετανοέω metanoeō met-an-o-eh'-o; From G3326 and G3539; to think differently or afterwards that is reconsider (morally to feel compunction):
>
> KJV - repent.
>
> **G3539**

νοιέω noieō noy-eh'-o; From G3563; to **exercise the mind** (observe) that is (figuratively) to comprehend heed:

KJV - consider, perceive, think, understand.

Go to G3563 > G1097 at UnlockBibleMeaning.com[6] to see how relevant the *mind, perception, understanding,* and *thinking* are to repentance.

Repentance is the *reversal of the mind* and the way we *perceive*. We reconsider how and what we *think*. We *understand* differently than *in the world*. It involves re-arranging our consciousness. Repentance leads to us coming out *of the world*.

One of the five components of consciousness is how humans function[7]. Here are the seven steps:

1. Two-faced Humanity.[8] We understand how we've followed the bad-dark side of our life.
2. Free Will[9]. We choose what we do with the seed God plants, whether we bear fruit or not.
3. Behavior.[10] The result of our choice. Accept God's calling or not. Repent or not.
4. Ethics[11]. We realize humans have their rules, and God has His commandments.

---

6. https://unlockbiblemeaning.com
7. https://theexplanation.com/psychology-best-bible-definition-for-humans/
8. https://theexplanation.com/two-faced-humanity-depraved-priests-and-kind-criminals/
9. https://theexplanation.com/free-will-we-all-possess-it-but-we-cant-always-utilize-it/
10. https://theexplanation.com/human-behavior-is-the-expression-of-human-nature-and-free-will/
11. https://theexplanation.com/ethics-are-the-blueprint-for-behavior-how-humanity-should-function/

5. Justice[12]. We begin to see that the *bad* is *sin*, the transgression of God's law (1 John 3:4).
6. Self-Reproach.[13] Biblically this is repentance. We're wrong and need a decisive change of mind.
7. Forgiveness[14]. The BELIEF Christ paid the heavy price for our sins.

When this process of God's goodness leads us to this realization and transformation of mind, one is forgiven and has their sins buried in the watery grave of baptism. That individual is still IN the *world* but no longer OF the *world*.

You can see this process impacts how a *called* and then *spiritually converted* person functions. It affects behavior concerning their purpose in life, socialization, and rulership. Since it primarily involves the mind, indeed their reasoning, all aspects of their neshama-consciousness are redirected from worldly to spiritual thinking, meditation, and decision-making.

Again the Greek for the word *world-kosmos* is revealing.

### G2889

> κόσμος kosmos kos'-mos; Probably from the base of G2865; orderly arrangement that is decoration; by implication the world (in a wide or narrow sense including its inhabitants literally or figuratively [morally]):
>
> KJV - adorning, world.

---

12. https://theexplanation.com/justice-goes-hand-in-hand-with-ethics-to-obtain-peace/
13. https://theexplanation.com/self-reproach-the-essential-beginning-step-toward-real-peace/
14. https://theexplanation.com/forgiveness-the-healing-bond-for-humans-to-function-peacefully/

### G2885

κοσμέω kosmeō kos-meh'-o; From G2889; to put in proper order that is decorate (literally or figuratively); specifically to snuff (a wick):

KJV - adorn, garnish, trim.

Interestingly, the word cosmetics derives from the Greek κοσμητικὴ τέχνη[15] ("kosmetikē tekhnē"), meaning "technique of dress and ornament," from κοσμητικός ("kosmētikos"), "skilled in ordering or arranging" and that from κόσμος ("kosmos"), meaning "order" and "ornament." There's a relationship between ornaments and how we *order*, *use*, or *organize* them. The emphasis is on the interior spiritual, not the exterior material.

### 1 Peter 3:3-4

3 Whose *adorning* (G2889 - kosmos) let it not be that outward adorning of plaiting the hair, and of wearing of gold, or of putting on of apparel;

4 But let it be the hidden man of the heart, in that which is not corruptible, even the ornament of a meek and quiet *spirit* (G4151 - pneuma), which is in the sight of God of great price.

We're still in the world, here and now, as others, but we're not OF this world (this does not mean we can't go to the hairdresser, wear jewelry, or fine clothes); we've had a profound change of heart. We are referring to the *pneuma-spirit*, the *mind* which is now in line with God's way, His behavior, ethics, and justice, including our outward appearance.

---

15. https://en.wikipedia.org/wiki/Cosmetics#Definition_and_etymology

In fact, those who accept and implement this calling have also had another change of clothing. They're ridding themselves of their *fig leaves*, not making their decisions based on intuition and their ideas of philosophy, science, and religion. Even the *skin coats* God dressed them with to live decent lives in the world have given way to clothing, not of this world.

**Ephesians 6:14-17**

14 Stand therefore, having your loins girt about with truth, and having on the breastplate of righteousness;

15 And your feet shod with the preparation of the gospel of peace;

16 Above all, taking the shield of faith, wherewith you shall be able to quench all the fiery darts of the wicked.

17 And take the helmet of salvation, and the sword of the Spirit, which is the word of God:

Figure 51. Consciousness and mind in the world but not of the world

We're still *in the world* but not *of the world* because inwardly, we're clothed with righteousness, the gospel of peace, faith, salvation, the Holy Spirit, and the Word of God.

The outside circles *in the world* are still present. But we're no longer *of the world; we've* shifted direction from the outer to the inner rings. The internal and external influences on our minds align with God's mind. Romans 12:2 says, "be not conformed to this world: but be you transformed by the renewing of your mind, that you may prove what is that good, and acceptable, and perfect, will of God." That is living in the world but not of the world.

# 46. Genuine Spirituality. From Childish to Mature Decision-Making

**Genuine spirituality is considerably more than keeping a bunch of rules and traditions. Children can do that. Biblically, true spirituality is a transformation of the mind.**

The book's final Section addresses genuine spirituality, the biblical spiritual side of psychology. Both primarily treat the mind, one from a non-godly and the other from a Godly point of view. This chapter will discuss God's Word to define spiritual maturity.

## Genuine Spirituality and Putting Away Childish Things

The Apostle Paul talks a lot about mature spirituality, "When I was a child, I spake as a child, I understood as a child, I thought as a child: but when I became a man, I put away childish things" (1

Corinthians 13:11). What are childish and mature things? What's the difference in how a child and adult function, in how they exercise their free will choices?

## Apostles and the Law of Moses

Let me give you an exciting episode in Church history to which many refer concerning choosing what and whether to keep the law of Moses (Acts 15). It occurred in Jerusalem with Paul, Barnabas, the Apostles, and the Elders; everyone was present. "There rose up certain of the sect of the Pharisees which believed, [spiritually converted who were originally of pharisaical beliefs and practices] saying, "That it was needful to circumcise them, [new non-Jewish converts] and to command them to keep the law of Moses. And the apostles and elders came together for to consider this matter" (Acts 15:5-6).

Here's James' concluding declaration at the meeting.

>**Acts 15:19-20**
>
>19 Wherefore my sentence is, that we trouble not them, which from among the Gentiles are turned to God:
>
>20 But that we write to them, that they abstain from pollutions of idols, and from fornication, and from things strangled, and from blood.

Observance of the law of Moses was and is not necessary for the spiritually converted, except for the above provisions.

## Paul and Meat Offered to Idols

Now, look at what Paul wrote to the Church in Corinth, composed of members supposed to possess genuine spirituality.

## 1 Corinthians 8:4-13

4 As concerning therefore the eating of those things that are offered in sacrifice to idols, we know that an idol is nothing in the world, and that there is none other God but one.

5 For though there be that are called gods, whether in heaven or in earth, (as there be gods many, and lords many,)

6 But to us there is but one God, the Father, of whom are all things, and we in him; and one Lord Jesus Christ, by whom are all things, and we by him.

7 Howbeit there is not in every man that knowledge: for some with conscience of the idol to this hour eat it (Sam: meat, pollutions of idols) as a thing offered to an idol; and their conscience being weak is defiled.

8 But meat commends us not to God: for neither, if we eat, are we the better; neither, if we eat not, are we the worse. (Sam: one way or the other, it doesn't matter if we eat meat offered to idols)

9 But take heed lest by any means this liberty of yours become a stumblingblock to them that are weak.

10 For if any man see you which have knowledge sit at meat in the idol's temple, shall not the conscience of him which is weak be emboldened to eat those things which are offered to idols;

11 And through your knowledge shall the weak brother perish, for whom Christ died?

12 But when you sin so against the brethren, and wound their weak conscience, you sin against Christ.

13 Wherefore, if meat make my brother to offend, I will eat no flesh while the world stands, lest I make my brother to offend.

Paul says you can eat meat offered to idols IF you recognize idols are *just called gods* (verse 5) but are nothing; this contradicts the events in Acts 15. So how do we explain Paul's recommendation? I will explain, but first, let me return to a statement I made in the last chapter[1] that may have surprised you. Even if it didn't, please meditate on its full meaning.

> In fact, those who accept and implement this spiritual calling have also had another change of clothing. They're ridding themselves of their *fig leaves*, not making their decisions based on intuition and their ideas of philosophy, science, and religion. **Even the skin coats with which God dressed them to live decent lives in the world** *have given way* **to clothing that is not of this world**.

That says other clothing should replace Adam and Eve's God-given clothing (Gen. 3:21). Previously, I explained the clothes represent God's law as expressed in Proverbs, in more down-to-earth language for the 21st century. This affirmation brings up a fundamental biblical controversy over which basically all Christianity stumbles; the relationship of the New to the Old

---

1. https://theexplanation.com/not-in-the-world-total-makeover-neshama-ruach/

Covenant, including the place of the Ten Commandments and Old Testament Law in worshiping God in spirit and truth (John 4:24).

## Genuine Spirituality and Decision-Making

In the situation of meat offered to idols, Paul tells them to make their OWN decision based on their conscience AND that of a brother or sister with genuine spirituality. There are several circumstances here; Paul has no way of knowing about. The ministry cannot make decisions for individual cases and events. It is up to the individual to decide for themselves, in prayer and meditation, what the conduct of their genuine spirituality will be.

This example helps us understand what Paul meant by "... I put away childish things." Thinking idols are or represent God, offering them meat, and thinking that meat is somehow sacred are all childish things; Christians with genuine spirituality understand and know how to make their own decisions concerning these and many other matters.

## Circumcision

Is circumcision necessary? That was the Pharisees' original request to the Apostles in Acts 15. The spiritual answer is it is not required for genuine Christian spirituality. Paul states as much in Romans 2:28-29 "For he is not a Jew, which is one outwardly; neither is that circumcision, which is outward in the flesh: But he is a Jew, which is one inwardly; and circumcision is that of the heart, in the *spirit* (Sam: pneuma, the mind), and not in the letter; whose praise is not of men, but of God."

But can spiritually converted individuals decide to circumcise their baby boy? Here's what the WebMD[2] website says about this practice.

> The use of circumcision for medical or health reasons is an issue that continues to be debated. The American Academy of Pediatrics (AAP) found that the health benefits of newborn male circumcision (prevention of urinary tract infections, penile cancer, and transmission of some sexually transmitted infections, including HIV) outweigh the risks, but the benefits are not great enough to recommend universal newborn circumcision.

I won't answer the question; understanding and applying genuine spirituality is up to you.

## Ten Commandments Replaced by Two Commandments

Christ and the Apostles do refer to the Ten Commandments, but both bring it down to Two Commandments.

> **Matthew 22:36-40**
>
> 36 Master, which is the great commandment in the law?
>
> 37 Jesus said to him, you shall love the Lord your God with all your heart, and with all your soul, and with all your mind.
>
> 38 This is the first and great commandment.

---

2. https://www.webmd.com/sexual-conditions/guide/circumcision

39 And the second is like to it, you shall love your neighbour as yourself.

40 On these two commandments hang all the law and the prophets.

Is He minimizing the Ten? Absolutely not. Converted Christians with genuine spirituality understand that every single law in the Old Testament is included in the two commandments, as Christ emphasizes in verse 40. How so? Because you have to DECIDE how to apply them.

In the Old Testament, everything was spelled out, just as you do with a list of do's and don'ts, chores, and responsibilities you hang on a refrigerator or in a kiddie classroom; take out the garbage, wash your hands, brush your teeth, put away your books.

When you grow up, bye-bye to that kind of list, to childish things; you become a wo/man and make your own decisions. Do you still brush your teeth, put out the garbage, and put away your books? Of course, you do! Are the Ten Commandments still valid? Of course, they are! But for Christians with genuine spirituality, they are an integral part of the Two Commandments. *Love God* covers the first four, and *love neighbor* includes the last six. Christ elaborated on their spiritual application in His first and probably most important teaching.

**Matthew 5:2-3**

2 And he opened his mouth, and taught them, saying,

3 Blessed are the *poor* (G4434) in *spirit* (G4151 pneuma - spirit/mind): for theirs is the kingdom of heaven.

Interestingly, this is the first and only time Christ evokes the spirit, the mind in this context. Everything in genuine spirituality starts in the mind, the spirit in humans, coupled with the Holy Spirit. It's all about transformation of the mind.

**James 2:5**

> Hearken, my beloved brethren, Has not God chosen the *poor* (G4434, same as *poor* in spirit) of this world *rich in faith*, and heirs of the kingdom which he has promised to them that love him?

*Rich in faith* in God means humble in the human mind or *poor in spirit*. Read Matthew 5-7, the genuine spirituality attitudes: mourn, meek, righteousness, merciful, pure in heart, peacemakers, persecuted for righteousness, reviled. These mental approaches are the practical application of the two great commandments, and it is all a state of mind.

Mature Christians, guided into spiritual reasoning by the Holy Spirit, know how to make decisions. Am I saying we can decide whether to keep the fourth Commandment, the Sabbath? No, absolutely not. Is it part of *Love God*? Yes, it is. But how you rest on the Sabbath is each Christian's decision, just as with meats offered to idols. It's a question of one's conscience concerning God. That's spiritual maturity.

All those tricky, superficial questions come down to answering only one. Is my decision in conformity to Scripture showing love to God and love to my neighbor?

We can now add a further inner ring to our *circles of psychology and spirituality*™. It represents spiritual maturity. The experienced Christian is increasing their spiritual fruit ten, thirty, and a hundredfold. The attitudes of Matthew 5, meekness, righteousness, mercy, purity in heart, and peace, shine as God's light through the Holy Spirit.

## Why only Two Commandments? The Ultimate Purpose

We'll spend eternity with God and with our neighbor. Earth is a PHYSICAL TRAINING GROUND before SPIRITUAL REALITY. In everything we do on Earth, there's constant training BEFORE we're faced with the deep end. Sometimes, if a father dies prematurely, the wife, eldest son, or daughter acquires responsibility they hadn't planned on nor been prepared for; life happens. But under normal circumstances, we should train children for responsibilities and life.

Figure 52. Consciousness and mind with the two great commandments

In God's plan, every single person who has walked the face of the Earth will go through the PHYSICAL TRAINING CAMP, and receive the opportunity of being a child donned with coats of skins, the Ten Commandments, and then growing up to put on spiritual clothing, the Two Commandments. They will follow the path from childhood to adulthood, applying the two great Commandments with genuine spirituality in preparation for their eternal life. Everyone has the same opportunity; that's God's patience, justice, and attachment for every single human being and the transformation of their minds.

# 47. Christ is THE WAY. From Filthy Rags to Fulfilled Righteousness

**The way to use consciousness and mind is a mystery. Even more so the destination. Here's the way.**

*The Explanation* has opened up the Bible meaning of neshama and ruach, consciousness and mind, the two inseparable spiritual elements that constitute humans along with the dust body. In Chapter 35, I gave the biblical definition of psychology[1] from *psyche* and *logos*; it's the neshama and ruach (psyche) functioning according to God's Word (logos).

God gave humankind the qualities (neshama-consciousness: purpose, function, socialization, rulership, and reasoning) and the mind-power (ruach) to implement, exercise, and develop those traits. From the beginning, the first 7th day God spent with Adam and Eve[2] in the Garden of Eden, He has revealed to humans the WAY to use consciousness and mind to reach peace and harmony.

---

1. https://theexplanation.com/psychology-best-bible-definition-for-humans/

2. https://theexplanation.com/on-the-seventh-day-god-continues-finishing-his-work/

God has recorded His WAY in His WORD, the Bible, and preserved it for us down through history. The Apostle Paul states as much.

## The Way, Recorded for Humankind

### Romans 3:1-4

1 What advantage then has the Jew? or what profit is there of circumcision?

2 Much every way: chiefly, because that to them were committed the oracles of God (Sam: the Word of the Old Testament).

3 For what if some did not believe? shall their unbelief make the faith of God without effect?

4 God forbid: yea, let God be true, but every man a liar; as it is written, That you might be justified in your *sayings* (G3056 - logos - Word), and might *overcome* (G3528 - prevail) when you are judged.

No matter the unbelief, incompetence, fighting between sects, or whatever circumstances, the mighty God has preserved His Word, whether it be the Hebrew Old or the Greek New Testaments. We have the solid promise that God has kept it perfectly for us today, regardless of human subterfuge regarding Scripture.

So, we have the tools (neshama, ruach) and the instruction manual (logos); what's missing is an example of the WAY to reach our destination. God closed that road thousands of years ago.

## The Way, Closed and Reopened

**Genesis 3:24**

> So he drove out the man; and he placed at the east of the garden of Eden Cherubims, and a flaming sword which turned every way, to *keep the way* of the tree of life.

God clothed Adam and Eve with the way to live outside of Eden. Access to the Garden was closed; God barred the way into His presence. Later He opened and revealed to us the WAY,

**John 14:2-6**

> 2 In my Father's house are many mansions: if it were not so, I would have told you. I go to prepare a place for you.
>
> 3 And if I go and prepare a place for you, I will come again, and receive you to myself; that where I am, there you may be also.
>
> 4 And *whither I go* (the destination) you know, and *the way* (how to get there) you know. (Sam: *to know* is a function of the consciousness and mind)
>
> 5 Thomas said to him, Lord, we know not whither you go; and how can we know the way?
>
> 6 Jesus said to him, I am the way, the truth, and the life: no man comes to the Father, but by me.

If you want a place in the Father's house, then you need the map, the *way* to reach that destination. Jesus alone has safeguarded the *truth*, His Word, and breathed the breath of *life* (nishmat chayim - lives) into humanity. By His example, we have the way; He's mapped out the route for us, including John the Baptist's preparation.

**Matthew 3:1-8**

1 In those days came John the Baptist, preaching in the wilderness of Judaea,

2 And saying, *Repent you* (this is the initial part of the way): for the *kingdom of heaven* is at hand (the destination).

3 For this is he that was spoken of by the prophet Esaias, saying, The voice of one crying in the wilderness, Prepare you *the way* of the Lord, make his paths straight (Sam: ramp up the starting blocks).

5 Then went out to him Jerusalem, and all Judaea, and all the region round about Jordan,

6 And were *baptized* of him in Jordan, *confessing their sins*.

7 But when he saw many of the Pharisees and Sadducees come to his baptism, he said to them, O generation of vipers, who has warned you to flee from the wrath to come?

8 Bring forth therefore *fruits* meet for repentance:

John opened the way. Briefly, it involved him preaching *repentance* (verse 2) followed by *baptism* (6) after people *confessed their sins* (6) and showed *fruits* (8). Let's look at the meaning of *repent* from the Greek.

### G3340

μετανοέω metanoeō met-an-o-eh'-o; From G3326 and G3539; to think differently or afterwards that is reconsider (morally to feel compunction):

KJV - repent.

### G3539

νοιέω noieō noy-eh'-o; From G3563; to exercise the mind (observe) that is (figuratively) to comprehend heed:

KJV - consider, perceive, think, understand.

### G3563

νοῦς nous nooce; Probably from the base of G1097; the intellect that is mind (divine or human; in thought feeling or will); by implication meaning :

KJV - mind, understanding. Compare G5590

The bottom line is the basis for the word *repent* is *mind* and *understanding*. That's the reason God blew neshama-consciousness and gave ruach-mind to humans. So they can repent. One of the five qualities of consciousness is the ability to reason[3]. G3539 says to *exercise the mind* for what? Among other things, to know what sin is. How can you confess sin if one doesn't know what it is? That takes understanding God's Word with the help of the Holy Spirit, witnessing with the ruach, the spirit in humans. These steps are the only way to start one's journey to the destination, the kingdom (2).

---

3. https://theexplanation.com/5-types-of-reasoning-life-hangs-ultimate-choice/

Christ confirmed the way when he came to John.

**Matthew 3:13-17**

13 Then comes Jesus from Galilee to Jordan to John, to be baptized of him.

14 But John forbad him, saying, I have need to be baptized of you, and come you to me?

15 And Jesus answering said to him, Suffer it to be so now: for thus it becomes us to fulfil all righteousness. Then he suffered him.

16 And Jesus, when he was baptized, went up straightway out of the water: and, lo, the heavens were opened to him, and he saw the Spirit of God descending like a dove, and lighting upon him:

17 And lo a voice from heaven, saying, This is my beloved Son, in whom I am well pleased.

Have you ever asked yourself why Christ was baptized? After all, He didn't sin, didn't need to confess sin, and didn't need forgiveness. Moreover, he already had the Holy Spirit of God and was His beloved Son. All this appears superfluous. But, of course, it isn't; it was to *fulfill all righteousness*, as verse 15 tells us.

There's a process that leads to righteousness, and John and Christ showed us the way; repent, confess, produce fruit, baptism, followed by testing to help us grow (see Matthew 4:1-11). As a result, even before His baptism Luke reports that "Jesus increased in wisdom and stature, and in favour with God and man" (Luke 2:52).

God's purpose for our life's spiritual purpose can only be accomplished because He gave us consciousness and mind. The Bible constantly emphasizes that for humans to achieve their spiritual purpose, we must:

- Believe God's Word reveals the definition of sin
  - Realize we are sinners
- Confess our wrong-doing
- Repent, reverse our spiritual lifestyle
  - Accept Jesus as our Savior Who paid for our sins
  - Be baptized for forgiveness and the start of a new life
  - Readily accept trials to grow more spiritual fruit

This preparatory path for the sure arrival of God's Kingdom is only possible because we possess neshama and ruach.

Do a study using UnlockBibleMeaning.com[4] to see how the five qualities of consciousness are fundamental to creating humans in God's image: *purpose* (our spiritual destination), *function* (repentance and growing spiritually), *socialization* (growing in favor with man, being a light), *rulership* (preparing to be a King and Priest (Revelation 1:6), and *reasoning* (wielding the sword of God's Word - Ephesians 6:17).

Every human who has ever walked the face of this Earth will have the opportunity to follow this way, the way, the only way to fulfill righteousness and reach their destination. God treats all humans equally, past, present, and future.

## Job and the Way

Let's look at one historic biblical example of Job, to whom God revealed the way. This biography is what I'd call a highlighted

---

4. https://unlockbiblemeaning.com

portrait because of its intense nature, but all the elements of the way are present.

Job was a God-fearing man, following God's ways, wealthy with a wonderful family.

### Job 1:1-3

> 1 There was a man in the land of Uz, whose name was Job; and that man was perfect and upright, and one that feared God, and eschewed evil.
>
> 2 And there were born unto him seven sons and three daughters.
>
> 3 His substance also was seven thousand sheep, and three thousand camels, and five hundred yoke of oxen, and five hundred she asses, and a very great household; so that this man was the greatest of all the men of the east.

Job was exercising his mind to accomplish the goals of his consciousness: he had a *purpose* for his life, and he was *functioning* and basically *reasoning* per the way of God. He practiced *rulership* through his riches and *socialization* via his family.

But Job was unaware he had a serious spiritual problem.

Read Job 1. Satan accused Job, saying he'd abandon God if all his well-being were removed from him. God acquiesced and allowed Satan to remove everything, family, riches, and Job's health until he sat atop a pile of ashes covered in boils, just itching himself with a broken piece of pottery.

Three of the day's most influential and intelligent people came to comfort him and explain why such a devastating trial was happening. The entirety of the book, about 30 chapters, is devoted to this exchange of ideas, all wrong. The men told Job he had hidden wrong-doing, and Job defended his integrity.

Finally, a younger man, Elihu, enters the discussion (Job 32) and makes one of the most important statements of the book; "I will fetch my knowledge from afar, and will ascribe righteousness to my Maker" (36:3). Using his spiritual reasoning, Elihu correctly, attributed complete righteousness to the Creator.

Job's problem is in Job 35:2 "Think you [Job] this to be right, that you said, My righteousness is more than God's?" This man could only see how right he was. That is the fundamental problem of humanity and leaders today. Everyone thinks they are right; they are the norm to which everyone else should conform. They think they're above everyone else; their ideas, doctrines, teachings, and beliefs are THE WAY.

## Puny Job, Puny Humans

God enters and concludes the discussion with Job showing how puny, incapable, incompetent, and stunted he is in relation to God. Job and his friends get an earful of Godly reasoning, and Job comes to his spiritual senses.

### Job 42:1-6

1 Then Job answered the LORD, and said,

2 I know that you can do every thing, and that no thought can be withheld from you (Job recognizes God's *purpose*).

3 Who is he that hides counsel without knowledge? therefore have I uttered that I understood not; things too wonderful for me, which I knew not (Sam: Job starts *reasoning* spiritually).

5 I have heard of you by the hearing of the ear: but now mine eye sees you.

6 Wherefore I abhor myself, and repent in dust and ashes (Sam: spiritual *functioning*, deep repentance, realizing he's nothing but filthy rags but has the potential for fulfilled righteousness, proper *rulership*, seeing God as the Head, proper *socialization*, seeing himself as a baby child exhibiting honor to God his Father).

Through this trial, God *formed* (Genesis 2:7 yatsar) Job[5] in the spiritual use of his consciousness (neshama) and mind according to His purpose for the Creation of humankind, having children grow up in the image of God's Family. "Let this mind be in you, which was also in Christ Jesus" (Philippians 2:5); Christ and Job are examples of the way, the only way, to fulfill righteousness and occupy one of the many mansions in our Father's House

---

5. https://theexplanation.com/human-family-elohim-god-works-both-create-rule/

# 48. Believe and Repent = Faith & Works = Dress & Keep Garden = 2 Commandments

**God's message to His Creation, humankind, has always been the same, *believe and repent*—only the format changed at Christ's Crucifixion.**

In this seventh Section about spiritual conversion of consciousness and mind, the focus has been on repentance, a change of mind resulting in a change of behavior; it includes the application of the Second Great Commandment, love your neighbor. Now, let's meditate on *believe* in *believe and repent*, and reveal its relationship to love your God, the First Great Commandment, and see how this dual formula links God and humans.

We shall also take a moment to show how a Christian practicing *believe and repent* should feel emotionally. It's necessary because some equate repentance with extreme sorrowful penitence.

## Doctrine is Teaching

As we study these two subjects, I must broach the doctrinal side of *faith and works* and other topics. The Bible states clearly in 2 Timothy 3:16, "All scripture is given by inspiration of God, and is profitable for *doctrine* (G1319), for reproof, for correction, for instruction in righteousness." Unfortunately, we're misusing the term doctrine for isolated biblical subjects like the doctrines of repentance or faith and works, etc. *Doctrine* (G1319) is simply *learning, teaching* from G1321 didaskō, to teach.

The point is this; many churches have creeds, confessions, or statements of faith; a list of doctrines, teachings, or beliefs that identify them. True, it is a quick way to get to know Church teaching, but it hides the integration of these beliefs. Members will defend each doctrine by finding corresponding verses, while someone in disagreement will find opposing verses. One is trying to outshout, *outverse* the other. That's not teaching, didaskō, "For God is not the author of confusion, but of peace, as in all churches of the saints" (1 Corinthians 14:33). This book has endeavored to present the overall integrated plan of God.

It's a jigsaw puzzle where all the pieces (doctrines, if you will) assemble together to form that one unconfused plan of God. As such, I entitled this chapter, "Believe and Repent = Faith & Works = Dress & Keep the Garden of Eden = 10 Commandments = 2 Great Commandments." So, there's one of the first events of the Old Testament, the Garden, coupled with the Two Commandments of the New Testament. In one sense, it couldn't get more diverse than that. But, since there's no confusion and "Jesus Christ is the same yesterday, and to day, and for ever" (Hebrew 13:8), let's reveal the link between these two seemingly disparate concepts.

To set the stage, we'll see God's plan for the Creation of humankind and, in particular, to whom and why God freely gives eternal life. If I break it down a little further, we plow into the commonly talked about doctrines of "believe and you're saved" and "are works necessary for salvation?" Remember, we're broaching this subject because it directly involves spiritual conversion, the Holy Spirit working with consciousness and mind and turning it around to God's point of view.

## Believe = Worship = Faith = Love God, The First Commandment

We'll start at the beginning with a question. God created the entire world with its biodiversity of fauna and flora during the six days of Creation. Toward the end of the sixth day, his culminating action was that of the first human, adam. Why did God plant the Garden of Eden only AFTER He created the human? After all, He finished everything before the man came into existence. Note the sequence of events immediately following the verse, which is the key to the Mind-Body dilemma.

> **Genesis 2:7-10**
>
> 7 And the LORD God formed man of the dust of the ground, and breathed into his nostrils the breath of life; and man became a living soul.
>
> 8 And the LORD God planted a garden eastward in Eden; and there he put the man whom he had formed.
>
> 9 And out of the ground made the LORD God to grow every tree that is pleasant to the sight, and good for

food; the tree of life also in the midst of the garden, and the tree of knowledge of good and evil.

10 And a river went out of Eden to water the garden; and from thence it was parted, and became into four heads.

The first human, with his consciousness and mind fully functioning, and undoubtedly his eyes open as wide as saucers, witnessed God plant a magnificent garden. Adam, in amazement, glimpsed the trees sprout and elevate skyward; those two cornerstone trees were the centerpieces of the garden, surpassing all the others by their splendor. It's impossible to be in Adam's shoes (which he didn't have anyway) but meditate on the scenario. Adam was a first-row spectator of the awesomeness of what God is capable of. Then, God picked him up and gently placed him in the garden; he quickly realized this literal paradise was where he'd live with this extraordinary Creator God—planting the Garden after Adam's creation developed his faith and relationship with His Creator. What an introduction to life.

Soon after, God created Eve, and the couple spent the Sabbath in the presence of God's shared wisdom (Genesis 2:2-3[1]). Later, the Serpent was allowed into the Garden, with the subsequent succumbing to temptation. Then, God decided to expel them, and here's the reason.

**Genesis 3:22-23**

22 And the LORD God said, Behold, the man is become as one of us, to *know* (H3045) good and evil:

---

1. https://theexplanation.com/god-to-do-with-his-work-to-make-them-on-7th-day-to-take-care-his-creation/

and now, lest he put forth his hand, and take also of the tree of life, and eat, and live for ever:

23 Therefore the LORD God sent him forth from the garden of Eden, to *till* (H5647) the ground from whence he was taken.

Unfortunately, this translation hides the crucial figurative meaning for fuller comprehension. Humans had become "like God to *know* (H3045) good and evil."

## H3045

יָדַע yâdaʿ yaw-dah'; a primitive root; to know (properly, to ascertain by seeing); used in a great variety of senses, figuratively, literally, euphemistically and inferentially (including observation, care, recognition; and causatively, instruction, designation, punishment, etc.):

KJV - acknowledge, acquaintance(-ted with), advise, answer, **appoint**, assuredly, be aware, (un-) awares, can(-not), certainly, comprehend, consider, × could they, cunning, **declare**, be diligent, (can, cause to) **discern, discover**, endued with, familiar friend, famous, feel, can have, be (ig-) norant, instruct, kinsfolk, kinsman, (cause to let, make) know, (come to give, have, take) knowledge, have (knowledge), (be, make, make to be, make self) known, + be learned, + lie by man, **mark, perceive**, privy to, × prognosticator, regard, have **respect**, skilful, **shew**, can (man of) skill, be sure, of a surety, **teach**, (can) tell, understand, have (understanding), × will be, wist, wit, wot.

It's not just *knowing* good and evil; it's also the other translations, including *appointing, declaring, discerning, discovering, marking, perceiving, respecting, showing,* and *teaching* good and evil. From that point forward, humans took it upon themselves to decide what is good and evil, which is solely the prerogative of God. Human consciousness and minds disconnected from God's way to establish their own. Every country has a leader and legislature to establish laws about right and wrong. Some invoke God, but not one makes any effort to do what's good in God's eyes.

Therefore, two results impact *believe and repent*. First, people no longer believe in God, and second, they no longer wish to follow His way (repent). Hence, God sent Adam and Eve out of the Garden to till the ground. This consequence is the equivalent of Romans 1:28 "And even as they did not like to retain God in their knowledge, God gave them over to a reprobate *mind*, to do those things which are not convenient;" There's a mind-flip from *believe* and *repent* to disbelief and disobedience. Humankind replaced God's knowledge of good and evil with human knowledge of good and evil. God left them with their twisted mind.

God had put them in the "garden of Eden to *dress* (H5647) and *keep* (H8104) it[2]." Then He expelled them to "*till* (H5647) the ground from whence he was taken." Note that *dress* and *till* are identical in Hebrew.

### H5647

עָבַד 'âbad aw-bad'; a primitive root; to work (in any sense); by implication, to serve, till, (causatively) enslave, etc.:

---

2. https://theexplanation.com/dress-keep-garden-of-eden-man-destined-to-be-a-gardener/

KJV - × be, keep in bondage, be bondmen, bond-service, compel, do, **dress**, ear, execute, + husbandman, keep, labour(-ing man, bring to pass, (cause to, make to) serve(-ing, self), (be, become) **servant**(-s), do (use) service, till(-er), transgress (from margin), (set a) work, be wrought, **worshipper**,

God put humans in the garden to *believe* in and *worship* him. That's the meaning of *dress*; Paul called himself the "servant of God" (Titus 1:1). *Believe* is to have faith (faith and works); it is the first four of the Ten Commandments and the First Great Commandment, *love God*. It's always been the same injunction to humanity; focus your mind on God, *believe and repent*. Adam, Eve, and humanity didn't want to worship God; He turned them over to *till*, which means *worship* the ground. Today materialism, worshipping the ground, is the name of the game.

## Repent, Keep, Works; Reprobate or Righteous, It Starts in the Mind

Do a study of *keep* (H8104)[3] as in "dress and *keep* the garden" in Genesis 2:15. It means *observe,* identical to many verses in Deuteronomy, namely Deut. 31:12 "that they may hear, and that they may learn, and *fear the LORD your God*, and *observe* (H8104) to do all the words of this law:" *Believe* and *repent* is *fear the LORD your God* and *observe*. In the New Testament, Paul shows that non-observance has an identical origin to non-worship, the mind.

**Romans 1:28-31**

---

3. https://unlockbiblemeaning.com

28 And even as they did not like to retain God in their knowledge, God gave them over to a reprobate mind, to do those things which are not convenient;

29 Being filled with all unrighteousness, fornication, wickedness, covetousness, maliciousness; full of envy, murder, debate, deceit, malignity; whisperers,

30 Backbiters, haters of God, despiteful, proud, boasters, inventors of evil things, disobedient to parents,

31 Without understanding, covenantbreakers, without natural affection, implacable, unmerciful:

Being animated by a reprobate mind is sinning, breaking God's law, and doing those acts in verses 29-31. They start in and are controlled by the mind, ruach, and spirit in humans; from this conduct, we must *repent;* that's believe and repent. It is transforming our worldly behavior to the *faith* and *works* of God. It is the application of the Second Great Commandment, love your neighbor, as we see in the above context.

## Results of a Reprobate Mind

Allowing a person, who has been helped, warned, shown the way, encouraged, guided, and received all possible assistance BUT who insists on doing their own thing, to be abandoned to a reprobate mind might sound awful, but it has a specific purpose. Paul in the New Testament does precisely what God did in the Old Testament with the expulsion.

### 1 Corinthians 5:1-5

1 It is reported commonly that there is fornication among you, and such fornication as is not so much as named among the Gentiles, that one should have his father's wife.

4 In the name of our Lord Jesus Christ, when you are gathered together, and my spirit, with the power of our Lord Jesus Christ,

5 To deliver such an one to Satan for the destruction of the flesh, that the *spirit* (G4151 - pneuma - mind) may be saved in the day of the Lord Jesus.

The key here is the preeminence of the mind over the body. Today all the emphasis is on the comfort of the physical body. In the name of humanism, we've gone beyond the tolerance of unthinkable behavior. Our reprobate society is upside down. In this field, we need repentance and the works of the last six of the Ten Commandments. God focuses on how you and I believe and repent to maintain healthy psychological and spiritual minds.

## Believe and Repent. Both are Vital for Salvation.

It's not one or the other or an interpretation of the meaning of repentance. A change of mind is the basis. We saw that on expulsion from the Garden of Eden, God clothed Adam and Eve with coats of skins signifying their new way of life. Similarly, those who will live eternally with God must don the white clothes of righteousness. Eternal life is a free gift, but we have responsibilities now and forever.

### Matthew 22:1-14

> 12 And he [the King] said to him, Friend, how came you in hither [to the wedding] not having a wedding garment? And he [the guest] was speechless.
>
> 13 Then said the king to the servants, Bind him hand and foot, and take him away, and cast him into outer darkness; there shall be weeping and gnashing of teeth.

God will only allow appropriately dressed individuals into His House for all eternity, just as you wouldn't admit rebellious people into your home even if they somehow *believe* you're the house owner. *So believe and repent* go together.

## Believe and Repent Bring Peace of Mind

Some think a Christian who believes and repents will live a life of drudgery, tediousness, sadness, and struggle. Sure, God will try us but imagine knowing why the Universe exists, why humans are on Earth, why we have consciousness and mind, why the world is the way it is with its incurable ills, and why humans are so stubborn. And especially understanding what the future, beyond the turmoil, holds for all of humankind, past, present, and future, and ourselves for all eternity. That's why Christ makes this promise.

> **John 14:27**
>
> Peace I leave with you, my peace I give you: not as the world gives, give I to you. Let not your heart be troubled, neither let it be afraid.

The true gift of peace of mind and tranquility of consciousness comes from the ability to believe and repent. With its myriad physical and spiritual remedies, the world offers an illusionary, temporary calm.

The repentant believer sees their life and situation in light of God's plan; their mindset carries them through troubled waters. Hang on to this SOS buoy, the save-our-spirit lifebuoy, with which we can serve believers and, in the right way, those willing to address spirituality in their lives so they can benefit from God's peace of mind.

# 49. Consciousness and Mind, the Way to the Full Image of God

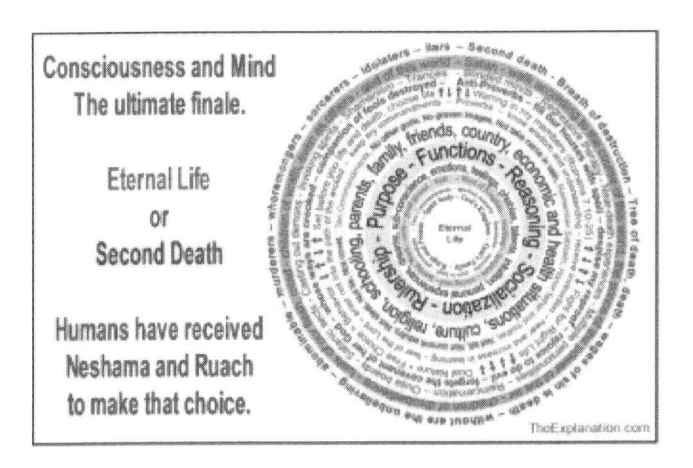

**Consciousness and Mind**
The ultimate finale.

Eternal Life
or
Second Death

Humans have received Neshama and Ruach to make that choice.

**This chapter is the finale of Mind-Body Problem Solved. Now, you know the biblical perspective of consciousness and mind.**

We've come a long way, but it's only the beginning. In 2023, nobody knows and shares this vital breakthrough knowledge. We'll come full circle and close the loop regarding consciousness and mind. We started in Genesis 2:7, and we will end there.

**Genesis 2:7**

And the LORD God formed man of the dust of the ground, and *breathed* (H5301) into his nostrils the *breath* (H5397) of life; and man became a living soul.

*God **breathed** the breath of life.* Easy to read, easy to understand. Yes, but the Hebrew reveals an enormous surprise. Check it at UnlockBibleMeaning.com[1]

### H5301

נָפַח nâphach naw-fakh'; a primitive root; to puff, in various applications (literally, to inflate, blow hard, scatter, kindle, expire; figuratively, to disesteem):

KJV - blow, breath, give up, cause to lose (life), seething, snuff.

*Cause to lose life*, wow, the opposite. We're not shocked because we know the first step to mastering Biblical Hebrew words; one can have many, even contradictory meanings[2]. Simultaneous with creating life, God has the power to snuff it out. You might think this is an anomaly, or Strong and Kneller are leading you up the garden path. Look at the root meaning of *breath* of life for confirmation of blowing out life, like a candle.

### H5397

נְשָׁמָה nᵉshâmâh nesh-aw-maw'; from H5395 (נָשַׁם); a puff, i.e. wind, angry or vital breath, divine inspiration, intellect. or (concretely) an animal:

KJV - blast, (that) breath(-eth), inspiration, soul, spirit.

### H5395

---

1. https://unlockbiblemeaning.com

2. https://theexplanation.com/fastest-bible-study-method-god-intended-meaning/

נָשַׁם nâsham naw-sham'; a primitive root; properly, to blow away, i.e. destroy:

KJV - destroy.

Again, **breath** *of life* includes *destruction*. This entire book has focused on that word and explained its *consciousness*, which it is. Now we see the flip side; consciousness means *annihilation;* it can be destroyed. By now, you should be putting two and two together and seeing how this assembles with God's plan.

Remember, in Genesis 2:7, it's the breath of liveS, chaYIM, plural. We have lives and death, destruction; in fact, we also have deathS, plural. Unfortunately, the translation hides this vital information from us, but Biblical Hebrew is clear.

### Genesis 2:9, 16-17

9 And out of the ground made the LORD God to grow every tree that is pleasant to the sight, and good for food; the tree of life (וְעֵץ הַחַיִּים – chaYIM – liveS is plural) also in the midst of the garden, and the tree of knowledge of good and evil.

16 And the LORD God commanded the man, saying, Of every tree of the garden you may freely eat:

17 But of the tree of the knowledge of good and evil, you shall not eat of it: for in the day that you eat thereof you shall *surely die* (מוֹת תָּמוּת – two deaths).

You can see the similarity of the last three letters, from the left, of those two words; dead, dead; it's plural, *you shall die die*. So, we have a double dose of death, just as we have multiple lives. The entire Bible story confirms this.

**Hebrews 9:27**

And as it is appointed to men once to die, but after this the judgment:

**Romans 6:23**

For the wages of sin is death; but the gift of God is eternal life through Jesus Christ our Lord.

The *wages of sin* is not the natural death that occurs to all humans; we're all appointed to die once. However, the Bible reveals there's a second death. The Bible corroborates a resurrection and second life AFTER the first death (Revelation 20:5, Ezekiel 37:1-14).

**Revelation 2:11, 21:8**

2:11 He that has an ear, let him hear what the Spirit says to the churches; He that overcomes shall not be hurt of the second death.

21:8 But the fearful, and unbelieving, and the abominable, and murderers, and whoremongers, and sorcerers, and idolaters, and all liars, shall have their part in the lake which burns with fire and brimstone: which is the second death (Sam: This fire is related to the meaning of *breathed* (H5301) which is *seething*).

We can now conclude the story of humankind. The Bible states two finalities: the second death or eternal life. Both are definitive. Of course, this is only the beginning of the story for those who receive the gift of God, eternal life. For the others, it is the end of the line.

You now know the reason WHY God gave each human neshama and ruach, consciousness and mind. To decide WHICH WAY they want to follow. There are two choices: God's and the Serpent's.

That's why God released the Serpent in the Garden of Eden and again at the end of the Millennium (Revelation 20:7-10). God always has total control over the Serpent, which He uses as needed for trials to see which way humans will choose.

Consciousness (neshama), with its five attributes, purpose, function, socialization, rulership, and reasoning, animated by the power of the spirit in humans (ruach), are God's qualities conferred on humans to make us temporary human beings in His image. He allotted humankind time to live and choose the way to God or the Serpent. Life is a human, temporary training ground to use the power of the mind applied to the five traits of consciousness. That way of life is directed to the Serpent or God; the choice is ours. The last chapter of Revelation makes this clear.

### Revelation 22:12-15

12 And, behold, I come quickly; and my reward is with me, to give every man according as his work shall be.

13 I am Alpha and Omega, the beginning and the end, the first and the last.

14 Blessed are they that do his commandments, that they may have right to the tree of life, and may enter in through the gates into the city (Sam: The gift of God is eternal life, but this verse shows the relationship

between the necessity for works/commandments and access to the tree of life).

15 For without are dogs, and sorcerers, and whoremongers, and murderers, and idolaters, and whosoever loves and makes a lie.

God's Family, composed of those who follow Christ's way[3], are IN New Jerusalem. Those who have made an unequivocal and unchanging choice to continue in their own way are OUTside of God's Kingdom.

Please understand. At this moment in history, God's plan for humans is NOT complete; there are numerous steps to come, too long to elaborate on here. But every human will have the full opportunity of being called to know the truth about God and deciding with complete knowledge and lucidity whether they want the second death or eternal life.

We can now complete our diagram of the *circles of psychology and spirituality*™, the roles of consciousness and mind in human well-being.

---

3. https://theexplanation.com/christ-is-the-way-filthy-rags-to-righteousnesss/

Figure 53. COnsciousness and Mind in Psychology And Sound Spirituality™- COMPASS

The ultimate goals are the second death for the unbelievers and unrepentant, or New Jerusalem, God's Kingdom and Family for those who choose to believe, repent, and "let the mind be in them, which was also in Christ Jesus" (Philippians 2:5).

## It's Always About Free Will Choice

From the beginning, God gave Adam and Eve a choice between the two trees. As discussed in the sixth Section[4], the psychology of the Old Testament with UNconverted people was and still is a choice.

---

4. https://theexplanation.com/psychology-best-bible-definition-for-humans/

As *The Explanation* pointed out, for the UNconverted in the 21st century, Proverbs is the best psychology book[5] we could have. It reveals the way to a sane and stable life, the way to avoid the unfortunate mental turmoil which describes our world today. Again, God says to choose.

> **Proverbs 1:22-23**
>
> 22 How long, you simple ones, will you love simplicity? and the scorners delight in their scorning, and fools hate knowledge?
>
> 23 Turn you at my reproof: behold, I will pour out my spirit to you, I will make known my words to you.

Whether it's the UNconverted before God calls them and opens their minds with the Holy Spirit to spiritual understanding OR for the converted who live in Christ, God's Word, Scripture, is first and foremost the book of Human Well-Being. God addressed it to humankind as the instruction manual for an abundant life.

## The Bible is the Book Leading to Life

Scripture reveals how to reach eternal life; it's not an elixir, a magical potion; it's how to use the Holy Spirit to "Set your affection on things above, not on things on the earth. And put on the new man, which is renewed in knowledge after the image of him [Jesus Christ] that created him:" (Colossians 3:2-10). Who, in all circumstances, directed His consciousness and mind in the five areas to accomplish His Father's will. He left us the perfect example to do likewise.

## Get Over the Pride of Life

---

5. https://theexplanation.com/everyday-psychology-everybody-healthy-mentality/

I suggest you study the verses with "...*of life.*" Here are two that show the negative implication of consciousness and mind.

### 1 John 2:16

For all that is in the world, the lust of the flesh, and the lust of the eyes, and the *pride (G212) of life*, is not of the Father, but is of the world.

### James 4:16

But now you rejoice in your *boasting* (G212): all such rejoicing is evil.

Another translation is *boaster* or *self-confidence*; this is not referring to being pleased with one's skills. It's an exaggerated consciousness and mindfulness of one's own dignity to the exclusion of giving God the credit. We've got to get over that, and the only way is by the Father's calling and giving us a portion of the Holy Spirit, the "*Spirit of life* in Christ Jesus has made me free from the law of sin and death" (Romans 8:2). Do you see the choice between pride *of life* and Spirit *of life*?

## The Lives of the Tree of Lives

When he was called, the future Apostle Peter reasoned with his consciousness and mind, "Then Simon Peter answered him, Lord, to whom shall we go? you have the *words of eternal life*" (John 6:68). God's Words are also called the *statutes of life* "If the wicked restore the pledge, give again that he had robbed, walk in the *statutes of life*, without committing iniquity; he shall surely live, he shall not die" (Ezekiel 33:15).

Spiritual conversion of the consciousness and mind means accepting the *Prince of Life* (Acts 3:15), Christ, the *Bread of Life* (John 6:48), Who is the *Way of Life* (Proverbs 6:23), distilling the *Reproof of Life* (Pro. 15:31) that puts us on the *Path of Life* (Pro. 5:6).

It's this teaching, the *Doctrine of Life* (2 Timothy 3:10), that helps us walk in *Newness of Life* (Romans 6:4) thanks to the *Water of Life* (Rev. 21:6), which represents the *Spirit of Life* (Rev. 11:11). The Holy Spirit transforms our consciousness and mind as we drink from the *Fountain of Life* (Psalm 36:9). These rivers will issue from the Garden of Eden and quench the spiritual thirst of all humankind in the future.

All who believe and repent will access a guiltless consciousness and mind "by the righteousness of one the free gift came upon all men to justification of life (Romans 5:18). They will have access to the Grace of Life (1 Peter 3:7) and the Crown of Life (Rev. 2:10) as Kings and Priests, and will benefit from the Resurrection of Life (John 5:29) with their names written in the Book of Life (Rev. 22:19) for all eternity.

God laid out His plan for humankind before the foundation of Earth; He will accomplish His purpose. Neshama and ruach, consciousness and mind, will be transformed into the image of God, which has been and always will be the work of Jesus Christ. Haste the day when humankind will understand.

# Epilogue

# The Bible is the Fabulous Story of Humankind. What a Human is.

**The Bible refers to God, but the focus is on God's Creation and the salvation of humans.** *Mind-Body Problem Solved* **explains what a human being is.**

Why write a book, *Mind-Body Problem Solved*, essentially around one Bible verse, Genesis 2:7? The Bible is, first and foremost, the story of humankind. And the paradox is that we don't know who we are, why we're here, or where we're headed. This book has answered all those queries.

Science, philosophy, religion, and the Bible cannot be divorced from our daily experiences. Yet often, we box those disciplines into separate segments of our reasoning. Yet, the Bible has revealed how the physical and spiritual are integrated into coherent completeness, with humans being the primary example.

Consciousness and mind, neshama and ruach, are central to God's plan for humans. Only when we understand this basis and why God imbued each physical human with these spiritual attributes can we build out other subjects in the Bible.

## God's Image

For instance, humans possess God's image[1]. They have free will to decide their purpose in life and how they will function, including their style of relationships, rulership, and, most importantly, reasoning. Will they reason along the lines of God or not? Humans, alone, can accomplish these feats thanks to God breathing the *breath of life* (neshama) into them.

## God's Family

Humans have the unprecedented opportunity of being God's sons and daughters and can enter God's family[2]. One of the primary misunderstood subjects in Genesis 1 is when Elohim (plural) says, "let US make *man* (adam - humans) in OUR image, after OUR likeness." God is a Family with a Father, a Son, and a Bride, who is also the Mother, the Church, or the Assembly of family members.

The Apostle Paul uses this analogy "For I am jealous over you (the Church members) with godly jealousy: for I have espoused you to one husband, that I may present you as a chaste virgin to Christ" (2 Corinthians 11:2). The human family institution, as exposed in Genesis 1, with a male and female multiplying and having children is in the image of God.

## The Bible Answers All the Questions About Genesis 2:7

---

1. https://theexplanation.com/consciousness-and-mind-the-way-image-of-god/

2. https://theexplanation.com/all-time-hidden-truth-elohim-god-is-a-family/

In the Introduction, I penned a promise about the outcome of *Mind-Body Problem Solved*.

Nobody understands Genesis 2:7.

Wow, Sam, that's a strong allegation. What do you mean? Let's take a closer look at this verse.

**Genesis 2:7**

And the LORD God formed man of the dust of the ground, and breathed into his nostrils the breath of life; and man became a living soul.

- Who is the Lord? What is the relation to the Higher Power?
- Why are *Lord* (Yahveh) singular and *God* (Elohim) plural?
- What does *formed* mean? For instance, why doesn't it say *created*?
- Why from the dust? What's the difference between dust and ground?
- Why breathe into the nostrils? Why breathe at all? God could've used any *method*.
- Did you know that *breathed* and *breath* are two different words in Hebrew? What does each mean? What is their relationship?
- The Hebrew says the *breath of liveS*. It's plural. What's that all about? By the way, the Tree of Life is also the *Tree of LiveS*, plural. Yes, you're getting an eyeful today.
- Does *man* in Hebrew only refer to the masculine gender or something else?
- What is a *soul*? That's the $1.000.000 question! Everybody talks about it, but for a definition, there's as much

confusion as for the *mind*.
- *Living* soul is singular. So why and how can a singular soul have a plural *breath of liveS*?

Many singulars, plurals, and variations of the same word are invisible in English. If we want appropriate answers, we have no choice but to delve into Biblical Hebrew. The solution must be coherent and relate to every human being, past, present, and future. God is the God of humankind, or He isn't. We might have a *spiritual* component, but we live in a *physical* world; they must relate.

When you can answer all those questions about Genesis 2:7 and many others, you will answer the mind-body problem with assurance and verity.

- Understand the Higher Power and the relationship with the mind.
- Grasp WHAT the mind is and WHY the Higher Power gave it.
- Fathom WHO possesses a mind and WHY they have one.
- Realize HOW TO USE your mind to the best of its potential. You'll understand the role of the mind now and, amazingly, in the future.

This book, the *Mind-Body Problem Solved*, will explain Genesis 2:7 and answer all the above questions and many more.

I believe *The Explanation* reached and surpassed that purpose. Meditation and guidance have taken *The Explanation* much further than ever expected over the year of writing this book. One of the main ingredients has been the ability to easily and quickly master Biblical Hebrew with the Bible tools available at UnlockBibleMeaning.com[3].

## The Fastest Method to Unlock the Bible's Original Meaning

The fourth step of the Bible study method[4] to reach the God-intended meaning of Scripture is the key destination for every Biblical Hebrew word. ALL the translations/meanings (multiple, contradictory, figurative, roots) for a given Biblical Hebrew word must tell ONE STORY. That's it. Bibles give us basically a word-for-word translation.

However, each Biblical Hebrew word tells ONE COHERENT STORY. ALL the multiple meanings weave together to narrate the original God-intended meaning.

We've prayed, meditated on, and studied to reach that, and that alone. Each word is a puzzle piece with its one-and-only shape. The various meanings reveal the contours of each word. When we really tell the word story, we understand WHERE and HOW it assembles with ALL the other puzzle pieces.

The Bible study method *The Explanation* uses for all its Bible commentaries narrates the word stories and assembles them with adjoining words until we build the complete puzzle. It reveals the God-intended meaning of His purpose for the universe and humankind.

---

3. https://unlockbiblemeaning.com

4. https://theexplanation.com/fastest-bible-study-method-god-intended-meaning/

Figure 54. How to reach coherent completeness

*Mind-Body Problem Solved* has answered all the above questions. We've narrated the exciting stories of each Biblical Hebrew word and assembled them into the God-intended, original message of Scripture. We've clarified the contours of neshama and explained why it's both a giver and snuffer of life. Finally, we've reached coherent completeness illustrated by the image Full Definition: Mind, Body, Consciousness.

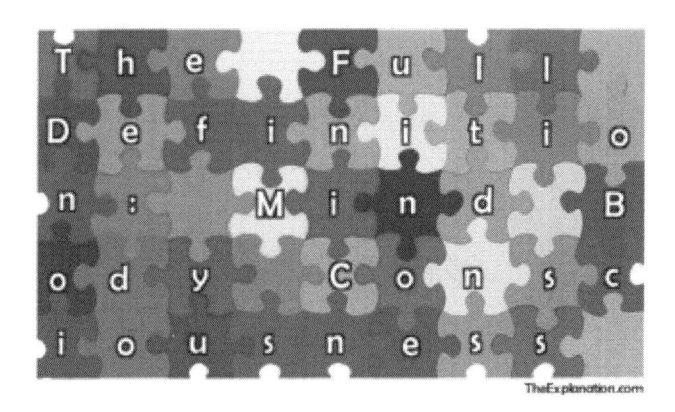

Figure 55. Coherent completeness

In the first Part, the book addressed universal conundrums science, philosophy, and religion can't answer. Section II revealed where to locate the explanation; then we went deep into the meaning of neshama (Section III - consciousness ) and ruach (IV - the power associated with the mind), showing how the latter animates the entire Universe (V). Finally, getting very practical, the book unveiled God's implication for the welfare of all humankind by granting them the path to an abundant life (VI) and, specifically, the way to spiritual calling and conversion (VII).

With that in mind, I'd like to draw your attention to one of the Apostle Paul's insights regarding God's Word in this epilogue. It's the elegance, practicality, and especially the simplicity of God's plan.

> **2 Corinthians 11:3**
>
> But I fear, lest by any means, as the serpent beguiled Eve through his subtilty, so your minds should be corrupted from the simplicity that is in Christ.

That verse covers the book, the outer and inner forces of the circles of psychology and spirituality[5]™, impacting the human mind and the simplicity of God's plan for humankind. Scripture is straightforward for those led by the Holy Spirit; God's plan shines through. "But the natural man receives not the things of the Spirit of God: for they are foolishness to him: neither can he know them, because they are spiritually discerned" (1 Corinthians 2:14). I cannot say it better than Paul.

## Now, You Have the Definition of *Human*; Where to From Here?

*Mind-Body Problem Solved* has so many ramifications it wasn't possible to broach all of them. Hence the reason for links to various

---

5. https://theexplanation.com/consciousness-and-mind-the-way-image-of-god/

books for further details. Other subjects like the Biblical Feasts, Passover, Unleavened Bread, and Pentecost resonate with how humans function, and terms like *begotten*, *babes*, and *born again* have been omitted to keep the book's length a reasonable size and still fully cover the subject.

The Mind-Body subject is far from exhausted, just as the Bible story is far from detailed. Many other pieces of the Bible puzzle still need to be put in their correct one-and-only slot. This process takes time and necessitates more spiritual learning and experience. I'm sure you have questions.

I suggest reading *The Explanation* 7 book series[6], a commentary of Genesis 1-3 based on the same Biblical Hebrew word mastery method as this book. In addition, you can follow online Bible courses[7] during which Sam will participate in live Q&A. Finally, please leave a review of this book where you purchased it, and join our no-obligation, total privacy, no-spam newsletter[8].

Sam continues to blog and write at TheExplanation.com[9] and produce videos at Youtube.com/theexplanation[10] and is working on numerous other projects, including *History, News, Prophecy, a biblical chronology of the Universe's and Humankind's events*. The Bible reveals the definite chain of circumstances leading to the climax of the Story of Humankind.

---

6. https://theexplanation.com/books

7. https://theexplanation.com/marketplace

8. https://theexplanation.com/subscribe

9. https://theexplanation.com/

10. https://www.youtube.com/theexplanation

# Practical Mind Transformation. First steps

## COnsciousness and Mind, Psychology And Sound Spirituality™ (COMPASS)

Here's a pragmatic method to begin preventing and healing mental disorders like anxiety and depression. Activities that include all five aspects of consciousness and can be practiced at all ages with no experience or advanced levels of competency. That's the ideal. Cooking and sports come to mind as themes that fit these criteria.

There are others like games and art, but the former have the added value of improving health and helping people become self-dependant in areas that impact us daily. They are worldwide occupations that necessitate little equipment and can be practiced by everyone anywhere. They could even lead to a money-earning occupation. There are many other ideas.

So, let's plot your COMPASS course.

Think about a ship leaving port and heading to its destination.

1. It must know its END destination
2. It must know how to get out of its present port. For this maneuver, its second-by-second surveillance often requires a local pilot and even tug-boats

That is the same as the trip of life.

1. What is your FUTURE destination for:
    a. Your PURPOSE in life: Train driver, derelict, doctor, social worker, artist
    b. How you will FUNCTION as a human being: behavior, readiness to change your actions, how you handle others' mistakes
    c. Your SOCIALIZATION: Single, married, divorced, integrated into society
    d. Your RULERSHIP: In control of yourself and your surroundings, salaried, independent
    e. Your REASONING: Based on rumors, fake news, erroneous information, truth

Those are big destination decisions where you'll be navigating some rough waters. You'll gain experience during the trip and make course changes to keep on track. You must know yourself, your capacities, and your mindset. You cannot do this alone, but you are ultimately responsible in all these areas to reach the proper ports of call and, finally, your destination.

You don't have to make FINAL destination choices at age 18, 20, or even 30, but you need an excellent idea of some intermediary ports, or you will be doing circles in shark-infested waters. Goals change; it's *flexible steadfastness*.

1. How are you maneuvering to get out of the harbor TODAY? In the next hour? NOW?
    a. Your PURPOSE today: What's today's ONE step forward toward becoming a better train driver, derelict, doctor, social worker, or artist?
    b. How will you FUNCTION in the next few minutes as a human being: your choices, accepting your errors, and making amends?
    c. Your SOCIALIZATION: What will be your subsequent five exchanges with people around you? Your mate, parents, children, colleague, person in the street.
    d. Your RULERSHIP: What will be your following three decisions in managing yourself and your surroundings? Will it improve or degrade your life?
    e. Your REASONING: How will your mind react and weigh the following two thoughts, situations, news, and information that come your way?

With your COMPASS in hand, you can modify a course, even one small degree, to align yourself in the right direction. As a parent, psychologist, teacher, manager, or coach, it's your responsibility to help point a child, patient, student, employee, or client in the right direction and show them HOW to take the FIRST step. Help them DEVELOP a plan and receive the TRAINING and EQUIPMENT necessary to cast off from the dock.

The five primary areas of life are daunting and may be beyond you. That's ok. Choose one domain and take just a short footstep in the right direction. Cast off just ONE of the ropes attached to the moorings, the first detaching of a shackle imprisoning you in the harbor. Jump the first, even lowest, hurdle in front of you. That's your initial victory.

Realize you did it. Help the person monitor their performance, even if you/they make a mistake. A cruise starts with one maneuver.

Map out the subsequent two or three actions to get out of port. Break it down, ONE stage at a time, the what and how you'll accomplish it. Do not overwhelm yourself or another person. Time is not the significant factor here; the person and their initial stride forward are.

A mistake in accomplishing the task is not a critical issue here; trying is; we all make mistakes. Analyze why the person tripped over the hurdle and how I can help myself or the person jump better. Maybe reduce the height. Perhaps you need to add a stage you hadn't thought of, like getting a more adapted pair of shoes or doing some leg-muscle building first if you're helping a sedentary person become more active.

My Departure: Myself, coach, manager, employer, teacher, parent, adult, adolescent, child.

- Consider their age, mental level, intellectual, and manual skills
- Consider whether you're proposing personal, spiritual, and/or civic advice
- Consider establishing a detailed *how to* reach each benchmark
- Make each step attainable *quickly* so they can know they've crossed the finish line
- Discuss the stage with them. It cannot be imposed. It must be their free-will choice
- They're responsible for their decision. They set the goal

and are accountable

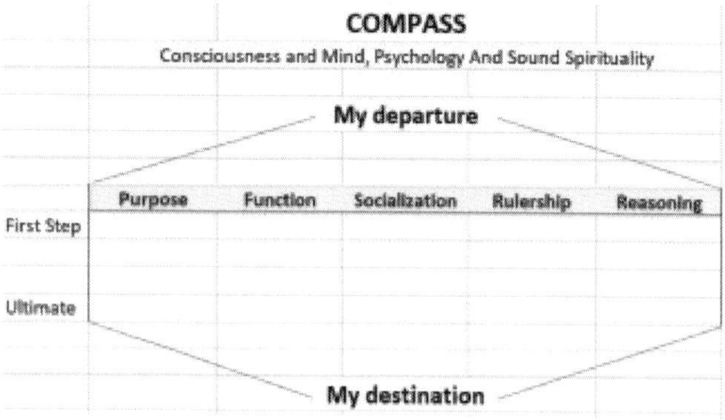

*Figure 56. Your mind transformation COMPASS*

Download (Google Doc)[1] and give a printed copy to the adventurer so they can plot and follow their cruise.

You'll find more details and examples about COMPASS there, and you can leave comments and suggestions[2].

**Example:**

Many years ago, in London, I went into this food store with a grill behind the counter. A disabled young man was learning to fry eggs. His manager patiently showed him how to clean, prepare the grill, break the egg (no shells and no broken yolk), and use a spatula to position it on the plate... A few days later, I returned, and he was doing a perfect job. One by one, he'd mastered the cooking steps and was autonomous.

---

1. https://theexplanation.com/compass

2. https://theexplanation.com/practical-mind-transformation-first-steps

Go fry an egg and break down all the steps. If you have a young child, watch, guide, envision, and see the detailed steps to make scrambled, 3-minute or hard-boiled eggs and how to peel them, then move on to an omelet, eggs Benedict. Every kid and adult should know such basics.

### 1. Purpose (Chapter 15)

All five areas of consciousness are essential, and the first step must be taken for each of them. But five steps can already be distressing, which we want to avoid. We don't organize life in one discussion. Let's focus on one aspect, and I suggest it be Purpose in Life. I think it's easier to define because it's pragmatic, and the physical tools for its accomplishment are easier to come by. Map it out. Your kids will love the experience, especially eating the results of their *labor*, they'll have a purpose. Map this out for all five areas of consciousness, but go molo-molo, slowly and delicately, at their pace, not yours.

Usually, a person's purpose depends on their talents, skill level, and particularly their likes and dislikes. If all those criteria line up, then you get a direction. It's good to have a medium-term objective in mind so the mentee can see how the first and intermediary steps lead to a bigger feasible goal. The slightest movement to the destination activates the neurotransmitters that reduce anxiety and depression. Once an individual embarks on regular steps, no matter how minute, their mental health takes an upswing.

We can get immediate, measurable, and positive results with Purpose orientation, which is a tremendous encouragement. Here is a non-exhaustive list of general ideas to narrow down to those first few steps.

**Suggestions:**

- **Mastery of space**: clean up; organize a drawer, cupboard, room, all the way up to a factory or office; it depends on the capacity and state of the individual
- **Learn** a subject or skill, enhance a talent they've always been intrigued by. Get one fact, move, and add more. Coaching might be necessary
- Let their **creativity**, physical or mental, begin to simmer. Help their **imagination** to flow. Just so long as it's legal and edifying. Compose stories, drawing, pottery, and many other endeavors

Remember, you might have to develop the **how to** step-by-step for yourself or with the person. Ask them how they will proceed; their method to get from A to Z. Let's be sure they're equipped to reach the goal.

**Proverbs 14:23** In all labor there is profit (mental health is a benefit): But the talk of the lips tend only to penury (staying tied to the mooring doesn't get you anywhere).

**Psychology shows us:** Benefits of cooking on mental health[3]. Why eggs with a recipe?[4]

**Quote:** You don't have to see the whole staircase; just take the first step.

**Five fundamental aspects of** *consciousness*

And the practical everyday application by the *mind*. Choose where to take the one little step forward among these characteristics and plan the way.

### 1. Purpose – Chapter 15

---

[3]. https://www.news-medical.net/health/Mental-Health-and-Cooking.aspx

[4]. https://www.wellandgood.com/brain-benefits-eggs/

# MIND-BODY PROBLEM SOLVED

Nature of Humans, Consciousness & Mind[5], Space-Time[6], Creativity[7], Imagination[8], Learning[9], Choices[10], Growth Mindset[11], Facing Challenges[12], Rule Life Responsibly[13].

## 2. Function – 16

Two-faced Humanity[14], Free Will[15], Behavior[16], Ethics[17], Justice[18], Self-Reproach[19], Forgiveness[20].

---

5. https://theexplanation.com/nature-of-humans-consciousness-mind-reveal-adroit-humans/
6. https://theexplanation.com/space-time-is-not-only-scientific-theory-its-also-a-human-singularity/
7. https://theexplanation.com/creativity-sets-humankind-apart-from-and-above-all-other-life-on-earth/
8. https://theexplanation.com/imagination-another-singularity-of-humankind-in-your-mind/
9. https://theexplanation.com/bears-dont-learn-to-ride-bicycles-humans-learn-that-and-much-more/
10. https://theexplanation.com/your-choices-tell-us-who-you-are-in-fact-they-identify-you/
11. https://theexplanation.com/growth-mindset-unique-humankind/
12. https://theexplanation.com/challenge-accompanied-courage-needed-face-new-struggles-another-human-singularity/
13. https://theexplanation.com/rule-life-responsibly-the-key-human-singularity/
14. https://theexplanation.com/two-faced-humanity-depraved-priests-and-kind-criminals/
15. https://theexplanation.com/free-will-we-all-possess-it-but-we-cant-always-utilize-it/
16. https://theexplanation.com/human-behavior-is-the-expression-of-human-nature-and-free-will/
17. https://theexplanation.com/ethics-are-the-blueprint-for-behavior-how-humanity-should-function/
18. https://theexplanation.com/justice-goes-hand-in-hand-with-ethics-to-obtain-peace/
19. https://theexplanation.com/self-reproach-the-essential-beginning-step-toward-real-peace/
20. https://theexplanation.com/forgiveness-the-healing-bond-for-humans-to-function-peacefully/

## 3. Socialization – 17

Human Society[21], Unique Individuals[22], Gender Equality[23], Bride and Groom[24], Couple Relationship[25], Marriage[26], Family[27], Parenting[28], Extended family[29], Ethnicity[30], Nations[31], Languages[32], Globalization[33].

## 4. Rulership – 18

Human Government[34], Governance Structure[35], Government for the People[36], Human Needs[37], Inner Peace[38], Peace of Mind[39], National and Individual Prosperity[40], History of Individuals and

---

21. https://theexplanation.com/human-society-the-only-global-social-species/

22. https://theexplanation.com/you-are-a-unique-individual-among-7-billion-on-earth/

23. https://theexplanation.com/gender-equality-gender-inequality-or-gender-compatibility/

24. https://theexplanation.com/bride-and-groom-is-a-cross-cultural-worldwide-phenomenon/

25. https://theexplanation.com/couple-relationship-binding-husband-and-wife-in-marriage/

26. https://theexplanation.com/healthy-marriage-a-happy-twosome-with-abundant-benefits/

27. https://theexplanation.com/family-the-cornerstone-of-human-society/

28. https://theexplanation.com/parenting-father-mother-have-essential-complementary-roles/

29. https://theexplanation.com/extended-family-many-generations-world-population/

30. https://theexplanation.com/ethnicity-clans-tribes-where-did-they-all-come-from/

31. https://theexplanation.com/nations-identified-by-their-own-patriotic-ethnic-culture/

32. https://theexplanation.com/origin-of-language-an-unsolvable-scientific-mystery

33. https://theexplanation.com/globalization-integration-segregation/

34. https://theexplanation.com/human-government-personal-world-peace/

35. https://theexplanation.com/governance-structure-important-role-in-rulership/

36. https://theexplanation.com/government-for-people-concern-for-poor/

37. https://theexplanation.com/human-needs-basics-person-expect/

38. https://theexplanation.com/inner-peace-citizen-goal-government/

39. https://theexplanation.com/peace-mind-tranquil-result-leadership/

# MIND-BODY PROBLEM SOLVED 521

Nations[41], Individual Rights vs. Collective Rights[42], Peace[43], Government Organization[44], Best Form of Government[45].

## 5. Reasoning – 19

Observation-Intuition[46], Philosophy[47], Science[48], Religion[49], Theology[50].

The COMPASS is simply a tool to establish the *now-steps* to help individuals be comfortable with themselves and society through proper purpose, conduct, socialization, management, and reasoning.

What goal are you aiming for in the next hour? Today? This month? For your life? As long as the purpose, socialization, rulership, reasoning, and how you function to reach your destination are biblical and legal, follow the COMPASS and go for it.

---

40. https://theexplanation.com/prosperity-nation-prosperity-citizen/

41. https://theexplanation.com/history-of-individuals-and-nations-practical-bible-wisdom

42. https://theexplanation.com/individual-rights-vs-collective-rights-the-bible-balance/

43. https://theexplanation.com/peace-national-international-government-concern/

44. https://theexplanation.com/government-2-choices-bottom-up-top-down/

45. https://theexplanation.com/best-form-government-aiming-common-good/

46. https://theexplanation.com/observation-first-way-human-reasoning/

47. https://theexplanation.com/philosophy-love-wisdom-whose-wisdom/

48. https://theexplanation.com/science-world-savior-human-reasoning/

49. https://theexplanation.com/religion-solution-world-peace/

50. https://theexplanation.com/deity-and-sound-reasoned-words-are-the-crux-of-theology/

# www.TheExplanation.com

Join The Explanation Newsletter[51] No spam, total privacy

Sam's latest blog post notifications and information about

*The Explanation.*

Join the **Bible course**: *Unlock Bible Meaning with 7-Keys*

*to Master Biblical Hebrew, with no Fuss.*

Reach the God-intended meaning of Scripture in the original language without investing much time or money.

NO learning a new alphabet, vocabulary, grammar, syntax, conjugations... with this groundbreaking course

that disrupts traditional Biblical Hebrew learning methods.

Quickly and easily grasp the mind of God and His Plan

for you and all of humanity.

Join the Bible course NOW

https://TheExplanation.com/challenge

---

51. https://theexplanation.com/subscribe/

# Index

**A**
able (G1410), 223, 227-228
adam, 80-83
adorn (G2885), 459
adorning (G2889), 458-459
afraid (H2296), 360
afraid (H2729), 419-420
age (H3117), 355-356
air (G109), 407-408
alive (G2227), 330-331
Almighty (H7706), 134-135
animal cognition, 45-46
animal mind, 47-50
apron (H2290), 355, 359
argument (H8433), 386-387
arm (H3802), 361-362
assurance (G4102), 454
aware (G1097), 457), 476

**B**
beatitudes, 158, 198
behavior, 158, 361, 365, 375, 387, 396, 422, 457, 482
belief, 9, 56, 87, 453-455, 482
believe (G4100), 453-455
bell (H6472), 317
betray (G3860), 432-433
Bible, 14, 68-70
    corroboration, 94, 100, 106
Bible study method, 71-78
biology of life, 27-34
BIOS, 231-232, 239
bond (H4148), 386
brain, 39-50, 115-122, 231, 266-276,
brainwaves, 320, 334
breast (H7699), 134-135
breath (H5397), 72-74, 85, 125-134, 203-216, 493-494

**B** continued
breath, spirit (H7307), 72-73, 128, 203-208, 211-216, 223-224, 250-251, 260-264, 287-288, 293-297, 316, 345-346, 355-356
breathe (H5301), 72-73, 125, 493-494, 496

**C**
chakras, 325-326
chemical life, 32
Christ, 95, 100, 108, 159, 226, 284, 361, 368-370, 439, 442, 445, 472, 502
circumcision, 466-467
clothe (H3847), 360-361
coat (H3801), 360-361
code of ethics, 365, 382, 388
codec, 270
cognition, 45, 141, 182, 259
cognitive neuroscience, 50
coherent completeness, 5, 58
Commandments, 363
    Ten, 363, 370, 388, 467
    Two, 108, 158, 470
computer program, 239, 243
    software, 229, 241
conscious will. 38
consciousness, 133, 139-141, 147, 151, 160, 180, 186, 189, 208, 241, 257, 389. 417, 493,
    hard problem, 40
    map of, 326
consider (G3539), 456, 476
conversion, 286, 429-438, 449, 484
create (H1254), 111

**C continued**
Creation, 10, 83, 95,
  physical, 109, 130, 196
    208, 220, 251, 273, 278
    288, 290, 328,
  spiritual, 288, 431, 449,
    482, 504
creativity, 145, 518

**D**
desolation (H7701), 134
destroy (H5315), 76, 125, 133,
  494
distressed (H3334), 111
DNA, 28
dominion (H7287), 176
dual conduct, 153,157, 161
dust (H6083), 120-121

**E**
emotions, 38, 160, 323, 344
ethics, 154, 375
exist (H1933), 92

**F**
family, 113, 163, 198
F/father, 95-100, 157, 372
father, parent (G3962), 98-99
firmware, 232, 238
five senses, 181, 292-294, 341
flesh (G4561), 407-410
forgiveness, 155-159, 458
formed (H3335), 111, 121, 143
free will, 153, 158, 457, 499
frequency, 294, 295, 311,
  318-327, 335
fundamental constants, 22

**G**
Garden of Eden, 109,484, 488
G/god, 15, 55-62, 71, 87-96
  97, 354, 417, 429
  Family, 97, 113, 498, 505
  Image, 103, 160, 493, 505
  Kingdom, 478, 498
  Plan, 191, 471, 484, 492
  Way, 198, 364, 379, 473
  Word, 145, 348, 462, 501
God (H430), 88-90
god, idol (H410), 89-90

**H**
health, 389, 399, 419, 512
  mental, 2, 6, 265, 384, 417
heart (G5590), 346-347, 408, 476
heart (H3820), 345
hertz, 294, 320
hide (H2244), 355, 357-358
higher power, 9, 13, 56, 87
Holy Spirit, 203, 222, 251, 287,
  295, 299, 306, 318, 328,
  443, 452, 469, 500
human, 4, 180, 190. 238, 375,
  405, 429, 504
  behavior, 153-158
  conduct/function, 151, 386
  purpose, 142, 389
  reasoning, 54, 180, 353
  responsibility, 171
  rights, 174
  rulership, 170, 390
  socialize, 160, 390
  software, 239
human being (H119), 81

**I**
imagination, 3, 145, 240
imagination (H3336), 186-187, 345
introspection, 38, 155
intuition, 182, 259, 344, 379 460, 465

**J**
James Webb Space Telescope, 19
justice, 154, 158, 380, 458

**K**
know (H3045), 139-140, 486
knowledge (H4486), 137-139, 181

**L**
law of conservation of energy, 307
learning, 145, 189, 230, 259
life biology, 27-34
life purpose, 142-150
living soul, 247-256
living thing (H2416), 248, 346
logogram, 56-57
Logos, 347-348, 473
logos, 57, 291, 340, 347, 513
Lord (H3068), 88, 91-94
love (H2245), 358

**M**
magpie, 49
man (H2145), 82
matter, 12, 22
mind 35, 229, 229-245, 257-265, 315-322, 342, 405, 417, 431, 449, 462, 493

**M** continued
mind (G1271), 407, 409-410
mind (G3563), 345, 457, 476
mind-body problem, 14, 191
modem, 269
move (H7363), 281-283
move at times (H6470), 316-317

**N**
naked (H5783), 362-363
natural law, 378-379
nature (G5449), 407-410
neshama, 74, 110, 132-141, 190-191, 210-218, 240, 257, 341, 449

**O**
observation, 182, 379
operating system, 238-244

**P**
personal growth, 389
persons (H120), 81-82
philosophy 9-14, 183-184
plan (H2154), 345
power (G1411), 222-228, 300
power (G1849), 407-408
power (H3581), 223-224, 227
prehistoric beings, 234-237
prevail ( G3528 ), 422
Prince (G758), 407
professional goals, 389
Proverbs, 384, 388, 500
psyche, 340, 345-349
psychology, 148, 193, 340-353, 355, 376, 405, 417, 444, 499, 512

## Q
quantum field, 280, 290, 308
quantum fluctuations, 307-312
quantum physics, 277, 283
quantum wave, 310-311
quick understanding (H7306), 204-205, 261-263, 289, 293-296, 356

## R
reasoning, 180-189, 191, 195, 198, 348, 353-364, 426
relational laws, 380
relationships, 160, 245
  animals, 45, 104
  God, 94, 101, 105, 357
  human, 97, 163
  marriage, 163
  Spirit, 203, 220, 278, 430
  spiritual, 16, 285, 295, 321
religion, 14, 24. 184-185
repent (G3340), 453, 456, 476
repentance, 158, 437
repentance (G3341), 456
rod (H7626), 386
ruach, 127, 141, 203-208, 210-218, 219, 227, 235, 256. 278, 286, 316, 328
rulership, 109, 113, 170-178, 195, 199, 259, 352, 390,
rulership laws, 380-381

## S
sacred books, 64-70
Satan, 405-416, 479, 490
savour (H7381), 292-294
science, 2, 9-11, 184, 217, 328
  ironic, 11, 37, 55
self-reproach, 155, 194, 437, 458
seventh day, 109-110

S continued
shut (H6095), 358
skin (H5785), 362
social relationships, 160, 167-169, 351, 390
software, 229-232, 238
soul (H5315), 85, 248, 345-346
space-time, 144, 280, 357
S/spirit, 127-128, 201-209, 210-218, 278-285, 286-295-303, 328-338, 34-347, 429
spirit (G4151), 222, 288, 346-347, 407-408, 459, 468, 490
spiritual calling, 439
spiritual conversion, 429-438, 449, 482
spirituality, 150, 210
  genuine 462
stardust, 54
strike at times (H6471), 317-18
subdue (H3533), 176

## T
Ten Commandments, see Commandments
theology, 55-62, 105-106, 185-186
theory of relativity, 22
thought (H4284), 186-187
till (H5647), 486-487
transducer, 269, 272, 276
tree (H6086), 355), 358
transformation,
  material, 25, 29, 101 269, 289, 302
  spiritual, 429, 434, 462, 512, 516
Tree, 182, 190, 355, 359
  Life, 15, 357, 495
  Good, Evil, 183, 495
Two Commandments, see Commandments
two-faced humanity, 457

## U
understanding (H995), 134, 136, 138, 168, 181, 188, 219
Universe, 19-26

## V
vibrations, 294, 323

## W
warring Proverbs, 394
waves, 269, 280, 301, 322
  brain, 320, 324
  sight, 294, 321
  smell, 293
  sound, 292, 320
  taste, 294
  touch, 294
wisdom 394
  Godly, 398, 401
  human, 399, 402
wisdom (H2451), 401-402
wit (H7919), 402-403
word (G3056), 422
word (H1697), 420
world, 46, 170, 376, 395
  material, 4, 159, 186 285, 304. 319
  spiritual, 12, 295, 319, 32, 3281
worldview, 185, 189
wrath (G3709), 407. 409-411

## Y
Yahveh Elohim, 87, 99
Yahweh (Yahveh), 91-94
YHVH to be (H1961), 92-94

# Scripture Index – Old Testament

**Genesis**
1:1, 88, 101, 333
1:1-2, 316
1:1-3, 281
1:2, 278, 284-285, 288, 290, 356
1:2-3, 287
1:11, 101
1:25, 101, 103, 251
1:26, 83, 90-91, 104, 430
1:26-27, 103, 109
1:26-28, 175-176
1:27, 111, 142
1:27-28, 166-167
1:28, 112, 191, 337, 367
1:29, 366
1:30, 109, 251-252
2:3, 91, 109
2:4, 88, 91, 109
2:7, 14-16, 76, 81, 84, 88, 111, 119, 124, 133, 203, 251, 267, 329, 493
2:7-10, 484-485
2:9, 495
2:15, 191, 488
2:16-17, 495
2:20, 191
2:24, 167
3, 190-191, 451
3:2-6, 182-183
3:6, 402
3:6-8, 355
3:7, 451
3:8, 359
3:19, 119
3:20, 235
3:21, 451
3:22-23, 485-486
3:24, 474
4:1, 91, 316

**Genesis** continued
4:12,14, 400
6:5, 186, 203
6:17, 203
7:15, 203, 206, 216
7:20-22, 125, 206-8
7:20-23, 126
7:22, 127-128, 196, 203, 209, 211
41:8, 316
49:25, 135

**Exodus**
3:13-15, 93
12:38, 370
20:19-21, 435
34:28, 420

**Numbers**
15:13, 292
31:35, 82

**Deuteronomy**
4:5-6, 363
4:5-9, 382
6:5-7, 392-393
7:13, 364
11:16, 186
12:8, 364
15:7-11, 380
17:13, 380
19:2,14,15,22 380
21:10,13,15,18,22,25, 380
21:18-21, 385
22:1-6, 381
23:24, 380
24:1,6,7,8,10,14,19 380-381
25:4, 381
29:4,19, 364

**Deuteronomy** continued
31:12, 488
32:11, 282
32:39, 213

**Joshua**
10:40, 84-85, 128
11:11, 85, 129
11:14, 85, 129, 202, 206

**Judges**
13:25, 318
14:6, 297
14:19, 297

**1 Samuel**
1:15, 263-264
16, 326

**2 Samuel**
22:16, 212, 215

**Nehemiah**
4:10, 121

**Job**
1:1-3, 479
4:9, 213
15:2, 432
16:3, 432
26:13, 284
27:3, 130, 213
32:8, 130-135, 138, 181, 201-
    202, 214, 260, 329, 445
32:18, 264
33:4, 129, 214-15
34:14, 141, 214-215, 260
35:2, 480
36:3, 480
38:31-36, 336
42:1-6, 480-481

**Psalms**
1:2, 195
8:3-4, 337
18:15, 215
33:6, 251
36:9, 502
51:1-19, 437-438
51:10, 263
77:4, 318
104:30, 251, 284
150:6, 131

**Proverbs**
1:7, 396
1:20, 398
1:22-23, 500
2:2, 397
2:6, 398
2:10, 398
3:13, 399
5:1-8, 399-400
7:7-14, 400-401
7:27, 401
8:1,35, 395
9:10, 188,
12:24, 396
13:24, 386
14:23, 518
15:32, 396
18: 21, 396
20:3, 396
21:2, 396
21:30, 395
22:15, 386
23:9, 396
29:15, 386

**Ecclesiastes**
3:19, 229
3:19-21, 250
12:7, 250
12:12, 189

**Isaiah**
29:15-16, 188-189
30:21, 420-421
42:5, 130, 215
45:9, 188
57:16, 216
64:4, 434-435
64:6, 121
64:6-8, 435
64:8, 112

**Jeremiah**
23:9, 282
27:5, 224
32:17, 224

**Ezekiel**
20:41, 292
28:12, 401
33:11, 383, 387
33:15, 501
37:1-14, 496

**Daniel**
1:4, 227
2:1, 318
4, 181
4:24-25, 137
4:33-36, 137-138
4:34-36, 202
4:36, 181
11:6, 224

**Micah**
2:2, 421, 424
3:8, 223
4:2-4, 371, 419

**Zechariah**
4:6, 297-298
12:1, 266

# New Testament

**Matthew**
3:1-8, 475
3:13-17, 477
5, 158, 198, 469. 470
5:2-3, 468-469
6:24, 27, 228
12:5-8, 110
12:31-32, 287
13:15-23, 440-441
22:1-14, 490-491
22:14, 448
22:36-40, 467-468
24:37-39, 168, 186
25:14-15, 245
25:15, 227, 300

**Mark**
1:14-15, 453
5:30, 225, 298
9:28-29, 298
10:42-44, 199

**Luke**
1:35, 225
2:52, 477
3:17, 158
4:14, 225
8:11, 348
24:27-49, 446
24:49, 222

**John**
1:12-14, 99, 100
2:16, 501
3:34, 225, 298, 330
5:17, 435
5:29, 502
6:44, 372, 440
6:48, 502
6:68, 501
14:2-6, 474
14:27, 491
17:1-11, 106-107
17:11,14, 450
17:20-21, 455
17:21-22, 95
20:20-23, 444-445
20:24-31, 304-305
20:31, 455

**Acts**
1:8, 222
10:38, 298
11:29, 228
15, 463, 465, 466
15:5-6, 463
15:19-20, 463
17:30-31, 158-159

**Romans**
1:19-31, 431-432
1:20, 234, 313
1:28, 487
1:28-31, 488-489
2:4, 456
2:8, 341
2:14-15, 379
2:28-29, 466
3:1-4, 473
6:4, 502
6:23, 496
7:10-14, 373-374
8:2, 501
8:14-16, 286
8:11, 331
8:16, 295, 331
10:8,9,17. 454
10:13-17, 447
12:2, 461

**1 Corinthians**
2:4, 226
2:9-13, 443
2:11, 377
2:11-14, 403-404
2:14, 510
5:1-5, 489-490
8:4-13, 464-465
12:4-11, 299
13, 198
13:11, 462-463
15:22-24, 108
15:27, 171
15:38-39, 233
15:45,47, 235, 445
15:49, 306
15:50-53, 337

**2 Corinthians**
3:7, 381
4:3-4, 411-412
11:2, 505
11:3, 510

**Galatians**
3:22-26, 369
4: 1-5, 372
6:7, 378

**Ephesians**
1:13, 368
2:2-3, 407
3:14-15, 98
5:25-6:1,4, 168-169
6:12, 406
6:14-17, 362, 460, 478

**Philippians**
1:27, 347
2:5, 198, 431, 481, 499

**1 Thessalonians**
1:5, 300

**1 Timothy**
2:14, 183

**2 Timothy**
1:7, 226
2:15, 201
3:10, 502
3:16, 483

**Hebrews**
1:1-3, 94
9:27, 496
11:23, 99

**James**
2:5, 469
2:26, 231
4:16, 501

**1 Peter**
1:3, 100
3:3-4, 459
3:7, 502
3:18, 330

**2 Peter**
3:2, 393
3:15, 368

**1 John**
2:16, 501
3:4, 458
4:1, 416
4:8, 213

**Revelation**
1:6, 478
2:10, 502
2:11, 496
5:8. 292
5:10, 178
11:11, 502
19:7, 100
19:13, 348
20:5, 496
20:7-10, 497
21:6, 502
21:8, 496
21-22, 95
22:12-15, 497-498
22:14-15, 158
22:17, 288
22:19, 502

# Strong's Index - Hebrew

H119 (human being) 81
H120 (persons) 81-82
H410 (god, idol) 89-90
H430 (God) 88-90
H995 (understanding) 134, 136, 138, 168, 181, 188, 219
H1254 (create) 111
H1697 (word) 420
H1933 (to exist) 92
H1961 (YHVH to be) 92-94
H2143 (memorial) 93
H2145 (man) 82
H2154 (plan) 345
H2244 (hide) 355, 357-358
H2245 (love) 358
H2290 (apron) 355, 359
H2296 (afraid) 360
H2416 (living things) 248, 346
H2451 (wisdom) 401-402
H2729 (be afraid) 419-420
H3045 (know, acknowledge) 139-140, 486
H3068 (Lord) 88, 91-94
H3117 (age) 355-356
H3334 (be distressed) 111
H3335 (formed) 111, 121, 143
H3336 (imagination) 186-187, 345
H3533 (subdue) 176
H3581 (power) 223-224, 227
H3801 (coat) 360-361
H3802 (arm) 361-362
H3820 (heart) 345
H3847 (clothe) 360-361

H4148 (bond) 386
H4284 (thought) 186-187
H4486 (knowledge, reason) 137-139, 181
H5301 (breathe) 72-73, 125, 493-494, 496
H5315 (soul) 85, 248, 345-346
H5395 (destroy) 76, 125, 133, 494
H5397 (breath) 72-74, 85, 125-134, 203-216, 493-494
H5647 (till), 486-487
H5783 (be made naked) 362-363
H5785 (skin) 362
H6083 (dust) 120-121
H6086 (tree) 355, 358
H6095 (shut) 358
H6470 (move at times) 316-317
H6471 (strike at times) 317-18
H6472 (bell) 317
H7287 (dominion), 176
H7306 (quick understanding) 204-205, 261-263, 289 293-296, 356
H7307 (breath, spirit) 72-73, 128, 203-208, 211-216, 223-224, 250-251, 260-264, 287-288, 293-297, 316, 345-346, 355-356
H7363 (move) 281-283
H7381 (savour) 292-294
H7626 (rod) 386
H7699 (breast) 134-135
H7701 (desolation) 134
H7706 (Almighty) 134-135
H7919 (wit) 402-403
H8433 (argument) 386-387

# Greek

G109 (air) 407-408
G758 (prince) 407
G1097 (be aware) 457, 476
G1271 (mind) 407, 409-410
G1410 (be able), 223, 227-228
G1411 (power), 222-228, 300
G1849 (power) 407-408
G2227 (make alive) 330-331
G2885 (adorn) 459
G2889 (adorning) 458-459
G3056 (word) 422
G3340 (repent) 453, 456, 476
G3341 (repentance) 456
G3528 (prevail) 422
G3539 (consider) 456, 476

G3563 (mind) 345, 457, 476
G3709 (wrath) 407. 409-411
G3860 (betray) 432-433
G3962 (father, parent) 98-99
G4100 (believe) 453-455
G4102 (assurance) 454
G4151 (spirit) 222, 288, 346-347, 407-408, 459, 468, 490
G4561 (flesh) 407-410
G5449 (nature) 407-410
G5590 (heart) 346-347, 408, 476

# List of Figures

1. Central Paradigm of Molecular Biology (Dr. Sahai), 28
2. Chemical life, 32
3. Puzzle of coherent completeness, 78
4. Coherent completeness, 78
5. Apoptosis, 117
6. Genesis 7:22, the breath of the spirit, 127
7. Job 32:8 El Shaddai, 134
8. Genesis 49:25 Almighty of the breasts, 135
9. Maslow's hierarchy of human needs, 193
10. Pyramid of human consciousness, 194
11. God's Creation, 197
12. Pyramid of biblical consciousness, 197
13. Search results for breath of life, 204
14. Genesis 7:22, The breath of the spirit, 207
15. Genesis 7:22 Two Biblical Hebrew words nishmat ruach (breath of the spirit), 211
16. Computer programs, 240
17. God's Creation. Neshama and Ruach, 246
18. Genesis 1:30, in which life is living, 249
19. Junction, transmission, connection, 268
20. Modem, 270
21. Transformation and transmission, 270
22. Codec, modem. Brain, transducer, 272
23. Computer programs, 274
24. Immaterial consciousness, mind, and material brain, 276
25. Shaking down to his bones, 283
26. God's Ruach – Holy Spirit: Power of Creation & Transformation, 306
27. Point emitting energy resembles an exploding firecracker, 309
28. Presentation of a two-dimensional quantum field, 310
29. Superimposed sphering points, 312
30. Quantum (vacuum) fluctuation, 313
31. Sound waves, 320
32. The Electromagnetic spectrum, 321
33. Brainwave frequencies, 324
34. Emotional, solfège, chakras, color frequencies, 326
35a. Theory of everything based on frequencies, 332
35b. Theory of everything based on frequencies, 333
36. Five elements of consciousness, 342
37. Consciousness and mind, 343

38. Consciousness and mind, internal & external influences, 344
39. Consciousness and mind guarded by God's Word, 349
40. Godly ethics and psychology, 376
41. Wisdom and anti-wisdom in Proverbs, 397
42. Satan's influence on our consciousness and mind, 415
43. Five elements of consciousness, 422
44. Consciousness and mind, internal & external influences, 423
45. Consciousness and mind, positive & negative influences, 425
46. Psychological requirements to maintain peace, 436
47. Circles of psychology with the things of God, 444
48. Consciousness and mind, 451
49. Consciousness and mind, internal & external influences, 451
50. Consciousness and mind in the world, 452
51. Consciousness and mind in the world but not of the world, 460
52. Consciousness and mind with the two great commandments, 470
53. COnsciousness and Mind in Psychology And Sound Spirituality™ – COMPASS, 499
54. How to reach coherent completeness, 509
55. Coherent completeness, 509
56. Your mind transformation COMPASS, 516

# TheExplanation.com/subscribe

## Join The Explanation Newsletter.
No spam, total privacy

Sam's latest blog post notifications and information about *The Explanation*

Did you love *Mind-Body Problem Solved*? Then you should read *Origin of the Universe* by Sam Kneller!

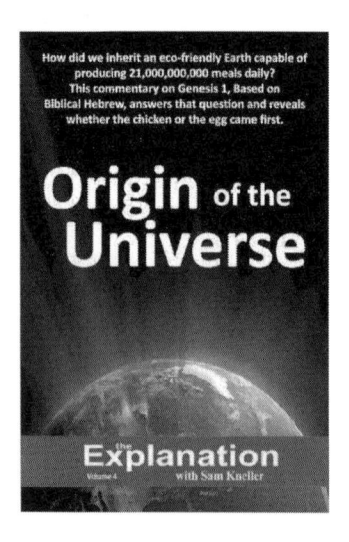

What is the *Origin of the Universe?* And the fight is on. In the red corner, Science. In the blue corner, Religion. For hundreds of years, the scuffling continues, and there's no clear winner. Now, there is, and it's neither!

Think. The *Origin of the Universe* can only have ONE explanation. To reach that, we must show coherent completeness between Science and God.

Your faith in Science and God hangs in the balance. You can't have confidence in the Big Bang and Creation if you think there are conflicting stories.

Meet the mediator and winner, Theology.

*Origin of the Universe*[1] makes sense of the Creation story in Genesis 1 and the Big Bang. Based on The *7*

1. https://books2read.com/rl/TheExplanation

*Keys to Master Biblical Hebrew*, a Bible study method used by thousands, Sam will help you unlock bible meaning. You'll have sound evidence that God's Word and scientific facts are coherent, WHY there's confusion, and how to resolve it. That's true theology.

Sheli said, "It is something I have been searching for, a way to get past the translations and get to the deeper meaning of God's word."

Whether you're an unbeliever, novice, or knowledgeable Bible or Science enthusiast, there's a wealth of wisdom at your fingertips. Each page of *Origin of the Universe* will enhance your insight and become a reference you'll refer to often when studying the Bible and Science.

Buy the e-book or paperback[1] at your favorite online store for a foray into scripture and science.

Read more at https://TheExplanation.com

---

1. https://books2read.com/rl/TheExplanation

# Also by Sam Kneller

**The Explanation**
Inventory of the Universe
Audit of the Universe
Audit of Humankind
Origin of the Universe
Origin of Humankind
Origin of Woman
Agony of Humankind and the Antidote

**Standalone**
Evidence for Bible Wisdom
7 Keys to Master Biblical Hebrew
Mind-Body Problem Solved

All e-books and print versions are available now, at your favorite bookstore[1].
Please write a review for each book and use this link to go to your bookstore[1]. Scroll to *customer review*.
Thanks.

Watch for more at https://TheExplanation.com

---

1. https://books2read.com/rl/TheExplanation

## About the Author

After spending twenty-five years in the Christian ministry, Sam Kneller taught at the American University in Paris, was a technical writer, and founded BonjourLaFrance.com, a successful site for travel and tourism in France.

Sam assists truth seekers overcome Bible turbulence and unlock the original God-intended meaning of Scripture via *7 Keys to Master Biblical Hebrew, with no fuss*™[1].

He is the author of the 7-book series *The Explanation*, a commentary on Genesis 1-3 based on Biblical Hebrew. Find Christ and see His amazing role in these chapters on creation.

He teaches and writes about God's Plan and the big questions in life at *https://TheExplanation.com*.

---

1. https://books2read.com/rl/TheExplanation

The mission of *The Explanation* is to make accessible[1] the God-intended meaning, in Scripture, of His plan and way of life to believers and non-believers.

Applying Bible benefits transforms into a saner, purposeful life here and now and eternal life in the future.

Join the **Bible course**: *Unlock Bible Meaning with 7-Keys to Master Biblical Hebrew, with no Fuss.*

Reach the God-intended meaning of Scripture in the original language without investing much time or money.

NO learning a new alphabet, vocabulary, grammar, syntax, conjugations… with this groundbreaking course that disrupts traditional Biblical Hebrew learning methods.

Quickly and easily grasp the mind of God and His Plan for you and all of humanity.

Join the Bible course NOW

https://TheExplanation.com/challenge

---

1. https://books2read.com/rl/TheExplanation

Made in the USA
Columbia, SC
15 December 2024